NEW THEORIES
ON THE
ANCIENT MAYA

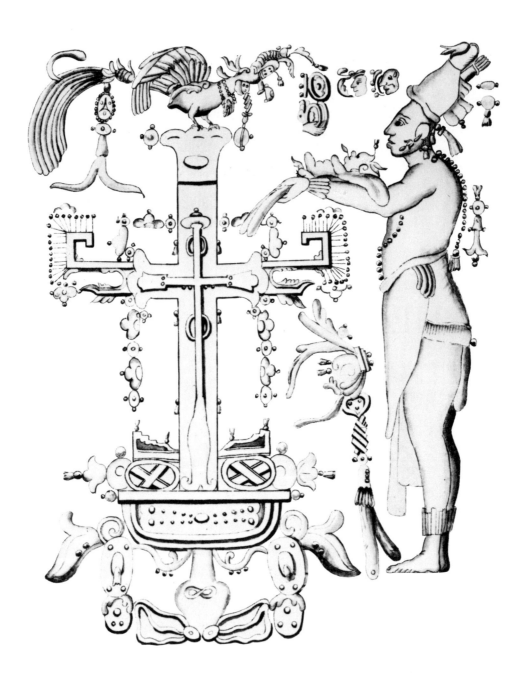

DEDICATION

To the hundreds of avocational Mayanists everywhere, with gratitude for their
(frequently unrecognized) contributions to Maya scholarship.

University Museum Monograph 77

UNIVERSITY MUSEUM SYMPOSIUM SERIES
VOLUME 3

NEW THEORIES ON THE ANCIENT MAYA

Elin C. Danien
Robert J. Sharer

Editors

Published by

The University Museum
University of Pennsylvania
1992

Layout and production:
   Bagnell & Socha
Printing:
   Cypher Press

Library of Congress Cataloging-in-Publication Data
New theories on the ancient Maya / Elin C. Danien,
   Robert J. Sharer, editors
   p. cm. — (University Museum symposium series :
   v. 3)
   (University Museum monograph : 77)
      Includes bibliographical references.
      ISBN 0-924171-13-8
      1. Mayas—Congresses. I. Danien, Elin C. II.
Sharer, Robert J. III. University of Pennsylvania.
University Museum of Archaeology and
Anthropology. IV. Series.
V. Series: University Museum monograph : 77.
F14235.N45 1992
972.81'016—dc20   92-8116
                                                     CIP

Frontispiece and endpapers: Armendáriz drawings of
   Palenque, 1787: The Tablet of the Temple of the
   Cross

TABLE OF CONTENTS

LIST OF ILLUSTRATIONS vii

PREFACE...xiii

INTRODUCTION...xv

THE PAST AS PRELUDE

    I.   Quest for Decipherment: A Historical and Biographical Survey of Maya Hieroglyphic Investigation 1
          George E. Stuart

EPIGRAPHY AND ICONOGRAPHY:
CURRENT STUDIES AND INTERPRETATIONS

    II.   Classic Maya Politics 65
          Stephen D. Houston

    III.   From Double Bird to Ah Cacao: Dynastic Troubles and the Cycle of Katuns at Tikal, Guatemala 71
          William A Haviland

    IV.   Preclassic Notation and the Development of Maya Writing..............81
          David W. Sedat

    V.   Excavating Among the Collections: A Reexamination of Three Figurines 91
          Elin C. Danien

    VI.   Pure Language and Lapidary Prose 99
          Clemency Chase Coggins

    VII.   The Myth of the Popol Vuh as an Instrument of Power 109
          Justin Kerr

THE ARCHAEOLOGICAL PERSPECTIVE:
NEW INSIGHTS INTO DEVELOPMENTS AND RELATIONSHIPS

    VIII. New Ceremonial and Settlement Evidence at La Venta, and its Relation to Preclassic Maya Cultures.......................................123
          William F. Rust, III

    IX.   The Preclassic Origin of Lowland Maya States...................131
          Robert J. Sharer

    X.   Preclassic Maya Civilization 137
          Norman Hammond

    XI.   The Development of a Regional Tradition in Southern Belize 145
          Richard M. Leventhal

    XII.   Beyond Temples and Palaces: Recent Settlement Pattern Research at the Ancient Maya City of Sayil (1983-1985).....................155
          Jeremy A. Sabloff and Gair Tourtellot

    XIII. Variations on a Theme: A Frontier View of Maya Civilization.........161
          John S. Henderson

THE MAYA WORLD VIEW:
THE ANCIENT WAYS AND THE MODERN LEGACY

    XIV.   Deciphering Maya Architectural Plans 173
            Wendy Ashmore

    XV.   Burials as Caches; Caches as Burials: A New Interpretation of the
            Meaning of Ritual Deposits Among the Classic Period Lowland
            Maya 185
            Marshall J. Becker

    XVI.   Rebellious Prophets 197
            Grant D. Jones

    XVII.   Divination and Prophecy in Yucatan 205
            Bruce Love

    XVIII. Mayan Calendars, Cosmology, and Astronomical
            Commensuration 217
            Barbara Tedlock

    XIX.   The Popol Vuh as a Hieroglyphic Book 229
            Dennis Tedlock

THE PRESENT AS PAST

    XX.   The Future of Tikal 241
            Christopher Jones

LIST OF ILLUSTRATIONS

Figure 1.1. A room in "Mexican taste": the earliest illustration of ancient Maya art. 3

Figure 1.2. The earliest known drawings of the ruins of Palenque: (*a*) the central scene on the Tablet of the Temple of the Sun; (*b*) temples at the site. 3, 4

Figure 1.3. Armendáriz drawings of Palenque, 1787: (*a*) The Tablet of the Temple of the Cross; (*b*) stucco relief on Pier E of House A of the Palace. 5, 6

Figure 1.4. Reliefs and other objects sent to Madrid in 1787 by Del Río to Madrid. 6

Figure 1.5. A portion of the Dresden Codex and a Palenque relief as published in 1810 by Humbolt: (*a*) five pages of the Dresden Codex; (*b*) Relief initially labeled in error as being from "Oaxaca." 7

Figure 1.6. Palenque monuments as published to accompany the English Publication of the Del Río narrative, 1822: (*a*) the Tablet of the Temple of the Cross; (*b*) the Palace House A pier. 8, 9

Figure 1.7. Constantine Samuel Rafinesque and his work: (*a*) portrait ; (*b*) the "tabular view" of glyphs. 9, 11

Figure 1.8. The "Castañeda" rendering of the Tablet of the Temple of the Cross at Palenque..12

Figure 1.9. Page 3 of the Dresden Codex, 1825-1975: (*a*) as drawn by Aglio, 1825; (*b*) as it appears today. 13, 14

Figure 1.10. Original Waldeck drawings of Palenque sculpture: (*a*) the Oval Tablet in Palace House E; (*b*) the West Sanctuary Jamb in the Temple of the Cross...14, 15

Figure 1.11. John Lloyd Stephens and Frederick Catherwood: (*a*) Stephens; (*b*) Catherwood. 15

Figure 1.12. Engravings of Catherwood drawings: (*a*) a stela from Copan; (*b*) the Tablet of the Temple of the Cross at Palenque. 16, 17

Figure 1.13. Drawings of Tikal by Lara and/or unknown artist, 1848............19

Figure 1.14. The manuscript of Landa's *Relación de las cosas de Yucatán*. ..20

Figure 1.15. The "Alphabet" from Bishop Landa's manuscript. 21

Figure 1.16. Leon de Rosny with Palenque stuccos. 22

Figure 1.17. Ernst Förstemann. 23

Figure 1.18. Alfred Percival Maudslay and his work: (*a*) Maudslay at Copan; (*b*) a page from Maudslay 1889-1902. ....24, 25

Figure   1.19.   Daniel Garrison Brinton. 26

Figure   1.20.   Eduard Georg Seler..27

Figure   1.21.   Joseph T. Goodman..28

Figure   1.22.   Teobert Maler. 28

Figure   1.23.   Sylvanus G. Morley. 30

Figure   1.24.   The Maya type font of William E. Gates............................32

Figure   1.25.   Sir Eric Thompson..34

Figure   1.26.   Yurii Valentinovich Knorozov. 36

Figure   1.27.   Tatiana Proskouriakoff..39

Figure   1.28.   David Humiston Kelley..40

Figure   1.29.   The Primera Mesa Redonda de Palenque, 1973..................42

Figure   1.30.   A page of the Grolier Codex. 43

Figure   1.31.   Ixkun Stela 1 as published in various sources: (*a*) Lara(?)
                    drawing; (*b*) rubbing by Merle Greene Robertson; (*c*) drawing
                    by Ian Graham. 45

Figure   1.32.   Ian Graham 46

Figure   2.1.   Political hierarchy proposed by Joyce Marcus (A), contrasting
                    with more recent interpretations of such relationships (B).........66

Figure   2.2.   *Ilah* glyph. 66

Figure   2.3.   Dos Pilas Panel 7. 67

Figure   2.4.   Place names, including those of Dos Pilas (A), Aguateca (B),
                    and Palenque (C). 68

Figure   3.1.   The Lords of Tikal...72

Figure   3.2.   Stelae 17 and 30. 73

Figure   3.3.   Burial 195, the tomb of Animal Skull...................................74

Figure   3.4.   Two manikin scepter figures from the tomb of Animal Skull. 74

Figure   3.5.   Structure 5D-43..75

Figure   3.6.   Miscellaneous Texts 216 and 217,......................................75

Figure   3.7.   Miscellaneous Text 25...76

Figure   3.8.   Shield Skull was probably responsible for a Twin Pyramid group
                    constructed in 9.12.0.0.0. Another possible Twin Pyramid group
                    may have been the first he ordered built, in 9.11.0.0.0...............77

Figure   3.9.   Altar 14. 78

Figure   3.10.   Burial 23, which could be Shield Skull's. 78

Figure   3.11.   Tikal Stela 22..79

Figure   3.12.   Shield Skull appears to have been memorialized by construction
                    of the first of Tikal's seven "Great Temples," Structure
                    5D-33-1st..79

Figure   4.1.   Monuments 13 and 14 from the Salama Valley, Guatemala........82

Figure   4.2.   Monument 21 from the Salama Valley, Guatemala....................83

Figure   4.3.   Drawing of the incised text on the Tuxtla Statuette. 85

Figure   4.4.   Some Classic period glyphs with infixed Cupulate Tradition
                  signs. 86

Figure   4.5.   Examples of Preclassic cylinder seals with inscribed abstract
                  notation:
                  (a) from the Salama Valley
                  (b) from El Jocote in the Chixoy Valley, Guatemala, and
                  (c) from San Andres Sajcabaja, Guatemala. 87

Figure   4.6.   Preclassic cylinder seals with abstract notation in three registers:
                  (a) from Tlatilco, Mexico;
                  (b) from El Jocote in the Chixoy Valley, Guatemala. 87

Figure   5.1.   Robert Burkitt. 92

Figure   5.2.   Figurine in the form of a shaman transformed into a jaguar. 93

Figure   5.3.   Seated figure of shaman, in the process of transforming from
                  human into jaguar. 93

Figure   5.4.   Figurine from Roknimaa in the form of a man holding a jaguar
                  cub. 94

Figure   7.1.   Hero Twins. Photo #1183.* 110

Figure   7.2.   Metropolitan vase. Photo #521. 110

Figure   7.3.   Blowgunner vase. Photo #1226. 111

Figure   7.4.   Hero Twins. Photo #1004. 111

Figure   7.5.   Drawing of Izapa stela 25. 112

Figure   7.6.   Slate scepter. Photo #3408. 112

Figure   7.7.   Slate scepter reverse. Photo #3409. 113

Figure   7.8.   Drawing of a Copan ball game marker. 113

Figure   7.9.   Drawing of Dumbarton Oaks tablet. 114

Figure   7.10.   Cutting-up of JGU. Photo #1370. 115

Figure   7.11.   Drawing of Tablet 14, Palenque. 115

Figure   7.12.   Drawing of Naranjo stela 12. 116

Figure   7.13.   Hero Twin with blowgun. Photo #2715. 117

Figure   7.14.   Drawing from Temple of Inscriptions. 117

Figure   7.15.   Drawing of panel from Temple of the Cross, Palenque. 118

Figure   7.16.   Drawing of panel from Temple of the Sun, Palenque. 118

Figure   7.17.   Humiliation of the Lords of the Underworld. Photo #1560. 119

Figure   7.18.   Drawing of panel of the Temple of the Foliated Cross, 119
                  Palenque. 119

Figure   7.19.   Women dressing Hun Hunaphu. Photo #1202 120

Figure   7.20.   Carved bone from Copan. 120

Figure   7.21.   Resurrection plate. Photo #1892 120

Figure   8.1.   Map of the La Venta region showing levee occupational sites
                  along the abandoned Río Bari channels 124

Figure   8.2   Portion of a Late Preclassic carved and incised ceramic vessel
                  from San Miguel, ca. 500-200 B.C. 127

*All photograph numbers refer to the Justin Kerr photograph collection.

Figure   11.1.   Archaeological sites of Southern Belize.....................................146

Figure   11.2.   Map of Uxbenka. 147

Figure   11.3.   Photograph of Stela 19, Uxbenka. 147

Figure   11.4.   Photograph of Stela 15, Uxbenka. 148

Figure   11.5a.   Photograph of Stela 11, Uxbenka. 149

Figure   11.5b.   Drawing of Stela 11, Uxbenka (drawing by Linda Schele)........150

Figure   12.1.   The Maya lowlands showing the location of the Puuc region and the site of Sayil...156

Figure   12.2.   The remains of a perishable structure at Sayil. 157

Figure   12.3.   At the heart of Sayil, the Mirador Complex and nearby basal platform units bracket an unusual area that might have been the central marketplace. 159

Figure   13.1.   Eastern Mesoamerica. 162

Figure   13.2.   Sula Valley and Southeast Periphery chronology. 162

Figure   13.3.   Olmec greenstone figurine (scale 10 cm)...................................163

Figure   13.4.   Sula Valley: Middle Preclassic and Playa phase settlements. 163

Figure   13.5.   Playa de los Muertos figurines (scale 10 cm). 164

Figure   13.6.   Sula Valley: Early Chamelecon phase settlements. 165

Figure   13.7.   Sula Valley: Middle and Late Chamelecon phase settlements...165

Figure   13.8.   Sula Valley: Ulua phase settlements...166

Figure   13.9.   Ulua polychrome vessel (scale 10 cm). 166

Figure   13.10.   "Stela" from Calabazas (note stylized outline face near top). ...167

Figure   13.11.   Ulua polychrome vessel; seated in stylized building (scale 10 cm)..168

Figure   13.12.   Sula Valley: Santiago phase settlements. 168

Figure   13.13.   Sula Valley: Botija phase settlements...169

Figure   13.14.   Sula Valley: Naco phase settlements...169

Figure   14.1.   Map showing locations of sites mentioned. 174

Figure   14.2.   Reconstruction drawing of Tikal Twin Pyramid group 4E-4. 174

Figure   14.3.   Map of Great Plaza area of Tikal. 175

Figure   14.4.   Map of the central portion of Tikal, Guatemala, with Twin Pyramid groups highlighted. 177

Figure   14.5.   Map of Cerros, Belize, with ball courts highlighted...................179

Figure   14.6.   Map of site core of Quirigua, Guatemala. 180

Figure   14.7.   Map of Gualjoquito, Honduras..181

Figure   17.1.   Days marked *utz* ("good") and *lob* ("bad") in the Chilam Balam of Tizimin...206

Figure   17.2.   Days marked "good" and "bad" in the Dresden Codex. 206

Figure   17.3.   A series of 13 consecutive days from 1 Imix to 13 Ben in the Madrid Codex...208

Figure   17.4.   A portion of a 260-day series in the Madrid Codex.................208
Figure   17.5.   A portion of a katun series from the Chilam Balam of
                       Tizimin..210
Figure   17.6.   Three katun pages from the Paris Codex. 211
Figure   17.7.   Katun 13 Ahau from the Paris Codex. 211
Figure   17.8.   Katun 11 Ahau from the Paris Codex. 213
Figure   17.9.   Katun 9 Ahau from the Paris Codex. 213
Figure   17.10.   A tun sequence from the Chilam Balam of Kaua....................214
Figure   17.11.   A uinal sequence from the Chilam Balam of Ixil......................214
Figure   17.12.   Ten Ahau to Four Ahau; a possible uinal sequence from the
                       Paris Codex..215
Figure   17.13.   Eleven Ahau to Five Ahau; a possible uinal sequence from the
                       Paris Codex..215
Figure   19.1   Glyph for *Ahaw*. 236
Figure   20.1   Temple I, Tikal, in 1988......................................242
Figure   20.2   North Acropolis summit behind Structure 5D-33 in 1980..........242
Figure   20.3   Lost World Pyramid, west side, in 1988......................243
Figure   20.4   Temple V in 1969..243
Figure   20.5   Temple I and Central Acropolis in 1969......................244
Figure   20.6   Stela 13, a monument to Kan Boar, ruler of Tikal (A.D. 457-
                       488). 245

PREFACE

When it began, it was known as the Free Museum of Science and Art. Over the years, the official name was altered once or twice, and it has been known colloquially as the University of Pennsylvania Museum, or simply Penn's Museum. In order to make clear its purpose and the nature of its collections, in 1990 it was officially renamed The University Museum of Archaeology and Anthropology of The University of Pennsylvania, usually shortened to The University Museum. In 1987, the Museum celebrated its centennial with academic and popular symposia devoted to those areas that have been the focus of its scholarly research in archaeology and ethnology. The annual Maya Weekend was chosen as a most appropriate venue for an overview of current Maya studies, reflecting the Museum's active involvement in the study of the ancient Maya during the past seventy-five years. The Maya Weekend, which began in 1983 as one of the Museum's special programs for the public, has become a forum of interest to academics as well; the yearly two-day event is a meeting ground for all those—professional and amateurs alike—who are fascinated by the Maya and by the research that continues to reveal their history.

We would like to thank the authors, who heeded our requests for papers and were patient and cooperative through all the changes and delays on the way to publication. Elizabeth Graham was helpful at an early stage of preparation. Wendy Bacon and Toni Montague were involved in early stages of copyediting; Tobia Worth undertook the final copyediting and the enormous task of putting twenty different bibliographies into coherent stylistic agreement. Her painstaking care and eye for detail are matched by a sure sense of scholarship. Karen Vellucci, Coordinator of Publications at The University Museum, was patient, stern, coaxing, and demanding in turn, and never lost sight of the final product. Her amazing good nature in the face of innumerable problems was—and is—extraordinary, and very much appreciated.

INTRODUCTION

Of all the regions where recent archaeological discoveries have changed our views of past civilizations, the Maya area must qualify as one where some of the most startling revisions are taking place. The remarkable breakthroughs in the decipherment of Maya hieroglyphics, the new technological frontiers in excavation techniques and artifact analysis, and the change in the approach archaeologists take to the problems they consider, as well as the nature of the problems themselves, have resulted in a dramatic shift in our perception of the ancient Maya and in our ability to interpret their material remains.

Speakers at the 1987 Maya Weekend were asked to consider a broad range of current topics in Maya iconography, epigraphy, ethnohistory, and cultural anthropology as well as the implications of recent archaeological discoveries. With some changes, additions, and updates where the authors deemed them necessary, those papers are offered here.

The categories into which we have placed the articles need no further explanation; each section attempts to address a different aspect of the Maya enigma.

The book begins and ends with articles of a slightly different nature; one deals with the eccentric lurches and swoops in the understanding of Maya epigraphy; the other, with the aftermath of excavation.

Clues to the history of hieroglyphic decipherment lie strewn in hundreds of libraries, archives, and attics. Nowhere has this history been gathered and presented in as concise and comprehensive a fashion as in the article by George Stuart with which the book begins. Some of the names will be familiar to those who have followed the sinuous path of hieroglyphic decipherment; many others will undoubtedly surprise. Anyone wishing to delve into the more esoteric byways of decipherment will find here a treasure of previously scattered source material.

The last article, by Christopher Jones, deals with subjects of growing concern to us all: the responsibility of the archaeologist to the site excavated and the past culture it represents; the sometimes ambiguous relationships with modern governments; the role of archaeology in the society within which we function; and the need to reach out to the students of the future. The example Jones cites, of the current problems facing Tikal, possible solutions, and the obstacles in their path, is a salutary reminder that we dare not limit our involvement to the period of excavation.

Some of the theories and discoveries described in the following pages may suggest a marked change from previous theories and earlier interpretations of archaeological excavation. Given the past history of Maya archaeology and the quickening pace of discovery, these articles may well be seen in the future as the platforms from which other theoretical approaches and newer interpretations will be launched toward different paths of knowledge.

Elin C. Danien
Robert J. Sharer

Philadelphia
October 1991

I
Quest for Decipherment:
A Historical and Biographical Survey of
Maya Hieroglyphic Investigation

George E. Stuart

National Geographic Society and The Center for Maya Research

Any unreadable or undeciphered piece of writing, whether the fragmentary inscription of an extinct culture or a trivial modern text rendered into code or cipher, holds an inherent and uncommon fascination for the beholder. The ancient Maya script is no exception. Many have pursued the secrets of its workings and content over the decades, and they are the protagonists of the intellectual and anecdotal history that forms the subject of the present essay.

PERIODS OF MAYA HIEROGLYPHIC RESEARCH

For the sake of discussion, I have divided the progress of Maya hieroglyphic research into six periods that more or less reflect major trends of concentration and accomplishment.

The first, that of the Eyewitnesses (1517-1740), begins with the appearance of the Spaniards in Yucatan, and ends around the time of the deaths of the last witnesses of the conquest of the Itza Maya of Tayasal, in the interior of present Guatemala. The second period (1740-1840) belongs to the Pioneers. It saw the earliest exploratory expeditions to the "lost cities" of the Maya area, the first publication of examples of Maya hieroglyphic writing, and the first "modern" attempts to read the glyphs.

The era of the Early Documentors (1840-1880) begins with the travels of John Lloyd Stephens and Frederick Catherwood, and includes the later accomplishments of Charles Etienne Brasseur de Bourbourg in the discovery and publication of manuscripts indispensable to all future Mayanists. Next, the period of the Early Scholars (1880-1910)

begins with the research of Ernst Förstemann and ends with the publication of Charles Pickering Bowditch's synthesis of Maya calendrics and numeration. This period also includes the extraordinary documentation of monumental inscriptions by Alfred P. Maudslay and photographer Teobert Maler. The half-century or so after that (1910-1958) I label the Period of the Institutions. It includes the indefatigible fieldwork of Sylvanus G. Morley and the far-reaching hieroglyphic researches of J. Eric S. Thompson, mainly under the auspices of the Division of Historical Research of the Carnegie Institution of Washington, whose active program of Maya studies virtually defines the span.

My final period, that of the past three decades (1958 on), is the most difficult to label, for it witnessed many different kinds of important advances in Maya glyphic research. These include the overriding concern with the historical content of the inscriptions that began in earnest with key contributions by Heinrich Berlin, Tatiana Proskouriakoff, and David H. Kelley, and the serious reemergence of the consideration of the phonetic character of Maya writing initiated by Yurii V. Knorozov. These and more recent trends in the continuing evolution of Maya hieroglyphic studies will be considered in greater detail below.

Like all such devices of convenience, these periods are only general reflections of the past expressed with the somewhat flawed perspective afforded by a blend of hindsight and subjectivity. Others have subdivided the history somewhat differently for reasons important to their aims (Kelley 1962a; Bernal 1980; Hammond 1982). Whatever system of periods is used, none is free of fault for the simple reason that the reality of complex human activity over long periods never conforms to a neat scheme of segments or labels.

THE EYEWITNESSES (1517-1740)

The record is silent as to who of non-Maya descent first laid eyes on a Maya hieroglyphic text, but mention of "books" and the peculiar writing in them appears early among the works of the European historians of the conquest.

The earliest account known is that of Peter Martyr d'Anghiera, or Peter Martyr (1459-1526), the famed chronicler of the Spanish conquest. Of his eight "decades"—these refer to the varying segments of time into which Martyr divided the span of time between 1493 and 1525—the Fourth Decade (Martyr 1530, 1555, 1912) contained a passage describing native books, at least some of which, according to Thompson (1972:4), may have been Maya. The passage, from the earliest translation into English, provides not only a detailed account of how the books were made, but also a first impression of hieroglyphic writing:

> The formes of their letters are nothynge lyke vnto owres. But are muche more crooked and entangeled, lyke vnto fyshehookes, knottes, snares, starres, dise, fyles, and suche other muche lyke vnto the Egiptian letters, and written in lynes lyke vnto owres. Here and there betwene the lynes, are pictured the shapes of men and dyuers beastes: And especially the Images of kynges and other nobel men . . . In these bookes are furthermore comprehended their lawes, rytes of ceremonies and sacrifyces, annotation of Astronomie, accomptes, computations of tymes, with the maner of graffynge, sowyng, and other thyngs perteinyng to husbandry. (Martyr [1530] 1555:162).

Michael D. Coe (1989) reinforces the contention that Martyr's description indeed referred to a Maya book, citing new evidence in a 1520 letter of Archbishop Ruffo, papal nuncio to the Spanish Court in Valladolid. Based on other evidence, Coe also proposes that the source of it and other such items included in Cortés's "Royal Fifth" was a Maya town on Cozumel Island.

Whatever the case, the content of the Martyr account serves as a representative sample of the *kinds* of information that appeared in the published record during the 200 or so years that followed the conquests of the Spaniards. Almost unfailingly, it consisted of brief treatments based either on hearsay or, as in Martyr's case, on the actual handling of screen-fold books. As Thompson notes in his detailed review of early sources (1972:3-14), Maya hieroglyphic books were also mentioned by Acosta (1590), Lizana (1633), Sánchez de Aguilar (1639 [1937]), and Villagutierre Soto-Mayor (1701).

One of the relatively few publications of the period that dealt with the Maya in some depth was the folio *Historia de Yucathan* by Fr. Diego López de Cogolludo, printed in Madrid in 1688. Among other things it described the ruins in Yucatan and, more importantly for future hieroglyphic research, provided the Yucatec names for the months and some of the days in the native calendar (López de Cogolludo 1688:176-177, 185-186).

While the imprints of the chroniclers and the ethnohistorians of New Spain were generally available for scholarly pursuit, many unique manuscripts pertinent to the Maya and their writing system reposed in various national, colonial, and ecclesiastical archives. Many such sources came to light only sporadically in the centuries that followed their actual writing—and many more doubtless still await discovery. This pattern of temporal lag in the availability of many enormously important documents of the period of the Eyewitnesses profoundly affected the pace of all subsequent research.

A detailed guide to the early published sources of the period of the Eyewitnesses appears in Volumes 13-15 of the *Handbook of Middle American Indians* (Cline 1972-1975). Wilgus's historiography of the early Spanish writers (1965) remains a useful sourcebook as well.

The period of the Eyewitnesses ended with the generation of Spaniards who died out in the half century that followed the conquest of the Itza Maya of Tayasal in 1697. Accounts of that episode by Villagutierre Soto-Mayor (1701) and Elorza y Rada (1714)—to mention only the main published sources—hold the last contemporary glimpses of Maya culture in its near-pristine state.

THE PIONEERS (1740-1840)

As the middle of the eighteenth century approached, characters of a new cast began to fill the stage for the next act in the drama of Maya hieroglyphic research. One was a librarian who gained an immortality of sorts through a fortunate purchase. The rest, with the exception of Rafinesque, were the explorers, who perhaps best typify the main activity of the period. With the collective contribution of these Pioneers began the accumulation and publication of actual examples of Maya writing and the first

Figure 1.1. A room in "Mexican taste": the earliest illustration of ancient Maya art. (From Racknitz 1796, Plate 34, courtesy of Wayne Ruwet and the Powell Library of the University of California at Los Angeles)

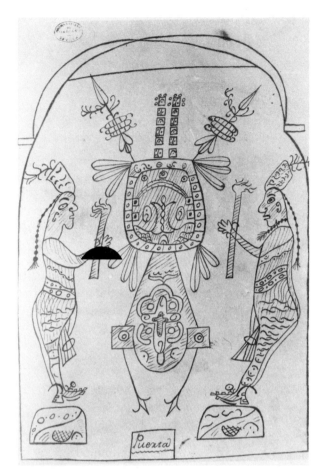

Figure 1.2a. The earliest known drawings of the ruins of Palenque: the central scene on the Tablet of the Temple of the Sun (by José Calderón 1784, from Angulo Iñiguez 1934).

scholarship devoted to its decipherment.

The first episode of note involved the screen-fold book that we know as the Codex Dresdensis or Dresden Codex. Strangely painted in color with delicate images that recall Martyr's description, the exotic piece was purchased in 1739 from a private owner in Vienna by Johann Christian Götze, then director of the Royal Library in Dresden. The book was cataloged the next year as "an invaluable Mexican book with hieroglyphic figures" (Deckert and Anders 1975:13). The first published mention of the Dresden Codex appeared in 1744 in Götze's *Merckwürdigkeiten* . . . , described as containing "characters" as well as hieroglyphic figures. In 1796, images copied from the manuscript served to illus-

trate a model design for a room in "Mexican taste" (see Fig. 1.1) in the *Darstellung und Geschichte des Geschmacks der vorzuglichsten Volker*, a five-volume treatise on interior decoration by Joseph Friedrich, Baron von Racknitz (or Rackwitz), published in Leipzig. The decorative motifs employed also include adaptations of Aztec art and architecture derived from illustrations in the *Storia antica del Messico* . . . by Clavigero (1780-1781), which had been translated into German and published in Leipzig in 1789-1790. As Michael D. Coe, discoverer of this bibliographical curiosity, points out (1963:40), the illustration in von Racknitz's *Darstellung*, although useless for research, remains the earliest known publication of Maya glyphs and figures.

Throughout the first 50 years of the Dresden epic,

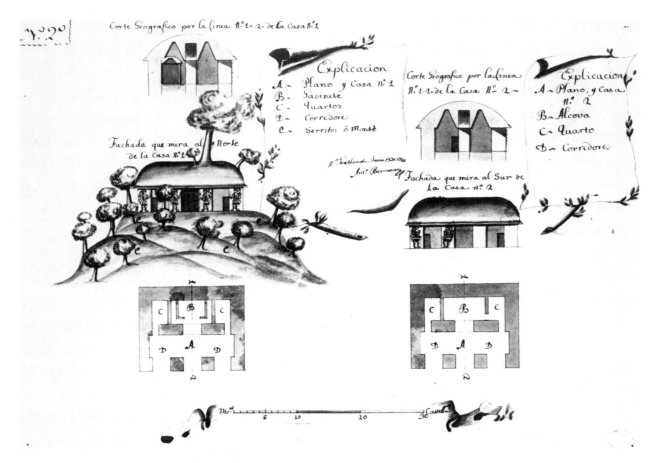

Figure 1.2b. The earliest known drawings of the ruins of Palenque: temples at the site (by Antonio Bernasconi 1786) (from Angulo Iñiguez 1934).

events were taking place elsewhere that began to provide additional samples of Maya writing. These, however, had nothing to do with manuscripts—they would always be of superlative rarity in any case—but rather with the numerous stone sculptures that lay among the forest-shrouded ruins in the interior of the Maya area. And it all began at Palenque.

That gem of a ruined city, so famous today, lay in obscurity until the middle of the eighteenth century. In the earliest known printed description of the site, the Guatemalan historian Domingo Juarros attributes its discovery to "some Spaniards having penetrated the dreary solitude" (Juarros [1808-1818] 1823:18). According to another account (Brasseur de Bourbourg 1866:3-4), relatives of Antonio de Solís, Licentiate of Tumbala (and no relation to the earlier historian of the same name), moved to the town of Santo Domingo del Palenque (founded in 1567) and came upon the nearby ruined city around 1746. In

1773, after word of the "stone houses" had spread, a small group organized by Ramón Ordoñez y Aguiar of Ciudad Real (later San Cristobal de las Casas) visited the ruin and later reported it to José Estachería, Governor General of Guatemala (Bernal 1980:87).

In 1784, a second exploring party, sent by Estachería and led by José Antonio Calderón, entered Palenque and remained for three days. The resulting report was accompanied by four drawings—images of part of the Tablet of the Temple of the Sun (Fig. 1.2a) two standing figures, and the Tower (Castañeda Paganini 1946:22-29). These are presently in the Archives of the Indies, Seville (Angulo Iñiguez 1934:pl. 137, 138).

A third expedition, led by architect Antonio Bernasconi the following year, produced his renderings of a site map, building plans and elevations (Fig. 1.2b) reliefs, and a throne, copies of which are also in the Archives of the Indies (Angulo Iñiguez

Figure 1.3a. Armendáriz drawings of Palenque, 1787: The Tablet of the Temple of the Cross.

1934:pl. 133-138), the British Museum (I. Graham 1971:50), and Mexico's Library of Anthropology (Maricruz Pailles, personal communication). Manuscript copies of accounts of these two expeditions are presently in the Archives of the Indies as well.

The fourth, the largest, and the most consequential of the early exploring parties to reach Palenque was headed by Captain of Artillery Antonio del Río and included the artist whose name appears in the scanty and inconsistent sources as either Ricardo Alméndariz (Castañeda Paginini 1946:15) or, more likely, Ignacio Armendáriz (Berlin 1970:111). The group entered the ruined city in force in May of 1787 and worked for several weeks until "there remained neither a window nor a doorway blocked up; a partition that was not thrown down, nor a room, corri-

dor, court, tower, nor subterranean passage in which excavations were not effected" (Del Río and Cabrera 1822:3).

Del Río's investigations at Palenque—fortunately exaggerated with regard to the damage done—resulted in the lengthy manuscript report now in the Academía Real de Historia, Madrid. Copies of Armendáriz's original drawings (Fig. 1.3a, b)—30 figures drawn on 26 sheets—are in the Biblioteca de Palacio, Madrid. The artifacts removed from Palenque by Del Río, including pottery vessels, flints, and parts of stone and stucco sculpture (Fig. 1.4) are among the collections of Madrid's Museo de América (Lothrop 1929; Cabello Carro 1984:42)

With the numerous copies of the Armendáriz drawings, or partial sets of them, which circulated soon after 1787, there began a complicated biblio-

Figure 1.3b. Stucco relief on Pier E of House A of the Palace. (From copies of the lost originals made in 1789 by order of Charles IV of Spain. Photographs courtesy of Consolación Morales, Director, Biblioteca de Palacio, Madrid.)

Figure 1.4. Reliefs and other objects sent to Madrid in 1787 by Del Río to Madrid: Photograph, ca. 1885, by Leon de Rosny in the courtyard of the Museo Arqueológico Nacional (now the Museo de América), Madrid. Appearing in the picture: Heinrich Schliemann (left), famed excavator of Troy and Tiryns, and Juan de Díos de la Rada y Delgado (right), whose publications include a Spanish translation of Rosny's work on Mayan writing and the Cortés fragment of the Madrid Codex. (From a heliograph in Rosny 1904).

graphic saga, discussed in some detail by Berlin (1970). Suffice it to say that during the century after they were drawn, various versions of these earliest reasonably accurate renderings of Palenque and its inscriptions appeared under different names and in a variety of works, nearly always without credit or acknowledgment.

In 1807, Guillermo Dupaix, retired captain of dragoons, and the artist José Lucian Castañeda visited Palenque during the last of their three expeditions commissioned by the Viceroy of New Spain for the exploration of ancient ruins. With the exception of a hieroglyphic panel (I. Graham 1971:50-51) that

Armendáriz had failed to record, the Castañeda drawings, which remained unpublished for more than a score of years in any case, contributed little in the way of new Maya glyphic texts, although they constitute a landmark of the first order in the historiography of Mexican archaeology. The detailed study of the various copies of the Castañeda drawings and their fate by José Alcina Franch (1949) is a minor masterpiece of bibliographic inquiry.

In 1810, Alexander von Humboldt, then just preparing for print the narrative of his Mexican scientific travels with the botanist Aimé Bonpland, heard of the Dresden Codex from the German antiquary Carl August Boettiger. Through him and a Count Marcolini, Humboldt procured copies of five pages of the manuscript (Fig. 1.5a) in time to illustrate them in the folio "atlas pittoresque," or *Vues des Cordillères, et monumens des peuples indigènes de l'Amérique* (Humboldt 1810:pl. 45). This elegant work of 69 plates with accompanying descriptions was designed to supplement the quarto *Voyage aux regions equinoctiales du nouveau continent* (Humboldt and Bonpland 1814-1825). However, it stands as an independent source of more than rou-

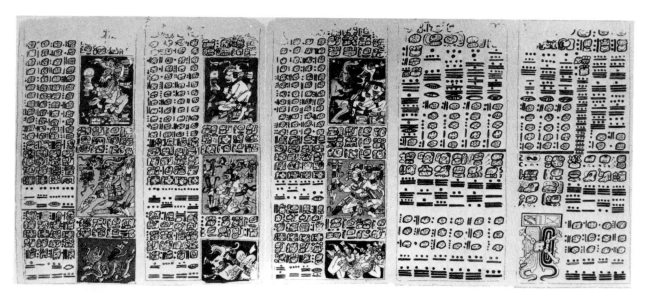

Figure 1.5a. A portion of the Dresden Codex and a Palenque relief as published in 1810 by Humboldt: five pages of the Dresden Codex (Humboldt 1810: pl. 45).

tine importance in the history of Maya research, for it contained not only the first relatively accurate publication of part of the Dresden Codex but an illustration (Fig. 1.5b) apparently derived ultimately from an Armendáriz original, of one of the stucco bas-reliefs from Palenque (Humboldt 1810:pl. 11). Unfortunately, the latter was misidentified in Humboldt's caption as having come from Oaxaca (although the error was noted in an obscure later passage in the work).

Parts of two of the Dresden pages also appeared in later, and abbreviated, octavo editions of the work in English (Humboldt 1814, 2:144-47, pl. 17) and French (Humboldt 1816, 2:268-72, pl. XVI). In the French version, the codex excerpts appear as "Aztec Hieroglyphic Pictures from the Dresden Manuscript."

The potential significance of Humboldt's publication of the Palenque stucco was largely negated by its unfortunate initial misidentification. One must therefore turn elsewhere for the appropriate recognition of the first illustrated publication dealing with a Maya ruin. As Ian Graham (1971:9) and others have noted, that distinction belongs to a thin quarto volume published by Henry Berthoud of London in 1822 (Del Río and Cabrera 1822).

The book, whose ringing title begins *Description of the Ruins of an Ancient City . . .*, was actually two volumes in one. It contained the *editio princips* of the report on Palenque by Captain Don Antonio Del

Figure 1.5b. Relief initially labeled in error as being from "Oaxaca" (Humboldt 1810: pl. 11). The mistake was later corrected. (Courtesy of the Center for Maya Research, Washington, DC)

Figure 1.6a. Palenque monuments as published to accompany the English publication of the Del Río narrative, 1822: the Tablet of the Temple of the Cross (Del Río and Cabrera 1822).

Río, as well as a longer treatise, *Teatro critico Americano,* by Paul Felix Cabrera, an Italian graduate of civil and canon law who had lived in New Spain and Guatemala from 1765 until his death in 1800 (Berlin 1970:109-110). Most importantly, the volume contained among its 17 plates the very first published depictions of Maya writing carved in stone (Fig. 1.6a, b). The engravings, made from a partial set of the Armendáriz drawings (with three illustrations added from an unknown source), bore the initials of Jean Frederic Maximilien Waldeck, a peripatetic artist who was in London at the time and made the engravings for this landmark volume.

In order to see the impact of the discoveries in Dresden and Palenque in proper historical perspective, it is appropriate to consider the general relationship between Latin America and the rest of the

world in the early decades of the nineteenth century. While Humboldt's prodigious output of scientific publications (30 folio and quarto volumes between 1805 and 1834) served to trigger initial public interest in Mexico, Central America, and South America, other forces were also at work.

Napoleon's invasion of Spain and the abdication of Charles IV in 1808 set the stage for the patriotic movements that, despite the restoration of the Spanish Bourbons in 1814, culminated in the political independence of most of Spanish America by 1825. This, in turn, opened up the entire area for travelers, traders, scientists, and merchants, who appeared in droves to take advantage of the new age. Those who followed in the footsteps of Humboldt and Bonpland thus found a ready market in Europe and North America for any publication

Figure 1.6b. The Palace House A pier (Del Río and Cabrera 1822). Note the initials JFW—Jean Frédéric Waldeck—on each engraving. (Both courtesy of the Center for Maya Research, Washington, DC)

Figure 1.7a. Constantine Samuel Rafinesque and his work: portrait (Rafinesque 1815: frontispiece).

dealing with the new American nations. As noted by McNeil and Deas (1980:23), the number of travel books on various parts of Spanish and Portuguese America reached a peak between 1815 and 1830 that would not be equaled until the last half of the century.

Berthoud's publication of the Del Río report, the Cabrera treatise, and the illustrations of Palenque—all apparently "liberated" from the archives of Guatemala by a mysterious "Dr. M. Quy" (Larrainzar 1875-1878, 1:43)—makes sense in this greater context. Paradoxically, the work appears to have been received indifferently by the public, perhaps because of the negative comments of its reviewer in the London *Literary Gazette* of November 9, 1822 (No. 303:705). Over the next decade, however, interest increased, and versions or copies of the illustrations of the work appeared in Germany and in France.

Thus, by late 1822 two important samples of Maya

hieroglyphic writing had appeared in print: Humboldt's depiction of the mysterious manuscript in Dresden (1810, etc.) and Waldeck's engravings, after Armendáriz, of hieroglyphs from Palenque (Del Río and Cabrera 1822). Today, we take the cultural connection between the two for granted, but at the time the relationship was far from obvious: as late as 1851, an excerpt from Humboldt's illustration continued to be captioned as "Azteck" (Heck 1857:pl. 423.8). However, that all-important link was soon to be made.

Some five years after the London publication of the Palenque illustrations, one of the most remarkable characters in the history of American science made his appearance on the Maya scene. Born in 1783, Constantine S. Rafinesque or, with his matronymic, Rafinesque-Schmaltz (Fig. 1.7a), has been described as "brilliant, egotistical, hypersensitive, hypercritical, indefatigible, erratic, and eccentric" (Ewan 1967:ii). Rafinesque himself perhaps put it best in his autobiography: "Versatility of talents and of professions, is not uncommon in America, but those which I have exhibited . . . may appear to exceed belief" (Rafinesque 1836:148). Primarily a botanist, he published even more new generic names than did Linnaeus, but of those 2,700, only 30 are accepted today. He even toyed briefly with seeking the post of official botanist for Lewis and Clark on their famed western journey (Ewan 1967:ii-iv). Deeply interested in languages and writing systems, Rafinesque is perhaps best known to Americanists for his transcription of the now-lost—and highly controversial—original of the *Walam Olum*, the migration legend of the Lenape, or Delaware, Indians (Indiana Historical Society 1954). He was, above all, an obsessive reader.

Rafinesque was 2 years old when Del Río entered Palenque; nearly 40 when the illustrated account was printed—and by then he had seen Humboldt's works. In the mid-1820s he turned his attention to the mysterious inscriptions of "Otolum," or Palenque.

In *The Saturday Evening Post* of January 13, 1827, there appeared a Rafinesque letter to the French philologist Peter Duponceau. Although much of the text was taken up with an attempt to assign alphabetical values to the Maya glyphs and to compare them to "Old Lybian" of North Africa, the remarkable letter contained a noteworthy paragraph that not only distinguished the Palenque hieroglyphs from the "Azteca or Mexican paintings" and other American symbol systems but also related them to those of the whole Maya area. Most importantly, Rafinesque attributed their linguistic connection specifically to the Chontal and Tzeltal languages.

Rafinesque continued his precocious pursuit of the elusive solution of the Maya glyphs in the succeeding years. In four *Saturday Evening Post* letter-articles addressed to the antiquarian James H. McCulloh of Baltimore (Rafinesque 1828), he noted among other things that he had read the descriptions of the ancient books, language, and customs in the works of López de Cogolludo (1688), Villagutierre Soto-Mayor (1701), and other available histories.

The Rafinesque-McCulloh relationship proved momentous for the beginnings of serious investigation of the Maya hieroglyphs. McCulloh, who had

written an admittedly simplistic commentary on ancient America a decade earlier (McCulloh 1817), now turned to the subject in earnest, spurred by the irrepressible Rafinesque, and produced his landmark *Researches, Philosophical and Antiquarian, concerning the Aboriginal History of America* (1829). In it, he made the first connection in print between the monumental inscriptions of Palenque, on the one hand, and the painted glyphs in the Dresden Codex on the other. McCulloh's illustration of ten hieroglyphs from the Tablet of the Temple of the Cross at Palenque (from Waldeck's plate in Del Río and Cabrera 1822) was the very first illustration of Maya writing to appear in print in America (G. E. Stuart 1989).

Rafinesque, meanwhile, was not idle. He corresponded with Jean Frédéric Waldeck, who had begun his own residency and exploration of Palenque in 1832, and with Dr. Francois Corroy of Tabasco, another frequent visitor to those ruins during the same period. The culmination of Rafinesque's contribution to Maya hieroglyphic studies came in various articles for his *Atlantic Journal* (Rafinesque 1832a, b). The most important of these was the second of three letters to the Egyptologist Champollion "on the Graphic Systems of America and the Glyphs of Otolum or Palenque, in Central America—Elements of the Glyphs," to which he appended a chart of the "Alphabets and Glyphs of Africa and America" (Fig. 1.7b). In the letter, he reiterated and elaborated on those points communicated to Duponceau some five years before, and also the results of his collaboration with McCulloh:

> Besides this monumental alphabet, the same nation that built Otolum, had a Demotic alphabet . . . which was found in Guatimala and Yucatan at the Spanish conquest. A specimen of this had been given by Humboldt . . . from the Dresden Library, and has been ascertained to be Guatimalan instead of Mexican, being totally unlike the Mexican pictorial manuscripts. This page of the Dresden Codex has letters and numbers, these represented by strokes meaning 5 and dots meaning unities, as the dots never exceed 4. This is nearly similar to the monumental numbers. The words are much less handsome than the monumental glyphs; they are uncouth glyphs in rows formed by irregular or flexous heavy strokes,

inclosing within, in small strokes, nearly the same letters as in the monuments.

Prophetically, Rafinesque ended his discussion: "It might not be impossible to decypher some of these manuscripts . . . since they are written in languages yet spoken, and the writing was understood in Central America, as late as 200 years ago. If this is done, it will be the best clue to the monumental inscriptions" (Rafinesque 1832b:40-44).

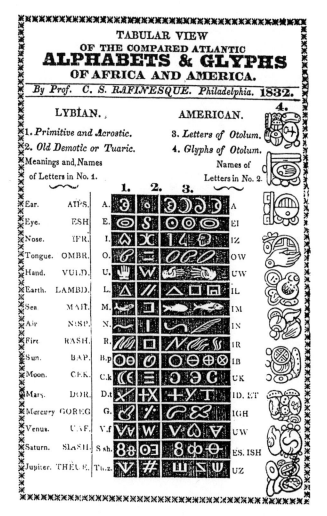

Figure 1.7b. Constantine Samuel Rafinesque and his work:the "tabular view" of glyphs, as it appeared in the Atlantic Journal and Friend of Knowledge in 1832. Note part of the text from the Tablet of the Cross, Palenque, copied from Del Río and Cabrera 1822 (see Fig. 1.6a). (Both courtesy of Charles Boewe, Louisville, KY)

Rafinesque's tracts, though brief and scattered throughout the extensive bibliography of his life's work (Fitzpatrick 1911; Boewe 1982), contain the seeds of scholarship, the first serious attempts at interpretation that we know of in Maya hieroglyphic research. We must therefore agree with Zimmermann (1964:246-47) in recognizing this controversial scientist as the prime mover in the earliest studies of the Maya glyphs.

In 1830, two sets of illustrations relevant to Maya hieroglyphic research appeared in what must be the single most ambitious publishing venture in the history of Americanist studies. *Antiquities of Mexico . . . ,* financed by Edward King, Viscount Kingsborough, and illustrated by the Italian artist Agustino Aglio, grew out of Kingsborough's obsessive belief that the American Indian had descended from Hebrew ancestors—a view, incidentally, that came under vehement attack by Rafinesque (1832c:99). To support his belief, Kingsborough commissioned Aglio to search out, copy, and later color any "Mexican" manuscripts that could be found in the libraries of Europe. To these were added any texts, descriptions, or illustrations that might bolster Kingsborough's case.

Words are hardly adequate to describe these volumes, for in their original bound and untrimmed state, depending upon thickness, each volume weighs between 20 and 40 pounds. Seven volumes of the set were issued in 1829 and 1830, and two more in 1848, 11 years after Kingsborough had died in debtors' prison. Only the first four carried illustrations. Among these, Volume 3 included the first reproduction of the entire Dresden Codex, and Volume 4 held pictures of Palenque, including hieroglyphic panels, and "Ocosingo" (Tonina). The latter were none other than the Castañeda drawings that accompanied the text of the Dupaix survey, both of which Kingsborough had obtained. The work of Dupaix and Castañeda did not appear in its own independent edition until 1834, when the folio *Antiquités Mexicaines* was published in Paris under the editorship of H. Baradère (1834; Fig. 1.8).

As Berlin has noted (1970:116-117), three of the drawings of Palenque attributed to Castañeda that appear in the 1830 and 1834 publications of the Dupaix survey are but copies of Armendáriz's original renderings, which Dupaix may have obtained from Ordoñez y Aguiar in Ciudad Real en route to Palenque in 1807. A comparison of the various edi-

Figure 1.8. The "Castañeda" rendering of the Tablet of the Temple of the Cross at Palenque. (First published in Baradère 1834. From the facsimile edition of Villaseñor Espinosa 1978. Courtesy of the Center for Maya Research, Washington, DC)

tions raises questions regarding other illustrations credited to Castañeda. Curiously, a total of 15 Castañeda illustrations that appear to be direct copies of the Armendáriz renderings corresponds almost precisely to the partial set used in the London publication of 1822.

Aglio's rendition of the Dresden Codex for Kingsborough (Fig. 1.9a) at last made all 74 pages of the precious manuscript available for scholars elsewhere. Moreover, both the hand-colored published version (Kingsborough 1830, vol. 3) and Aglio's original tracing, now in the British Museum, allow a glimpse of the manuscript in its earliest knowable state, a useful privilege since the original (particularly the fine brown linework) has not only faded since the tracing was made but also suffered extensive water damage during World War II (Fig. 1.9b).

The increasing activity on the Maya scene of the early 1830s is reflected in the appearances in the popular press of various articles dealing with American antiquities. For the Maya area, this trend had begun with Rafinesque's prolific correspondence, exemplified by the letters to Duponceau, McCulloh, and Champollion published in the *Saturday Evening Post* and Rafinesque's own *Atlantic Journal*, cited above. In 1833 and 1834, two New York magazines took up the cause. In its November 1833 issue (Vol. II, No. 5:371-82), *The Knickerbocker* published Dr. Samuel Akerly's—the name is spelled "Ackerly" in some sources—report

to the Lyceum of Natural History of New York (Akerly 1833). It included excerpts of Akerly's correspondence with both Waldeck and Corroy regarding their work at Palenque, and part of a now-lost letter from Corroy to Rafinesque (Boewe 1985).

Between December 7, 1833, and March 29, 1834, the *Family Magazine, or Weekly Abstract of General Knowledge*, another New York periodical, noting that "public attention has recently been excited in relation to an ancient city in Guatemala," ran installments of Antonio Del Río's report on Palenque and Dr. Cabrera's "Teatro Critico Americano." Both were taken essentially verbatim from the 1822 London imprint, and five of the installments carried full-page illustrations taken from the same work. Whatever triggered this series—and the date suggests that it was the earlier article in *The Knickerbocker* (which the *Family Magazine* had repeated in four installments in early 1834)—it resulted in the first American edition of Del Río and Cabrera and brought public knowledge of Palenque to a head in the United States.

The decade of the 1830s was shared by two others who had only recently entered the Maya field. Juan Galindo, a colonel in the service of Central America, visited Palenque, Copan, and Yaxha between 1831 and 1835 and produced a few drawings of sculptures and hieroglyphs. Of Galindo's brief career, examined by Ian Graham (1963:12-35), the main contribution to Maya glyph studies was the conclusion, published in 1832, that the hieroglyphic inscriptions of Palenque and Copan were indeed identical writing systems and a uniquely Maya achievement (I. Graham 1963:32).

Only a year after Galindo's sojourn in Palenque, Jean Frédéric Waldeck, mentioned above, reentered the Maya field, this time in earnest. The long life and wanderings of this engaging character have been chronicled by Brunhouse (1973:50-83) and critically examined by Cline (1947:278-300). Some four years after he had appeared in London to engrave the plates from the Berthoud edition of Del Río and Cabrera, Waldeck's journeys took him to Mexico and ultimately to Palenque, that irresistible magnet for early travelers in the Maya area.

Waldeck lived and worked at Palenque from May 1832 to July 1833, producing drawings and paintings of the architecture, some of the hieroglyphic inscriptions, and scenes in the town. "I dwell in a house in the ruins, having been driven from the palace by the

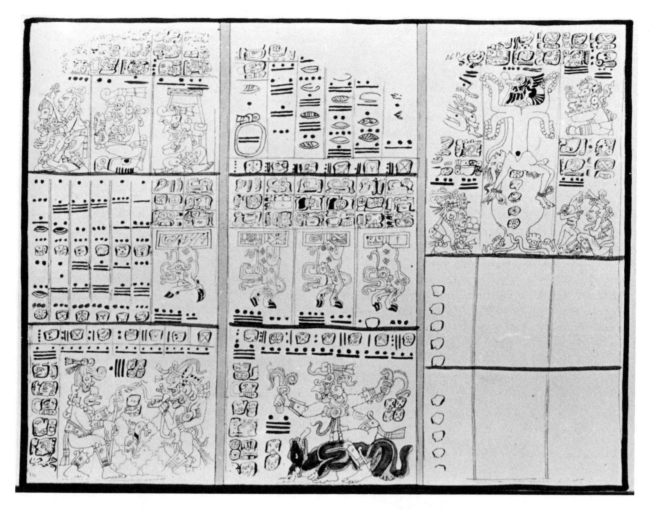

Figure 1.9a. Page 3 of the Dresden Codex, 1825-1975: as drawn by Aglio, 1825 (Kingsborough 1829-1848:3).
(Courtesy of the Library of the National Geographic Society, Washington DC)

Bats," he wrote to Rafinesque on one occasion. "The reliefs and inscriptions are very complicated and difficult to copy, it took me 20 days to copy 114 glyphs" (Rafinesque 1835:6).

The published versions of Waldeck's drawings of bas-reliefs and hieroglyphic inscriptions (Waldeck 1838; Brasseur de Bourbourg 1866) appear as idealized shaded renderings that would be more at home in the art of classical antiquity than in the ancient Maya tradition. This is not so, however, in the case of many of Waldeck's originals, now in the Edward Ayer Collection of the Newberry Library, Chicago. Among those are numerous fine-lined ink and pencil renderings of bas-reliefs and hieroglyphs that exceed all preconceived expectations of Waldeck's output and amply repay a visit and perusal (Fig. 1.10a, b).That

none of these reached print with the accuracy of their original rendering has unfortunately diminished Waldeck's perceived contribution to the field of Maya studies.

Although Waldeck lived well beyond the period of the Pioneers, he and his work typify it, and it seems appropriate to end this span with the appearance, in 1838, of his major publication, the imposing *Voyage pittoresque et archéologique dans la province d'Yucatan* . . . Its meticulous depictions of Palenque and Uxmal, as we know now, are for the most part accurate only in general appearance. Three more years passed before a truer aspect of the ruins and their inscriptions became available to a fascinated public.

THE EARLY DOCUMENTORS
(1840-1880)

As Hammond (1982:31) has pointed out, the year 1840 proved to be a watershed in the history of Maya research. Before that, study was both sporadic and uneven in quality, and focused almost exclusively on the ruins of Palenque. Almost immediately afterward, however, the unsuspected variety of Maya remains was laid before the world, and in the four decades that followed, the documentary foundations for future research were firmly laid. This accomplishment, achieved in both field and library, was shared mainly by a famed American traveler, an English architect, a Yucatecan scholar, and an energetic French cleric.

The story of John Lloyd Stephens and Frederick Catherwood (Fig. 1.11a, b) has been related in detail by von Hagen (1973). The incredible story of their journey of exploration between October 3, 1839, and

Figure 1.10a. Original Waldeck drawing of Palenque sculpture: the Oval Tablet in Palace House E.

Figure 1.9b. Page 3 of the Dresden Codex, 1825-1975: as it appears today. (Photograph courtesy of Ferdinand Anders)

the last day of July 1840, and that of the subsequent expedition of 1841-1842 has been told best by Stephens himself in two separate works: *Incidents of Travel in Central America, Chiapas, and Yucatan,* published by Harper and Brothers in 1841, and *Incidents of Travel in Yucatan,* which appeared in 1843. Both two-volume sets contain vivid narratives of hardship, illness, and discomfort mixed with blessed episodes of local friendship and hospitality; of incidents of political turmoil and civil war tempered by the awesome natural setting; and, of course, descriptions of the ruins themselves.

While Stephens wrote his descriptive narrative, Catherwood was drawing and painting, at first frustrated by the strange art style and the intricacies of a bewildering alien iconography. Unlike his predecessor, Catherwood soon proved himself master of the

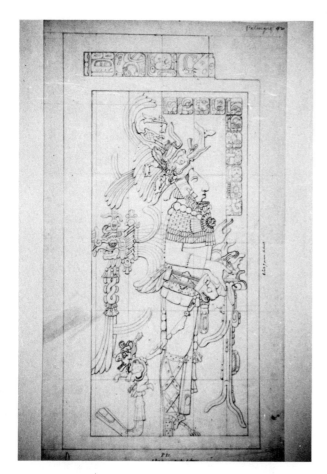

Figure 1.10b. Original Waldeck drawing of Palenque sculpture: the West Sanctuary Jamb in the Temple of the Cross. (Both courtesy of the Newberry Library, Chicago)

Figure 1.11a. John Lloyd Stephens, from a woodcut after a daguerreotype (Stephens 1854).

Figure 1.11b. Frederick Catherwood, the only known portrait (Catherwood 1844). (Both courtesy of the Center for Maya Research, Washington, DC)

problem and, despite illness and the rigors of the trail, produced a huge body of meticulous plans, architectural renderings, records of hieroglyphic inscriptions, artifacts, and scenery.

Catherwood occasionally used the camera lucida, a portable apparatus with a prism that enabled the artist to see and draw the images of scenes or objects projected onto paper (Turner 1983:299). This aided him greatly in the most difficult subjects, particularly the intricate and complicated sculptures of Copan, the scene of his initiation into the Maya art style (Stephens 1841,1:240). The engravings—some 200 in all—that appeared in the Stephens volumes (Fig. 1.12a, b) were therefore much more accurate than those engraved from the renderings of earlier draftsmen. They not only set new standards for the recording of ancient Maya remains but also helped make the works unprecedented best-sellers of their day.

The Stephens-Catherwood trips served to inspire, then to eclipse, another expedition of some note. In November 1839, the Englishmen John Herbert Caddy and Patrick Walker made an arduous journey overland from Belize (then British Honduras) to Palenque. They arrived at the site in February of 1840, well ahead of Stephens and Catherwood, and remained for two weeks. The account of the Walker-Caddy expedition, including Walker's sketches and paintings of the site, has been published in a definitive edition by Pendergast (1967).

One poignant note underscores the year 1840 as a station of separation between the Pioneers and Early Documentors: according to von Hagen (1947:187-188), only a month or so after his return from the first trip, Stephens received a letter from Rafinesque in Philadelphia in which the dying scientist reminded Stephens of his priority in discovering the nature of the hieroglyphs. Stephens acknowledged the priority in a letter which is mentioned by von Hagen but without citation. That letter would have reached Philadelphia just as Rafinesque's friends, seeking to save his cadaver from sale to the medical school, were spiriting it away from his Race Street landlord, for the eccentric and poverty-stricken scientist had just died with his rent badly in arrears (Ewan 1967:ii; Boewe 1982:52).

In the light of today's routine bestsellers, it is difficult to appreciate either the impact of the Stephens volumes or their popularity on both sides of the Atlantic. In the four decades or so that followed their appearance, each set went into several editions and nearly two dozen reprintings. In addition, illustrations copied or derived from those of Catherwood appeared for decades in works ranging from the serious (Laranaudière and Lacroix 1844; Larrainzar 1875-1878) to episodes of flagrant exploitation like that perpetrated by P. T. Barnum in the notorious episode of the pamphlet proclaiming the discovery of the "remarkable Aztec children" in the "idolatrous city of Iximaya" (Velasquez 1850).

Whether the popularity of books on Mexico in the 1840s was merely an extension of the enthusiasm of the previous decades or the result of a growing interest enhanced by events on the Texas border, or both, the output of other works that coincided with the appearance of the Stephens books was enor-

Figure 1.12a. Engraving of Catherwood drawing that appeared in Stephens 1841 and 1843: a stela from Copan.

mous. The year 1843 alone saw the appearance of Fanny Calderón de la Barca's *Life in Mexico,* William H. Prescott's classic three-volume *History of the Conquest of Mexico,* and *Rambles in Yucatan . . .* by Benjamin M. Norman, a traveler whom Stephens himself had encouraged. The last work contained addenda, taken mostly from *American Antiquities and Discoveries in the West,* an anthology of historical articles by others published in numerous—and differing—editions by the Albany harness maker Josiah Priest between 1833 and 1841. The bewildering bibliography of Priest's work, which contained articles on Palenque and Mexico lifted from various sources, has been summarized by Boewe (1982:15-18). It is of interest here for its role in the popular dissemination of various Rafinesque articles (Priest

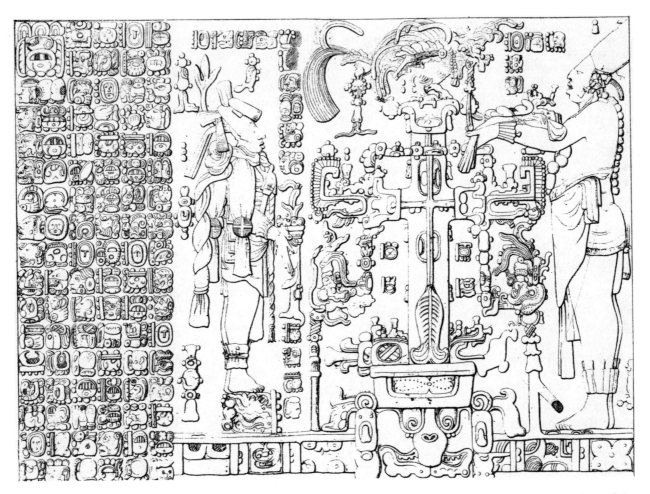

Figure 1.12b. Engraving of Catherwood drawing that appeared in Stephens 1841 and 1843: the Tablet of the Temple of the Cross at Palenque. Note that the right-hand slab is missing. (Both courtesy of the Center for Maya Research, Washington, DC.)

1841:120-129, etc.). Among the items picked up by B. M. Norman from Priest was the late scientist's first letter to Champollion on Palenque and its hieroglyphs (Rafinesque 1832a, b:4-6; Norman 1843:292-296).

To the 1843 volumes—devoted mainly to Yucatan—Stephens appended two short works by the Yucatecan scholar Juan Pio Pérez, then *Jefe Político* of the town of Peto. The first (Stephens 1843, 1:284-307), drew upon ancient manuscript chronicles collected by Pérez and sought to explain the workings of the old calendar. Like López de Cogolludo's 1688 history, it provided a list of the month names and also gave the first published list of the 20 days along with explanations of calendrical mechanics that are remarkably free of error. To the

second volume of *Incidents of Travel in Yucatan*, Pérez contributed the transcript of part of the Mani chronicle (Stephens 1843, 2:305-308).

The brevity of Pérez's contributions, in both the Stephens volumes and, later, in the pages of the magazine *El Registro Yucateco* (Pérez 1846), belied their importance. Here for the first time in accessible sources were excerpts from a manuscript chronicle written in Mayan during the centuries immediately following the conquest. It and others laboriously and accurately copied by Pérez were published more than a century later in an important anthology, the *Codice Pérez*, named for him (Solís Alcalá 1949). Thus did Juan Pio Pérez help to reveal an entire new category of data pertinent to Maya calendrics, language, history, and custom. These and other colonial documents soon took an important place among the diverse clues to the nature and meaning of the glyphs.

The decade that followed the spectacular success earned by Stephens and Catherwood witnessed little of import directly related to Maya writing. Catherwood published his *Views of Ancient Monuments in Central America, Chiapas, and Yucatan*, a large folio of 25 colored lithographs of selected Central American ruins and scenes, in 1844. That same year, a young scholar, Ernst Förstemann, of whom we will say more below, received his doctorate in philology.

In late February of 1848, Ambrosio Tut, Governor of the district of El Peten, Guatemala, and Colonel Modesto Méndez, chief magistrate, conducted the first official exploration of the huge ruined city of Tikal. They were accompanied by the artist Eusebio Lara. In 1852, Méndez discovered the important Peten ruins of Ixkun and Ixtutz. The first account of Tikal reached print in the *Gaceta de Guatemala* in April and May of 1848. The drawings of buildings and monuments by Lara and perhaps another artist who remains unknown appeared in print shortly afterward in Germany (Ritter 1853). The renderings at once revealed the wonders of the hitherto unknown reaches of the Peten region but set the standards of draftsmanship back at least a century (Fig. 1.13). Hammond (1984) gives a detailed account of these early explorations in Peten, along with the complete Méndez narrative and the illustrations accompanying it, from copies now in the library of the Society of Antiquaries of London.

John Lloyd Stephens died in the autumn of 1852. Catherwood revised the publication of their first collaboration, added a memorial notice to "his fellow-traveller and intimate friend," and published it as a single volume in 1854. In September of the same year, Catherwood himself, en route from London to New York, was lost at sea in the fog-shrouded collision that sank the S.S. *Arctic* (von Hagen 1950:114-117).

The era that ended with the loss of Catherwood saw another beginning of sorts, for the occurrence of the sea disaster coincided with the presence of a French priest, Etienne Charles Brasseur de Bourbourg, in New York City. In October 1854, Brasseur departed for Central America for the third, and most fruitful, of his trips up to that time (Adams 1891:277). He, like Stephens before him, had become captivated by the available literature on Mexico and Central America and its antiquities. Brasseur devoted his considerable energy not to ruins but instead, in the manner of Juan Pio Perez, to the recovery of manuscripts related to the history of the region. At this he excelled. On an earlier trip, at a bookstall in Mexico City, Brasseur had purchased the 1,200-page manuscript now known as the Motul Dictionary for four pesos (Martínez Hernández 1930:xvi).

In Guatemala, Brasseur de Bourbourg borrowed and copied the now-indispensable manuscripts of the Popul Vuh (1861) and the Annals of the Cakchiqueles, and later transcribed the first dictation of the Maya drama, the *Rabinal Achi*, which was soon published as an addendum to his important grammar of Quiche (Brasseur de Bourbourg 1862). To facilitate his pursuit of material, Brasseur learned Nahuatl, Quiche, and Cakchiquel, thus becoming the first scholar of note to fully realize the benefits of knowing the native languages of his area of study.

Brasseur's greatest accomplishment lay neither in his unprecedented 2,600-page *Histoire des Nations Civilisées du Mexique et de l'Amérique Centrale . . .* (1857-1859) nor in his interpretative studies, which became increasingly colored by his obsession with the "lost continent" of Atlantis, but rather in the rapid publication of the key manuscript material that he saved from possible oblivion. His series of such contributions began in 1861 with the publication of the Popul Vuh, the enormously important Quiche manuscript, set down by Dominican Father Francisco Ximenez, that provided later scholars with a vast treasury of ancient Maya mythology. Although a German translation had appeared four years earlier (Scherzer 1857), Brasseur was the first to publish the original Quiche version of the text, to which he added numerous notes.

While Paris printers labored over the fourth and final volume of Brasseur's massive *Histoire . . .* , a discovery of note was taking place in a dingy chimney corner of the Bibliothèque Imperiale. There in a basket of old papers, Leon de Rosny, a young scholar of Maya writing, found the 22-page fragment of the Maya hieroglyphic book that we now know as the Paris Codex.

Actually, the codex that Rosny "discovered" had been known for at least a quarter of a century, for it was acquired by the Bibliothèque Imperiale in 1832 (Zimmermann 1954). In 1835, the artist Augustine

Figure 1.13. Drawings of Tikal by Lara and/or unknown artist, 1848. (From Ritter 1853, courtesy of Norman Hammond)

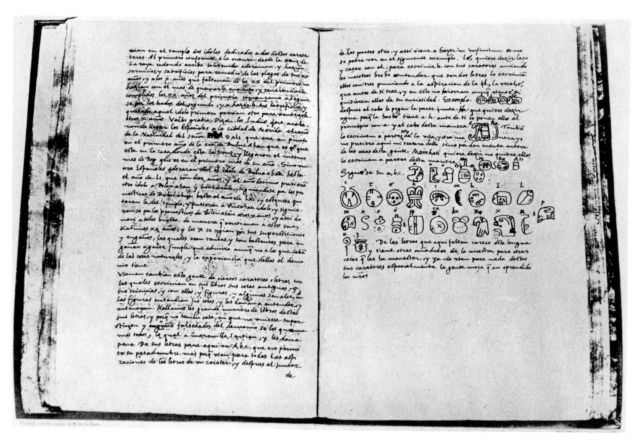

Figure 1.14. The manuscript of Landa's Relación de las cosas de Yucatán. *(From Rosny 1876. Courtesy of the Center for Maya Research, Washington, DC)*

Aglio drew the Paris Codex in the course of his ongoing commission for Lord Kingsborough (it was to have appeared in the tenth volume of Kingsborough's *Antiquities of Mexico*, but because of Kingsborough's death it never reached print). In 1849, the first known published reference to the Paris Codex had appeared in a short descriptive text by Joseph M. A. Aubin (1849; Anders 1968:9 n. 10; Glass 1975a:179). Late in 1855, Mexican scholar José F. Ramírez wrote a report on 11 codices in the Bibliothèque Imperiale. His description of the unprepossessing Maya book (then Number 2 of the collection) noted its close resemblance to the Dresden Codex, which Ramírez had seen in the work of Kingsborough (1829-1848, 3). The short commentary, relegated to the files of the library, did not appear in print for almost a century (Zimmermann 1954:63-64).

In 1859, one José Pérez published two descriptions of the Paris Codex (Pérez 1859a/b) and illustrated one of them (Pérez 1859a) with a reproduction of a single page (Anders 1968:9, n.10; Glass 1975a:179; 1975b:675). All in all, however, the first 25 years or so of the known existence of the Paris Codex constitute a kind of "lost generation," during which time the precious manuscript remained all but unknown to the world in general.

When Rosny rediscovered the Paris Codex, it was wrapped in a paper (now lost) bearing the word "Pérez"—perhaps a reference to José Pérez, who certainly must have handled the document shortly before. Whatever the origin of the mysterious wrapper label, Rosny named the manuscript the "Codex Peresianus," or "Codex Pérez" after it. The manuscript has since become more generally known as the Paris Codex in order to avoid confusion with the compendium of colonial-period documents named for Juan Pio Pérez (Solís Alcalá 1949), noted above. Despite the tardiness of Rosny's find in relation to the known history of the manuscript, the

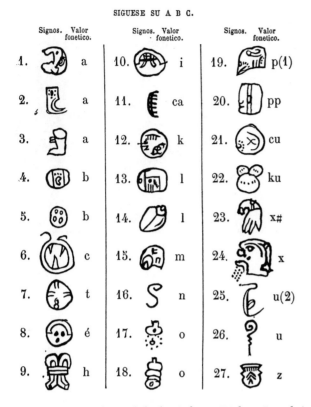

SIGUESE SU A B C.

Figure 1.15. The "Alphabet" from Bishop Landa's manuscript, as first published. (Brasseur de Bourbourg 1864. Courtesy of the Center for Maya Research, Washington, DC)

now-famous episode still pervades the historical literature as the "official" beginning of the modern history of the Paris Codex, 120 years after the purchase of the Dresden Codex (Rosny 1856, 1860, 1864).

In 1863, the tireless Brasseur made the single find that, even if he had made no other, would have immortalized him among Mayanists. In the Biblioteca de la Academia de la Historia, in Madrid, he came upon an abbreviated copy (the longer original remains lost) of Bishop Diego de Landa's *Relación de las cosas de Yucatan*, originally written around 1566 (Landa 1966). One of the fundamental source documents of Mesoamerican ethnohistory, the Landa account (Fig. 1.14) provides an astonishingly complete look at Maya culture as it was in the very first decades of the conquest—a work that does for the northern Maya what SahagDn's much longer *Historia general de las cosas de Nueva España* (Sahagún 1950-1969) did for the Aztecs. Brasseur's

publication of most of Landa's *Relación* . . . the following year (Brasseur de Bourbourg 1864) constitutes a milestone of the first importance in Maya glyphic studies, for it furnished two critical sets of information. First, the names of the Yucatec Maya days and months, previously known from López de Cogolludo (1688) and Pérez (Stephens 1843, 1:284-307), were linked for the first time to illustrations of their respective hieroglyphs. Second, the manuscript contained an illustration, with accompanying discussion, of a Maya hieroglyphic "alphabet" (Figs. 14, 15). The first of these resulted in the solving of the mechanics of the ancient Maya calendar two decades later. The second thrust scholars into a controversy that plagued Maya hieroglyphic studies for the next century.

In 1866—the same year he published the text that accompanied Waldeck's corpus of drawings of Palenque, Uxmal, and other sites—Brasseur discovered the third Maya hieroglyphic book to come to light in modern times. What Brasseur found was actually a 70-page codex fragment in the possession of Don Juan Tro y Ortolano, Professor of Spanish palaeography at the Escuela Superior de Diplomática in Madrid (Anders 1967:51). Brasseur obtained permission to publish this "Codex Troano" and issued it under the auspices of Napoleon III in two large volumes that included not only a reliable color version of the manuscript but also a lengthy treatise on ancient Maya writing (Brasseur de Bourbourg 1869-1870). Unfortunately, this summary was tarnished by Brasseur's ill-conceived use of the Landa alphabet, his interpretation of signs as representing personified powers of nature, and a reading of the codex in reverse order (Brunhouse 1973:133-134).

In 1875, still another codex fragment found safe haven in a European institution. Offered for sale in Paris and London as early as 1867, the 42-page hieroglyphic manuscript was purchased in 1872 by the collector José Ignacio Miro, who sold it to the Museo Arqueológico of Madrid three years later. The piece was named the "Codex Cortesianus" from information that it had been brought from Mexico by the conquistador himself (Anders 1967:51). Both Brasseur, shortly before his death in 1874, and Leon de Rosny had heard of the existence of the piece. In 1880, the latter saw it in Madrid, photographed it, and soon proved it to be the missing portion of the Codex Troano (Rosny 1882:79-83). The two parts

(Fig. 1.16), joined again as the Codex Tro-Cortesianus or the Codex Madrid, can still be seen in Madrid's Museo de América.

In the summer of 1873, the first International Congress of Americanists convened at Nancy, France. Its distinguished delegates included William Bollaert of England, Francisco García Pimentel of Mexico,and Joseph Henry of the United States. In that initial session, Leon de Rosny presented a study of Maya numeration (1875). Since then, that learned gathering—held every two years with astonishingly few interruptions of regularity—has proved a durable and useful arena for the dissemination of scholarly research on the Maya and their hiero-glyphic writing.

In Yucatan, meanwhile, Juan Pio Pérez, who died in 1859, had left unfinished his largest work, a Maya-Spanish dictionary of Yucatec. The task of complet-ing it was taken up by the Yucatecan cleric-historian Don Crescencio Carrillo y Ancona and Dr. Carl Hermann Berendt, exiled German physician and political activist who had turned to Maya ethnology and linguistics. Publication of Pérez's *Diccionario de la lengua Maya*, begun in 1866, was not finished until 1877 because of civil war in Yucatan (Brinton 1900:4). It became the principal source for Yucatec Maya as an aid to glyph decipherment until the pub-lication of the much longer (and earlier) Motul Dictionary (Marteinez Hernández 1930).

Berendt, who died in Coban, Guatemala, in 1878, accumulated rare publications and manuscripts and made handwritten copies of some 120 important sources related to the various Mayan languages. These and other materials now form the notable Berendt Linguistic Collection at the University of Pennsylvania (Brinton 1900).

With the work of Brasseur de Bourbourg and of Leon de Rosny, we come to the end of the period of the Early Documentors. The break in time periods between them and later scholars of the calendar, set rather arbitrarily at 1880, is, however, neither a clean nor a clear separation, partly because the amount of data available for Maya hieroglyphic research was, at the time, growing rapidly. Often, too, the data-gath-erers were themselves the interpreters, and the enthusiasms of discovery often propelled these researchers into overinterpretations of their material. But, as we must remind ourselves, appropriate guidelines for proper research were only beginning to crystallize in the 1870s.

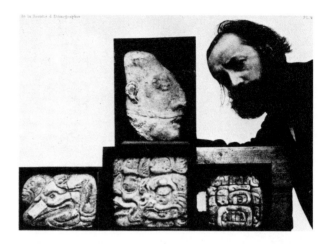

Figure 1.16. Leon de Rosny with Palenque stuccos. (Rosny 1882. Courtesy of the Center for Maya research, Washington, DC)

Brasseur's shortcomings in scholarship were tem-pered by some enduring contributions to glyphic interpretation. Apparently independent of Rafinesque's earlier work, Brasseur correctly inter-preted the Maya bar-and-dot numbers. He also veri-fied the meanings of the day signs, the hieroglyph for *kin*, or "day" (Thompson 1950:29), the *tun* sign for the 360-day period (Brunhouse 1973:134), and, most importantly, the sign for the possessive pro-noun *u* (Kelley 1962a:6).

Leon de Rosny performed great service by his publications of the Paris Codex (1887, 1888), and his scholarship seems, in retrospect, to be more even-handed than that of Brasseur. He elicited the mean-ings of the world direction glyphs (Rosny 1876:204) and accurately identified certain phonetic elements reflected in the day and month signs (Kelley 1962a:7). Rosny's *Essai sur le déchiffrement de l'écri-ture hiératique de l'Amérique Centrale*, issued in lim-ited folio and octavo editions dated 1876 (although neither actually appeared in complete form until 1883), constitutes the first general book of any merit on Maya hieroglyphic writing. Because of the time in which it was written, the work is confined to the material in the three hieroglyphic codices then known.

In 1879, Charles Rau, Chief of the Archaeological Division of the National Museum of the Smithsonian Institution in Washington, DC, published a short, excellent work on the "Palenque Tablet." The sculp-tured slab had been acquired in 1842 by the short-lived National Institute for the Promotion of Science and later transferred to the Smithsonian Institution (Rau 1879:1-3). By means of comparison with the earlier drawings by Waldeck and Catherwood and a photograph published by the explorer Désirée Charnay (1863:pl. 21), Rau verified the conclusion by Matile (1868, cited in Rau 1879) that the piece constituted the right-hand portion of the Tablet of the Temple of the Cross at Palenque. For purposes of his discussion, Rau adopted the system, now standard practice, of lettering and numbering hieroglyphic texts by columns and rows. Rau's meticulous treatment of the hieroglyphic text, his comparisons of its glyphs with the calendrical signs in the Landa account, and his utilization of the earliest truly useful photographic representation of a carved text all contributed to this early example of model research. Happily, the Palenque table was returned to Mexico in 1910 as a good-will gesture, and the entire panel, incomplete for over half a century, was restored to its original state.

Rau's monograph on the Palenque tablet, along with its translation into Spanish (Davis and Pérez 1882), serves well as a preview of the best of the events that followed in the rigorous study of the monumental inscriptions.

THE EARLY SCHOLARS (1880-1910)

For this epoch of research, we must return first to Dresden, and then to the field, since the story of the earliest intensive scholarship devoted to Maya writing had its beginnings almost simultaneously in both settings.

By 1880 the philologist Ernst Förstemann (Fig. 1.17) had been Librarian of the Königlichen Bibliothek (the Royal Library) of Dresden for 15 years (Deckert 1962:26). During that time he had corresponded with both Rosny in Paris and William Bollaert, a London scholar who published short works on the Maya codices (e.g., Bollaert 1870). In addition, Bishop Landa's *Relación . . .* had been available throughout Förstemann's tenure, and the librarian-philologist could not fail to note that its "alphabet," in the incautious hands of Brasseur and others, had yielded virtually nothing of use in deciphering any of the available Maya codices. The year 1880 marked, in fact, a low point of sorts for the reputation of the Landa data: the researcher Philipp

Figure 1.17. Ernest Förstemann. (From Ian Graham 1971. Courtesy of the Peabody Museum of Archaeology and Ethnology, Harvard University)

Valentini had stated in print his contention that the alphabet was nothing more than a Spanish contrivance—a fabrication, in effect, forced by Landa from his hapless informant (Valentini 1880).

Thus the time was ripe in 1880 for Förstemann to undertake what surely must be the ultimate in "library research." With ready and unlimited access to the original Dresden Codex, and with the methodical analytical approach that characterized his entire career in Maya studies, Förstemann began to reveal the entire working mechanism of the Maya calendar system and the functional interpretation of most of the hieroglyphs involved.

Förstemann began with the publication of a facsimile of the Dresden Codex (Förstemann 1880). Printed in Leipzig, it was limited to 60 copies and thus is of superlative rarity today. In the facsimile, each page of the manuscript appeared separately, at actual size and in color, all but perfectly replicated by the process of chromolithography, a method of reproduction utilizing photography and lithographic stones. The quality of this facsimile and its second edition (Förstemann 1892) has never been surpassed.

Between 1880 and 1906, the year of his death at age 84, Förstemann produced some 50 publications on the interpretation of Maya writing. These dealt mainly with the calendrical, astronomical, and mathematical sections of the Dresden manuscript, but also treated of the carved inscriptions as they appeared in publications of the time. In his commentary accompanying the facsimile (1880), and in successive papers, he identified the Dresden's month signs. In his seminal *Erlauterungen . . .* (1886), he worked out the essential mechanics of the "long-count" system of recording dates, and soon after calculated what had to be the base date of the count (Förstemann 1887). In the course of these pursuits, he recognized the hieroglyphs for zero and 20 in the Maya vigesimal, or base-20, system of arithmetic and worked out the complicated multiplication charts of the manuscript. In short papers of 1891 and 1893, Förstemann identified the period glyphs used to express long-count dates, and even recognized that the ancient calendarists counted lunar months by using alternating 29- and 30-day intervals (Förstemann 1893:32). He followed this with an explanation of the complex Venus tables and the correct reading of long-count dates on eight Copan monuments (1894), while identifying the head variants of the period glyphs.

A comprehensive bibliography of Förstemann's work appears with the reprint of the 1892 facsimile of the Dresden Codex (Deckert 1962:57-59). As Thompson (1950:30) noted in tribute to this astonishing scholar, "he stands shoulders above any other student of Maya hieroglyphs."

One of the principal factors in the great productivity of Förstemann and his contemporaries lay in the sudden availability of new Maya hieroglyphic texts, not only the two additional codices in Paris and Madrid, but, more importantly, accurate representations of the inscriptions in stone as well. Before the time of Förstemann, even the best published copies of the monumental texts (Stephens 1841, 1843) were simply not quite adequate for the kind of

Figure 1.18a. Alfred Percival Maudslay and his work: Maudslay at Copan (Maudslay 1889-1902).

careful analysis to which the codices could be subjected. The tide turned abruptly in 1889, with the publication of a thin oblong folio of 22 plates—plans, photographs, and drawings of Copan and its monumental inscriptions. Its author was the English traveler and scientist Alfred Percival Maudslay (Fig. 1.18a), whose first of many scientific working trips deep into the Maya area had taken place in 1882. The work in question was the first of 16 such fascicles dealing with various sites that appeared, along with text installments, irregularly over the next 13 years. The whole of this monumental work, consisting of four large volumes of plates and one of text, titled simply *Archaeology*, appeared in final form in 1902 as the third section (Vols. 55-59) of the *Biologia Centrali-Americana* (Godman and Salvin 1879-1915), an encyclopedic compendium of natural his-

Figure 1.18b. A page from Maudslay 1889-1902. (Both courtesy of the Center for Maya Research, Washington, DC)

tory published in London.

The labor involved in the compilation and production of the data for the great work was enormous. Maudslay not only made the taxing journeys to remote sites with the cumbersome gear necessary for glass-plate photography and the making of numerous moulds of the great stones, but later he also supervised the drawings of the inscriptions that accompanied the photographic coverage.

The finished work contained, in its 402 plates, splendid details of art and architecture, mainly of Copan, Quirigua, Yaxchilan, Chichen Itza, Tikal, and Palenque. In the treatment of hieroglyphic texts, Maudslay pioneered new standards. The photographic images—masterpieces of sharpness and subtle contrast—were reproduced at a scale usable by the epigraphist and accompanied by drawings of

identical size for maximum clarity. Maudslay's achievement, and that of those who helped, in particular photographer Henry Sweet and artist Annie Hunter, cannot be overstated. They set the highest of standards for scholarly work for the century to come (Fig. 1.18b).

Just as Förstemann's work typifies the beginning of the period of the Early Scholars in terms of pure research, that of Maudslay reflects it in terms of excellence in the field, a quality that separates the English gentleman-scholar from all who preceded him in the twin endeavors of exploration and documentation.

During the early 1880s, while Maudslay's field trips continued in Mexico and Guatemala, and Förstemann's short and incisive papers on his inspired gleanings from the Dresden Codex appeared in print at a relentless rate, others entered the field of Maya studies.

In 1881, Don Crescencio Carrillo y Ancona of Izamal, Yucatan, who had helped bring the Pérez dictionary into print, culminated 16 years of part-time study of his beloved local history in the 671-page *Historia Antigua de Yucatan* (1881). Throughout his adult life, and as Bishop of Yucatan from 1887 to 1897, Carrillo y Ancona continued the intensive pursuit of colonial-period Maya chronicles begun earlier by Juan Pio Pérez. At one time or another, he had in his possession the manuscripts of the Books of Chilam Balam of Chumayel, Kaua, Tizimin, Ixil, the Codex Pérez, and others (Rivera Figueroa and Canton Rosado 1918:41-42)—each of them a major source on the early Maya that might have been lost to posterity without his intervention.

Between 1884 and 1899, the French linguist Count Hyacinthe de Charency published several short but important works dealing with the contemporary Tzotzil Mayan language and calendar, including the eighteenth-century vocabulary of Manuel Hidalgo (Charency 1885) and one of his own compilation (1899). These added substantial linguistic data to the body of material that had begun to accumulate from early colonial sources (e.g., Coronel 1620; Beltran de Santa Rosa 1859 [1746]), and the works of Brasseur de Bourbourg (1862, 1869-1870) and others.

Daniel Garrison Brinton (Fig. 1.19), a Philadelphia physician and later Professor of American Archaeology and Linguistics at The University of Pennsylvania, began his studies shortly before the American Civil War (in which he served at

Figure 1.19. Daniel Garrison Brinton. (Oil portrait courtesy of the Library of The University Museum of Archaeology and Anthropology, The University of Pennsylvania, Philadelphia)

Gettysburg as battlefield surgeon) with a bibliographical work on the aboriginal history of Florida (Brinton 1859). Eventually he published more than 70 books or articles on Native American languages and literature (Brinton 1898). His work in the realm of ancient Maya writing began with a note on the Landa alphabet (Brinton 1870) and went on to include extremely valuable publications of the colonial-period chronicles accumulated by Pérez, Carrillo y Ancona, and others (Brinton 1882a, 1882b). His *A Primer of Mayan Hieroglyphics* was "intended as a summary of what had been achieved up to that time [1895] by students in this branch" (Brinton 1898:16-17). It achieved just that—a careful appraisal of the field with few original contributions by Brinton himself, except for the insistence that Maya hieroglyphic writing could never be successfully read without drawing upon knowledge of the Mayan languages. This seemingly obvious point of method, first suggested by Rafinesque (1832a, b), was not thoroughly exploited for another half century. In this respect, Brinton's work seems decades ahead of its time (Kelley 1962a:10-11) and helps make the *Primer . . .* of 1895 the first important general summary of Maya hieroglyphic writing to appear in the literature.

Another American, Cyrus Thomas of the Bureau of American Ethnology of the Smithsonian Institution in Washington, former lawyer, minister, and entomologist of some note, appeared on the Mayanist roster in 1882 with a study of the Troano Codex. In that work, he followed up on Rau's treatise on the Palenque Tablet of the Temple of the Cross (Rau 1879), applied principles evident in the codices, then tested and refined them with a close analysis of repeating hieroglyphic "clause" sequences on the carved stone. This study settled for all time the fundamental question of the reading order of the Maya inscriptions (Thomas 1882:199-292), as the exhaustive reexamination of the problem by Gunckel (1897) demonstrated. In the actual interpretation of the hieroglyphs, much of Thomas's work revolved around his premise that Maya writing was, as Landa had indicated, mainly phonetic, and only occasionally alphabetic. However, his efforts to establish a phonetic key came mostly to naught, as Thomas himself ultimately admitted (Kelley 1962a:9).

Eduard Seler (Fig. 1.20), whose profoundly important researches reached across all of Mesoamerica, provided, in the huge corpus of his works (Seler 1902-1923), so many potential paths of fruitful inquiry that subsequent scholars have often found their ideas to have been first broached by this great scholar. Seler's curiosity dealt not only with his specialty—the interpretation of the Borgia Codex and other central Mexican manuscript books and the belief system that underlay them (Seler 1904)—but with almost everything else as well, including the Maya codices (1887, 1888, 1904) and the ruins of Chichen Itza (Seler 1902-1923, 5:197-388), Palenque (Seler 1915), and Uxmal (Seler 1917).

Among the Maya texts, Seler identified the color signs and other extremely important glyphs, including those for "dog," "fire," and "capture" (Kelley 1962a:7-8). He also subjected the work of J. T. Goodman, whom we will discuss below, to rigorous testing, apparently concerned with the American's

Figure 1.20. Eduard Georg Seler. (Drawing by Hans Krausz, December 1901, courtesy of the Museum für Völkerkunde Preussischer Kulturdesitz, Berlin)

lack of acknowledgment of the work of the German scholars (Seler 1899). Perhaps the most lasting of Seler's contributions was his demonstration of the essential cultural unity of Mesoamerica. As we shall see below, this point was made especially clear in his survey of the meanings of the days of the sacred calendar cycle (Seler 1888; 1902-1923, 1:417-503).

Paul Schellhas, Förstemann's friend and colleague, made his own mark on Maya glyph studies in a series of short works that began in 1887 and culminated a decade later in a key study of the deities depicted in the Dresden Codex (Schellhas 1896). There, Schellhas provided the first "catalog" of Maya supernaturals by labeling them with letters—a practice continued by those who later expanded Schellhas's work (e.g., Zimmermann 1956). In his treatise, Schellhas also isolated the hieroglyphs referring to each deity, thus making the first inroad into the important category of names in Maya writing.

The period of research between Förstemann's

entry into the field in 1880 and Cyrus Thomas's final publication in 1904, while unusually productive of basic contributions on both sides of the Atlantic, was also notable for the first culmination of the "phonetics war" that had its roots in the 1864 publication of Bishop Landa's "alphabet" (Brasseur de Bourbourg 1864).

The fundamental problem lay in whether the Maya hieroglyphic system was (1) pictographic, where written elements are pictures with the inherent meaning or sound of the object depicted; (2) ideographic, in which the depiction represents a more complex set of meanings, as a picture of fire might represent "heat"; or (3) phonetic, where a written element might stand for a sound—either a syllable, in which each sign represents a possible vowel-consonant (consonant-vowel) set, or parts of an alphabet, where each sign stands for a pure sound, either a vowel or a consonant. The choices lay among these possibilities and a fourth, in which the system might be logographic, that is, a mixture of representations of words and sounds. Attempts to resolve the important question underlay the work of virtually all scholars in the decades following the appearance of Landa's putative key.

The protagonists that emerged to embrace the opposing sentiments of the 1880s and 1890s included Cyrus Thomas, on the one hand, who advocated the view that the Maya writing system was mainly phonetic, as Brasseur and Rosny had thought, and Eduard Seler, on the other, who considered the system mainly ideographic, a view shared by Schellhas and Förstemann. The latter, in fact remained obdurately disdainful of the applicability of phoneticism: "No one," he wrote, "will misconstrue my silence with regard to the so-called alphabet of Diego de Landa" (Förstemann 1894, 1904:501). The middle road was taken by Brinton, who consistently viewed Maya writing as a composite system of pictures, ideograms, and phonetic signs (Brinton 1882:xxvii, 1895:13). There the matter rested—at least for a while.

By the beginning of 1897, nearly half of Alfred P. Maudslay's prodigious record had appeared in seven fascicles of the now familiar and sought-after folios, providing a steady flow of new monumental inscriptions for Maya scholars. That year there appeared a large work, *The Archaic Maya Inscriptions*, based almost solely on the Maudslay material, that stands as the first major interpretative work on the Maya

Figure 1.21. Joseph T. Goodman. (Courtesy of Philip Earle, The Nevada Historical Society, Reno, NV)

Figure 1.22. Teobert Maler at Piedras Negras, Guatemala. (Courtesy of the Peabody Museum of Archaeology and Ethnology, Harvard University)

inscriptions. Its author was the American Joseph Thompson Goodman of San Francisco (Fig. 1.21), former owner of the Virginia City, Nevada, newspaper *The Territorial Enterprise*. There Goodman had given Mark Twain his start in writing; later he amassed a mining fortune (Brunhouse 1975:42).

Since the appearance of the first of Maudslay's fascicles, Goodman had used them eagerly, and soon began to make many important breakthroughs in the realm of calendrical and numerical glyphs. Among other things, Goodman correctly identified most of the head variant glyphs used for the numbers 1 to 19; and the glyphs for several important time periods. Many of his interpretations match conclusions published earlier by Förstemann, and Thompson (1950:30) notes the curious lack of appropriate citations in Goodman's work. That notwithstanding, the contributions attributable to

Goodman proved crucial in reading the inscriptions, and his lengthy table of Maya dates is still used by scholars (I. Graham 1975a:28-55). Maudslay himself, hearing in 1892 of Goodman's studies, encouraged the retired editor and soon arranged for his work to appear as a full-fledged appendix to the text volume of the completed Maudslay opus (1889-1902).

Goodman's second major effort addressed the problem of correlating the Maya dates in the inscriptions, which by their nature "floated" together in time, with dates in the Christian calendar. His correlation formula (Goodman 1905) was rejected at first, them modified later by Juan Martínez Hernández (1926) and J. Eric S. Thompson (1927, 1950:App. II). As we will see below, one of Thompson's two modifications of Goodman's original formula has remained a top contender among the multitude of correlations that have been proposed.

While Goodman's work progressed toward fruition, another explorer-photographer entered the Maya field. Teobert Maler (Fig. 1.22), born in Rome in 1842 of German parents, ended up in Mexico 23 years later among the French forces sent to support the Emperor Maximilian. He remained there after the fall of the regime (Brunhouse 1975:5-6). The year 1877 found Maler at Palenque, sketching the ruins as had so many before him, and photographing the site and its surroundings. Eventually, he settled in Merida, Yucatan.

For the next two decades Maler followed a field itinerary that ranged from northern Yucatan to the remote reaches of the Usumacinta Valley and the most inaccessible ruins of the Peten, continually photographing, mapping, and writing descriptions of his findings. His great contribution to Maya hieroglyphic studies lay in the meticulous photographic documentation of inscriptions and monuments that, in many cases, would otherwise have been unavailable for posterity. Working without institutional support most of the time, Maler chose for himself what must appear to have been a life of extreme rigor and loneliness for the cause of Maya archaeology.

In 1901, many of the best of his images of monuments at Yaxchilan, Piedras Negras, Chinikiha, and other important sites began to appear in print in the *Memoirs* of Harvard University's Peabody Museum of Archaeology and Ethnology—a series of major works (Maler 1901, 1903, 1908a, b, 1910, 1911) that ended with the publication of his Tikal photographs. In 1911, the decade-long official relationship between the Peabody Museum and the explorer was terminated, and Maler died six years later in Merida. The bulk of his photographic output, maps, and notes lies scattered in repositories from Mexico to Europe, and one hopes that someday it will be cataloged and published.

In another of those coincidental links between successive generations of Mayanists, it is appropriate to note that Maler, during his final years in Merida, had an informal "student"—none other than Alfredo Barrera Vásquez (David H. Kelley, personal communication). The young Barrera Vásquez who visited with Maler about once a week to discuss Maya matters later married a niece of Edward H. Thompson (himself famed for the dredging of the Sacred Cenote at Chichen Itza). After studying under the great Alfred M. Tozzer at Harvard, Barrera Vásquez went on to become perhaps the greatest Maya scholar to emerge from the actual land of the Maya. His work in linguistics culminated in the great Diccionario Maya Cordemex (1980), and his collected works appeared soon afterward (Barrera Vásquez 1980-1981).

In one sense, Teobert Maler's documentary work was a continuation of a tradition begun by Désiré Charnay (1863). The ruins themselves or portraits of people, however, and not glyphic texts, formed the major portion of Charnay's accomplishment (Davis 1981:38-99). Therefore his contribution lies outside the scope of the present survey. Maler's work is thus best compared to that of Maudslay, whom he immediately succeeded in print. In fact, the publication

dates of the two form a 30-year "golden age" in the documentation of the Maya inscriptions. Anyone inspecting the negatives or the photographic images of these pioneer photographers in the Maya area must surely feel a sense of regret at the loss of both the routine use of the large-format camera and the publication techniques that did full justice to the resulting images.

Coincident with the years of the Maler publications were those of our last important scholar of the period. Charles Pickering Bowditch had been the moving force behind the funding of Maler's work for the Peabody Museum, much as he had been for George Byron Gordon at Copan and Edward H. Thompson in northern Yucatan (Weeks 1984:3). During his years of productive study, Bowditch raised the hand of caution and subjected many of the findings of his contemporaries, particularly Goodman, to rigorous testing. In a series of privately printed pamphlets beginning in 1901, Bowditch made refinements in the consideration of Maya dating methods (1901a) and explored the nature of the mechanics of certain Calendar Round dates (1901b). After having seen Maler's report on Piedras Negras, Bowditch speculated on specific points of historical content in the hieroglyphic passages (1901c:13). This astonishing insight anticipated by nearly six decades the more complete and rigorous analysis by Proskouriakoff (1960). Other publications by Bowditch dealt with the inscriptions of Tikal (1903) and the Tablet of the Temple of the Cross at Palenque (1906).

One of the greatest services performed on behalf of Maya scholarship in the United States was Bowditch's successful effort to have the original contributions of Förstemann, Seler, Schellhas, and others translated into English and published as a collection by the Smithsonian Institution (Bowditch 1904). At the Peabody Museum, he supervised a translation of Schellhas's key work on the Maya gods in the Dresden Codex (1904) and of the most important of Eduard Seler's collected works (Seler 1902-1923), later distributed in mimeograph form to scholars.

Bowditch's major work, the summary of knowledge on Maya numeration, calendrics, and astronomy, privately printed in 1910, synthesized the knowledge of the time, and thus serves as a fitting end to our period of the Early Scholars. In July of the same year, Cyrus Thomas died at his Washington home at the age of 85.

Up to this time, we have seen enormous gains in the interpretation of the codices, the beginning of the mass publication of photographs and drawings of the monumental inscriptions, and the first culmination of the scholarly debate over the matter of phoneticism in Maya writing. By 1910, no single faction had "won" these engagements. Phoneticism as an issue seemed dead, but such was not the case. The question simply lay dormant while the next generation of scholars devoted themselves mainly to elaborations of the growing knowledge of Maya calendrics and the attempts to match Maya dates with those of the Christian era (Kelley 1962:4).

THE PERIOD OF THE INSTITUTIONS (1910-1958)

In September 1910, Mexico City celebrated the centennial of the nation's revolution for independence and prepared for the inauguration of Porfirio Díaz for an eighth presidential term. At the same time a small group of scholars, including Eduard Seler, Franz Boas, and Ezequiel Chávez, signed the bylaws of the Escuela Internacional de Arqueología y Etnología, a new organization that served for 10 years as a sponsor of international scientific endeavor (Bernal 1980:160).

The first set of events in that fateful Mexican autumn ended in armed revolution that engulfed the country for decades. The second created an institution that, though short-lived, helped transform archaeology from the mere collecting of artifacts and sculpture to something nearer true science.

The excavations by Manuel Gamio at San Miguel Amantla in the Valley of Mexico employed, for the first time in any area of Mesoamerica, the stratigraphic method by which the Indian past could be elicited, at least in terms of relative chronological order (Bernal 1980:164). This archaeological innovation played a crucial role in putting the ruins, the ceramics, and other cultural remains of the ancient Maya in order. Those data, in turn, could for the first time be compared with the ongoing findings related to the chronological content of the Maya hieroglyphic inscriptions.

The year 1910 also saw Sylvanus Griswold Morley (Fig. 1.23), a 26-year-old archaeology student out of Harvard, beginning his first of three seasons of excavation in the Maya area (Brunhouse 1971:52). The

Figure 1.23. Sylvanus G. Morley at Chichen Itza, 1924. (Photograph by Jerome O. Kilmartin)

project, under the pioneer Southwestern archaeologist Edgar Lee Hewett, Director of the School of American Archaeology in Santa Fe, settled on the site of Quirigua, Guatemala, for the recording of monuments, excavation, and consolidation of architecture (Hewett 1911, 1912). Here, Morley not only indulged his rapidly growing interest in the hieroglyphic inscriptions acquired in Alfred M. Tozzer's Harvard classroom, but he also learned something of the administration of an archaeological project as well (Brunhouse 1971:53). Both experiences served well in the subsequent history of Maya glyphic research.

In 1912, the Board of Trustees of the Carnegie Institution of Washington appropriated funds for archaeological research, and in 1914 Morley was appointed Research Associate of the Institution (Brunhouse 1971:63-75). However, his initial plan—

the archaeological investigation of Chichen Itza (Morley 1913)—was delayed by the Mexican Revolution. Morley quickly adapted, devoting himself instead to "the preparation of a work containing descriptions and decipherments of all known Maya texts . . . as a ready and standard reference on Maya chronology" (Morley 1914).

Morley was well prepared for this immense task. Early in 1914 he had completed *Introduction to the Study of the Maya Hieroglyphs* (Morley 1915). This general work was designed to do what Bowditch's 1910 summary had done—to provide a single source for the many otherwise inaccessible works of earlier scholars. However, it also had another aim—to make the subject comprehensible to the layperson. Morley's *Introduction . . .* , still one of the most readily understandable treatments of Maya calendrics ever written, also contains a cogent argument for the high probability of historical content in the inscriptions (1915:33-34), the very point that Bowditch had touched upon in 1901).

The matter of history in the inscriptions, however, was simply not ready for pursuit for various reasons. For one, there existed no known methodology for tackling the problem. There was also the simple matter of momentum: the productive efforts of Förstemann and others in Maya calendrics, and the overriding concern of the archaeology of the period with chronology alone, served well to sublimate any inclination toward historical pursuits. Whatever the causes, Morley almost immediately turned to the calendrical and chronological content of the texts, to the exclusion of all else. The two paragraphs that constitute the formal notice of the Carnegie Institution's sponsorship of Morley's glyph project (doubtless penned by Morley himself) state the matter officially and succinctly: "The Maya hieroglyphic inscriptions, so far as they have been deciphered, deal exclusively with the counting of time either in relation to the Maya calendar or certain astronomical phenomena with which the Mayas were familiar" (Morley 1914:333).

The beginning of Morley's association with the Carnegie Institution serves well as a milestone in our research history. He and others who later joined the staff made Carnegie the dominant force in Maya studies for nearly half a century. The 60 major publications issued between 1913 and 1962 are works on archaeology, botany, entomology, ethnohistory, architecture, ceramics, ethnology,

and hieroglyphic writing.

The first major report that resulted from the Carnegie Institution's archaeological program was Morley's *The Inscriptions at Copan* (1920). In the gigantic work, the first result of the hieroglyphic project, he provided detailed interpretations of the calendrical matter on the monuments, even those with badly eroded inscriptions, for no one bettered Morley in his determination—and ability—to wrest dates from even the most damaged monuments. Texts dealing with noncalendrical matters, however, were generally ignored, in both discussion and illustration, for at this time there was simply no apparent strategy for attacking those mysterious glyphs with no numbers attached.

Morley followed an identical policy in the multivolume *The Inscriptions of Peten* (1937-1938), thereby setting the general pattern for most Maya text treatments published by Carnegie and other institutions of the time (Palacios 1928; Thompson, Pollock, and Charlot 1932; Ruppert and Denison 1943). Thus did Morley and others gradually build a relative chronology for the Maya lowlands based on the time spans of the dates found at sites throughout the region. Morley's contributions, although demanding some corrections in the light of later work and discoveries of missing fragments, remain among the most productive efforts ever made in the gathering of dated Maya texts for scholars.

In working with the growing number of calendrical texts, Sylvanus G. Morley made many noteworthy breakthroughs, including the pioneering work on the "supplementary series," the string of glyphs including lunar data that follows Initial Series dates, and certain period-ending glyphs.

Morley's landmark volume on Copan contained, in addition to the calendrical data in the inscriptions themselves, two valuable early accounts of the site and a section on Mayan languages (Morley 1920:541-550, 605-615). These were the contributions of William E. Gates, then 57, one of the more curious characters in our growing roll of Mayanists. Above all else, Gates was a collector and bibliophile. Around the turn of the century, he had begun amassing rare books and manuscripts dealing with native Mexico and, in particular, the Maya. Originals that he could not obtain, he had photographed; ultimately, he owned some 7,000 items (Brunhouse 1975:159), many of which have proved indispensable to the study of Mayan languages, Postconquest Maya history, and, indirectly, the study of Maya hieroglyphic writing.

In 1920, Gates created The Maya Society, an organization of specialists, including Morley, who served as a kind of trust for Gates's vast library. Unfortunately, it quickly foundered in the turmoil of political and personal conflicts that marked Gates's brief tenure at the Department of Middle American Research at Tulane University, a new institution in 1924, which purchased much of the Gates Collection and hired Gates himself as its first director.

Although collecting as an end in itself appears to have dominated his mentality, Gates did publish occasional works relative to the study of Maya hieroglyphs, particularly after 1930, when he revived The Maya Society. These, however, typically appeared in extremely limited editions. Among them were versions of the three codices, issued either as photographic copies or in versions employing Gates's font of Maya glyph "type," by which he sought to clarify the variations inherent in the originals (Fig. 1.24). Gates's *An Outline Dictionary of Maya Glyphs* (1931), although superseded by the work of Zimmermann (1956) and Thompson (1962), represented the first attempt to catalog all the hieroglyphs of the Dresden, Paris, and Madrid Codices in a systematic manner.

The books, manuscripts, photographs, and miscellanea that made up the original Gates Collection are housed, in the form of originals or photographic copies, and only in part, in various repositories: mainly Tulane, Harvard, Princeton, and Brigham Young Universities, the Library of Congress, and the Newberry Library. The publication of the vast corpus of the Gates material would be of immense value to future Maya scholarship. Meanwhile, a useful—indeed indispensable—guide to those portions of the Gates Collection held by various repository institutions has recently been published by John Weeks (1990).

In 1937, the year of the first appearance of part of Morley's enormous *Inscriptions of Peten*, the Carnegie Institution published another work, which, by virtue of its focus and approach, was quite the opposite of Morley's opus. It dealt with the inscriptions of Chichen Itza, and its author was Hermann Beyer of the Middle American Research Institute—formerly the Department of Middle American Research—at Tulane University.

Beyer was born in Cologne, Germany, the year

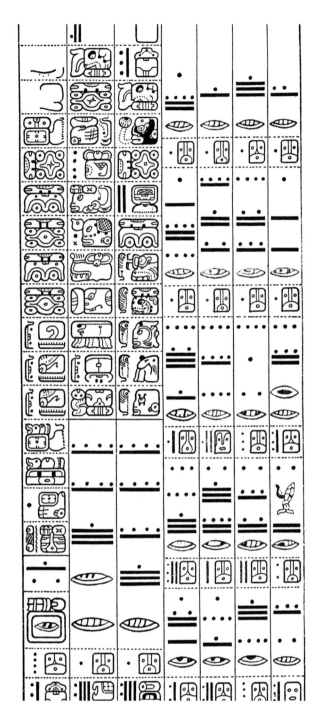

Figure 1.24. The Maya type font of William E. Gates. (Courtesy of the Center for Maya Research)

that Ernst Förstemann began his studies of the Dresden Codex. Following his education at the University of Berlin and the Sorbonne in Paris, he settled in Mexico City where, in 1915, he became Inspector of Monuments. Afterward Beyer occupied the chair of Mexican Archaeology at the Universidad Nacional Autónoma de México, where he taught until 1927, when his tenure at Tulane began (Caso 1959:24-25). In 1919, Beyer launched the journal *El México Antiguo*, to which he contributed for two more decades.

As Eric Thompson—who knew them both well—noted, the differences between Morley and Beyer transcended even their appreciable contrasts in personality: "Morley was wrapped up in the very restricted aspects of the Maya Initial Series, and to Hermann, I think, he seemed like a child playing with that single toy; Hermann saw Maya glyphs as something more than a string of dates" (Thompson 1959:18). It was this viewpoint that gave Beyer's study of the inscriptions at Chichen Itza (Beyer 1937) its enduring value. In concept, the work is little more than what many modern scholars of Maya epigraphy take for granted—a comparative structural analysis of glyph groups of "clauses" of apparently identical meaning or function that nonetheless possess certain variations in their component signs and in details of arrangement.

Beyer's meticulous methodology was far ahead of its time. His purely graphic approach isolated sets of component signs in the inscriptions that possibly shared identical meanings or functions and served to make a breach in the nearly impenetrable realm of noncalendrical glyphs. The principal problem with Beyer's approach may have been, as Barthel suggested in 1952, "his method of dissecting graphical elements so far that their meaning as entities was destroyed and they fell apart into a heap of fragmentary uncoordinated symbols" (Kelley 1962a:14). Nonetheless, Beyer's innovative method at least began to reveal some of the conventions and substitution patterns inherent in the Maya writing system, and for that we are greatly indebted to him.

Beyer's publications on Maya writing appeared between 1921 and 1945. Among the many concerned with calendrical matters, the most important of them was the one demonstrating that the variable element of the Initial Series Introductory Glyph varied in accordance with the month of the date in question (Beyer 1931). He also dealt with such matters as the stylistic change in certain glyphs over time (1932) and the graphic rules that appeared to govern the pattern of the attachment of affixes (the smaller elements of Maya writing) to main signs (1934, 1934a, 1936). Hermann Beyer's death, in 1942, in the wartime camp for interned aliens at Stringtown, Oklahoma, provided a sad finale to one of the most productive careers in Maya hieroglyphic research.

The years between 1910 and 1940 saw other students of Maya writing make their mark in the rapidly expanding field. Among them, Herbert Spinden, a contemporary of Morley's, whose career included curatorships at the American Museum of Natural History, the Peabody Museum at Harvard, and the Brooklyn Museum, pioneered in the systematic study of Maya art (Spinden 1913). Spinden's other specialty lay in the correlation of Maya and Christian dates, and in 1924 he proposed a formula that assigned Maya dates to a time approximately 260 years earlier than those derived by means of Goodman's formula. He then spent much of his career defending it (Thompson 1950:33). Spinden also made more attempts than most to come to terms with noncalendrical as well as calendrical glyphs, but virtually all of his interpretations came to naught (Kelley 1962a:12-13).

In the realm of astronomy, Spinden was one of the earliest scholars to deal rigorously with the complex subject both in Maya terms and in terms of real time (Spinden 1924, 1928, 1949).

John Edgar Teeple, a chemical engineer by profession and a Mayanist by avocation, proved that the function of most of the hieroglyphs that comprise the lunar series attached to Maya Initial Series dates (Teeple 1925, 1925a, 1928). In 1930, he summarized his work in *Maya Astronomy*, a landmark study published by the Carnegie Institution. In it, Teeple proposed, among other things, his theory of "determinants"—putative numerical corrections for reconciling the true solar year with the fractionless Maya calendrical units. This proposal ultimately faltered in the light of criticism by Satterthwaite (1947:125-142) and the subsequent recognition of those intervals as historical periods of time, rather than astronomical spans (Kelley 1976:213). However, Teeple's summation represented a culmination of work on the astronomical aspect of the content of Maya writing that had begun with Förstemann and Seler. It also provided a baseline study for future work on the all-important subject by Spinden (1940), Makemson (1943), and others.

In 1926, John Eric Sidney Thompson (Fig. 1.25), a young Englishman born in Argentina, joined

Figure 1.25. Sir Eric Thompson in his study at Ashdon, Saffron Walden, Essex, 1972. (Photograph by Otis Imboden, courtesy of the National Geographic Society, Washington, DC)

Morley's project at Chichen Itza as Assistant Archaeologist. The next year he moved into an assistant curatorship at the Field Museum of Natural History in Chicago, where he remained until joining the permanent staff of the Carnegie Institution of Washington in 1935 (Hammond 1977:181). More than any other individual in the history of the field, Thompson came to dominate Maya studies, in particular those of the hieroglyphic writing system.

In his first major interpretative publication (1927), Thompson reinvestigated the formula for the correlation of Maya and Christian chronology proposed by Goodman (1905) and reaffirmed by the Yucatecan scholar Juan Martínez Hernández (1926), and modified it. By 1941, no less than 70 separate publications by Thompson had appeared, including works in ethnology (1930) archaeology (1931), and ethnohistory (1938), along with an important work on the moon goddess in ancient Mesoamerica (1939). In the specific field of hieroglyphs, Thompson's contributions were both numerous and important. In 1929 he recognized the function of Glyph G of the supplementary series. In 1934, he deciphered the "15-*tun*" time-period glyph and produced an important interpretative summary on the significance of colors and directions in the Maya inscriptions. In 1937, he deciphered the peculiar style of dating at Chichen Itza. And this was only the beginning.

In 1930, Juan Martínez Hernández published the Maya-Spanish portion of the massive *Diccionario de Motul*, the earliest known and largest of such works

on Yucatec Maya. According to Brinton (1900:2), it contained roughly three and a half times the number of entries in Pérez's earlier work (1866-1877). The Motul Dictionary has proved to be a fundamental aid in eliciting readings of the glyphs, particularly those in the Postclassic (and presumably Yucatec-based) codices. Recent investigations by Rene Acuña of the Universidad Nacional Autónoma de México indicate that the Motul Dictionary is none other than the great Calepino of Antonio de Ciudad Real. A photographic facsimile of the Maya-Spanish portion of the work, along with an exhaustive commentary, has recently appeared (Acuña 1984).

Other contributions of the 1930s include translations by Médiz Bolio (1930) and Ralph Roys (1933) into Spanish and English, respectively, of the Book of Chilam Balam of Chumayel, the enormously important eighteenth-century compendium of chronicle and prophecy which Brinton had published in part (1882) and which now is part of the collection of the Princeton University Library. The relevance of the Chumayel manuscript and other such colonial native documents to the study of Maya writing lies in the high probability that phraseology and specific patterns in the transcriptions of words reflect characteristics derived directly from the earlier hieroglyphic system (Bricker 1989).

Up to now we have seen how the three decades that preceded World War II witnessed a quantum leap in the intensity of effort devoted to understanding the ancient Maya. That effort was largely channeled by ongoing archaeological fieldwork under the auspices of institutions such as the Carnegie, which had its inception during the period, and other, older programs whose research began in earnest after 1910.

Between 1923 and 1937, Carnegie's growing archaeological staff, under the direction of Morley and, later, Alfred Kidder, undertook successive field programs at Chichen Itza and Uaxactun and published the first full-fledged reports on Tulum, Coba, and other key sites. In Belize—then British Honduras—Thomas A. Joyce of the British Museum excavated at Lubaantun and Pusilha from 1926 to 1930, while his countryman Thomas Gann, a physician and tireless Mayanist, continued his steady output of popular volumes on explorations and discoveries reaching back to 1894 (Carmichael 1973:34).

In 1928, Frans Blom, Gates's successor at Tulane's

Middle American Research Institute, undertook an exploration of the Lacandon Forest, a journey of incredible hardship—the very kind that Blom relished (Brunhouse 1976:88-113). It revealed numerous new sites in that remote area of Chiapas (Blom and Duby 1955-1957). The University of Pennsylvania's University Museum spent the decade of the 1930s investigating Piedras Negras. In 1934, the Museo Nacional de Arqueología, Historia, y Etnografía of Mexico (recast in 1939 as the Instituto Nacional de Arqueología e Historia) began more than a decade of archaeological and conservation work at Palenque under the direction of Miguel Angel Fernández (Molina Montes 1979:4-6). Among its accomplishments, that effort succeeded in uncovering several long inscriptions of great importance in the Palace (Palacios 1935).

Harvard's Peabody Museum of Archaeology and Ethnology, on the other hand, did little in the way of actual fieldwork in the Maya area after the time of Maler's explorations and the sponsorship of R. E. Merwin's excavation of Holmul in 1912. Instead, its publication program on Maya subjects concentrated almost exclusively on important results of nonfield pursuits that included work on colonial history (Means 1917), the Dresden Codex (Guthe 1921), astronomy (Willson 1924), phonetics in Maya writing (Whorf 1933), and the substantial contributions by Alfred M. Tozzer culminating in the completion of the definitive, annotated English translation of Landa's *Relación* . . . (1941).

For present purposes, the short work by Benjamin Lee Whorf is of much more than routine interest, for its appearance marked the beginning of the second stage of a controversy that had lain dormant since the time of Seler and Thomas. Tozzer, in the introduction to Whorf's monograph, put it best: "With great acumen and courage Whorf dares to reopen the phonetic question" (Whorf 1933:ix).

Whorf believed that "Landa's list of characters has certain earmarks of being genuine and also of being the reflex of a phonetic system" (1933:2) but took this reasonable premise and proceeded through a chain of arguments that contained more than a few fatal flaws, including the misidentification of glyphs and an inconsistency in dealing with the linguistic rules (Kelley 1962a:8). Whorf's single acceptable reading—*hax* for the "drill" glyph in the Dresden Codex—appears to be one of those right answers that derive from a wrong approach. A second paper

by Whorf on his phonetic approach (1942) fared no better, either in the methods employed or in the reaction of others. Thompson's devastating critique (1950:311-313) is still the most telling appraisal of this second revival of the question of phoneticism.

Aside from the brief rise and, as we shall see, temporary fall of phoneticism as a viable consideration in defining the nature of Maya writing, the decade of the 1940s saw a corresponding increase in the output of scholars dealing with dates (Lizardi Ramos 1941) and numbers (Berlin 1945). In retrospect, Satterthwaite appears to have dominated this period of consideration of chronological matters by his rigorous defense of Thompson's correlation formula and his meticulous 1947 summation, *Concepts and Structures of Maya Calendrical Arithmetics*.

J. Eric S. Thompson, meanwhile, continued his amazing output of research papers on virtually all aspects of Mesoamerican culture while leaning more and more toward considering the matter of the Maya noncalendrical glyphs. His most important contributions during the 1940s included discovery of the important ritual cycle of 819 days (1943) and the regional pattern of the aberrant "Yucatecan-style" dates (with Proskouriakoff 1947). Most important of all, however, was a short paper issued in mimeograph in 1944 for distribution by the Carnegie Institution. It dealt with the "count" glyphs and proposed that the main sign, the head of a shark, *xoc* in Yucatec Mayan, served also as *xoc*, the root of the verb "to count." Today, this kind of relationship between the written and spoken language, where a sign refers to two different things, seems both simple and obvious. Although Thompson's interpretation of it is in question, the *xoc* reading constituted an innovation of the highest order for its time (Kelley 1962a:16). Indeed, the very suggestion that the system could work in such a manner opened new vistas for future research. In the same paper Thompson demonstrated that the element that Landa had labeled *ti* indeed appeared in the inscriptions and functioned as the locative "to" or "at," just as the dictionaries said it should.

In another area of study, the Yucatecan linguist Alfredo Barrera Vásquez collaborated on two important and useful compendiums of parallel texts in the various Books of Chilam Balam, one in Spanish (Barrera Vásquez and Rendón 1948), the other in English (Barrera Vásquez and Morley 1949).

Sylvanus Morley died in September 1948. One of

ATION

RAN

FST

Thompson's last publications of the 1940s was the obituary of his close friend and colleague (Thompson 1949). Morley's passing dealt a serious blow to Maya studies, for with him exited the irreplaceable spirit and enthusiasm that characterized the whole period of his presence on the scene. It is fitting, in the history of research and publications, to acknowledge Morley's great popular work, *The Ancient Maya*. Its appearance in 1946 coincided not only with the spirit of hope that followed the end of World War II but also with the time when available information on the Maya had reached all but critical mass. Morley wrote it in a readable and informative style that inspired many Mayanists in the field today. The work is now in its fourth edition (Morley, Brainerd, and Sharer 1983).

In 1950, Eric Thompson published the most remarkable of all his works—*Maya Hieroglyphic Writing: An Introduction*. Far more than an introduction, the work provided the landmark summation of knowledge on the subject up to that time. Thompson's awesome knowledge of Maya archaeology, ethnohistory, and ethnology pervaded every section of the book, as did his clear and elegant writing style. As Kelley noted (1962c:278-279), Thompson's 1950 summary substantially increased the knowledge of both the hieroglyphs themselves and the principles of the writing system, particularly with respect to grammatical patterns evident in the codices. About half of some 40 new readings introduced by Thompson—often only casually—have since proven acceptable to modern scholars (Kelley 1962b:14). Among these, the most important is perhaps *te*, which, as Thompson showed (1950:282-84), could function as the word "tree," as the grammatical particle that served as a numerical classifier, or as part of the deity name *Bolon-yoc-te* (Kelley 1962b:16). This reinforced the very important principle that a single sign could function grammatically in a variety of ways.

With the *te* argument, Thompson entered the realm of sign-sound relationships, much as he had in the case of the *xoc* reading of 1944. In that key question, which lay at the very core of the problem of the nature of Maya writing, he had no problem with the logographic or "rebus" use of either *te* or *xoc*. Each of those, no matter what else it did, could function as an independent speech particle—*te* as "tree" or "wood," and *xoc* as "shark." What Thompson opposed was any contention that a hieroglyphic sign

Figure 1.26. Yurii Valentinovich Knorozov. (Courtesy of Valery Gulayev, Akademiya Nauk, USSR)

could work solely as a phonetic syllable or, indeed, as anything below the grammatical level of an independent morpheme. He adhered steadfastly to this view for the next two decades (Thompson 1972:28-31).

In 1952, Yurii Valentinovich Knorozov (Fig. 1.26), a young Russian scholar, published the first of several papers arguing in favor of the very point opposed by Thompson. He began with the assumption of the fundamental validity of Landa's "alphabet" as a series of signs with "the exact phonetic meaning that he attributed to them" (Knorozov 1952:14). He then proposed a series of phonetic readings of various sign combinations in the codices, including a pair possessing a sign—which Knorozov read as *tzu*—in common. One, long recognized as having some association with "dog" (e.g., Seler 1902-

1923, I:476) came out *tzul*, a word for "dog" in Yucatec Mayan (Pérez 1866-1877:XXX); the other, *cutz*, the common Yucatec word for "turkey" (Martínez Hernández 1930:214). In this and subsequent papers (1952, 1955a, b) Knorozov offered readings for some 100 signs and 200 glyphic combinations, of which 50 or so were new (Kelley 1962a:18).

At first, reactions to Knorozov were almost unanimously negative for many reasons, including the polemic character of the 1952 article and Knorozov's carelessness or misidentifications in dealing with certain parts of his data. Reactions from Thompson (1954:174-178; 1959) and Barthel (1958) were particularly severe, attacking the obvious weaknesses of Knorozov's work, and concentrating largely on the proposed readings themselves, (Kelley 1962a:18). In the climate of rather heated exchanges that characterized this revival of the phonetics war in the 1950s, the main point of Knorozov's work—the establishment of a principle governing the very workings of Maya writing—seemed to have been lost as the appropriate focus for dispassionate testing.

Simply stated, what Knorozov proposed was that the Maya could, if they wished, utilize glyphs as purely phonetic syllables. Each such syllable was composed of a certain initial consonant (C) and a certain final vowel (V). Such a CV phoneme, in combination with another (CV-CV) or others (CV-CV-CV), could form words. Furthermore, the final vowel of such a combination was but a purely orthographic device that could be dropped. Thus the example *tzul*, noted above, was actually written *tzu-lu,* with *cutz* likewise rendered as *cu-tzu* (Knorozov 1955a, b).

While the Knorozov-Thompson dispute ran its course through the mid-1950s toward culmination in the pages of *American Antiquity* (Knorozov 1958; Thompson 1959), Günter Zimmermann of the University of Hamburg sought to systematize the hieroglyphs and deity representations in the three Maya codices—an effort to rectify the inadequacies of William Gates's 1931 work and to refine the classifications of Schellhas (1897). The Zimmermann catalog (1956), welcomed by virtually all concerned Mayanists, proved to be a meticulous work that not only provided a systematic reference for the hieroglyphic signs and deities, but also produced important insights into the relationships between the text and image in the manuscript books. Key among

these was the recognition of "attributive" glyphs. These apparently conveyed augural information related, not to lucky or unlucky days themselves, but rather to deities of "negative" or "positive" aspect pictured in association with those days (Zimmermann 1956:161-168).

The closing years of the 1950s were marked by events of both negative and positive consequence to Maya studies in general and to hieroglyphic studies in particular. In 1958, the Carnegie Institution of Washington abruptly abolished its Division of Historical Research in order to devote more funds to nuclear research—this in the wake of the Sputnik scare. Thus ended the program of research begun by Morley more than 40 years earlier. Its accomplishments over that period were summarized by Pollock (1958:435-449), and its extensive archive was turned over to the Peabody Museum of Archaeology and Ethnology at Harvard University.

With the demise of the Division of Historical Research of the Carnegie Institution, Maya research lost one of its organizational mainsprings as well as a principal publication vehicle. Although Carnegie had been taken to task at times for a tendency to neglect interpretation in favor of data (Kluckhohn 1940; Taylor 1948), its contribution was enormous and included many of the key works of hieroglyphic scholarship cited above, ranging from Morley's compendiums of site-by-site calendrical text analysis (1920, 1937-1938) to Thompson's summary of Maya writing (1950). Under Carnegie's auspices, more than a score of minor works on specific texts had appeared as well.

The momentum of institutional research that characterized the Carnegie years was, toward the end of the period, reinforced by the acceleration of activities by others. In 1956, The University Museum of the University of Pennsylvania began the long-term Tikal Project, which, among other things, resulted in the redrawing of the numerous inscriptions of that great site and the discovery of new texts (Satterthwaite 1958; Coe, Shook, and Satterthwaite 1961; Jones and Satterthwaite 1982). Shortly afterward, Tulane's Middle American Research Institute under Robert Wauchope initiated field research at Dzibilchaltun in northern Yucatan directed by E. Wyllys Andrews IV, a rare scholar who was equally at home in archaeology and epigraphy. Mexico's National Institute of Anthropology and History, meanwhile, had begun a second major program of archaeology and architectural conservation at Palenque in 1949 under the direction of Alberto Ruz Lhuillier (Molina Montes 1979:7).

In the nearly half century that elapsed between 1910 and 1958, Carnegie and other institutions brought a vast amount of new material to light. In terms of major trends of research, we have seen how the decades before World War II witnessed an almost exclusive concern by Morley and others with calendrical, astronomical, and chronological matters. These new data were derived largely from monumental inscriptions, which generally replaced the codices as the primary focus of attention. Among Mayanists of the pre-World War II era, Beyer stands out by virtue of his interest in noncalendrical hieroglyphs, but his contribution remains more in the realm of the methodology of his structural approach than in specific and testable readings. The long-dormant phonetics question was revived briefly in the 1930s and 1940s but without useful results.

During the postwar period, on the other hand, an increased movement into the area of noncalendrical texts took place. Thompson's great summary of 1950 created an established baseline, both for his own future work and for that of other Western scholars who together constituted virtually the entire body of those working on Maya writing. Into that intellectual climate suddenly came Knorozov's proposal of actual phonetic rules for the reading of Maya hieroglyphic signs. While the controversy over the very nature of the writing system continued through the 1950s, tangible progress in eliciting its historical content began in 1958. It is that point at which we begin our consideration of the next—and most recent—period of Maya hieroglyphic research.

THE RECENT PAST (1958-1984)

Among the continuing contributions of the 1950s, few individuals surpassed Heinrich Berlin in terms of far-reaching significance. Berlin had come to Mexico from his native Germany in 1935, and five years later he found himself working for Miguel Angel Fernández at Palenque, where he became interested in the hieroglyphic inscriptions of the site, just as had many before him. In 1943, Berlin published the first of many papers on Maya hieroglyphs. In the beginning, these dealt with chronological matters (Berlin 1943), and included important identifications

such as the rare head variant of the number 11 (1944). By the 1950s, he had begun to concentrate increasingly on the noncalendrical content of Maya writing. In 1958, this effort resulted in a key breakthrough.

Berlin had noticed that certain hieroglyphs were distinguishable from all others by virtue of the presence of certain essentially consistent affixes attached to a larger main sign. The latter, on the other hand, varied greatly, and almost always each variant main sign appeared to be confined to a particular site. Moreover, the distinctiveness of these particular hieroglyphs was only reinforced by their consistency of location at the ends of texts or at the end of recognizable clauses. Berlin concluded that these "emblem glyphs," as he termed them (Berlin 1958), must refer to sites in some specific manner, either as actual place names or as names of lineages or families at those places. Since 1958, other emblem glyphs have come to light, and their pattern of distribution and context only reinforces Berlin's original conclusions.

The major accomplishment of Berlin's 1958 paper lay in its rigorous proof of the existence of actual historical information in the Maya monumental inscriptions. This alone set off a chain reaction of related decipherments and interpretations that helped to realign the direction of much of Maya glyphic research during the next decade.

It must be remembered that, up to the late 1950s, the identification of the figures portrayed in Maya monumental art—and thus the likely subject matter of the texts that accompanied them—remained ambiguous. A perusal of popular works by leading Mayanists of the period shows this most effectively: Morley (1946:368) labels the principal figure on Piedras Negras Wall Panel 3 as a *halach uinic*, the Yucatec term for a local ruler. Brainerd (1954:58) notes the subject matter of the stelae as "either priest, ruler, or god" and, in his revision of Morley two years later, settles on "priest" to replace Morley's earlier term. Thompson, in the first edition of his notable *Rise and Fall of Maya Civilization,* also favors "priest" (1954:175) and states further that the hieroglyphic texts of the Classic period "do not appear to treat of individuals at all" (1954:168).

Alberto Ruz's discovery of the astonishing crypt inside the Temple of the Inscriptions on June 15, 1952, helped greatly in resolving the ambiguity attending the identity of the protagonist of the mon-

Figure 1.27. Tatiana Proskouriakoff. (Photograph courtesy of the Peabody Museum of Archaeology and Ethnology, Harvard University)

his arguments on the occurrences of nominal glyphs in the texts of the Palenque tomb, Tatiana Proskouriakoff (Fig. 1.27) was engaged in a critical analysis of certain inscriptions from Piedras Negras. Her findings forever changed our fundamental knowledge of the content of the vast majority of Maya hieroglyphic texts.

Earlier in her career, Proskouriakoff had worked at Piedras Negras under the auspices of The University Museum of The University of Pennsylvania. Later, as a staff member of the Carnegie Institution, she participated in fieldwork at Copan and Mayapan. An artist, she specialized at first in archaeological illustration, producing superb reconstruction renderings of Maya sites and architecture (Proskouriakoff 1946; Smith 1955). Another of her key contributions lay in the field of art history, in work that systematized the motifs and stylistic changes in Maya sculpture through the Classic period (1950).

Proskouriakoff's fruitful investigation of Piedras Negras monuments was partly rooted in Eric Thompson's relatively routine revision of a damaged date on Stela 14 (Thompson 1943). Specifically Thompson took a date proposed earlier by Teeple (1930:58), which, according to the correlation formula, fell in the year 790 and, using better photographs of the glyphs, revised the reading of the date to one corresponding to the year 758.

The unusual pattern of monument erection at Piedras Negras then came into play, for it was known that, at five-year intervals, stelae were placed in rows fronting particular structures at the site, each such cluster thus constituting a "set" bridging a particular period of time. As Thompson noted (1943:115), his revision made Stela 14 the earliest of the set of six monuments in front of Structure O-13. So the matter had rested for nearly two decades.

Proskouriakoff noted, as had others, that Stela 14 was an example of an unusual monument type marked by the representation of a niche containing a seated figure. In addition, monuments of this type featured two other noteworthy motifs—a band of footprints ascending to the niche and, most of the time, the depiction of a sacrificial victim in the lowermost register. Proskouriakoff believed that a careful study of Stela 14 and other "niche" monuments at the site—all of which were now provable as the first to be erected in their respective sets—might possibly yield the hieroglyphic expression for sacrifice. Her

uments. Drilling soon showed the massive block of stone in the chamber, with its carved top and sides, to be a sarcophagus instead of an elaborate altar, as was first believed (Ruz Lhuillier 1955:91). This, at long last, placed hieroglyphic texts in direct association with the physical remains of a human being who, even by the most ungenerous laws of probability, was likely to be a primary referent of these texts.

In 1959, Heinrich Berlin published an important paper on this very point. He systematically analyzed the portraits and hieroglyphic captions on the sides of the great sarcophagus and the lengthy text on the perimeter of the lid. These, he convincingly demonstrated, included names of historical individuals (Berlin 1959).

At about the same time that Berlin was preparing

analysis instead led to something much more important.

It was initially apparent that each set of monuments constituted a separate hieroglyphic record that contained an earliest date, a subsequent date, and later notations of the anniversaries of the second date. More importantly, the total time span covered in three sets of monuments where such data were complete proved to be 60, 64, and 56 years. These, Proskouriakoff suggested, were all possible life spans for individuals. Further analysis served to isolate hieroglyphs tentatively identifiable as event designations meaning "birth" and "accession," along with others that appeared to be names and/or titles. Moreover, they corresponded neatly with portraits, including those of women and children, on the monuments. In addition, the putative "verbs" and "subjects" followed the grammatical order noted by Whorf (1933:5) in the short texts of the Dresden Codex.

The summation of the Piedras Negras study appeared in a landmark article in *American Antiquity* (Proskouriakoff 1960), and it firmly established the "historical hypothesis," which was immediately accepted by Thompson (1960:v) and others. Since then, it has withstood all tests, including detailed analyses of the inscriptions of Quirigua (Kelley 1962b) and Yaxchilan (Proskouriakoff 1963, 1964).

As we have seen, patterns of text structure have proved to be the primary key to virtually all the breakthroughs in noncalendrical texts since Bowditch's brief and remarkable anticipation of Proskouriakoff's Piedras Negras analysis (1901c:13). In 1963, Heinrich Berlin carried the application of structural analysis in the hieroglyphic texts to a new high with his key study of the noncalendrical texts of an entire architectural complex—the Cross Group at Palenque.

By careful comparison of text structure in the inscriptions of the Temple of the Cross, the Foliated Cross, and the Sun, Berlin was able to isolate the names of three supernaturals or divine personalities, which he labeled GI, GII, and GIII—collectively, "The Palenque Triad" (Berlin 1963). This work, in short, not only reinforced the method of structural analysis as a key tool in working out the noncalendrical texts, but also served to show that, indeed, such texts could deal with supernatural as well as historical subjects.

Figure 1.28. David Humiston Kelley. (Photograph by Jane Kelley)

Meanwhile, on the phonetics front, Knorozov's output of proposed readings of the Maya script continued to be a subject of controversy (e.g., Thompson 1960). In 1962, David H. Kelley (Fig. 1.28) published two very important papers dealing with the problem. In the first (1962a), he summarized the overall history of attempts to decipher Maya writing beginning with Brasseur de Bourbourg's publication of the Landa manuscript in 1864. Following a cogent definition of the major trends of the decipherment effort—which we have drawn upon heavily in the present work—Kelley presented a summary tabulation of glyphs and the agreements or disagreements of their interpretation among some 30 past and present scholars, including Knorozov (Kelley 1962a:23-45).

The second paper (Kelley 1962c) focused on phoneticism in particular and carefully examined the arguments put forth for numerous readings by Whorf, Thompson, Knorozov, and others. In his conclusion, Kelley acknowledged the evidence for some use of phoneticism in Maya writing, accepted Knorozov's general principle on how this worked, agreed with some of the Russian's readings, and disagreed with others. By virtue of its rigorous testing methods and remarks on proper approaches to the problems of decipherment, Kelley's summary of 1962 stands as an important station in the history of Maya hieroglyphic studies.

That same year saw the appearance of *A Catalog of Maya Hieroglyphs*, Eric Thompson's concordance of hieroglyphic signs, grouped and tabulated according to all their occurrences and contexts within the known corpus of Maya writing (Thompson 1962). The catalog vastly improved upon the pioneering attempt by Gates (1931) to do the same thing, and expanded the coverage of Zimmermann's similar work (1956), which was limited to the hieroglyphs of the three codices. By means of the Thompson catalog, some 800 different elements of the Maya script could be transcribed by the use of numbers assigned to them. In the subsequent literature utilizing the Thompson catalog, these transcriptions appear as the now familiar "T" numbers.

In July 1962, a small group in Merida, Yucatan, including Wolfgang Cordan and William Brito Sansores, initiated what they called the "Mérida System" of Maya hieroglyphic decipherment (Brito Sansores 1962; Cordan 1963:9). The approach applied Swadesh's work on glottochronology to various Mayan languages, including Chorti, Chol, Mam, and, of course, Yucatec, in order to reconstruct the "archaic" Maya reflected in the codices. Then, utilizing the work of Zimmermann, Thompson, and others, they produced a series of phonetic readings for signs in the texts of the three Maya codices (Cordan 1963:1101-1103). Despite the shortcomings of its results, which did not survive the tests of subsequent scholarship, the Merida School achieved a distinction of sorts by its then-innovative emphasis on linguistic methods.

In 1963, Knorozov published a general work, *Pis'mennost' Indeitsev Maiia*, summarizing his studies to date. Its Spanish translation by Mimo de Pintos (Knorozov 1965) and English version by Sophie Coe (Knorozov 1967), abridgments of the original, made the results of Russian scholarship more readily accessible for testing and application. As Proskouriakoff pointed out in her preface to the Coe translation, there was at the time "still no consensus on the value of Knorozov's contribution to Maya epigraphy" (1967:i).

In 1965, David Kelley followed up on Berlin's study of the Palenque Triad with a much more elaborate analysis that related the dates associated with the divinities of the Triad to their births. These dates, in turn, defined their respective calendar names in much the manner of the conquest-period codices of central Mexico. In this paper, Kelley drew upon complex iconographic and astronomical associations to place the Triad in the general context of pan-Mesoamerican religion and cosmology—a scope and approach reminiscent of Seler's earlier studies, which demonstrated, as much as anything else, the kinds of information to which hieroglyphic analysis could lead.

Before the 1960s, the effort devoted to Maya hieroglyphic research was mainly one of individual contributors whose intercommunication was achieved through correspondence or sporadic meetings such as those afforded by the International Congresses of Americanists. In contrast, the last 20 years of Maya hieroglyphic research has seen an increasing incidence of scholarly meetings devoted solely to the subject of Maya writing and its adjunct specialties: art history, iconography, and linguistics. In December 1966, such a meeting took place in Mexico City, and it helped set a pattern that has obtained since.

The Primer Seminario para el Estudio de la Escritura Maya was sponsored by the Comisión para el Estudio de la Escritura Maya (CEEM) of the Universidad Nacional Autónoma de México. It was organized by Alberto Ruz, director of the university's Seminario de Cultura Maya, and Alfredo Barrera Vásquez, director of the Instituto Yucateco de Antropología e Historia (Hopkins 1967:91). The purpose was to discuss the international effort then in progress on Maya glyphic research, and the scholars who attended included Günter Zimmermann and Thomas Barthel of Germany; Mauricio Swadesh, William Brito Sansores, and Maricela Ayala of Mexico; and Norman McQuown, Marshall Durbin, David H. Kelley, and Michael D. Coe of the United States. The sessions served as forums for progress reports followed by discussion of various aspects of hieroglyphic research with an emphasis on linguistics that, until this time, had only rarely been integrated into the specialty.

The Mexico City seminar was a success, not so much for the individual contributions, which varied from excellent to routine, but for the sum of the presentations and the indefinable "chemistry" that often adds a special and intangible dimension to scholarly interaction—and for the full-fledged entry of the international community of linguistic scholars into the arena of glyphic research.

Among the more important papers to emerge from the Primer Seminario was that by Kelley on the occurrence of the name "Kakupacal" in the hieroglyphic inscriptions of Chichen Itza (Kelley 1968). Not only did this reading serve as a promising test of the phonetic system proposed by Knorozov, but it also tied the content of the inscriptions to that of various colonial Maya documentary sources, where a certain Kakupacal, an Itza "captain," is mentioned (Kelley 1968:262-263).

The practice of having meetings on the subject of Maya hieroglyphic writing was given fresh impetus in late 1971 with the Conference on Mesoamerican Writing Systems at Dumbarton Oaks, in Washington, DC, organized by Elizabeth Benson, Michael Coe, and Floyd Lounsbury. The resulting publication (Benson 1973) included five important papers ranging in geographical focus from central Mexico through the Maya area. Among these, Lounsbury's paper dealing with the glyphic element customarily nicknamed the "*ben-ich* prefix" stands as a minor masterpiece of meticulous analysis, bringing to bear not only the best of traditional text analysis but also complex linguistic data, ethnohistorical accounts, and rigorous hypothesis testing. It is this conjunctive approach, as exemplified by the work of Lounsbury and others in recent years, that, from the perspective of the present writing, seems to represent a most productive pathway to ultimate success in Maya hieroglyphic research. The 1971 conference quickly led to a fruitful series of "mini-conferences" held annually at Dumbarton Oaks between 1974 and 1979 by a small group of scholars including Elizabeth Benson, Floyd Lounsbury, Peter Mathews, and Linda Schele. Though never published as such, these informal sessions nonetheless proved crucial in the interchange of data and ideas on both the nature and the specific content of the Maya inscriptions.

In August 1973, a small group of Palenque enthusiasts headed by Merle Greene and Lawrence W.

Figure 1.29. The Primera Mesa Redonda de Palenque, 1973. (Photograph by George E. Stuart)

(Bob) Robertson conceived the idea of having a "round table" of invited scholars to deal with the art, iconography, and hieroglyphic inscriptions of the great site, which, as we have seen, played such an enormous role in the history of Maya research. The first such meeting (Fig. 1.29), held that December, exceeded all expectations: by dividing up the areas of concentration, major breakthroughs took place on a variety of fronts. Perhaps the most spectacular was the decipherment, by Floyd Lounsbury, Peter Mathews, and Linda Schele, of the dynastic list of Palenque's rulers (Mathews and Schele 1974). That basic analysis of dates and names, was partially but firmly based on earlier work by Berlin, Kelley, and others—and it literally opened the core content of the Palenque inscriptions. The Palenque Mesas Redondas have been held at intervals since, drawing an ever increasing number of epigraphists, art historians, archaeologists, and others who attend simply to share their enthusiasm for things Maya.

In 1973, Michael D. Coe published a work that, by virtue of its subject matter and interpretations, has since become a classic in Maya hieroglyphic research. *The Maya Scribe and His World*, actually a detailed and beautifully published catalog issued on the occasion of an exhibit of Maya hieroglyphic art by the Grolier Club of New York, opened another all-but-ignored world for the epigraphist: the hieroglyphic texts and, most often, the scenes painted or carved on Maya ceramics. Such texts, Coe contended, were not, as earlier scholars had believed, merely ornamental, but very sophisticated ritual texts (which he termed "primary standard sequences") often supplemented by historical data much like that in the monumental inscriptions (Coe 1973:18). Coe went on to note the apparent close relationship between certain scenes on Maya ceramics—particularly the polychrome cylinder vases of the Late Classic period—and the myth of the Hero Twins recorded in the *Popol Vuh,* the sacred book of the Quiche Maya copied down by Father Francisco Ximénez more than four centuries earlier (Estrada Monroy 1973). Coe's analysis effectively demonstrated the longevity of what must have been a basic pan-Mesoamerican myth and the intimate connection between the ancient Maya of the lowlands and their historical counterparts in the highlands.

As if all these new data were not enough, Coe's 1973 publication also contained the first published photographs of a newly discovered 11-page fragment of a Maya manuscript book (Fig. 1.30), which he named the "Grolier Codex" (Coe 1973:150). At first thought by Thompson (1975) and others to be a falsification, the Grolier Codex is now generally regarded as genuine, based on iconographic and astronomical evidence in its contents (Carlson 1982).

Michael D. Coe's work, with glyphic text and scenes on Maya pottery, in effect introduced a whole new context for the endeavors of the epigraphist. Since publication of *The Maya Scribe and His World,* several additional source volumes by Coe himself (1978, 1982) and others (e.g., Foncerrada de Molina and Lombardo de Ruiz 1979) have added much in the way of new material.

The popularity and portability of Maya vases has unfortunately resulted in a recent increase in the mass looting of such vessels from Maya tombs for sale on the international art market, as well as an increased amount of vase "restoration" to enhance sales. This has resulted in a twofold problem for Maya hieroglyphic research. First, such vases are without archaeological provenance, a circumstance that alone may not diminish their value for the study of the glyphic texts, although such provenance is a guarantee of both known archaeological context and authenticity. Second, many vases are restored so skillfully that the boundary between the paintings of the ancient and the modern artist may not be clear, and if hieroglyphs are involved they become, needless to say, useless, if not dangerous, as data for analysis.

In 1976, Joyce Marcus took Berlin's pioneering study of the Emblem Glyphs and expanded it into an

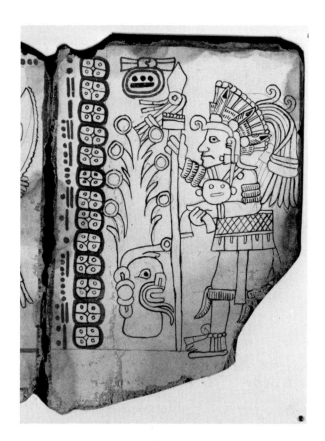

Figure 1.30. A page of the Grolier Codex. (Photograph by Enrico Ferorelli, courtesy of the National Geographic Society, Washington, DC.)

innovative distributional analysis that resulted in the first rigorous definition of ancient Maya polities to be based on epigraphic evidence (Marcus 1976). That same year, both Berlin and Kelley published general summary works on Maya writing. Berlin's *Signos y significados . . .* (1977) provided a much-needed and straightforward treatment of the subject in Spanish that is particularly useful for its efficiently balanced treatment of both the calendrical and noncalendrical content of Maya writing. Kelley's much larger *Deciphering the Maya Script* (1976), written over a period of many years, not only embraces the entire subject in great detail but also presents a rigorous appraisal of the role of phoneticism in the hieroglyphic texts.

All in all, the grand result of the quarter-century or so of epigraphic research and publication that took place after 1958 may be seen as a blend of two major achievements: the confirmation of Proskouriakoff's (1960) Historical Hypothesis (and one can never overestimate the momentous impact this had on the field); and the gradual confirmation of the phonetic component of the Maya script by a consensus of scholars. The latter is perhaps best reflected in the remarkable anthology *Phoneticism in Mayan Hieroglyphic Writing,* issued under the editorship of John S. Justeson and Lyle Campbell (1984)—the results of a conference held in Albany in 1978 (see also D. Stuart 1987; Houston 1988). At the same time, Linda Schele brought to print her doctoral dissertation, *Maya Glyphs: the Verbs* (1984), in which a single grammatical category of the hieroglyphic texts was thoroughly cataloged and analyzed.

THE RECORDING AND AVAILABILITY OF MAYA HIEROGLYPHIC TEXTS

It should be obvious by now that the publication of accurate recordings of Maya texts has proved perhaps the single most important factor in the pacing and success of research that has taken place since the middle of the nineteenth century. As in the case of monumental Egyptian texts (Caminos 1976), the Maya inscriptions present their would-be recorder with one of the most exacting and difficult tasks in the entire field of specialized scientific illustration. In an age in which the effort of interpretation has been eased by the superb draftsmanship of Ian Graham (1975b), Eric Von Euw (1977), William R. Coe (Jones and Satterthwaite 1982), Peter Mathews (1983), and a very few others, we have come to take such work for granted. In the history of Maya hieroglyphic research, however, even a minimum standard of duplication of texts has been all too rare.

We have seen how the earliest artists, beset by the rigors of the field and contemplating a totally alien symbol system of which absolutely nothing was known at the time, drew with the best of intentions, but nearly always drew badly. We have noted a turn for the better in some of Waldeck's renderings of Palenque material and Catherwood's superior drawings, occasionally helped by the *camera lucida.* And we have noted the superb photography of Maudslay and Maler, as well as the extraordinary quality of the Hunter drawings that accompanied the published work of the former.

John Graham and Stephen Fitch (1972:42) point out the abrupt decline in the quality of both photography and drawing that characterize the period after Maudslay and Maler, and go on to discuss the merits of rubbings and the stereographic, or photogrammetric, recording of Maya texts.

Rubbings of Maya relief carving, as used by Denison in the early 1930s (Ruppert and Denison 1943:1-2) and later utilized by Merle Greene Robertson (1967, 1983-1985) and John Graham (1972), have a distinct place in epigraphic utility, for they often reveal details of carving that are not apparent in any other medium. They also serve to show very accurately the overall "map" of the carving that neither routine photography nor line renderings derived from it can produce. More importantly, they eliminate the subjective element that is the single most telling basis for the criticism of many drawings.

Proper photography of Maya monuments is nearly as difficult as their drawing, for it involves matters of both lenses and lighting—the former to avoid distortion in the prints; the latter to ensure the revelation of pertinent detail. Only a multiple set of prints, each lit from a different direction and scanning angle, will help show latent configurations and details of eroded glyphs—and provide a basis for judgment between manmade and natural lines in the carving. Leyrer (1935) was the first fully to describe night photography of Maya monuments with the aid of a portable generator—a method that is now standard practice.

In the drawings of Maya inscriptions that have appeared in the last half century of the published literature, techniques have ranged from stipple shading (Andrews IV and Stuart 1968: Fig. 1) to the juxtaposition of rubbings and photographs (J. Graham 1972). The combination of line rendering and background stipple adopted for the Tikal Project (Jones and Satterthwaite 1982) has now become the general standard. We have selected a single Maya monument, Ixkun Stela 1, to show the various ways in which it has been rendered since its discovery in the middle of the last century (Fig. 1.31a, b, c).

The most ambitious and important single project for the recording of Maya monumental texts was begun in 1968 by Ian Graham (Fig. 1.32) Research Associate of Harvard University's Peabody Museum of Archaeology and Ethnology. The *Corpus of Maya Hieroglyphic Inscriptions* has for its long-range goal the accurate recording of every known Maya hieroglyphic text, excluding those in the codices or on pottery vessels (I. Graham 1975a:7).

The concept is nothing new, but its tangible results are. We have already noted Morley's (1914:33) idea for much the same thing. Whereas Morley planned "descriptions and decipherments," however, the present Corpus Project is concerned solely with the accurate recording of the texts in question. For this, Graham, in 1968, spent some six months in library research in order to ascertain the scope of the problem and to establish the methods and meticulous standards of illustration that he detailed in the introductory volume (I. Graham 1975a). This done, he spent a field season the following year at Naranjo and Uxmal to test the efficiency of various recording methods. The first fascicle of drawings (of Naranjo monuments), accompanied by photographs, soon followed (I. Graham 1975b). As its volumes and parts accumulate in the manner of the appearance of Alfred P. Maudslay's great work almost a century earlier—there are a dozen at this writing—the *Corpus* becomes more and more indispensable as the primary research tool for all present and future students of ancient Maya writing.

Figure 1.31b. Ixkun Stela 1: rubbing by Merle Greene Robertson.

Figure 1.31a. Ixkun Stela 1: Lara(?) drawing (Ritter 1853).

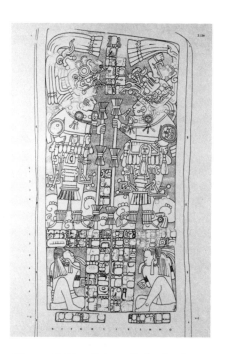

Figure 1.31c. Ixkun Stela 1: drawing by Ian Graham.

Figure 1.32. Ian Graham at Yaxchilan, 1975. (Photograph by Otis Imboden, courtesy of the National Geographic Society, Washington, DC)

Meanwhile, the monumental inscriptions of various sites have been published in more or less complete form. Among them are the Altar de Sacrificios (J. Graham 1972), Tikal (Jones and Satterthwaite 1982), Caracol (Beetz and Satterthwaite 1981), and Toniná (Bequelin and Baudez 1979-1982). Each, of course, reflects its own set of standards and quality, with some approaching, perhaps even matching, the exacting guidelines and character of Ian Graham's *Corpus*, but lacking, by definition, its overall consistency. Of special note is the remarkable ongoing publication of Merle Greene Robertson's meticulous photography and drawing of the art—the carved architectural stone and stucco—of Palenque, perhaps the most ambitious documentation of a site ever accomplished (Greene Robertson 1983-1985).

The study of nonmonumental Maya texts carries its own unique set of problems, ranging from the question of availability of usable reproductions to matters of ethics created by the vast art collectors' market. The former tend to govern scholarly access to the four known codices; the latter is particularly evident to those who would turn their attention to in the carved, incised, or painted vases, stones, and other artifacts, usually portable, that end up in private collections.

We are fortunate to have recent and excellent facsimiles or reproductions of the Maya codices in the Akademische Druck-und Verlagsanstalt of Graz, Austria, imprints of the Dresden, Madrid, and Paris codices (see, respectively, Deckert and Anders 1975; Anders 1967, 1968). The Grolier Codex is repro-

duced in color at a reduced but usable scale by Michael Coe (1973). Thomas Lee (1985) provides full-scale color reproductions of all four Maya codices, three of them taken directly from the Graz facsimiles, and provides an excellent bibliography. Meanwhile, the traditional "workhorse" of codical study, the 1930 black-and-white edition of the Dresden, Madrid, and Paris manuscripts by Villacorta and Villacorta (1930), has reappeared in print.

The huge corpus of painted and inscribed Maya vases is becoming more generally available through catalogs of special gallery exhibits (e.g., M. Coe 1973, 1978, 1982) or compendiums that bring together illustrations of a large number of individual pieces (e.g., Robicsek and Hales 1981). Of particular note in this regard is the ongoing series of volumes by Justin Kerr (1989-1990), in which he utilizes his now-famous roll-out camera with great success. Another primary source lies in the large collection of 35mm transparencies showing pieces in private collections in both the Americas and abroad taken over the years by Nicholas Hellmuth, of which many scholarly institutions possess full or partial sets.

We are now entering an era in which the digitized imagery of computer graphics is beginning to come into its own as a medium for epigraphic investigation. The most ambitious endeavor along these lines is the Art and Archaeology Database Project of the Pre-Columbian Art Research Institute of San Francisco, where Merle Greene Robertson and Martha Macri are in the process of converting drawings and rubbings into "read only" compact discs and, eventually, laser videodiscs. The successful utility of any such data base, of course, will ultimately depend upon the integrity of the source drawings and other data used for it. Thus, we can never overestimate the necessity for accuracy on the part of those who document the writings left us by the ancient Maya.

CONCLUSION

Having now arrived at a point so close in time to the present that proper perspective is impossible, I think it appropriate to draw this historical survey of Maya hieroglyphic investigation to a close. Suffice it to say that research since the mid-1980s seems to continue at a steadily increasing rate and by more and more students of the hieroglyphs. The effort, happily, continues to be one of international range. In Germany, the work of Berthold Riese, Dieter Dütting, and Nikolai Grube, among others, is paced by that of Michael Closs, Stephen Houston, Bruce Love, Peter Mathews, David Stuart, and other epigraphists in the United States and Canada; by Michel Davoust in France; Yasugi Yoshiho in Japan; and by many, many others. Among the more important conferences in terms of bringing together epigraphists from many nations was the First World Symposium on Maya Epigraphy held in Guatemala City in August 1988. Sponsored jointly by the Instituto de Antropología e Historia de Guatemala, the Asociación Tikal, and the National Geographic Society, it was fittingly dedicated to Heinrich Berlin and to the memory of Tatiana Proskouriakoff, who had died the year before.

The recent years have also seen an increasingly rigorous application of linguistic principles to problems of Maya writing, as is evident in the work of Victoria Bricker, Nicholas Hopkins, Kathryn Josserand, John Justeson, and others on problems ranging from patterns of discourse to the presence of loan words in the inscriptions (e.g., Bricker 1986; Justeson et al. 1985). Meanwhile, ongoing work by Lyle Campbell, William Hanks, Terrence Kaufman, Robert Laughlin, William Norman, and their colleagues in the field of linguistics itself has led to the increased recognition and use of Mayan languages other than Yucatec, particularly those of the Cholan group, as crucial keys to the old writing system (e.g., Kaufman 1984; MacLeod 1984). This correction of imbalance extends as well to the increased use of archaeological data by the epigraphist and, in turn, a growing regard by archaeologists for the kinds of data that can be gleaned from the inscriptions (e.g., Freidel and Schele 1988; Culbert 1989; Fash 1989; Houston 1989a).

The role of the art-historical viewpoint as a productive approach to the problems of interpreting ancient Mesoamerican remains—an effort begun almost single-handedly by George Kubler (1962, 1969)—has also come into its own recently. The combined iconographic and hieroglyphic treatments evident in the work of Jeff Kowalski, Arthur Miller, Mary Miller, Linda Schele, and Karl Taube, among others, provide profound insights, not only into specific problems at hand but also into the very mentality of the Maya (e.g., M. Miller 1986; Schele and Miller 1986).

Mesoamerican ethnological data, so profitably used by Eric Thompson and others, are once again being brought to bear on the cultural implications of the glyphic texts. Noteworthy among such studies are the independent epigraphic investigations by Stephen Houston, David Stuart, and Nikolai Grube that have revealed the shamanistic dimension of those texts in the frequent and explicit mention of "companion spirits" (Houston and Stuart 1989).

In astronomy, Anthony Aveni, John Carlson, and their coworkers have refined the tradition of contributions reaching back to Teeple and beyond to give us an even greater appreciation of the intricacies of the Maya view of their celestial world (see Aveni 1980).

An increasing interest on the part of archaeologists and other Mayanists who are nonspecialists in the study of hieroglyphs, and of the general public as well, has recently culminated in participatory workshops. Among the most successful are those given annually since 1978 by Linda Schele under the auspices of the Institute of Latin American Studies of the University of Texas at Austin, and, since 1983, another sponsored by The University Museum in Philadelphia.

Many new data continue to emerge from all this activity—so much so that it becomes increasingly difficult to keep up. In closing this brief history, I can only recommend the latest published general works on the subject, specifically the treatments by James A. Fox (in Morley, Brainerd, and Sharer 1983) and Michael Coe (1987), along with the summaries by Houston (1989b) and D. Stuart and Houston (1989). Thus, I leave it to those sources to lead the reader anew into whatever degree of detail on the subject is desired.

And while the present seems to its inhabitants as perhaps the most exciting of all the eras of Maya research, it must be remembered that it is also but one point in time on a continuum—and that the future of the field is, as always, brightened by the prospects of new scholarship and new inscriptions for its application and testing.

As we have seen throughout, the story of Maya glyphic research is one punctuated by alternating episodes of action and reaction, advance and retreat—cycles often followed by reappraisals that gradually bring balance and refinement to our state of knowledge. With that in mind, it must also be clear that in a sense the point in the story at which we now find ourselves is much like any other time in the long history of research that has been sketched above. The only major difference between the present and past stages of progress in the effort to understand the nature and the content of Maya hieroglyphic writing lies in the amount of accumulated debt that we owe to the labors of our colleagues.

BIBLIOGRAPHY

Acosta, J. de
1590   *Historia natural y moral de las Indias.* Seville: Juan de León.

Acuña, R. (editor)
1984   *Calepino Maya de Motul.* 2 vols. México: Universidad Autónoma de México. Photographic copy of the original with facing-page transcription.

Adams, H.
1891   Life and Works of Brasseur de Bourbourg. In *Proceedings of the American Antiquarian Society, No. 80.* Worcester, MA: Charles Hamilton.

Akerly (or Ackerly), S.
1833   American Antiquities, A report read to the Lyceum of Natural History of New York, September 23, 1833. *The Knickerbocker* 2(5):371-382. *The Knickerbocker* was later renamed *The Federal American Monthly.* Akerly's report—based on correspondence with Francisco Corroy of Tabasco—also appeared in installments in the *Family Magazine, or Weekly Abstract of General Knowledge* 1(39):307-309; 1(40):315-317; 1(41):323-325; and 1(42):331-332. These installments carried three illustrations from Del Río and Cabrera 1822.

Alcina Franch, J.
1949   *Guillermo Dupaix: expediciones acerca de los monumentos de la Nueva España, 1805-1808.* 2 vols. (text and plates). Colección Chimalistac de Libros y Documentos acerca de la Nueva España, nos. 27 and 28. Madrid: Ediciones José Porrúa Turanzas.

Anders, F.
1967   *Codex Tro-Cortesianus (Codex Madrid) Museo de América, Madrid: Einleitung und Summary.* Codices Selecti, vol. 8. Graz, Austria: Akademische Druck-und Verlagsanstalt. Accompanies facsimile in two screenfold sections of 70 and 42 pages.

1968   *Codex Peresianus (Codex Paris), Bibliothèque Nationale, Paris: Einleitung und Summary.* Codices Selecti, vol. 9. Graz, Austria: Akademische Druck-und Verlagsanstalt. Accompanies 22-page screenfold facsimile of the manuscript.

Andrews, E. W., IV, and G. E. Stuart
1968   The Ruins of Ikil, Yucatan, Mexico. In *Archaeological Investigations on the Yucatan Peninsula,* Middle American Research Institute, Tulane University. Publication 31, pp. 69-80. New Orleans.

Angulo Iñiguez, D.
1934   *Planos de monumentos arquitectónicos de América y Filipinas existentes en el Archivo de Indias. Catálogo, II.* Seville: Universidad de Sevilla, Laboratorio de Arte. Contains copies of the Calderón and Bernasconi drawings of Palenque in Plates 133-138.

Aubin, J. M. A.
1849   *Mémoire sur la peinture didactique et l'écriture figurative des anciens Mexicains.* Paris: Paul Dupont.

Aveni, A. F.
1980   *Skywatchers of Ancient Mexico.* Austin: University of Texas Press.

Baradère, H. (editor)
1834   *Antiquités Mexicaines.* Paris: Jules Didot. Two volumes of text and one of plates contain the narrative of the Dupaix expeditions of 1805-1807 and the illustrations of Castañeda, along with many articles on American antiquities by other authorities of the time (see also Villaseñor Espinosa 1978).

Barrera Vásquez, A.
1980   *Diccionario Maya Cordemex, Maya-Español, Español-Maya.* Mérida, Yucatán: Ediciones Cordemex.

1980-1981   *Estudios Linguisticos: obras completas.* 2 vols. México: Fondo Editorial de Yucatán.

Barrera Vásquez, A., and S. G. Morley
1949   *The Maya Chronicles*. Carnegie Institution
           of Washington. Publication 585, Contribu-
           tion 48. Washington, DC.

Barrera Vásquez, A., and S. Rendón
1948   *El libro de los libros de Chilam Balam*.
           México: Fondo de Cultura Económica.

Barthel, T. S.
1958   Die gegenwärtige Situation in der
           Erforschung der Mayaschrift. In
           *Proceedings of the 32d International
           Congress of Americanists (1956)*, pp. 476-
           484. Copenhagen.

Beetz, C. P., and L. Satterthwaite
1981   *The Monuments and Inscriptions of
           Caracol, Belize*. The University Museum
           Monograph 45. Philadelphia: The
           University Museum, The University of
           Pennsylvania.

Beltrán de Santa Rosa, Fr. P.
1859   *Arte del idioma maya reducido a sucintas
           reglas, y semilexicon Yucateco*. 2d ed.
           Mérida, Yucatán: J. D. Espinosa. First pub-
           lished Mexico City, 1746.

Benson, E. P. (editor)
1973   *Mesoamerican   Writing   Systems*.
           Washington, DC: Dumbarton Oaks.

Bequelin, P., and C. F. Baudez
1979-1982 *Toniná, une cité Maya du Chiapas*. Mission
           archéologique et ethnologique Français au
           Mexique, collection études Meso-
           américaines, no. 6. 3 vols. Paris: Editions
           Recherche sur les Civilisations.

Berlin, H.
1943   *Notes on Glyph C of the Lunar Series at
           Palenque*. Carnegie Institution of
           Washington. Notes on Middle American
           Archaeology and Ethnology, no. 24.
           Cambridge, MA.

1944   *A Tentative Identification of the Head
           Variant for Eleven*. Carnegie Institution of
           Washington. Notes on Middle American
           Archaeology and Ethnology, no. 33.
           Cambridge, MA.

1945   A Critique of Dates at Palenque. *American
           Antiquity* 10:340-347.

1958   El glifo "emblema" en las inscripciones
           mayas. *Journal de la Société des
           Américanistes* (n.s) 47:111-119. Paris.

1959   Glifos nominales en el sarcófago de
           Palenque. *Humanidades* 2(10):1-8.
           Guatemala.

1963   The Palenque Triad: A Study in Method.
           Journal de la Société des Américanistes
           (n.s.) 52:91-99. Paris.

1970   Miscelánea Palencana. *Journal de la Société
           des Américanistes* (n.s.) 59:107-128. Paris.

1977   *Signos y significados en las inscripciones
           Mayas*. Guatemala: Instituto Nacional del
           Patrimonio Cultural de Guatemala.

Bernal, I.
1980   *A History of Mexican Archaeology*. London
           and New York: Thames and Hudson.

Beyer, H.
1931   The Analysis of the Maya Hieroglyphs.
           *Internationales Archiv für Ethnographie,
           vol. 31*. Leiden: E. J. Brill.

1932   *The Stylistic History of the Maya
           Hieroglyphs*. Middle American Research
           Institute, Tulane University. Publication 4,
           pp.71-102. New Orleans.

1934   The Position of the Affixes in Maya
           Writing. *Maya Research* 1(1):20-29. New
           York: The Alma Egan Hyatt Foundation
           (for the Department of Middle American
           Research, Tulane University).

1934a   The Position of the Affixes in Maya
           Writing: II. *Maya Research* 1(2):101-108.
           New York: The Alma Egan Hyatt Founda-
           tion (for the Department of Middle
           American Research, Tulane University).

1936   The Position of the Affixes in Maya
           Writing: III. *Maya Research* 3:102-104. New
           Orleans: Maya Research (for the Depart-
           ment of Middle American Research, Tulane
           University).

1937   *Studies on the Inscriptions of Chichen Itza*.
           Carnegie Institution of Washington.
           Publication 483, Contribution 21.
           Washington, DC.

Blom, F., and G. Duby
1955-1957 *La Selva Lacandona: Andanzas
           Arqueológicas*. 2 vols. México: Editorial
           Cultura. Frans Blom's map of the Lacandon
           Forest, which accompanies this set,
           remains the most useful and complete
           work of its kind for the location of archae-
           ological sites.

Boewe, C.
1982   *Fitzpatrick's 'Rafinesque: A Sketch of His
           Life with Bibliography.'* Weston, MA: M & S
           Press. The 1911 edition of Fitzpatrick is
           superseded by this enlarged revision. The

numbering of the publications by Rafinesque—the "Fitzpatrick-Boewe" numbers—are based on this work.

1985   A Note on Rafinesque, The Walam Olum, the Book of Mormon, and the Mayan Glyphs. *Numen* 32, fasc. 1 (July):101-113. Amsterdam.

Bollaert, W.
1870   *Examination of Central American Hieroglyphs in Yucatán. Including the Dresden Codex, the Guatemalien of Paris and the Troano of Madrid; the Hieroglyphs of Palenque, Copán, Nicaragua, Veraguas and New Granada; by the Recently discovered Maya Alphabet.* Anthropological Society of London, Memoirs LLL, pp. 288-314. London.

Bowditch, C. P.
1901a   *A Method Which May Have Been Used by the Mayas in Calculating Time.* Cambridge, MA: The University Press.
1901b   Memoranda on the Maya Calendars Used in the Books of Chilam Balam. *American Anthropologist* 3:129-138.
1901c   *Notes on the Report of Teobert, Maler, in Memoirs of the Peabody Museum, vol. II, no. I.* Cambridge, MA: The University Press.
1903   *A Suggestive Maya Inscription.* Cambridge, MA: The University Press.
1906   *The Temples of the Cross, of the Foliated Cross and of the Sun at Palenque.* Cambridge, MA: The University Press.

Bowditch, C. P.(editor)
1904   *Mexican and Central American Antiquities, Calendar Systems, and History.* Smithsonian Institution, Bureau of American Ethnology Bulletin 28. Washington, DC: Government Printing Office.

Brainerd, G. W.
1954   *The Maya Civilization.* Los Angeles: The Southwest Museum.

Brasseur de Bourbourg, E. C., Abbé
1857-1859   *Histoire des Nations Civilisées du Mexique et de l'Amérique-Centrale, durante les siècles antérieurs a Christophe Colomb.* 4 vols. Paris: Arthus Bertrand.
1861   *Popol Vuh: le livre sacré et les mythes de l'antiquité Américaine, avec les livres héroïques et historiques des Quichés.* Paris: Arthus Bertrand.

1862   *Grammaire de la langue Quiché servant d'introduction au Rabinal-Achi.* Paris: Arthus Bertrand.
1864   *Relacion des choses de Yucatan de Diego de Landa . . . .* Paris: Arthus Bertrand.
1866   *Recherches sur las ruines de Palenque et sur las origines de la civilization du Mexique.* Paris: Arthus Bertrand. This 84-page folio accompanied the *Monumens anciens du Mexique*, the 1866 folio of 56 lithographic plates by J. F. Waldeck.
1869-1870   *Manuscrit Troano: études sur le système graphique et la langue des Mayas.* Mission Scientifique au Mexique et dans l'Amérique Centrale. 2 vols. and supplement. Paris: Imprimerie Impérale. Contains color lithographs of the "Troano" portion of the Codex Tro-Cortesianus, or Madrid Codex.

Bricker, V. R.
1986A   *Grammar of Mayan Hieroglyphs.* Middle American Research Institute, Tulane University. Publication 56. New Orleans.
1989   Convenciones de abreviatura en la inscripciones Mayas y los libros de Chilam Balam. In *Memorias II: colóquio internacional de Mayistas* (Campeche, August 17-22, 1987), vol. 1, pp. 45-58. 2 vols. México: Universidad Nacional Autónoma de México.

Brinton, D. G.
1859   *Notes on the Floridian Peninsula, Its Literary History, Indian Tribes and Antiquities.* Philadelphia: Joseph Sabin. A useful bibliographical study based on observations made during a residence in the peninsula; edition limited to 100 copies.
1870   The Ancient Phonetic Alphabet of Yucatan. *American Bibliopolist* 2:143-148.
1882a   *The Maya Chronicles.* Library of Aboriginal American Literature, no. 1. Philadelphia.
1882b   The Graphic System and Ancient Records of the Mayas. In *Contributions to American Ethnology*, vol. 5, pp. xvii-xxxvii. Washington, DC.
[1895] *A Primer of Mayan Hieroglyphics.* The University of Pennsylvania Series in Philology, Literature, and Archaeology, vol. 3, no. 2. Philadelphia.
1898   *A Record of Study in American Aboriginal Languages.* Media, PA. Printed for private distribution.
1900   *Berendt Linguistic Collection at The University of Pennsylvania.* Philadelphia.

Brito Sansores, W.
1962   Sistema de Mérida para el deciframiento de los jeroglíficos Mayas. *Revista de la Universidad de Yucatán*, no. 24 (año 4, vol. 4):74-85. Mérida.

Brunhouse, R. L.
1971   *Sylvanus G. Morley and the World of the Ancient Maya*. Norman: University of Oklahoma Press.
1973   *In Search of the Maya*. Albuquerque: University of New Mexico Press.
1975   *Pursuit of the Ancient Maya*. Albuquerque: University of New Mexico Press.
1976   *Frans Blom, Maya Explorer*. Albuquerque: University of New Mexico Press.

Cabello Carro, P.
1984   Palenque: primeras excavaciones sistemáticas. *Revista de Arqueología*, a:o 5(38). Madrid.

Calderón de la Barca, F.
1843   *Life in Mexico*. 3 vols. Boston: Little, Brown.

Caminos, R.
1976   The Recording of Inscriptions in Tombs and Temples. In *Ancient Egyptian Epigraphy and Paleography*, pp. 1-25. New York: Metropolitan Museum of Art. Bound together with article by Henry G. Fischer.

Carlson, J. B.
1982   The Codex Grolier: New Light on the Authenticity of a Thirteenth-Century Maya Venus Calendar. *Archaeoastronomy* 5(4):6-9. College Park, MD. Abstract of a paper for presentation at the Third Annual Meeting of the Historical Astronomy Division of the American Astronomical Society, Boston, January 1983.

Carmichael, E.
1973   *The British and the Maya*. London: The British Museum.

Carrillo y Ancona, C.
1881   *Historia antigua de Yucatan*. Mérida: Espinosa y Companía.

Caso, A.
1959   Homenaje a Hermann Beyer. *El México Antiguo* 9:23-30. México.

Castañeda Paganini, R.
1946   *Las ruinas de Palenque: su descubrimiento y primeras exploraciones en el siglo XVIII*. Guatemala.

Catherwood, F.
1844   *Views of Ancient Monuments in Central America, Chiapas, and Yucatan*. London. Short text accompanying 25 color lithographs. The rare original was limited to 300 copies—250 tinted in sepia, and 50 hand-colored; of the several modern facsimiles available, that of the Editora del Sureste, Mexico, 1984, is probably the best.

Charency, H. de
1885   Vocabulaire de la langue tzotzil. *Memoires de l'Academie Nationale de Sciences, Arts et Belles-Letters de Caen*. Caen: Blanc-Herdel. Extracted from a 59-page manuscript attributed to Fr. Manuel Hidalgo, probably 1735. The original is in La Bibliothéque Nationale, Paris (Mexicain 412).
1899   Vocabulario tzotzil-español: dialecto de los indios de la parte oriental del Estado de Chiapas (Mexico). *Revue de Linguistique et de Philologie Comparée* 22:247-273. Orléans.

Charnay, D.
1863   *Cités et ruines Américaines: Mitla, Palenqué, Izamal, Chichen-Itza, Uxmal*. Paris: Gide and A. Morel. Text volume accompanying the Charnay photographic portfolio, with contribution by M. Viollet-le-Duc.

Ciudad Real, Fr. A. de
(1600)   See Acuña 1984.

Clavigero, F. J.
1780-1781   *Storia antica del Messico . . . .* 4 vols. Cesena. Many editions followed this first, including the 1789 Leipzig version in German.

Cline, H. F.
1947   The Apocryphal Early Career of J. F. Waldeck. *Acta Americana* 5:278-300. México.

Cline, H. F. (volume editor)
1972-1975   *Handbook of Middle American Indians*, R. Wauchope, general editor, vols. 12-15 (*Guide to Ethnohistorical Sources*). Austin: University of Texas Press.

Coe, M. D.
1963   Una referencia antigua al códice de Dresde. *Estudios de Cultura Maya*, vol. 3, pp. 37-40. México: Centro de Estudios Mayas, Universidad Nacional Autónoma de México.

1973   *The Maya Scribe and His World.* New York: The Grolier Club.

1978   *Lords of the Underworld: Masterpieces of Classic Maya Ceramics.* Photographs by Justin Kerr. Princeton: The Art Museum, Princeton University (distributed by Princeton University Press).

1982   *Old Gods and Young Heroes: The Pearlman Collection of Maya Ceramics.* Photographs by Justin Kerr. Jerusalem: The Israel Museum.

1987   *The Maya.* 4th ed., fully revised. London and New York: Thames and Hudson.

1989   *The Royal Fifth: Earliest Notices of Maya Writing.* Research Reports on Ancient Maya Writing, no. 28. Washington, DC: Center for Maya Research.

Coe, W. R., E. M. Shook, and L. Satterthwaite
1961   *The Carved Wooden Lintels of Tikal.* Tikal Reports, nos. 5-11, pp. 15-112. Philadelphia: The University Museum, The University of Pennsylvania.

Cordan, W.
1963   *Introducción a los glifos Mayas* Serie Origo, no. 1. Mérida, Yucatán: Universidad de Yucatán.

Coronel, Fr. J.
1620   *Arte en lengua de Maya, recopilado, y enmmendado.* México: Adriano César.

Culbert, T. P.
1989   Political History and the Decipherment of Maya Glyphs. *Antiquity* 62(234):135-152.

Davis, K. F.
1981   *Désiré Charnay, Expeditionary Photographer.* Albuquerque: University of New Mexico Press.

Davis, J., and M. Pérez (translators)
1882   *El tablero del Palenque en el Museo Nacional de los Estados Unidos, por Ch. Rau.* Anales del Museo Nacional, época 1, vol. 2, pp. 131-203. México. See Rau 1879.

Deckert, H.
1962   *Maya Handschrift der Sächsischen Landesbibliothek Dresden: Codex Dresdensis.* Berlin: Akademie Verlag. Accompanies facsimile of the codex.

Deckert, H., and F. Anders
1975   *Codex Dresdensis, Sächsische Landesbibliothek Dresden (Mscr. Dresdensis R 310). Kommentar.* Graz, Austria: Akademische Druck-und Verlagsanstalt. Accompanies facsimile of the manuscript.

Del Río, A., and P. F. Cabrera
1822   *Description of the ruins of an ancient city discovered near Palenque, in the Kingdom of Guatemala, in Spanish America. Translated from the original report of Captain Antonio del Río, followed by Teatro Critico Americano, or a Critical Investigation and Research into the History of the Americans, by Dr. Paul Felix Cabrera, of the City of New Guatemala.* London: Henry Berthoud and Suttaby, Evance and Fox.

Dupaix, G.
1834   See Baradère 1834.

Elorza y Rada, D. F. de
1714   *Nobiliario de el valle de la Valdorba, ilustrada con los escudos de armas de sus palacios, y casas nobles; con el extracto de la Conquista de el Ytza en la Nueva España, por el Conde de Lizarraga-Vengoa, natural del valle.* Pamplona: Francisco Antonio de Neyra. English translation and facsimile published by Editions Genet, Paris, 1930.

Estrada Monroy, A. (editor)
1973   *Popol Vuh.* Facsimile edition. Guatemala: Editorial "José de Pineda Ibarra."

Ewan, J. (editor)
1967   *Florula Ludoviciana, or a Flora of the State of Louisiana, by C. S. Rafinesque.* Clasica Botanica Americana, vol. 5. New York and London: Hafner. Facsimile of the 1817 edition.

Family Magazine, or *Weekly Abstract of General Knowledge*
1833   See Ackerly 1833; Del Río and Cabrera 1822.

Fash, W. L., Jr.
1989A   New Look at Maya Statecraft from Copán, Honduras. *Antiquity* 62(234):157-169.

Fitzpatrick, T. J.
1911   *Rafinesque: A Sketch of His Life with Bibliography.* Des Moines: Historical Department of Iowa. See Boewe 1982.

Foncerrada de Molina, M., and S. Lombardo de Ruiz
1979   *Vasijas pintadas Mayas en contexto arqueológico (catálogo).* México: Universidad Nacional Autónoma de México.

Förstemann, E. W.
1880   *Die Mayahandschrift der Königlichen Öffentlichen Bibliothek zu Dresden.* Leipzig: Verlag der A. Naumann'-schen

Lichtdruckerei. Chromolithographic reproduction of the 74-page manuscript; a second such reproduction was issued in 1892, printed in Dresden by Richard Bertling.

1886 *Erläuterungen zur Mayahandschrift der Königlichen Öffentlichen Bibliothek zu Dresden*. Dresden: Warnatz and Lehmann.

1887 *Zur Entzifferung der Mayahandschriften*. Dresden.

1891 *Zur Entzifferung der Mayahandschriften, II*. Dresden.

1892 *Zur Entzifferung der Mayahandschriften, III*. Dresden.

1893 Die Zeitperioden der Mayas. *Globus* 63:30-32. Brunswick.

1894 *Zur Entzifferung der Mayahandschriften, IV*. Dresden.

1904 Translations of various papers in Bowditch 1904 (see entry above).

Freidel, D., and L. Schele

1988 Symbol and Power: A History of the Lowland Maya Cosmogram. In *Maya Iconography*, eds. E. P. Benson and G. G. Griffin, pp. 44-93. Princeton: Princeton University Press.

Gates, W. E.

1931 *An Outline Dictionary of Maya Glyphs*. Maya Society Publication 1. Baltimore. Limited to 207 copies; reprinted by Dover Publications, New York, 1978, with additions.

Glass, J. B.

1975a A Census of Native Middle American Pictorial Manuscripts. In *Handbook of Middle American Indians*, vol. 14, eds. R. Wauchope (general editor), H. F. Cline (volume editor), and C. Gibson and H. B. Nicholson (associate volume editors), pp. 81-253. Austin: University of Texas Press. In collaboration with Donald Robertson.

1975b Annotated References. In *Handbook of Middle American Indians*, vol. 15, eds. R. Wauchope (general editor), H. F. Cline (volume editor), C. Gibson and H. B. Nicholson (associate volume editors), pp. 537-724. Austin: University of Texas Press.

Godman, F. D., and O. Salvin (editors)

1879-1915 *Biologia Centrali-Americana; or, Contributions to the Knowledge of the Flora and Fauna of Mexico and Central America*. London: R. H. Porter and Dulau. The larger work to which Maudslay 1889-1902 and Goodman 1897 are appended.

Götze, J. C.

1744 *Die Merckwürdigkeiten der Königlichen Bibliothek zu Dresden*. Dresden: George Konrad Walther.

Goodman, J. T.

1897 *The Archaic Maya Inscriptions*. Appendix to *Archaeology: Biologia Centrali-Americana*, by A. P. Maudslay. London: R. H. Porter and Dulau. See Godman and Salvin 1879-1915; Maudslay 1889-1902.

1905 Maya Dates. *American Anthropologist* 7:642-647.

Graham, I.

1963 Juan Galindo, Enthusiast. *Estudios de Cultura Maya*, vol. 3, pp. 11-35. México: Universidad Nacional Autónoma de México.

1971 *The Art of Maya Hieroglyphic Writing. January 28-March 28, 1971: An Exhibition in the Art Gallery, Center for Inter-American Relations, Sponsored Jointly by the Peabody Museum of Archaeology and Ethnology, Harvard University, Cambridge, MA, and Center for Inter-American Relations, Inc., 600 Park Avenue, New York, New York*. Cambridge, MA: Harvard University Printing Office.

1975a *Corpus of Maya Hieroglyphic Inscriptions, Vol. 1: Introduction*. Cambridge, MA: Peabody Museum of Archaeology and Ethnology, Harvard University.

1975b *Corpus of Maya Hieroglyphic Inscriptions, Vol. 2, Part 1: Naranjo*. Cambridge, MA: Peabody Museum of Archaeology and Ethnology, Harvard University.

Graham, J. A.

1972 *The Hieroglyphic Inscriptions and Monumental Art of Altar de Sacrificios*. Peabody Museum Papers, vol. 64, no. 2. Harvard University.

Graham, J. A., and S. R. Fitch

1972 The Recording of Maya Sculpture. *Contributions of the University of California Archaeological Research Facility*, ed. J. A. Graham, no. 16, pp. 41-52. Berkeley.

Greene Robertson, Merle

1967 *Ancient Maya Relief Sculpture*. Introduction by J. E. S. Thompson. New York: The Museum of Primitive Art.

1983-1985 *The Sculpture of Palenque*. 3 vols. (of 5). Princeton: Princeton University Press. The volumes published through 1985 are 1:

The Temple of the Inscriptions, 2: The Early Buildings of the Palace and the Wall Paintings, and 3: The Late Buildings of the Palace.

Gunckel, L. W.
1897   The Direction in Which Mayan Inscriptions Should Be Read. *The American Anthropologist* 10:146-162.

Guthe, C. E.
1921   *A Possible Solution of the Number Series on Pages 51 to 58 of the Dresden Codex.* Peabody Museum Papers, vol. 6, no. 2. Harvard University.

Hammond, N.
1977   Sir Eric Thompson, 1898-1975: A Biographical Sketch and Bibliography. In *Social Processes in Maya Prehistory*, ed. N. Hammond, pp. 1-17. London, New York, and San Francisco: Academic Press.
1982   *Ancient Maya Civilization.* New Brunswick, NJ: Rutgers University Press.
1984   Nineteenth-Century Drawings of Maya Monuments in the Society's Library. *The Antiquaries Journal* 64 (1):83-103. Dorking, England: Adlard and Son, for the Society of Antiquaries of London.

Heck, J. G.
1857   *The Iconographic Encyclopaedia of Science, Literature, and Art.* New York: R. Garrigue. Reprinted as *The Complete Encyclopedia of Illustration* by Park Lane Publishers, New York, 1979.

Hewett, E. L.
1911   Two Seasons' Work in Guatemala. *Bulletin of the Archaeological Institute of America* 2(1910-1911):117-134. New York: Macmillan.
1912   The Excavations at Quirigua in 1912. *Bulletin of the Archaeological Institute of America* 3(1911-1912):163-171. New York: Macmillan.

Hopkins, N. A.
1967   Summary of the First Seminar for the Study of Maya Writing. *Latin American Research Review* 2(2):91-94.

Houston, S. D.
1988   The Phonetic Decipherment of Mayan Glyphs. *Antiquity* 62 (234):126-135.
1989a   Archaeology and Maya Writing. *Journal of World Prehistory* 3(1):1-32.
1989b   *Maya Glyphs.* London: British Museum.

Houston, S., and D. Stuart
1989   *The Way Glyph: Evidence for "Co-essences" among the Classic Maya.* Research Reports on Ancient Maya Writing, no. 30. Washington, DC: Center for Maya Research.

Humboldt, A. von
1810   *Vues des cordillères, et monuments des peuples indigènes de l'Amérique.* Paris: F. Schoell. An excellent photographic facsimile edition of the 1810 Humboldt folio, with plates in color, was published by Éditions Erasme of Paris, in 1989, under the editorship of Charles Minguet and Amos Segala.
1814   *Researches Concerning the Institutions and Monuments of the Ancient Inhabitants of America, with Description and Views of Some of the Most Striking Scenes in the Cordilleras.* 2 vols., octavo. London.
1816   *Vues des cordillères, et monuments des peuples indigènes de l'Amérique.* 2 vols., octavo. Paris: N. Maze.

Humboldt, A. von, and A. Bonpland
1814-1825   *Voyage aux regions equinoctiales du nouveau continent.* Paris.

Indiana Historical Society
1954   *Walam Olum, or Red Score: The Migration Legend of the Lenni Lenape or Delaware Indians.* Indianapolis.

Jones, C., and L. Satterthwaite, Jr.
1982   *The Monuments and Inscriptions of Tikal: The Carved Monuments.* University Museum Monograph 44: Tikal Report No. 33, Part A. Philadelphia: The University Museum, The University of Pennsylvania.

Juarros, D.
1823   *A Statistical and Commercial History of the Kingdom of Guatemala, in Spanish America*, London. Translation into English by J. Baily of the original *Compendio de la historia de la Ciudad de Guatemala.* 2 vols. Guatemala: Ignacio Beteta, 1808-1818.

Justeson, J. S., and L. Campbell (editors)
1984   *Phoneticism in Mayan Hieroglyphic Writing.* Institute for Mesoamerican Studies, State University of New York at Albany. Publication 9. Albany, NY.

Justeson, J. S., W. M. Norman, L. Campbell, and T. Kaufman
1985   *The Foreign Impact on Lowland Mayan Languages and Script.* Middle American Research Institute, Tulane University. Publication 53. New Orleans, LA.

Kaufman, T. S.
1984   An Outline of Proto-Cholan Phonology, Morphology, and Vocabulary. In *Phoneticism in Mayan Hieroglyphic Writing*, eds. J. S. Justeson and L. Campbell, pp. 77-166. Institute for Mesoamerican Studies, State University of New York at Albany. Publication 9. Albany, NY.

Kelley, D. H.
1962a   A History of the Decipherment of Maya Script. *Anthropological Linguistics* 4(8):1-48.
1962b   Glyphic Evidence for a Dynastic Sequence at Quiriguá, Guatemala. *American Antiquity* 27:323-335.
1962c   Fonetísmo en la escritura Maya. *Estudios de Cultura Maya*, vol. 2, pp. 277-317. México: Universidad Nacional Autónoma de México.
1968   Kakupacal and the Itzas. *Estudios de Cultura Maya*, vol. 7, pp. 255-268. México: Universidad Nacional Autónoma de México.
1976   *Deciphering the Maya Script.* Austin: University of Texas Press.

Kerr, J.
1989-1990   *The Maya Vase Book.* 2 vols. New York. A continuing series, useful not only for its splendid roll-out photographs in black-and-white, but for commentaries on art and epigraphy by various scholars.

Kingsborough, E. K., Viscount
1829-1848   *Antiquities of Mexico, Comprising Facsimiles of Ancient Mexican Paintings and Hieroglyphics, Preserved in the Royal Libraries of Paris, Berlin, and Dresden; in the Imperial Library of Vienna; in the Vatican Library; in the Borgian Museum in Rome; in the Library of the Institute at Bologna; and in the Bodleian Library at Oxford. Together with the Monuments of New Spain, by M. Dupaix; with their Respective Scales of Measurement and Accompanying Descriptions. The Whole Illustrated by Many Valuable Inedited Manuscripts, by Augustine Aglio.* London: James Moynes (vols. 1-7) and Colnagi (vols. 8 and 9). This important work bears various dates: vols. 1 and 2, 1829, 1830, or 1831; vols. 3 through 7, 1830 or 1831; and vols. 8 and 9, 1848.

Kluckhohn, C.
1940   The Conceptual Structure in Middle American Studies. In *The Maya and Their Neighbors*, eds. C. L. Hay, R. L. Linton, S. K. Lothrop, H. L. Shapiro, and G. C. Vaillant. New York: D. Appleton-Century.

Knorozov, Y. V.
1952   ("The ancient script of Central America.") *Sovietskaya Etnografiya.* Moscow: Academy of Sciences.
1955a   *La escritura de los antiguos mayas (ensayo de descifrado).* Authorized Spanish translation. Moscow: Academy of Sciences.
1955b   *A Brief Summary of the Studies of the Ancient Maya Hieroglyphic Writing in the Soviet Union.* Authorized English translation. Reports of the Soviet Delegations at the 10th International Congress of Historical Science in Rome. Moscow: Academy of Sciences.
1958   The Problem of the Study of the Maya Hieroglyphic Writing. *American Antiquity* 23:284-291.
1965   Principios para descifrar los escritos mayas. *Estudios de Cultura Maya*, vol. 5, pp. 153-188. Translation by M. Mimo de Pintos. México: Universidad Nacional Autónoma de México.
1967   *The Writing of the Maya Indians.* Translation by S. Coe; collaborating editor, T. Proskouriakoff. Peabody Museum of Archaeology and Ethnology, Russian Translation Series, no. 4. Cambridge, MA.

Kubler, G.
1962   *The Art and Architecture of Ancient America.* Harmondsworth, England: Penguin Books. 2d ed., 1975.
1969   *Studies in Classic Maya Iconography.* Memoirs of the Connecticut Academy of Arts and Sciences, vol. 18. New Haven, CN.

Landa, Fray Diego de
1966   *Relación de las Cosas de Yucatán.* México: Editorial Porrua.

Larenaudière, M. de, and M. Lacroix
1844   *Mexique, et Guatemala, [et] Perou.* Paris: Didot Frères.

Larrainzar, M.
1875-1878 *Estudios sobre la historia de América, sus ruinas y antiguedades.* 5 vols. México: Villanueva, Villagelieu; Cárlos Ramiro.

Lee, T. A.
1985 *Los códices Mayas.* Introducción y bibliografía. San Cristóbal de las Casas, Chiapas: Universidad Autónoma de Chiapas. Contains full-color reproductions of all four known Maya codices, three of them taken directly from the facsimilies of the Dresden, Madrid, and Paris Codices issued by the Akademische Druck-und Verlagsanstalt, Graz, Austria. See Anders 1967, 1968; Deckert and Anders 1975.

Leyer, D.
1935 A New Method Used in Photographing Maya Hieroglyphs. *Maya Research* 2(1):61-63. New York: The Alma Egan Hyatt Foundation (for the Department of Middle American Research, Tulane University).

Literary Gazette
1822 (Review of Del Río and Cabrera 1822), no. 303 (November 9). London.

Lizana, B. de
1633 *Historia de Yucatan, devocionario de nuestra Se:ora de Izmal, y Conquista Espiritual.* Valladolid: Gerónimo Morillo. Reprinted by the Museo Nacional, Mexico City, in 1892 and 1893. The latter, based on a hitherto unknown complete copy, is the definitive modern edition.

Lizardi Ramos, C. (editor)
1941 *Los Mayas antiguos: monografías de arqueología, etnografía y linguistica Maya.* México: Colegio de Mexico.

López de Cogolludo, Fr. D.
1688 *Historia de Yucathan.* Madrid: Juan García Infanzón. Reprinted in Mérida and Campeche, 1842-1845; Mérida, 1867-1868; Campeche, 1955; and Mexico City, 1957. The 1842-1845 Campeche edition was issued in facsimile in Graz, Austria, by the Akademische Druck-und Verlagsanstalt, 1971. The best working edition is that of 1957, with prologue by Rubio Mañe, along with a photographic reproduction of the 1688 edition. It forms no. 3 of the *Colección de Grandes Crónicas Mexicanas,* published by the Editorial Academia Literaria.

Lothrop, S. K.
1929 Sculptural Fragments from Palenque. *Journal of the Royal Anthropological Institute* 59:53-63. London.

McCulloh, J. H., Jr.
1817 *Researches on America: Being an Attempt to Settle Some Points Relative to the Aborigines of America, &c.* Baltimore: Joseph Robinson.
1829 *Researches, Philosophical and Antiquarian, concerning the Aboriginal History of America.* Baltimore: Fielding Lucas, Jr.

MacLeod, B.
1984 Cholan and Yucatecan Verb Morphology and Glyphic Verbal Affixes in the Inscriptions. In *Phoneticism in Mayan Hieroglyphic Writing,* eds. J. S. Justeson and L. Campbell, pp. 233-262. Institute for Mesoamerican Studies, State University of New York at Albany. Publication 9. Albany, NY.

McNeil, R. A., and M. D. Deas
1980 *Europeans in Latin America: Humboldt to Hudson.* Catalog of an exhibition held in the Bodleian Library, December 1980-April 1981. Oxford: Bodleian Library.

Makemson, M. W.
1943 *The Astronomical Tables of the Maya.* Carnegie Institution of Washington. Publication 546, Contribution 42. Washington, DC.

Maler, T.
1901 *Researches in the Central Portion of the Usumatsintla Valley: Report of Explorations for the Museum 1898-1900.* Peabody Museum of Archaeology and Ethnology, Harvard University, Memoirs, vol. 2, no. 1. Cambridge, MA.
1903 *Researches in the Central Portion of the Usumatsintla Valley: Report of Explorations for the Museum.* Peabody Museum of Archaeology and Ethnology, Harvard University, Memoirs, vol. 2, no. 2. Cambridge, MA.
1908a *Explorations in the Department of Peten, Guatemala, and Adjacent Regions: Topoxte; Yaxha; Benque Viejo; Naranjo.*

Peabody Museum of Archaeology and Ethnology, Harvard University, Memoirs, vol. 4, no. 2. Cambridge, MA.

1908b   *Explorations of the Upper Usumatsintla and Adjacent Region: Altar de Sacrificios; Seibal; Itsimte-Sacluk; Cancuen.* Peabody Museum of Archaeology and Ethnology, Harvard University, Memoirs, vol. 4, no. 1. Cambridge, MA.

1910   *Explorations in the Department of Peten, Guatemala, and adjacent Regions: Motul de San José; Peten-Itza.* Peabody Museum of Archaeology and Ethnology, Harvard University, Memoirs, vol. 4, no. 3. Cambridge, MA.

1911   *Explorations in the Department of Peten, Guatemala: Tikal.* Peabody Museum of Archaeology and Ethnology, Harvard University, Memoirs, vol. 5, no. 1. Cambridge, MA.

Marcus, J.
1976   *Emblem and State in the Classic Maya Lowlands.* Washington, DC: Dumbarton Oaks.

Martínez Hernández, J.
1926   *Crónicas Mayas: Crónica de Yaxkukul.* Mérida: Tipografía Yucateca.

1930   *Diccionario de Motul maya-español atribuido a Fray Antonio de Ciudad Real y arte de lengua Maya por Juan Coronel.* Mérida: Talleres de la Companía Tipografica Yucateca.

Martyr d'Anghiera, P. (or Pedro Martír de Anglerá, etc.)
1530   *De Orbe Novo Petri Martyris ab Anglería Mediolanensis Protonotarij Cesarís Senatoris Decades.* Alcalá de Henares: Michael de Eguia. (in Latin.)

1555   *The Decades of the New World or West India, Conteyning the Nauigations and Conquests of the Spanyards, with the Particular Description of the Most Ryche and Large Landes and Islands Lately Found in the West Ocean Perteyning to the Inheritance of the Kings of Spayne.* Translation by R. Eden. London: William Powell.

1912   *De Orbe Novo, the Eight Decades of Peter Martyr d'Anghiera.* Translated from the Latin with notes and introduction by F. A. McNutt. 2 vols. New York and London.

Mathews, P.
1983   *Corpus of Maya Hieroglyphic Inscriptions, Vol. 6, Part 1: Tonina.* Peabody Museum of Archaeology and Ethnology, Harvard University.

Mathews, P. and L. Schele
1974   Lords of Palenque—The Glyphic Evidence. In *Primera Mesa Redonda de Palenque, Part 1*, ed. M. Greene Robertson, pp. 63-75. Pebble Beach, CA: The Robert Louis Stevenson School.

Matile, G. A.
1868   American Ethnology. *American Journal of Education.*

Maudslay, A. P.
1889-1902   *Archaeology.* 5 vols. (one of text, four of plates). London: R. H. Porter and Dulau. Appendix to *Biologia Centrali-Americana*, edited by Godman and Salvin, and includes Goodman 1897.

Means, P. A.
1917   *History of the Conquest of the Itzas and of the Itzas.* Peabody Museum Papers, vol. 7. Harvard University.

Médiz Bolio, A.
1930   *Libro de Chilam Balam de Chumayel.* San José, Costa Rica: Lehmann (Sauter and Co.).

Miller, M. E.
1986   *The Murals of Bonampak.* Princeton: Princeton University Press.

Molina Montes, A.
1979   Palenque: The Archaeological City Today. In *Tercera Mesa Redonda de Palenque, vol. 6*, eds. M. Greene Robertson and D. C. Jeffers, pp. 1-8. Monterey, CA: Herald Printers (for the Pre-Columbian Art Research Center).

Morley, S. G.
1913   Archaeological Research at the Ruins of Chichen Itza, Yucatan. In *Reports upon the Present Conditions and Future Needs of the Science of Anthropology*, pp. 61-91. Carnegie Institution of Washington. Publication 200. Washington, DC.

1914   Archaeology. In *Carnegie Institution of Washington, Year Book No. 13*, p. 333. Washington, DC. Distributed February 10, 1915.

1915   *Introduction to the Study of Maya Hieroglyphs.* Smithsonian Institution, Bureau of American Ethnology, Bulletin 57. Washington, DC: Government Printing Office.

1920   *The Inscriptions at Copan.* Carnegie Institution of Washington. Publication 219. Washington, DC.

1937-1938   *The Inscriptions of Peten.* 5 vols. Carnegie Institution of Washington. Publication 437. Washington, DC.

1946   *The Ancient Maya.* Stanford: Stanford University Press.

Morley, S. G., G. W. Brainerd, and R. J. Sharer

1983   *The Ancient Maya.* 4th ed., rev. Stanford: Stanford University Press.

Norman, B. M.

1843   *Rambles in Yucatan, including a Visit to the Remarkable Ruins of Chi-Chen, Kabah, Zayi, Uxmal, &c.* New York: J. and H. G. Langley.

Palacios, E. J.

1928   *En los confines de la Selva Lacandona: exploraciones en el Estado de Chiapas, 1926.* Secretaría de Educación Pública. México.

1935   *Guía arqueológica de Chichen-Itza.* Secretaria de Educación Pública. México.

Pendergast, D. M.

1967   *Palenque: The Walker-Caddy Expedition to the Ancient Maya City, 1839-1840.* Norman: University of Oklahoma Press.

Pérez, J.

1859a   Note sur un ancien manuscrit americaine inédit. *Revue Orientale et Américaine* 1:35-39. Paris. Illustrates one page of the Paris Codex.

1859b   Note sur un manuscrit Yucatèque inédit. *Archives de la Société Américaine de France* 1:29-32. Paris.

Pérez, J. P.

1846   Antigua cronología Yucateca. *El Registro Yucateco* 3:281-289; 323-332. Mérida: Castillo y Compañia.

1866-1877   *Diccionario de la lengua Maya.* Mérida: Imprenta Literaria de Juan F. Molina Solís.

Pollock, H. E. D.

1958   Annual Report of the Director of the Department of Archaeology. In *Carnegie Institution of Washington Year Book 57* (for the year July 1, 1957-June 30, 1958). Washington, DC.

Prescott, W. H.

1843   *History of the Conquest of Mexico.* 3 vols. New York: Harper and Brothers.

Priest, J.

1833   *American Antiquities and Discoveries in the West: Being an Exhibition of the Evidence That an Ancient Population of Partially Civilized Nations, Differing Entirely from Those of the Present Indians, Peopled America, Many Centuries Before Its Discovery by Columbus.* Albany, NY: Hoffman and White.

1841   See Priest 1833. The 1833 issue is labeled "second edition, revised." Other editions or issues are dated various years between 1833 and 1841.

Proskouriakoff, T.

1946   *An Album of Maya Architecture.* Carnegie Institution of Washington. Publication 558. Washington, DC.

1950   *A Study of Classic Maya Sculpture.* Carnegie Institution of Washington. Publication 593. Washington, DC.

1960   Historical Implications of a Pattern of Dates at Piedras Negras, Guatemala. *American Antiquity* 25:454-475.

1963   Historical Data in the Inscriptions of Yaxchilan. *Estudios de Cultura Maya*, vol. 3, pp. 149-167. México: Universidad Nacional Autónoma de México.

1964   Historical Data in the Inscriptions of Yaxchilan, Part 2. *Estudios de Cultura Maya*, vol. 4, pp. 177-202. México: Universidad Nacional Autónoma de México.

1967   Preface in *The Writing of the Maya Indians.* Translation by S. Coe; collaborating editor, T. Proskouriakoff. Peabody Museum of Archaeology and Ethnology, Russian Translation Series, no. 4. Cambridge, MA.

Racknitz, J. F., Baron von

1796   *Darstellung und Geschichte des Geschmacksder Vorzuglichsten Volker.* 5 vols. Leipzig.

Rafinesque, C. S.

1815   *Analyse de la nature, ou tableau de l'inivers et des corps organisés.* Palermo. (Fitzpatrick-Boewe No. 235.) See Boewe 1982.

1827   Important Historical and Philological Discovery. To Peter Duponceau, Esq. *The Saturday Evening Post* 6(285):[2], cols. [2-3], January 13, 1827. Philadelphia. (Fitzpatrick-Boewe No. 979.)

1828 Four Letters on American History by Prof. Rafinesque, to Dr. J. H. M'Culloh, of Baltimore. *The Saturday Evening Post* 7(358):[1], cols. [3-4], June 7, 1828 (First Letter); 7(360):[1], cols. [4-5], June 21, 1828 (Second Letter); 7(364):[2], cols. [1-2], July 19, 1828 (Third Letter); 7(371):[1], cols. [4-5], September 6, 1828 (Fourth Letter). Philadelphia.(Fitzpatrick-Boewe No. 979.)

1832a Philology. First Letter to Mr. Champollion, on the Graphic Systems of America, and the Glyphs of Otolum, or Palenque, in Central America. *Atlantic Journal, and Friend of Knowledge* 1(1):4-6. Philadelphia. (Fitzpatrick-Boewe No. 614.)

1832b Philology. Second Letter to Mr. Champollion, on the Graphic Systems of America, and the Glyphs of Otolum, or Palenque, in Central America—Elements of the Glyphs. *Atlantic Journal, and Friend of Knowledge* 1(2):40-44. Philadelphia. (Fitzpatrick-Boewe No. 640.)

1832c The American Nations and Tribes Are Not Jews. *The Atlantic Journal and Friend of Knowledge* 1(3):98-99.

1835 Otolum, near Palenque. *Bulletin No. 1 of the Historical and Natural Sciences*, pp. 5-6. Philadelphia. (Fitzpatrick-Boewe No. 851c.)

1836 *A Life of Travels and Researches in North America and South Europe, or Outlines of the Life, Travels, and Researches of C. S. Rafinesque, A.M., Ph.D., Professor of Historical and Natural Sciences, Member of Many Learned Societies in Europe and America, Author of Many Works, &c., Containing His Travels in North America and the South of Europe; the Atlantic Ocean, Mediterranean, Sicily, Azores, &c., from 1802 to 1835.* Philadelphia: F. Turner. (Fitzpatrick-Boewe No. 863.)

Rau, C.
1879 *The Palenque Tablet in the United States National Museum, Washington, DC.* Smithsonian Contributions to Knowledge, vol. 22, no. 5. Washington DC: Smithsonian Institution. See Davis and Pérez 1882.

Ritter, C.
1853 Ueber neue Entdeckungen und Beobachtungen in Guatemala und Yucatan. *Zeitschrift für Allgemeine Erdkunde* 1:161-193. Berlin.

Rivero Figueroa, D. J., and F. Canton Rosado
1918 *Dos vidas ejemplares: ensayos biográficos del Ilmo. Sr. Obispo de Yucatán Don Crescencio Carrillo y Ancona y de Monseñor Norberto Domínguez.* Havana: Avisador Comercial.

Robicsek, F., and D. M. Hales
1981 *The Maya Book of the Dead: The Ceramic Codex.* Charlottesville, VA: The University of Virginia Art Museum (distributed by the University of Oklahoma Press).

Rosny, L. de
1856 *Collection d'anciennes peintures mexicaines.* Paris: Maisonneuve et Cie.

1860 *Les écritures figuratives et hiéroglyphiques des differents peuples anciens et modernes.* Paris: Maisonneuve et Cie.

1864 *Collection d'anciennes peintures mexicaines (hiéroglyphes mexicains), publié avec des notices descriptives.* Paris. Glass 1975b:690 cites this as a possible second edition of Rosny 1856.

1875 *Mémoire sur la numération dans la langue et dans l'Ecriture sacrée des anciens Mayas (1).* Congrès International des Américanistes: Compte-Rendu de la Première Session, Nancy, 1875, vol. 2, pp. 439-458. Nancy: G. Crépin-Leblond.

1876 *Essai sur le déchiffrement de l'écriture hiératique de l'Amérique Centrale.* Paris: Maisonneuve et Cie. Appeared in both folio and octavo limited editions in French. A Spanish edition was printed in Madrid in 1884 under the editorship of Juan de Dios de la Rada y Delgado; it included a transcription of the Diego de Landa's *Relación de las cosas de Yucatán*—the first complete and accurate version of that work.

1882 *Les documents écrits de l'antiquité Américaine.* Paris: Maisonneuve et Cie.

1887 *Codex Peresianus. Manuscrit hiératique des anciens Indiens de l'Amérique Centrale conservé à la Bibliothèque Nationale de Paris. Publié en coleurs avec une introduction . . .* Paris: Bureau de la Société Américaine. Lithographic edition with errors of omission caused by manipulation of the base photographs.

1888 *Codex Peresianus. Manuscrit hiératique des anciens Indiens de l'Amérique Centrale conservé à la Bibliothèque Nationale de Paris, avec une introduction . . . seconde édition imprimée en noir.* Paris: Bureau de la Société Américaine. Unretouched images make this the most accurate of the early reproductions.

1904   *L'Amérique Pré-Colombienne: études d'histoire, de linguistique & de paléographie sur les anciens temps du nouveau-monde.* Paris: Ernest Leroux.

Roys, R.
1933   *Book of Chilam Balam of Chumayel.* Carnegie Institution of Washington. Publication 438. Washington, DC.

Ruppert, K., and J. H. Denison, Jr.
1943   *Archaeological Reconnaissance in Campeche, Quintana Roo and Peten.* Carnegie Institution of Washington, Publication 543. Washington, DC.

Ruz Lhuillier, A.
1955   Exploraciones en Palenque: 1952. *Anales del Instituto Nacional de Antropología e Historia,* epoch 6, vol. 6, pp. 79-110. México.

Sahagún, Fr. B. de
1950-1969   *Florentine Codex: General History of the Things of New Spain.* 12 books. Translated from the Aztec into English, with notes and illustrations, by A. J. O. Anderson and C. E. Dibble. Santa Fe, NM: University of Utah and School of American Research. The original manuscript of this superlatively important work, with numerous illustrations, is among the treasured holdings of the Medicea Laurenziana Library of Florence, Italy (no. 218-220 of the Palatine Collection). A superb facsimile edition (of 2,000) in three volumes was printed in 1979 by the house of Giunti Barbèra under the joint auspices and supervision of the Library and Mexico's Archivo General de la Nación. Published editions in Spanish include that of Robredo (México, 1938).

Sánchez de Aguilar, P.
1937   *Informe contra idolorum cultores del obispado de Yucatán.* 3d ed. Mérida: E. G. Triay and Sons. First published in Madrid, 1639; the second edition appeared in the Anales del Museo Nacional de México, epoch 1, vol. 6, pp. 13-122, México, 1900.

Satterthwaite, L., Jr.
1947   *Concepts and Structures of Maya Calendrical Arithmetics.* Joint Publications of The Museum of The University of Pennsylvania and the Philadelphia Anthro-

pological Society, no. 3. Philadelphia: The University Museum, The University of Pennsylvania.

1958   *The Problem of Abnormal Stela Placements at Tikal and Elsewhere.* Tikal Report No. 3, pp. 61-83. Museum Monograph 15. Philadelphia: The University Museum, The University of Pennsylvania.

Schele, L.
1984   *Maya Glyphs: The Verbs.* Austin: University of Texas Press.

Schele, L., and M. E. Miller
1986   *The Blood of Kings: Dynasty and Ritual in Maya Art.* Fort Worth, TX: Kimbell Art Museum (George Brazillier, Inc., Publisher).

Schellhas, P.
1886   Die Maya Handschrift der Königlichen Bibliothek sur Dresden. *Zeitschrift für Ethnologie* 24:12-42, 49-84. Berlin.

1897   *Die Göttergestalten der Mayahandschriften, 2: Ein mythologisches Kulturbild aus dem alten Amerika.* Dresden: Verlag von Richard Bertling.

1904   *Representation of Deities of the Maya Manuscripts.* Peabody Museum Papers, vol. 4, no. 1. Harvard University.

Scherzer, K.
1857   *Las historias del origin de los indios de esta provincia de Guatemala.* Vienna: Academia Imperial de las Ciencias.

Seler, E. G.
1887   Entzifferung der Maya-Handschriften. *Zeitschrift für Ethnologie* 19:231-237.

1888   Die Tageszeichen der aztekischen und der Maya-Handschriften und ihre Gottheiten. *Zeitschrift für Ethnologie* 20, pp. 10-97. Berlin. Reprinted in Seler 1902-1923, 1:417-503.

1899   Die Monumente von Copán und Quiriguá und die Altarplatten von Palenque. *Zeitschrift für Ethnologie* 31:670-738.

1902-1923   *Gesammelte abhandlungen zur Amerikanischen Sprach und Alterthumskunde.* 5 vols. Berlin: Ascher (vols. 1 and 2), Behrend (vols. 3-5). Reprinted 1960-1961 by the Akademische Druck-und Verlagsanstalt, Graz, Austria; Ferdinand Anders's *Wort- und sachregister . . . ,* an index to the set, was issued (as Vol. 6) in 1967.

1904   *Codex Borgia: Eine altmexikan Bilderschrift der Bibliothek der Congragatio de Propagande Fide (Rom).* Berlin. Reprinted in Spanish, with accompanying facsimile, by the Fondo de Cultura Económica, México, 1963.

1915   Beobachtungen und Studien in den Ruinen von Palenque. From *Abhandlungen der Königlichen Preussichen Akademie der Wissenschaften, Jahrgang, 1915, Phil.-Hist. Klasse,* no. 5. Berlin.

1917   Die Ruinen von Uxmal. From *Abhandlungen de Königlichen Preussichen Akademie der Wissenschaften, Jahrgang, 1917, Phil.-Hist. Klasse,* no. 3. Berlin.

Smith, A. L.
1955   *Archaeological Reconnaissance in Central Guatemala.* Carnegie Institution of Washington. Publication 608. Washington, DC.

Solís Alcala, E.
1949   *Códice Pérez.* Ediciones de la Liga de Acción Social. Mérida: Imprenta Oriente.

Spinden, H. J.
1913   *A Study of Maya Art.* Peabody Museum Memoirs, vol. 6. Harvard University.

1924   *The Reduction of Maya Dates.* Peabody Museum Papers, vol. 6, no. 4. Harvard University.

1928   *The Ancient Civilizations of Mexico and Central America.* 3d ed., rev. American Museum of Natural History Handbook Series. New York.

1940   Diffusion of Maya Astronomy. In *The Maya and Their Neighbors,* eds. C. L. Hay, R. Linton, S. K. Lothrop, H. L. Shapiro, and G. C. Vaillant, pp. 162-178. New York: D. Appleton-Century.

1949   Mexican Calendars and the Solar Year. In *Smithsonian Institution Annual Report for 1948,* pp. 393-406. Washington, DC.

Stephens, J. L.
1841   *Incidents of Travel in Central America, Chiapas and Yucatan.* 2 vols. New York: Harper and Brothers.

1843   *Incidents of Travel in Yucatan.* 2 vols. New York: Harper and Brothers.

1854   *Incidents of Travel in Central America, Chiapas, and Yucatan, by the late John Lloyd Stephens.* Revised from the latest American edition, with additions, by Frederick Catherwood. London: Arthur Hall, Virtue and Co.

Stuart, D.
1987   *Ten Phonetic Syllables.* Research Reports on Ancient Maya Writing, no. 14. Washington, DC: Center for Maya Research.

Stuart, D., and S. D. Houston
1989   Maya Writing. *Scientific American* 261(2):82-89.

Stuart, G. E.
1989   *The Beginning of Maya Hieroglyphic Study: Contributions of Constantine S. Rafinesque and James H. McCulloh, Jr.* Research Reports on Ancient Maya Writing, no. 29. Washington, DC: Center for Maya Research.

Taylor, W. W.
1948   A Study of Archeology. *American Anthropological Association Memoir 69.*

Teeple, J. E.
1925   Maya Inscriptions: Glyphs C, D, and E of the Supplementary Series. *American Anthropologist* 27:108-115.

1925a   Maya Inscriptions: Further Notes on the Supplementary Series. *American Anthropologist* 27:544-549.

1928   Maya Inscriptions, VI: The Lunar Calendar and Its Relation to Maya History. *American Anthropologist* 30:391-407.

1930   *Maya Astronomy.* Carnegie Institution of Washington. Publication 403, Contribution 2. Washington, DC.

Thomas, C.
1882   *A Study of the Manuscript Troano.* U. S. Department of the Interior, Contributions to North American Ethnology, vol. 5. Washington, DC: Government Printing Office.

Thompson, J. E. S.
1927   A Correlation of the Mayan and European Calendars. *Field Museum of Natural History, Anthropological Series,* vol. 17, no. 1. Chicago.

1930   Ethnology of the Maya of Southern and Central British Honduras. *Field Museum of Natural History, Anthropological Series,* vol. 17, no. 2. Chicago.

1931   Archaeological Investigations in the Southern Cayo District, British Honduras. *Field Museum of Natural History Anthropological Series,* vol. 17, no. 3. Chicago.

1938   Sixteenth and Seventeenth Century Reports on the Chol Mayas. *American Anthropologist* 40:584-604.

1939   *The Moon Goddess in Middle America with Notes on Related Deities.* Carnegie Institution of Washington. Publication 509, Contribution 29. Washington, DC.

1943   *Maya Epigraphy: A Cycle of 819 Days.* Carnegie Institution of Washington, Division of Historical Research. Notes on Middle American Archaeology and Ethnology, no. 22. Cambridge, MA.

1949   Sylvanus Griswold Morley, 1883-1948. *American Anthropologist* 51:293-297.

1950   *Maya Hieroglyphic Writing: An Introduction.* Carnegie Institution of Washington. Publication 589. Washington, DC.

1954   *The Rise and Fall of Maya Civilization.* Norman: University of Oklahoma Press.

1959   Systems of Hieroglyphic Writing in Middle America and Methods of Deciphering Them. *American Antiquity* 24:349-364.

1960   Preface. In *Maya Hieroglyphic Writing: An Introduction.* 2d ed. Norman: University of Oklahoma Press.

1962   *A Catalogue of Maya Hieroglyphs.* Norman: University of Oklahoma Press.

1972   *A Commentary on the Dresden Codex.* Memoirs of the American Philosophical Society, no. 93. Philadelphia.

1975   The Grolier Codex. In *Contributions of the University of California Archaeological Research Foundation*, no. 27, pp. 271-279. Berkeley, CA.

Thompson, J. E. S., H. E. D. Pollock, and J. Charlot
1932*A*   *Preliminary Study of the Ruins of Coba, Quintana Roo, Mexico.* Carnegie Institution of Washington. Publication 424. Washington, DC.

Thompson, J. E. S., and T. Proskouriakoff
1947   *Maya Calendar Round Dates Such as 9 Ahau 17 Mol.* Carnegie Institution of Washington, Division of Historical Research. Notes on Middle American Archaeology and Ethnology, no. 79. Cambridge, MA.

Tozzer, A. M.
1941   *Landa's Relación de las cosas de Yucatán.* Peabody Museum Papers 18. Harvard University.

Turner, G. L.
1983   *Nineteenth-Century Scientific Instruments.* London: Sotheby Publishers.

Valentini, P. J. J.
1880   The Landa Alphabet; A Spanish Fabrication. *Proceedings of the American Antiquarian Society*, no. 75, pp. 59-91. Worcester, MA.

Velasquez, P.
1850   *Memoir of an Eventful Expedition to Central America; Resulting in the Discovery of the Idolatrous City of Iximaya, in an Unexplored Region, and the Possession of Two Remarkable Aztec Children, Descendants and Specimens of the Sacerdotal Caste (now nearly extinct) of the Ancient Aztec Founders of the Ruined Temples of That Country, Described by John L. Stevens, Esq., and Other Travellers. Translated from the Spanish of Pedro Velasquez, of San Salvador.* New York: J. W. Bell. A variant of this inventive pamphlet was published in London by R. S. Francis, 1853, with additional illustrations.

Villacorta C., J. Antonio, and C. A. Villacorta
1930   *Códices Mayas.* Guatemala: Tipografía Nacional. Reprinted 1976 and 1977.

Villagutierre Soto-Mayor, J. de
1701   *Historia de la conquista de la Provincia de el Itza, redvcción, y progresos de la de el Lacandon, y otras naciones de Indios bárbaros, de la mediación de el Reyno de Gvatimala, a las provincias de Yvcatán, en la America Septentrional.* Part One. Madrid: Lucas Antonio de Bedmar y Narvaez. All published. The second edition of the work, edited by Pedro Zamora, was printed in Guatemala City by the Tipografía Nacional, 1933. An English translation by Brother Robert D. Wood, edited by Frank E. Comparato, was published by Labyrinthos, 1983. A facsimile of the 1701 edition, with introduction by Miguel Leon-Portilla, was done by the Grupo Condumex in Mexico City, 1985.

Villaseñor Espinosa, R. (editor)
1978   *Atlas de las antigüidades Mexicanas halladas en el curso de los tres viajes de la real expedición de antigüidades de la Nueva España emprendidos en 1805, 1806, y 1807. Contiene la reproducción facsimilar de las litografías ejecutadas a partir de los dibujos de José Luciano Castañeda, e impresas en Paris, en 1834, por Jules Didot; así como la relación de dichos viajes por el Capitán Guillermo Dupaix, jefe de la real expedición.* Preface by Miguel León-

expedición. Preface by Miguel León-Portilla. México: San Angel Ediciones, S.A. One of six works produced in "gift editions" under the auspices of Mexican President José López Portillo, this volume reproduces the portion of Baradère (ed.) 1834 that treats of the three expeditions of Dupaix, and includes color versions of all the plates made from the Castañeda illustrations of various Mexican and (then) Guatemalan ruins that appeared in that edition.

Von Euw, E.
1977   *Corpus of Maya Hieroglyphic Inscriptions, Vol. 4, Part 1: Itzimte, Pixoy, and Tzum.* Cambridge, MA: Peabody Museum of Archaeology and Ethnology, Harvard University.

Von Hagen, V. W.
1947   *Maya Explorer: John Lloyd Stephens and the Lost Cities of Central America and Yucatán.* Norman: University of Oklahoma Press.

1950   *Frederick Catherwood, Archt.* Introduction by Aldous Huxley. New York: Oxford University Press.

1973   *Search for the Maya: The Story of Stephens and Catherwood.* Farnsborough, England: Saxon House.

Waldeck, J. F. de
1838   *Voyage pittoresque et archéologique dans la province d'Yucatan (Amérique Centrale), pendant les années 1834 et 1836.* Paris: Bellizard Dufour et Cie. A Spanish version of this work, limited to 110 copies, was translated by Mestre Ghigliazza and edited by Carlos R. Menéndez, and was published in Mérida, Yucatán, 1930.

Weeks, J.
1984   *Manuscripts Relating to Middle American Indians at Tozzer Library, Harvard University.* Photocopy. Cambridge, MA: Tozzer Library.

1990   *Mesoamerican Ethnohistory in United States Libraries: Reconstruction of the William E. Gates Collection of Historic and Linguistic Manuscripts.* Culver City, CA: Labyrinthos.

Whorf, B. L.
1933   *The Phonetic Value of Certain Characters in Maya Writing.* Peabody Museum Papers, vol. 13, no. 2. Harvard University.

1942   *Decipherment of the Linguistic Portion of the Maya Hieroglyphs.* Smithsonian Institution Annual Report for 1941, pp. 479-502. Washington, DC.

Wilgus, A. C.
1965   *Histories and Historians of Hispanic America.* New York: Cooper Square Publishers. Other editions, 1936 and 1942.

Willson, R. W.
1924   *Astronomical Notes on the Maya Codices.* Peabody Museum Papers, vol. 6, no. 3. Harvard University.

Zimmermann, G.
1954   Notas para la historia de los manuscritos Mayas. *Yan* 3:62-64. México: Centro de Investigaciones Antropológicas de México.

1956   *Die hieroglyphen der Maya handschriften.* Hamburg: Cram, de Gruyter.

1964   La escritura jeroglífica y el calendario como indicadores de tendencias de la historia cultural de los Mayas. In *Desarrollo cultural de los mayas*, eds. E. Z. Vogt and A. Ruz Lhuillier, pp. 229-242. México: Universidad Nacional Autónoma de México.

II
Classic Maya Politics

Stephen D. Houston

Department of Anthropology
Vanderbilt University

The greatest Mayanist of his day, J. Eric Thompson, once said that Classic Maya political organization consisted of a "loose federation of states, each ruled by a small group of sacerdotal aristocrats" (1950:7). This was a reasonable view and, as we shall see, probably correct in its main thrust. But it had one drawback: it could not be confirmed or disproved on the basis of information available at the time. We must remember that Thompson and others of his generation regarded Maya writing as something highly unusual. It did not refer to politics or to the affairs of humans, as do so many other scripts, but rather to the obscure subjects of numerology, time worship, calendrical astronomy, and prophecy. Under these circumstances, scholars could not hope to say much about ancient political organization.

It now seems that Thompson was only partly correct in his ideas about Maya glyphs. According to recent research, most Classic inscriptions are also historical documents: they commemorate rulers and their relatives as well as some members of the nobility. Even more important, glyphs refer to political relations among the ruling dynasties of the Classic period. For the first time ancient Maya political organization can be discussed from the perspective of those it affected, and with some hope of evaluating interpretations of Classic politics.

Most studies of Classic politics correspond to one of two views, which may be labeled the "Imperial" and "City-State" models. The Imperial model assumes that a few dynasties, each attached to a particularly impressive site, controlled large areas of the Maya lowlands. Within such areas lay subordinate sites whose ruling families were dependent on the imperial dynasty. The site of Tikal is often regarded as such a "primate" city, controlling much of the southern Maya lowlands and even some areas

beyond (Adams 1986). In contrast, the City-State model describes a more fragmented political landscape in which the domain of a dynasty extended only a few kilometers beyond the limits of its home site. Of course, all models are simplifications, and these are no exception; most interpretations of Classic politics incorporate something of both views, with varying emphases. But the question remains: Which model, or variant model, accords best with the evidence from Maya epigraphy?

This and other questions cannot be answered without looking at some recent interpretations of Classic politics. One of the most influential of such studies is that of Joyce Marcus, who has used epigraphic evidence to propose a variant of the Imperial model (1976). From the evidence of two stelae, one from the site of Copan and the other from Seibal, Marcus believes the Classic Maya achieved a high order of political integration. To Marcus, the Classic Maya divided their world into quarters, each presided over by a regional capital of great size and influence. Crucial to her theory is the notion of an "emblem glyph," a glyphic title that evidently specifies dynasties or sites (Berlin 1958). By studying the distribution of these emblem glyphs, Marcus has devised a scheme fleshing out the relationships between capitals and sites subordinate to them (Fig. 2.1, with Roman numerals indicating levels in her hierarchy). For example, a primary or regional capital, identified by its emblem glyph, occupies the highest position in a hierarchy, and it is to this center that secondary, tertiary, and quaternary sites owe their allegiance. Lower-order centers are joined to higher ones by coercion, marriage alliances, or possibly economic ties. At the lowest level, centers tend not to use emblem glyphs, a title presumably reserved for only the most important sites.

In overview, Marcus's model represents a com-

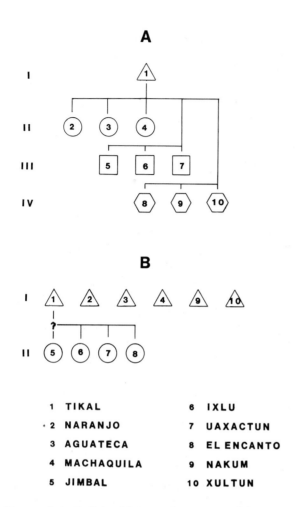

A

I

II

III

IV

B

I

II

1	TIKAL	6	IXLU
2	NARANJO	7	UAXACTUN
3	AGUATECA	8	EL ENCANTO
4	MACHAQUILA	9	NAKUM
5	JIMBAL	10	XULTUN

Figure 2.1. Political hierarchy proposed by Joyce Marcus (A), contrasting with more recent interpretations of such relationships (B).

Figure 2.2. Ilah glyph at Seibal.

position of the sign in this and other texts, such as the one illustrated in Figure 2.3 it may well be that the glyph simply indicates the presence of a ruler or his proxy at key dynastic rituals celebrated by a local lord—that is, the visitor "saw" or witnessed the ritual (David Stuart, personal communication). Similar visits by foreign nobility are documented elsewhere in the Maya area, such as in the Bonampak murals of Mexico (Miller 1986). There is no pressing reason, then, to assume that the references at Seibal and Copan reflect a quadripartite political division of the Classic Maya world; they simply record the participation of foreign lords in local rituals. Thus, Marcus's suggestion of large-scale, cosmologically based political organization, in this case embracing all the Maya lowlands, cannot be substantiated by glyphic evidence.

Another problem with Marcus's study is the lack of epigraphic justification for her hierarchies. This is especially true of the so-called Tikal regional state, in which Tikal appears as a primary capital, with several important centers beneath it (see Fig. 2.1). Among these are Naranjo, Aguateca, and Machaquilá at the secondary level; Jimbal, Ixlu, and Uaxactun at the tertiary; and El Encanto, Xultun, and Nakum at the quaternary. First, according to Marcus's model, Naranjo, Aguateca, and Machaquilá should acknowledge Tikal in some manner. They do not. Instead, the references cited by Marcus are to the rulers of Dos Pilas, who share with Tikal the same emblem glyph form but whose connection to Tikal is highly ambiguous (Houston and Mathews 1985). Second, the monumental record at Jimbal and Ixlu overlaps only slightly with that of Tikal; rather, it dates in large part to the period after Tikal's apparent disintegration as an important center. This pattern is unlikely to be coincidental, and may result from the reduction of the Tikal polity into smaller political groupings during the end of the Classic, a pattern paralleled near the Lake Petexbatún region of Guatemala. Finally, of sites at the lowest level

prehensive and well-argued effort, and some features of it, such as the emphasis on marriage alliances, continue to be valid. But it now seems that her overall model is less tenable. For one, Marcus's evidence for a set of primary capitals comes from two monuments, Stela A from Copan and Stela 10 from Seibal, which show three foreign emblem glyphs in addition to a local one. As mentioned above, Marcus feels that these references map the highest level of Classic polity, with each capital being fully independent of the other. Yet the texts from Copan and Seibal are exceptionally obscure, but for one glyph, which introduces the text at Seibal (Fig. 2.2). There is good reason to read this sign as *ilah,* based on a root meaning "to see." From the

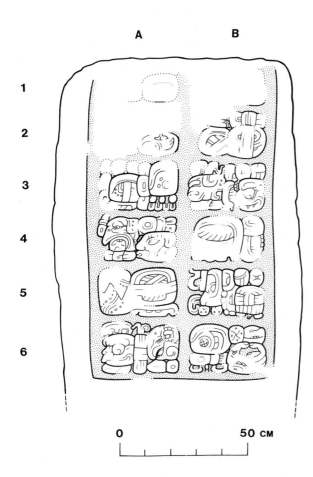

Figure 2.3. Dos Pilas Panel 7. Ilah glyph at B4.

Nakum has a poor record of monuments, with little bearing on Marcus's argument. Xultun is a case in point, because it possesses its own emblem glyph (presumably a mark of prominence) and seems to mention Tikal solely in the context of warfare. Thus, there is scant glyphic evidence that Tikal was politically paramount during the Late Classic. By extension, there exists small support for the Imperial model of lowland Maya politics, at least as this is deduced from inscriptions.

The Early Classic evidence for regional capitals is somewhat more complex (Mathews 1984). Tikal does seem to have been the most important and influential center during the Early Classic. Yet, if anything, early inscriptions from Tikal and other sites are more ambiguous than later ones. Too often, arguments about contacts between Tikal and its neighbors are based on points of artistic similarity

rather than on the specific historical arguments that inscriptions can provide (see Adams 1986). A more compelling picture of Early Classic political organization must await further work on this very difficult body of texts.

Of late, the City-State model of Classic politics has received more support (see Adams 1977:159). A key feature of this model is the close linkage between sites and polities, with the latter only occasionally embracing more than a single major center. Accordingly, the scale of political organization is much reduced from that envisaged by Marcus. Hierarchies may have existed, but only in the immediate hinterland of a site, beyond which allegiance to central authority grew progressively weak and more likely to be transferred to competing centers.

The City-State model, or at least a variant form of it, has much to recommend it. In the first place, it now seems that emblem glyphs are both titles and references to polities (Mathews 1984). In consequence, a site with an emblem glyph presumably functioned as the capital of a polity. There is also a good deal of epigraphic evidence that polities, as identified by emblem glyphs, were essentially autonomous: it is at this level that the Maya conducted most foreign policy, including the practice of warfare and the transfer of royal women. Higher-order relations, involving the subordination of one polity to another, occur in only a few instances and for brief periods. Nonetheless, while such relations lasted, the connection between overlord and tributary was, to judge from inscriptional evidence, a strong one (Houston and Mathews 1985; Houston 1987).

In a related development, recent work by David Stuart and the author indicates that the Classic Maya recorded the existence of several major sites within a single polity. The Maya apparently employed place name or toponym glyphs, of which a few are illustrated here (Fig. 2.4). Particularly good examples of toponyms come from near Lake Petexbatún. There, the sites of Dos Pilas and Aguateca contain inscriptions with the same emblem glyph and yet also employ different toponyms. The practical benefit of this arrangement is obvious; Maya scribes could record where events took place within a particular polity. Toponyms played a less useful role in polities with only one major center.

The discovery of toponymic signs suggests that the notion of the city-state among the Classic Maya

A   **B**   **C**

Figure 2.4. Place names, including those of Dos Pilas (A), Aguateca (B), and Palenque (C).

must be modified. On the whole, Classic polities possessed one large center, but, as we have seen, several contain more, often of substantial size and with monuments erected by a single ruling dynasty. For this reason, sites and polities are by no means synonymous.

Even with such modifications there can be little doubt that the Classic polities of the southern lowlands were relatively small, and nothing like the vast territories embraced by the Aztec of central Mexico. Indeed, the spacing of autonomous centers raises some interesting similarities with patterns from Old World archaeology. In the Maya region, political capitals averaged a mean distance of 32 km from their neighbors, with some being rather closer or more distant than this figure. On empirical evidence this matches (with allowances for individual differences in speed) the distance a person can walk in a day over the broken terrain of the Maya lowlands (Adams 1978:27). The figure corresponds strikingly to that of many early polities in the Old World, of a sort described by Colin Renfrew as "Early State Modules" (1982:282). One author has even discussed the figure in terms of administration, by stating that such control "was limited to a radius of about 20 km (a one-day round-trip distance) from a given high-order center" (Johnson 1982:415), beyond which effective control would presumably dissipate. He further suggests that one way to overcome this handicap was to place additional centers within a one-day round trip from the primary site, a pattern perhaps documented in the Lake PetexbatDn region of Guatemala. The sites of Aguateca and Dos Pilas, demonstrably ruled by the same family at the same time, lie approximately a day's walk from each other. Most likely, travel time and the spatial limits on

effective administration restricted the size of Classic polities and accounted for anomalous settlement patterns, such as those near Lake Petexbatun.

There is some evidence that the Classic Maya occasionally went beyond such limits, usually by means of warfare (Riese 1984). At a number of ruins, including Naranjo, Cancuen, and Seibal, it appears that foreign forces occupied sites long enough to erect victory monuments (Baudez and Mathews 1978). At other places, such as Tikal, failure in warfare may have contributed signally to dynastic weakness (Houston 1986). But despite such evidence, it is equally true that the control of foreign centers was in large part short-lived: the Maya seemed to have had as much difficulty in consolidating empire as their counterparts in Central Mexico had success.

The reasons for such difficulties are at present obscure. It may be that the Classic Maya took little interest in seizing territory and booty; their interests may rather have tended to the capture of individuals for enhanced prestige and eventual sacrifice, as J. Eric Thompson suggested many years ago (1950; see also Demarest 1978). A related explanation is that the very structure of Classic society prohibited the effective control of conquered territory. There is accumulating evidence, much of it assembled by Peter Mathews and David Stuart, that Classic rulers appointed representatives to positions of authority in subsidiary centers (Mathews and Justeson 1984). Some of these individuals were related to the ruling family, and even seem to have acceded to high office in the same fashion as paramount lords. An additional characteristic of the representatives is that monuments celebrating their subordinate status span a brief period. Conceivably, the chronology was brief simply because local lords did not long stay under the authority of paramount rulers; rather, they achieved independence because of the distance from overlords (who ordinarily might be inclined to a meddlesome interest in subordinates) and the temptation to install their own family as a ruling lineage. Unfortunately, it is not yet possible to document such changes of status with epigraphic evidence. Supporting texts will appear only with further investigation at sites with representatives, such as the poorly known ruins of El Cayo and La Pasadita.

In conclusion, the model that best fits the epigraphic evidence is a modified City-State model, in which polities included at most a few major sites.

The picture of political organization that emerges is not one of neatly ordered arrangements, disposed hierarchically. Rather, the pattern resembles a shifting mosaic, with the reversals and successes that so characterize human history. J. Eric Thompson may not have fully understood the content of Maya writing, but his intuitive grasp of Classic politics seems perhaps closer to the mark than the theories of those who followed him.

BIBLIOGRAPHY

Adams, R. E. W.
1977   *Prehistoric Mesoamerica.* Boston: Little, Brown.
1978   Routes of Communication in Mesoamerica: the Northern Guatemalan Highlands and the Peten. In *Mesoamerican Communication Routes and Cultural Contacts*, eds. T. A. Lee, Jr., and C. Navarette, pp. 27-35. Papers of the New World Archaeological Foundation 40. Provo, UT: Brigham Young University.
1986   *Rio Azul Reports 2: The 1984 Season.* San Antonio: Center for Archaeological Research, University of Texas.

Baudez, C. F., and P. Mathews
1978   Capture and Sacrifice at Palenque. In *Tercera Mesa Redonda de Palenque, Vol. IV*, eds. M. Greene Robertson and D. C. Jeffers, pp. 31-40. Palenque, Chiapas: Pre-Columbian Art Research Center.

Berlin, H.
1958   El glifo 'emblema' en las inscripciones Mayas. *Journal de la Société des Américanistes* 47:111-119.

Demarest, A.
1978   Interregional Conflict and "Situational Ethics" in Classic Maya Warfare. In *Codex Wauchope: A Tribute Roll*, pp. 101-111. New Orleans: Human Mosaic 12.

Houston, S. D.
1986   Appendix II: Notes on Caracol Epigraphy and Its Significance. In *Investigations at the Classic Maya City of Caracol, Belize: 1985-1987*, by A. F. Chase and D. Z. Chase, pp. 85-100. Monograph 3. San Francisco: Pre-Columbian Art Research Institute.
1987   *The Inscriptions and Monumental Art of Dos Pilas, Guatemala: A Study of Classic Maya History and Politics.* Ph.D. dissertation, Department of Anthropology, Yale University.

Houston, S. D., and P. Mathews
1985   *The Dynastic Sequence of Dos Pilas, Guatemala.* Monograph 1. San Francisco: Pre-Columbian Art Research Institute

Johnson, G.
1982   Organizational Structure and Scalar Stress. In *Theory and Explanation in Archaeology: The Southhampton Conference*, eds. C. Renfrew, M. J. Rowlands, and B. A. Seagrave, pp. 389-421. New York: Academic.

Marcus, J.
1976   *Emblem and State in the Classic Maya Lowlands.* Washington, DC: Dumbarton Oaks.

Mathews, P.
1984   Emblem Glyphs in Classic Maya Inscriptions. Paper presented at the meeting of the American Anthropological Association, Denver.

Mathews, P., and J. S. Justeson
1984   Patterns of Sign Substitution in Maya Hieroglyphic Writing: "The Affix Cluster." In *Phoneticism in Mayan Hieroglyphic Writing*, eds. J. S. Justeson and L. Campbell, pp. 185-231. Publication 9. Albany: Institute for Mesoamerican Studies, State University of New York at Albany.

Miller, M. E.
1986   *The Murals of Bonampak.* Princeton: Princeton University Press.

Renfrew, C.
1982   Polity and Power: Interaction, Intensification, and Exploitation. In *An Island Polity: The Archaeology of Exploitation in Melos*, eds. C. Renfrew and M. Flagstaff, pp. 264-290. Cambridge: Cambridge University Press.

Riese, B.
1984   Kriegsberichte der klassichen Maya. *Baessler-Archiv, Beitrage zur Völkerkunde* 30(2):255-321.

Thompson, J. E. S.
1950   *Maya Hieroglyphic Writing: An Introduction.* Publication 589. Washington, DC: Carnegie Institution of Washington.

From Double Bird to Ah Cacao: Dynastic Troubles and the Cycle of Katuns at Tikal, Guatemala

William A. Haviland

Department of Anthropology
The University of Vermont

Thirteen years have now passed since publication of Christopher Jones's seminal article (1977) in which he identified, and discussed the reigns of three Late Classic kings of Tikal. Since then great strides have been made at reconstructing the rest of that site's dynastic history (see Fig. 3.1) although some parts of it have proved more difficult to understand than others. One such part is that which falls between the dates of A.D. 573 and 692 (or 9.7.0.0.0 and 9.13.0.0.0 in the Maya calendar), a time in which no monuments are known to have been carved at Tikal. In this paper, I wish to take a new look at this difficult period of dynastic history, from which comes my suggestion that the cultural renaissance over which Ah Cacao presided after his inauguration in 9.12.9.17.16 (A.D. 682) might have come sooner had it not been for the fatalistic view of the Maya toward cyclical time and history.

EARLY DYNASTIC HISTORY AT TIKAL

At Tikal dynastic rule is probably as old as the earliest North Acropolis tombs, which date back to the last century B.C. This is suggested by their several similarities to the later tombs of Tikal's kings, for whom the Acropolis served (until the death of Ah Cacao) as royal cemetery. Written records pertaining to dynastic rule, however, date no further back than the reign of Yax Moch Xoc, who ruled sometime between A.D. 219 and 238 (Schele and Freidel 1990:134), while the earliest king of whom we have

a portrait, Scroll-Ahau-Jaguar (called Jaguar Paw in Fig. 3.1), appears on Stela 29 at 8.12.14.8.15 (A.D. 292). After his death, power passed through a number of men, in some cases from father to son and in others from brother to brother, until the end of the reign of Double Bird, 21st successor of Yax Moch Xoc (see Schele and Freidel in press: 134-161 for a summary of this dynastic history). Double Bird's accession took place in 9.5.3.9.15 (A.D. 537), and as far as we know, his monument (Stela 17), raised in 9.6.3.9.15 (A.D. 557), was the last one carved until Ah Cacao erected his first (Stela 30) in 9.13.0.0.0 (A.D. 692; Fig. 3.2). The question is, what went on between the reigns of these two monarchs?

FROM DOUBLE BIRD TO AH CACAO

Although Christopher Jones once postulated that a dynastic overthrow occurred between the reigns of Double Bird and Animal Skull (Jones and Satterthwaite 1982), two texts cite Double Bird and Animal Skull as the 21st and 22d successors of Yax Moch Xoc, strongly implying that the one directly succeeded the other. That Animal Skull was of the ruling dynasty, rather than an outsider, is indicated by his listing as the 22d successor of its anchoring ancestor. As pointed out by Clemency Coggins (1975), the presence of *Spondylus* shell, stingray spines, and jade tie his tomb, Burial 195 (Fig. 3.3), to the tradition of Tikal's royal tombs; furthermore, the ceramics (unlike some in the graves of several earlier

72

HAVILAND

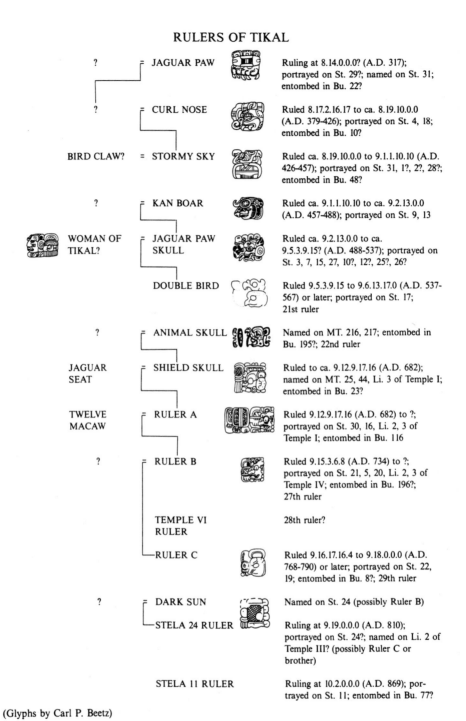

RULERS OF TIKAL

?	⊨ JAGUAR PAW		Ruling at 8.14.0.0.0? (A.D. 317); portrayed on St. 29?; named on St. 31; entombed in Bu. 22?
?	⊨ CURL NOSE		Ruled 8.17.2.16.17 to ca. 8.19.10.0.0 (A.D. 379-426); portrayed on St. 4, 18; entombed in Bu. 10?
BIRD CLAW? = STORMY SKY			Ruled ca. 8.19.10.0.0 to 9.1.1.10.10 (A.D. 426-457); portrayed on St. 31, 1?, 2?, 28?; entombed in Bu. 48?
?	⊨ KAN BOAR		Ruled ca. 9.1.1.10.10 to ca. 9.2.13.0.0 (A.D. 457-488); portrayed on St. 9, 13
WOMAN OF TIKAL?	⊨ JAGUAR PAW SKULL		Ruled ca. 9.2.13.0.0 to ca. 9.5.3.9.15? (A.D. 488-537); portrayed on St. 3, 7, 15, 27, 10?, 12?, 25?, 26?
	DOUBLE BIRD		Ruled 9.5.3.9.15 to 9.6.13.17.0 (A.D. 537-567) or later; portrayed on St. 17; 21st ruler
?	⊨ ANIMAL SKULL		Named on MT. 216, 217; entombed in Bu. 195?; 22nd ruler
JAGUAR SEAT	⊨ SHIELD SKULL		Ruled to ca. 9.12.9.17.16 (A.D. 682); named on MT. 25, 44, Li. 3 of Temple I; entombed in Bu. 23?
TWELVE MACAW	⊨ RULER A		Ruled 9.12.9.17.16 (A.D. 682) to ?; portrayed on St. 30, 16, Li. 2, 3 of Temple I; entombed in Bu. 116
?	⊨ RULER B		Ruled 9.15.3.6.8 (A.D. 734) to ?; portrayed on St. 21, 5, 20, Li. 2, 3 of Temple IV; entombed in Bu. 196?; 27th ruler
	TEMPLE VI RULER		28th ruler?
	└ RULER C		Ruled 9.16.17.16.4 to 9.18.0.0.0 (A.D. 768-790) or later; portrayed on St. 22, 19; entombed in Bu. 8?; 29th ruler
?	⊨ DARK SUN		Named on St. 24 (possibly Ruler B)
	└ STELA 24 RULER		Ruling at 9.19.0.0.0 (A.D. 810); portrayed on St. 24?; named on Li. 2 of Temple III? (possibly Ruler C or brother)
	STELA 11 RULER		Ruling at 10.2.0.0.0 (A.D. 869); portrayed on St. 11; entombed in Bu. 77?

(Glyphs by Carl P. Beetz)

Figure 3.1. The Lords of Tikal, as published by Jones and Satterthwaite (1982). The names of their Rulers A, B, and C are Ah Cacao, Yax Kin, and Chitam. This paper presents a revised version of the genealogy from Double Bird to Shield Skull.

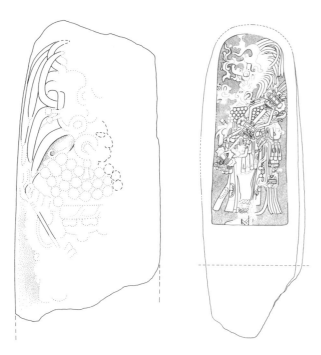

Figure 3.2. Here Stelae 17 and 30 are arranged in such a way that the rulers Double Bird (what little can be glimpsed of him) and Ah Cacao face each other, as if across the period of Tikal's "hiatus." The tastes of both rulers seem to have run to similar styles of beaded collars.

kings) were all local. Four "manikin scepter" figures (Fig. 3.4) of a sort associated with earlier and later members of the Tikal dynasty, were also included in Burial 195. Moreover, a device on the exterior base of a brown pottery vessel may correspond to an emblem worn on the anklets, bracelets, and staffs of the rulers on most Tikal stelae, which could be one of the oldest insignia of rule at this site. Finally, similar ceremonial deposits placed soon after inauguration of Ah Cacao in the rooms of the funerary temples of Animal Skull and the earlier rulers Stormy Sky and Curl Nose (see Fig. 3.1), suggest that all three, rather than Curl Nose and Stormy Sky alone, figure in the ancestry of Ah Cacao.

At Tikal inheritance of rule commonly passed from father to son or brother to brother, but whether it did in this case is open to question. In a text from his tomb (Fig. 3.5), Animal Skull is identified as the son of Lady Hand Sky and a man whose name appears without the Tikal emblem glyph. Although Schele (in Jones and Satterthwaite 1982:129) has sug-

gested that Double Bird might be named father, Jones thinks that someone else might be. He admits, however, that "we cannot be sure that the double-bird glyph is the correct or only characteristic nominal glyph for the person [Double Bird] on Stela 17" (Jones and Satterthwaite 1982:41).

If Double Bird was the father, it is surprising that the Tikal emblem glyph was omitted from his name, although there is precedence for this, for example on Stela 3, where the name of Jaguar Paw Skull occurs without the emblem glyph. Still, a father-son relationship cannot be proved, and there is a likely alternative: that Double Bird was succeeded by the son of his sister or cousin, the Lady Hand Sky named as Animal Skull's mother. If the 21st ruler died without male issue, or if he had a son who was lost, perhaps, in the war of 9.6.8.4.2 (A.D. 562) in which Tikal suffered defeat at the hands of Lord Water of Caracol (Schele and Freidel 1990:167), this would have served to prevent power from passing to someone who was not a direct descendant of the earlier kings of Tikal.

Animal Skull's death was associated with one of the most extensive modifications of the site center ever carried out: the Great Plaza and North Acropolis were given a major overhaul, in the course of which the old Great Plaza ball court was eliminated. The West Plaza was also repaved at this time, and on the East Plaza a Twin Pyramid group that had been in service since 9.4.0.0.0 (A.D. 514) was replaced by a ball court and a shrine, both of which were built in a foreign style (Fig. 3.5). The plaza itself was provided with a new pavement, along with a causeway (the first version of the Maler) leading off to the north. The replacement of the Twin Pyramid group by a ball court seems especially significant, for it implies a cessation of the particular katun celebrations (a katun consisted of twenty 360-day years) for which Twin Pyramid groups were built (Jones 1969), and no new one was built until the reign of Shield Skull. Since the katun celebrations had been a focus of dynastic ritual life since the time of Curl Nose, a break in succession seems likely. Similarly, elimination of the Great Plaza ball court, which was subsequently restored by Ah Cacao, seems indicative of a break in dynastic traditions. I suggested is that a dynastic overthrow took place upon the occasion of Animal Skull's death and that the massive reconstruction at the site center was an attempt by usurpers to put their own distinctive stamp on the

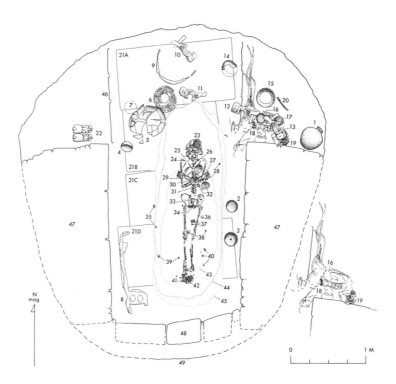

Figure 3.3. Burial 195, the tomb of Animal Skull.

political and ceremonial heart of the city, which then remained unchanged until after the accession of Ah Cacao in 9.12.9.17.16 (A.D. 682).

Although the date of Animal Skull's death is not known for sure, a text carved on boards in his tomb suggests that it could have been no earlier than 9.8.0.0.0 (A.D. 593). If Animal Skull's reign was of average length for Tikal's later rulers (about 29 years; Jones and Satterthwaite 1982:131), and if his predecessor died as a consequence of his defeat by Lord Water of Caracol in 9.6.8.4.2, as seems probable, then a death date of 9.8.0.0.0 or shortly thereafter for the 22d successor is reasonable. He could perhaps have lived into the next katun, as suggested by a probable two-katun-reign anniversary notation on a plate in his tomb (Fig. 3.6) but is unlikely to have lived much beyond ca. 9.9.0.0.0. (A.D. 613). My reason for this conclusion is that rarely (if ever) did a monarch hold power for as many as 50 years; thus, it is difficult to take seriously a date more recent than ca. 9.9.0.0.0 for the death of Animal Skull, and a date closer to 9.8.0.0.0 is even more likely.

The next ruler of record is Shield Skull, who must have been the 25th successor of Yax Moch Xoc, if

Figure 3.4. Two of four manikin scepter figures, made of stucco-covered wood, from the tomb of Animal Skull. About 40 cm high, they were originally mounted on the ends of wooden shafts.

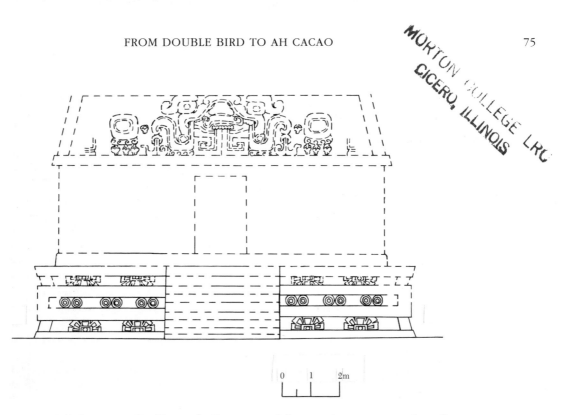

Figure 3.5. Structure 5D-43 was built as part of the massive reconstruction of Tikal's center that followed Animal Skull's death. Its style of architecture, and that of an associated ball court, is more Mexican than Mayan.

Figure 3.6. Miscellaneous Texts 216 and 217, painted on two plates in his tomb, record Animal Skull's name, those of his mother and father, the fact that he was 22d successor, and a probable two-katun-reign anniversary.

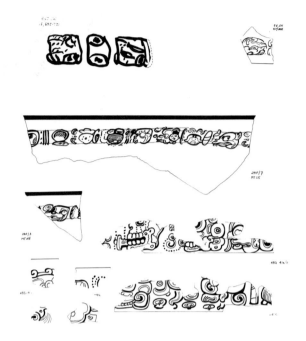

Figure 3.7. Miscellaneous Text 25 was painted on a pottery vessel, a piece of which was found in a chultun. A statement in it that Animal Skull was Shield Skull's father either is wrong or the Animal Skull referred to is someone other than the 22d successor of Yax Moch Xoc.

the Maya themselves are to be believed; several inscriptions combine to tell us that Tikal's 27th successor was Yax Kin, the son of Ah Cacao, whose father was Shield Skull. Because these texts contradict another (Fig. 3.7) appearing to name Animal Skull as Shield Skull's father, either the latter must be in error, or else the Animal Skull referred to is someone other than the 22d successor (his name glyph in fact differs slightly from those on plates in Animal Skull's tomb). In any event, there is clear evidence for two reigns between those of Animal Skull and Shield Skull, about which the inscriptions are silent. The logical inferences are that outsiders seized power from the legitimate dynasty and that whatever records were associated with their reigns were destroyed sometime after Shield Skull regained the seat of power for the old ruling line.

Precisely when Shield Skull regained the seat of power is unknown, but it may be marked by construction of the first Twin Pyramid group since destruction of the earlier one on the East Plaza. This

could be Group 5B-l, built in 9.12.0.0.0 (A.D. 672), although a good case can be made that Stela P 78 marks a Twin Pyramid group built in 9.11.0.0.0 (A.D. 652; see Fig. 3.8)

Assuming, for the sake of argument, Shield Skull's accession as early as 9.11.0.0.0, and Animal Skull's death as late as 9.9.0.0.0, 39 years are available for the reigns of two rulers in between. Considering that Tikal's 12th through 20th successors held power for no more than an average of eight years each (Schele and Freidel 1990:448 n.7), the time is adequate for the two reigns, especially if a coup by Shield Skull cut the second one short. On the other hand, if Animal Skull's death occurred just after 9.8.0.0.0 and Shield Skull's accession just before 9.12.0.0.0, the time is adequate for two reigns averaging about 39 years each.

One might expect Shield Skull's rise to power to have brought about something of a cultural renaissance at Tikal, but in fact it did not. Although the construction of Twin Pyramid groups was resumed, in neither of those for which he was responsible did Shield Skull erect a carved monument, as did his successors (Ah Cacao, Yax Kin, and Chitam) in theirs. Nor did he oversee important construction projects on the North Acropolis or Great Plaza (Coe 1990). Here, the traditional building and rebuilding of temples was resumed soon after the inauguration of Ah Cacao, the same ruler responsible for restoration of the Great Plaza ball court, and for the first monuments known to have been carved since Double Bird's. Indeed, that Shield Skull failed to purge Tikal of alien ways is suggested by the monuments (Fig. 3.9) and tombs (including what may be Shield Skull's own; see Fig. 3.10) dating toward the end of his reign that appear foreign by local standards. The question is, why did a ruler who was able to regain the seat of power for his dynasty do so little to revitalize Tikal? The answer, I think, lies in Maya beliefs concerning history and its relationship to cyclical time.

MAYA HISTORY AND THE CYCLE OF KATUNS

By the time the Spanish arrived in Yucatan, the Maya had long since abandoned the old long count—a sequential tally of days, 20-day months, and 360-day years (tuns)—in favor of the short

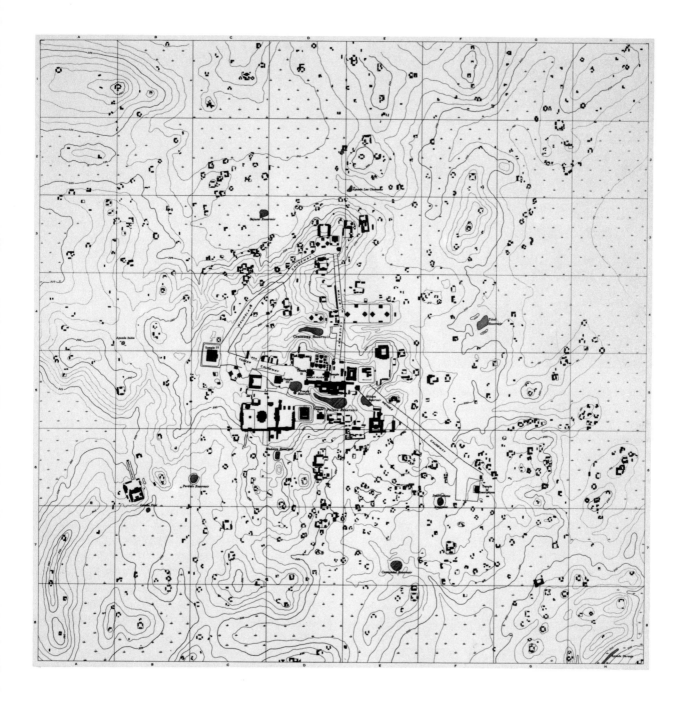

Figure 3.8. Shield Skull was probably responsible for a Twin Pyramid group constructed in 9.12.0.0.0. (lower left); later, perhaps when Temple IV was built, it was dismantled. Another possible Twin Pyramid group (right) may have been the first he ordered built, in 9.11.0.0.0. If so, it too was later dismantled.

Figure 3.9. Altar 14, which was paired with Stela 30 (Fig. 2), has more in common with the "giant Ahau" altars of Caracol than it does with any other at Tikal. Another Tikal monument, Stela 34, may even have been transported from Caracol, perhaps about 9.13.0.0.0 or a little before.

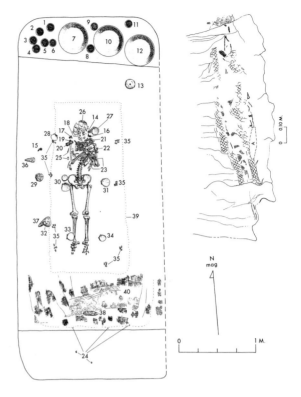

Figure 3.10. Burial 23, which could be Shield Skull's. Like its companion Burial 24, it has features reminiscent of royal tombs at Caracol.

count, by which time was reckoned by the passage of katuns. These were named for the day Ahau in the 260-day ritual calendar on which they ended, the number Ahau decreasing by two with each successive one. As there were 13 numbers, this produced a cycle in which each katun repeated itself after the passage of 260 tuns, or 256 of our years.

To the Maya, the katuns were not mere units of time; each had its own special patron deity, special rites, and prophecy. Examples of the latter abound in the native chronicles written after the Spanish conquest, and rulers had the important duty of conducting rituals of divination and promulgation of the prophecy of each particular katun. Since each katun repeated itself every 256 years, so too, believed the Maya, did whatever occurred in past katuns of the same name. As the late Maya scholar Ralph L. Roys pointed out (1967:184): "The events recounted in the Maya Chronicles . . . offer excellent grounds for believing that this belief was so strong at times as to actually influence the course of history." Indeed,

events surrounding the conquest of the Itza in 1697 appear to have been shaped significantly by such an outlook; believing their defeat to be inevitable, the Itza nonetheless resisted all attempts by the Spanish to conquer and convert them to Christianity until the proper katun rolled around. After 178 years of stout resistance, however, as the fateful time approached they submitted with no more than token resistance (Schele and Freidel 1990:193-194).

As is well known, the short count is a derivative of an abbreviated system of dating that made its appearance in the Classic period, whereby only the specific katun and the date on which it ended were specified, and at Tikal, carved monuments in Twin Pyramid groups in all but one case bear dates in this system (Fig. 3.11) Moreover, Twin Pyramid groups appear to have been used for ceremonies that served to determine the prophecies of the katun. Given this, a belief in the inevitability of history repeating itself every 260 tuns ought to be at least as old as the Twin Pyramid groups at Tikal, and may in fact go back to

Figure 3.12. Self-effacing though he may have been in life, Shield Skull appears to have been memorialized in grand style after death by construction of the first of Tikal's seven "Great Temples," Structure 5D-33-1st. Deep in its fill lies the temple built over the tomb of Stormy Sky, whose reign Shield Skull's son saw himself as restoring.

Figure 3.11.Tikal Stela 22, with its clear notation of "13 Ahau 18 Cumku, end of 17 katuns" at A1-B1, provides a good example of the abbreviated dating system from which the Postclassic "count of the katuns" derives. It also shows the ruler Chitam (Ah Cacao's grandson) scattering some substance (corn? blood?), perhaps part of the procedure to determine the prophecy of the katun.

the fourth century A.D.(see also Puleston 1979). In support of this, Ah Cacao's inaugural date falls within Katun 8 Ahau, which seems to have been an auspicious one for Tikal's traditional rulers; in the preceding one, the reign of Stormy Sky was one of unparalleled wealth, power, and prosperity. Coggins (1975) has argued persuasively that Ah Cacao's reign was a restoration of Stormy Sky's, and that his inaugural date was deliberately chosen for its commemoration of the 13-katun anniversary of his illustrious predecessor's. Indeed, the possibility exists that Ah Cacao saw himself as a reincarnation of Stormy Sky.

Such evidence for dynastic renewal at Tikal, occurring after a 13-katun interval, leads me to suggest that Shield Skull's fate was to be ahead of his time. Somehow, he was able to regain the seat of power for his dynasty before the prophetic Katun 8 Ahau rolled around, and for this reason he could do little more than mark time until history repeated itself. Had it not been for this fatalistic view of history, Shield Skull would likely have presided over a burst of creative activity similar to that which followed Ah Cacao's inauguration (Fig. 3.12). In any event, there is a lesson to be learned from all of this: in seeking to explain the events of ancient Maya history, it is not enough to concern ourselves with material causes alone, for ideological factors may play a determining role as well. "People," the late Frank Speck is reported to have said, "do not merely invent and recount myths; they actually live them."

BIBLIOGRAPHY

Coe, W. R.
  1990   *Excavations in the Great Plaza, North
                Terrace and North Acropolis of Tikal.* Tikal
                Report No. 14. Philadelphia: The University
                Museum, The University of Pennsylvania.

Coggins, C. C.
  1975   Painting and Drawing Styles at Tikal: *An
                Historical and Iconographic Recon-
                struction.* Ph.D. dissertation, Harvard
                University. Ann Arbor: University
                Microfilms.

Jones, C.
  1969   *The Twin Pyramid Group Pattern: A Classic
                Maya Architectural Assemblage at Tikal,
                Guatemala.* Ph.D. dissertation, University
                of Pennsylvania. Ann Arbor: University
                Microfilms.
  1977   Inauguration Dates of Three Late Classic
                Rulers of Tikal, Guatemala. *American
                Antiquity* 42:28-60.

Jones, C., and L. Satterthwaite, Jr.
  1982   *The Monuments and Inscriptions of Tikal,
                Part A: The Carved Monuments.* Tikal
                Report No. 33A. Philadelphia: The
                University Museum, The University of
                Pennsylvania.

Puleston, D. E.
  1979   An Epistemological Pathology and the
                Collapse, or Why the Maya Kept the Short
                Count. In *Maya Archaeology and Ethno-
                history,* eds. N. Hammond and G. R.
                Willey, pp. 63-71. Austin: University of
                Texas Press.

Roys, R. L.
  1967   *The Book of Chilam Balam of Chumayel.*
                Norman: University of Oklahoma Press.

Schele, L., and D. Freidel
  1990   *A Forest of Kings.* New York: William
                Morrow and Co.

IV

Preclassic Notation and the Development of Maya Writing

David W. Sedat

The University Museum of Archaeology and Anthropology
University of Pennsylvania

The origins of the hieroglyphic writing tradition that is so characteristic of Classic Maya civilization has long been a fascinating issue, but, despite recent progress in deciphering this most complex of all indigenous New World scripts, the actual process through which the Maya writing developed has remained an enigma. Conventionally, it has been believed that this hieroglyphic system, characterized by a graphic style that frequently depicts anthropomorphic and zoomorphic elements as central components in its main signs, crystallized out of earlier Mesoamerican pictographic traditions around the second or first century B.C. (see Marcus 1976). The most frequently mentioned areas where Classic script is thought to have originated—the southern highland and Pacific coastal regions of Chiapas, Mexico, and Guatemala (Norman 1973; Graham 1979)—lie outside the central Maya lowlands. The search for earlier forms of Maya glyphs has not been rewarding, however, and although the Olmec are often claimed as the inventors of Mesoamerican writing (Gay 1973), this precocious Gulf Coast civilization of the Early and Middle Formative (1200-400 B.C.) seems to have passed on only a very few recognizable symbols to later Maya writing (Coe 1976:111). Thus, aside from raw speculation, until quite recently the most we have been able to say about the origins of Mayan hieroglyphs is that, to quote Michael Coe, "there can be little doubt that the Classic Maya writing system did not spring into being at once, but that it evolved as a result of individual innovation over a long period of time" (Coe 1976).

In this discussion I would like to suggest that part of the stumbling block in unraveling the development of Maya writing has been a long-standing assumption that Mesoamerican hieroglyphic traditions evolved according to a preconceived Old World model—that is, a development through a series of stages beginning with depictive art followed by representational pictograms in which pictures are used for signs. Because Maya writing never climbed higher on the same idealized developmental ladder as Old World scripts to become alphabetic, we have tended to regard it as a system frozen at an arrested, albeit complexly elaborated, stage. Until recently, this conceptual handicap contributed to our long-standing failure to recognize that Maya writing comprised a mixed system of representational logograms and conventionalized phonetic elements that together served to reproduce and convey verbal messages (Morley, Brainerd, and Sharer 1983:532). As a result, not only has there been a long delay in deciphering the Maya hieroglyphic system, but most of the inquiry into its origins has been directed toward quests for the pictographic antecedents to each glyphic sign. This approach has led up a blind alley since the trail of such antecedent forms ends about 400-300 B.C., at a point where the system of writing and calendrics as a whole is already far too developed and widespread to be considered near its conception.

This paper presents evidence suggesting that the development of Maya writing, and New World writing systems in general, does not closely follow the Old World evolutionary model, but rather that it developed along a unique trajectory out of a widespread and far more ancient tradition of abstract nondepictive notation. I will also develop this evidence as a case study to support John Justeson's prediction that "writing probably develops, not within a single graphic system, but rather via conjoint use of more than one graphic system in a single context" (1986: 439).

PRECLASSIC MONUMENTS OF THE SALAMA VALLEY

The key evidence for this discussion of the process by which Maya writing developed is afforded by a number of monuments recovered during the course of The University Museum's research in the northern Maya highlands, a region that has long been recognized as strategically situated intermediate between the southern Maya area, where much Preclassic development has been revealed, and the

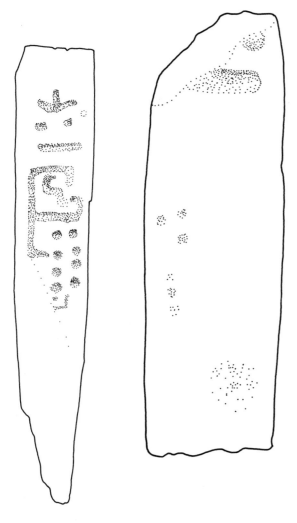

Figure 4.1. Monuments 13 and 14 from the Salama Valley, Guatemala (after Sharer and Sedat 1987: Pls. 18.10 and 18.12).

central Maya lowlands where Classic civilization flourished (Kidder 1940). Excavations in the Salama Valley (Sharer and Sedat 1987), one of the largest valleys of this northern highland zone, determined that the practice of erecting and sculpting stone monuments began at least by the end of the Middle Preclassic period, or about 500-400 B.C. But this research also discovered, somewhat surprisingly, that the monuments of this era shared two distinctive sculptural styles employing quite different graphic traditions (Sharer 1985). The first of these styles is a pecked and grooved technique evidenced on two rather unprepossessing small stone slabs or miniature stelae known as Monuments 13 and 14 (Fig. 4.1) found reused as lintels in a crypt burial (Burial 5) of a postulated village headman or shaman from the valley margin site of Los Mangales. A more familiar low-relief sculpted stela (probably depicting a ruler figure in the now largely destroyed central scene) with a Maya-style vertical column glyphic inscription, was revealed on a much larger stone, Monument 1, at the dominant valley center site of El Porton (see Sharer and Sedat 1973;1987: Pl. 18.1). Although disturbed by a looter's pit, the placement of Monument 1 is clearly associated with a radiocarbon date of 410-370 B.C (CRD-10 calibration; see Sharer and Sedat 1987:58-59). I will return to comment on the implications of these diverse coeval styles within the single context of the Salama Valley after considering more carefully the pecked-and-grooved sculptured elements on Monuments 13 and 14, and similar cupulate markings on another Salama Valley stone, Monument 21 (Fig. 4.2) an inscribed boulder from an indeterminate context at the site of Piedra de Sacrificios on the southern margin of the valley.

The most notable feature of the pecked-and-grooved monuments, particularly Monument 13, is a series of apparently nonrandom, nondecorative small dots or cupules, and linear grooved elements. Although these pecked lines and dots are quite simply executed and involve only minimal modification of the stone's surface, they are neither obvious pictographic nor decorative elements, but rather seem to represent symbolic motifs or signs. In other words, they appear to constitute an early form of message conveyance.

The signs on Monument 13 are arranged in two vertical rows on the upper two-thirds of the stone, leaving the lower third unaltered as if the stone were

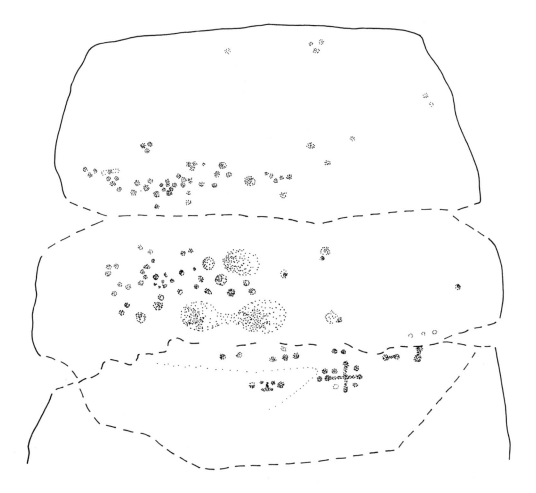

Figure 4.2. Monument 21 from the Salama Valley, Guatemala (after Sharer and Sedat 1987: Pl. 18.26).

intended to be displayed by being set erect in the ground. It is logical to assume that the signs on Monument 13 were meant to be interpreted in sequence, either from top to bottom (most likely) or vice-versa. In the case of Monument 21 the signs, particularly those on Panel C, clearly form horizontal bands. Such regular, intentional spacing would have promoted comprehension. Thus, cupulate markings the on these Preclassic monuments seem to be arranged according to a developed graphic heritage in which an abbreviated code was used to convey information. The existence of at least several stones with these elements in the Salama Valley implies a tradition of individuals who both inscribed the marks and interpreted their meaning. In other words, this Salama Valley tradition contains all the criteria of a

partial writing system as defined by Prem (1971:114), and may be designated a notational system. To distinguish this notational system from the more familiar conventional glyphic system, a very early form of which is represented by El Porton Monument 1, it will be referred to as the Cupulate Tradition after the pecked cuplike dots that are its most identifiable mode.

At present the sign inventory of the Cupulate Tradition as expressed on stone monuments of the Salama Valley is rather limited, given the conditions of archaeological preservation and the small number of monuments assignable to this corpus. Although the single cupule or dotlike mark might be an elemental sign, this is difficult to establish as most of these are arranged in pairs, clusters, or linear arrangements. It is logical to assume, however, that each dot represents a single symbol or event, especially if employed in a tally sequence or as part of a numerical system, as may be represented in the vertical rows on Monument 13. Other cupulate arrangements include the paired-dot motif; triadic groupings; T-shaped four-dot clusters (sometimes inverted); and V-shaped five-dot groups. These last-named higher-value arrangements seem to be derived from the frequently employed three-dot cluster, suggesting both that their composition involved additive concepts and that the triadic arrangement had special significance. Triadic clusters are particularly noticeable on the upper inclined face (Panel A) of Monument 21, where they are arranged in a horizontal band. Similarly, the deepest conical pits on the flat middle section (Panel B) are clustered in a triangle.

As integral or associated components of linear signs, cupulate arrangements include barbell-like motifs formed by two dots connected by a groove, as in Monument 21 Panel C. The crosslike design on the same panel is formed by grooves connecting four lateral cupules to a central dot, with dots in the four quadrants. The same method of connecting dots with lines is also seen in the E-shaped element on Monument 13 . Also included in the sign repertory on the same stone is a trilobed motif and a horizontal bar. On both Monuments 13 and 14 a single horizontal groove is seen below two paired dots, in the fashion of the Maya numeral seven.

EVIDENCE FROM OTHER PRECLASSIC MONUMENTS

Elsewhere throughout Mesoamerica similar pecked cupulate markings on boulders have been noted, but these have usually attracted only passing mention because of the greater attention given to later period representational sculpture and associated hieroglyphic inscriptions, and because of the difficulty in directly dating such stones. Where they have been studied in some depth, this pecked cupulate style and related abstract pecked-and-grooved designs have frequently been assigned to an early period in the local culture history (Gay 1971, 1973; Murray 1985). Overall, the widespread geographic distribution and lengthy temporal occurrence of pecked-and-grooved boulder sculpture argues for

the great antiquity of the style, which, according to Grieder (1982), spans some 7000 years and marks the first wave in the origins of Precolumbian artistic development.

Although it is as yet difficult to assess fully the function of cupulate texts because of their brevity, incomplete preservation, and simplistic graphic style, the sequential ordering of the signs presumably indicates the conveyance of a message. Part of this message was expressed by dots; by analogy to the later Maya numerical system, these dots could have expressed numerical values. In this regard, it may be of some significance that the early long count date (equivalent to A.D. 161) on the Tuxtla Statuette from Chiapas, Mexico, is expressed as a vertical column of incised lines and small pits or dots (Fig. 4.3). Except for introductory and terminating glyphs, these simply engraved numerals are unassociated with time-unit glyphs, as in later long count dates. They are also notable for being stylistically distinct from the more conventionally expressed glyphs and bar-and-dot numerals seen elsewhere on the statuette. This evident contrast between numerals and glyphic blocks is another suggestion of the early existence of two separate notational traditions, one a cursive form of numerical indicators, and the other a representational glyphic tradition, analogous to the presence of the two traditions found separately in the Salama Valley by the end of the Middle Preclassic. In the case of the Late Preclassic Tuxtla Statuette, however, these two traditions appear to be combined on a single artifact.

Further support of this distinction between abstract cupulate numerical notation and conventionalized glyphs comes from the pan-Mesoamerican use of the bar-and-dot numerical system and the more restricted distribution of Maya-style representational glyphs. The earliest known examples of long count dates rendered in stone show a similar heritage of bar-and-dot numerals without time-unit glyphs. On one of the earliest of these, Tres Zapotes Stela C from Veracruz, Mexico, dated to 31 B.C., the numerals of the calendric computation stand alone in a manner similar to the Tuxtla Statuette date. The same pattern can be seen for the comparable long-count dates on Stela 5 from Abaj Takalik, Guatemala, and Stela 1 from La Mojarra, Veracruz (Winfield C. 1988: Fig. 4.7). Other investigators have already presumed on theoretical grounds that bar-and-dot numerals are older than hieroglyphic writing (Coe

Figure 4.3. Drawing of the incised text on the Tuxtla Statuette.

1965:756) and ancestral to all Mesoamerican scripts (Justeson 1986:440).

An additional point of interest on the Tuxtla Statuette and the La Mojarra stela is the use of downward-facing brackets (some enclosing two side-by-side dots), which appear to function as grammatical indicators to separate the columns of glyphs into phraselike units. Other combinations of dots and abstract elements appear infixed within the individual glyph blocks, adding a possible phonetic value. Similar dotted brackets and related graphic forms are present in the sign inventory on cylinder seals where the text is purely abstract (see below and Fig. 4.6). Thus, it may be hypothesized that the intricately conjoined numerical, grammatical, and representational glyphic elements of Maya writing derived from the fusion in the Preclassic of distinct traditions in a manner similar to our own writing, in which numerals originated from Arabic notation and alphabetic signs evolved from a Phoenician system.

MEANINGS OF SOME ABSTRACT PRECLASSIC SYMBOLS

The triadic dot cluster seems to have had associations with important symbolic values far beyond the Preclassic era in the Salama Valley. The triadic cluster occurs as an infixed symbol of various early glyphs of the southern Maya area. Similarly, it is seen in earlier Olmec iconography, where it has been termed by Joralemon (1971:16) as Motif 153, or "Stacked Cannonballs." As an Olmec motif it occurs in association with regalia of rulers holding bloodlet-

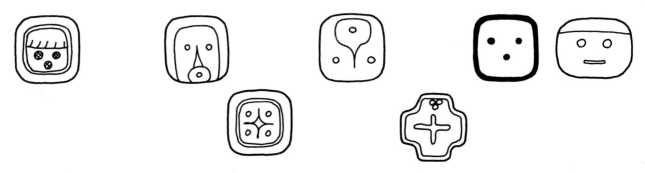

Figure 4.4. Some Classic period glyphs with infixed Cupulate Tradition signs. (From Thompson 1962)

ting paraphernalia (Reilly 1987; see also Coe 1965: Fig. 18). The same triadic cluster is an important component in the later Maya glyphic system (Fig. 4.4; see also Thompson 1962), particularly in the signs for the days Ix (T524), Ahau (T533), and Ahau semblants and variants (T534, 541, 542), among others. The sign for Lamat or Venus is a cross with a dot in each of its corners or a superfixed three-dot cluster (T510A and C).

An interesting example of the value of archaeological context to epigraphic research is provided by now considering the possible significance of the cupulate triadic clusters that occur repeatedly on Monument 21 in the Salama Valley, and the pattern of the three deep basins on the middle (Panel B) of the same boulder (see Fig. 4.2). In discussing Glyph T672 or the so-called fire fist, Thompson (1962:276) states "this fist with its three circles, the ancient Maya fire symbol . . . stands for an action connected with fire, such as to light a fire, to burn copal." The associated concepts of fire and fist linked to a triadic arrangement of elements are physically manifest in the Early Classic Special Deposit 21 at Quirigua, Guatemala. In this ritual deposit, seemingly dedicatory to a small platform that supported an early dynastic stela (Monument 26), three extensively burned pottery vessels and their covers were found in a crypt, arranged in a triangle. Among the offerings in this cache were two small carved jadeite fists (Ashmore 1980:37-39). The symbolism of this cache, consistent with Thompson's association of fire, fist, and triad, leads to the interpretation that the three triadically arranged deep conical basins on Salama Valley Monument 21 (Panel B) were receptacles for the burning of offerings. The extensive exfoliation of this area on Monument 21 may indeed have been caused by repeated burning.

Further light might be shed on triadic symbolism by considering three-pronged incense burners, so prevalent in the Maya highlands during the Preclassic (de Borhegyi 1951). Two such incense burners, adorned with modeled jaguar faces, were found at El Porton, partially covered by triadically placed stacks of pottery vessels (Cache 17; Sharer and Sedat 1987:82-86, Pl. 3.34). This deposit appears to have marked a transition between two building stages in the largest platform at the site, Structure J7-2, an event likely corresponding to the accession of a new ruler, perhaps symbolized by the two jaguar-effigy censers in Cache 17. Likewise, the Quirigua Special Deposit 21 mentioned above was probably associated with ceremonies marking the transition between two reigns (Jones and Sharer 1980). Of further note, Hatch (1982:8) has commented on the presence of the fire-fist glyph in clauses pertaining to political transition in Late Classic Quirigua. Thus, fire-related rituals including a triadic theme appear to refer to inaugural ceremonies.

Because in later times the triadic dot cluster and the sometimes associated dotted cross also relate to glyphs dealing with calendrical subjects, it can be plausibly postulated that cupulate notation was used to record cyclical events and associated rites. In this regard, the dotted-cross symbol has been interpreted as a device for computing, or symbolizing the computation of, calendrical counts and position since Preclassic times (Aveni, Hartung, and Buckingham 1978; Murray 1985). Coggins (1980) has also proposed that crosses or four-part figures denote cyclic completion of time periods.

By converging these lines of evidence, it may be suggested that Salama Valley Monument 21 was the

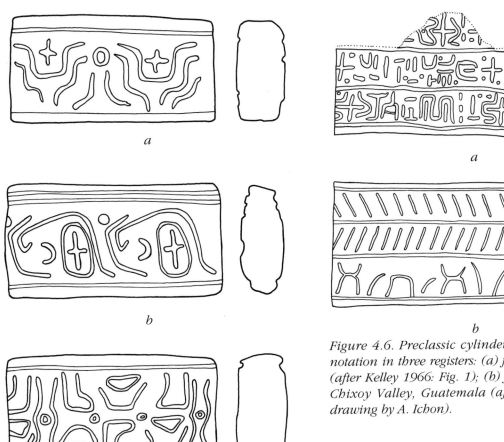

Figure 4.5. Examples of Preclassic cylinder seals with inscribed abstract notation: (a) from the Salama Valley (after Sharer and Sedat 1987: Pl. 4.11); (b) from El Jocote in the Chixoy Valley, Guatemala, and (c) from San Andres Sajcabaja, Guatemala (b and c from Ichon and Grignon 1981: Fig. 87).

Figure 4.6. Preclassic cylinder seals with abstract notation in three registers: (a) from Tlatilco, Mexico (after Kelley 1966: Fig. 1); (b) from El Jocote in the Chixoy Valley, Guatemala (after an unpublished drawing by A. Ichon).

focus for ceremonies involving the use of fire in rites connected to calendrical cycles or political transition. This monument is located in a side valley on the periphery of the Salama Valley. This may indicate that these rituals were not intended for public participation, but rather were part of an esoteric shamanistic cult, conducted by individuals such as those postulated to have used Monuments 13 and 14 and who were buried at Los Mangales. Drawing on accounts of shamanistic function and Maya belief system practice and function, we can further specu-

late that these early supernatural specialists boldly placed themselves as mediators between the three basic states of matter and existence in the Maya cosmos—the water below, the earth between, and the sky above. In this reconstruction, the rites conducted at Monument 21 might have involved the shaman's burning blood-smeared paper or copal on the altar, its smoke rising to beckon the life-giving rain from the sky above.

THE EVIDENCE FROM PRECLASSIC CYLINDER SEALS

The argument for monuments inscribed with cupulate notation as an important Preclassic phenomenon is strengthened by considering the dotted-cross or crosslike symbols and other abbreviated abstract, nondecorative signs present on numerous Preclassic cylinder seals. These have been found throughout Mesoamerica and include one example from the Salama Valley (Fig. 4.5a) excavated from an undisputable late Middle Preclassic context. Similar

Preclassic seals have been found in the Chixoy Valley, Guatemala (Fig. 4.5b, c) and at Chiapa de Corzo, Mexico (Lee 1969), as well as from such sites as Las Bocas and Tlatilco in Central Mexico, among others (Gay 1973). Excluding those seals that are purely decorative, a number of the examples from the areas cited employ a large number of different abbreviated, cursive abstract signs. Occasionally such notations are arranged in lengthy sequences and in distinct three-tiered registers or bands that surely indicate a complex communication function. One such example (Fig. 4.6a) the very complexly inscribed seal described by Kelley (1966) as coming from Preclassic Tlatilco, is compositionally similar in a number of details to one found in an excavated context from the Middle Chixoy valley of Guatemala (Fig. 4.6b) Until now most scholars of formative writing systems have disregarded such examples of notation by maintaining that if writing were involved, it would be the most advanced system achieved in Mesoamerica (Graham 1971:133; Kelley 1966:744). Perhaps as more examples of Preclassic seals are brought forward and studied, this preconception— that development of New World scripts must fit into a universal pattern in which the evolution of writing systems invariably progresses from pictographic beginnings toward more abstract forms—will be modified.

Although we can not yet say that the cylinder seal symbol complex and the Cupulate Tradition are part of the same information conveyance system, together they constitute convincing evidence that abstract, nonpictographic notation was in widespread use throughout Mesoamerica by the Middle Preclassic era, if not earlier, as a means to record and transmit a wide variety of messages. These early diverse traditions support Justeson's assertion that the bar-and-dot numerical system, a form of abstract notation, was a foundation for the emergence of writing, because "by conveying meaning segmentally, rather than in the integrated fashion of traditional depictive art, its conventions conformed closely to those by which concepts are encoded via language" (1986:444).

ORIGINS OF THE REPRESENTATIONAL MAYA GLYPHIC TRADITION

Returning now to the representational glyphic tradition and its associated sculptural style in the Salama Valley, the preserved text on the large low-relief carved Monument 1 seems clearly antecedent to the later Classic period Maya glyphic system (Sharer and Sedat 1987:382-383). Monument 1 and the altar that accompanied it required substantial public effort for their transport and a considerable degree of sophistication in the execution of the carving and text. Likewise, these sculptures were set in front of a shrine on a large-scale raised area as the focus of public ceremonial activity in the largest organizational center of the valley. This context indicates that the sculptured monument with its glyphic text, rendered in depictive artistic manner, was the prerogative of authority figures, used presumably to display their visages, record their achievements, justify their lineage memberships, and assert their claims to power. It might be argued that, within this Late Preclassic milieu, representational glyphs on public monuments would have been readily interpreted by the general populace as ideological icons and thus served effectively to reinforce the sociopolitical structure. The abstract and cursive elements of the cupulate system, on the other hand, would have required prior specialized training and initiation for its effective manipulation, a circumstance probably reserved for specialists in esoteric shamanistic cults. Thus, it seems reasonable that as El Porton emerged as the dominant Preclassic center for the valley, the representational glyphic tradition associated with this coalescing power attained a superior status and eventually superceded or even suppressed the older Cupulate Tradition. Yet some of the useful attributes of the Cupulate Tradition were retained, as in the survival of the bar-and-dot numerical system and the inclusion of cupulate elements within glyphic writing as symbolic or phonetic modifiers.

The association of an evolving glyphic writing system with the emergence of a regionally dominant valley center also suggests that such a system may have been transmitted to other areas by the widespread trade networks transporting jade, obsidian, quetzal feathers, and other goods that flourished during the Preclassic period. Such commercial links among the various Preclassic centers of southern Mesoamerica would have provided the means for the conveyance of written texts on a variety of different media; concomitantly this would have facilitated or even promoted the movement of related sociopolitical, ideological, and sculptural concepts intimately related to these graphic traditions. Economic, social, and ideological ranking of centers and the prestige of their associated ruling lineages, along with linguistic differences, would have influenced preferences in writing forms and conventions, resulting in some elements being abandoned and others being elaborated and emulated. In this intertwining-lattice model of evolving Preclassic writing

and communication, the Salama Valley would have functioned as an ideal intermediate station for travel and commercial exchange by its location astride the most direct and suitable land route between the southern highlands and Pacific coast to the south and the lowlands to the north. These networks through the Salama Valley would have been ideal conduits for the communication and spread of notational experimentation and innovation resulting from the conjoint use of different graphic systems, and they may typify the nexus from which Maya writing, and its associated sociopolitical and ideological systems, evolved towards its climax in the Classic period.

BIBLIOGRAPHY

Ashmore, W. A.
1980   Discovering Early Classic Quirigua. *Expedition* 23(1):35-44.

Aveni, A. F., H. Hartung, and B. Buckingham
1978   The Pecked Cross Symbol in Ancient Mesoamerica. *Science* 202:267-279.

Coe, M. D.
1965   The Olmec Style and Its Distribution. In *Handbook of Middle American Indians*, vol 3., ed. G. R. Willey, pp. 739-775. Austin: University of Texas Press.

1976   Early Steps in the Evolution of Maya Writing. In *Origins of Religious Art and Iconography in Preclassic Mesoamerica*, ed. H. B. Nicholson, pp. 107-122. Los Angeles: UCLA Latin American Center Publications/Ethnic Arts Council of Los Angeles.

Coggins, C. C.
1980   The Shape of Time: Some Political Implications of the Four-Part Figure. *American Antiquity* 45:727-739.

de Borhegyi, S. F.
1951   A Study of Three-Pronged Incense Burners from Guatemala and Adjacent Areas. *Notes on Middle American Archaeology and Ethnology*, no. 101. Washington DC: Carnegie Institution of Washington.

Gay, C.
1971   *Chalcacingo*. Graz, Austria: Akademische Druck-und Verlagsanstalt.
1973   Olmec Hieroglyphic Writing. *Archaeology* 26:278-288.

Graham, J. A.
1971   Commentary on: Calendric and Writing in Mesoamerica. In *Contributions of the University of California Archaeological Research Facility* 11:133-140. Berkeley.
1979   Maya, Olmecs, and Izapans at Abak Takalik. In *Actes du XLIIe Congrès International des Américanistes* 8:179-188. Paris.

Grieder, T.
1982   The Origins of Pre-Columbian Art. Austin: University of Texas Press.

Hatch, M. P.
1982   The Identification of Rulers at Quirigua. *Journal of New World Archaeology* 5(1):1-9.

Ichon, A., and R. Grignon
1981   *Archéolgie de Sauvetage dans la vallée du Rio Chixoy 3-El Jocote*. Centre National de la Recherche Scientifique, Institut d'Ethnologie, Paris. Guatemala: Editorial Piedra Santa.

Jones, C., and R. J. Sharer
1980   Archaeological Investigations in the Site Core of Quirigua, *Expedition* 23(1):11-19.

Joralemon, D.
1971   *A Study of Olmec Iconography.* Dumbarton Oaks Studies in Pre-Columbian Art and Archaeology, no. 7. Washington, DC: Dumbarton Oaks.

Justeson, J.
1986   The Origin of Writing Systems: Preclassic Mesoamerica. *World Archaeology* 17(3):437-458.

Kelley, D. H.
1966   A Cylinder Seal from Tlatilco. *American Antiquity* 31(5):744-746.

Kidder, A. V.
1940   Archaeological Problems of the Highland Maya. In *The Maya and Their Neighbors*, eds. C. L. Hay et. al. New York: D. Appleton-Century.

Lee, Jr., T. A.
1969   *The Artifacts of Chiapas de Corzo, Chiapas, Mexico*. Papers of the New World Archaeological Foundation, no. 26. Provo, UT: Brigham Young University.

Marcus, J.
1976   The Origins of Mesoamerican Writing. In *Annual Review of Anthropology*, vol. 5, eds. B. Siegel, A. Beals, and S. Tyler, pp. 35-67.

Morley, S. G., G. C. Brainerd, and R. J. Sharer
1983   *The Ancient Maya* (4th ed. rev.). Stanford: Stanford University Press.

Murray, W. B.
1985   Petroglyphic Counts at Icamole, Nuevo Leon (Mexico). *Current Anthropology* 26:276-279.

Norman, V. J.
1973   *Izapan Sculpture, Part 1: Album*. Papers of the New World Archaeological Foundation, no. 30. Provo, UT: Brigham Young University.

Prem, H.
1971   Calendrics and Writing in Mesoamerica. In *Contributions of the University of California Archaeological Research Facility*, no. 11. Berkeley.

Reilly, F. K., III
1987   Symbolism and Meaning in the Olmec Royal Costume. Paper given at the 3d Texas Symposium, Austin, TX.

Sharer, R. J.
1985   Archaeology and Epigraphy Revisited. *Expedition* 27(1):25-29.

Sharer, R. J., and D. W. Sedat
1973   Monument 1 El Port<n, Guatemala, and the Development of Maya Calendric and Writing Systems. In *Contributions of the University of California Archaeological Research Facility*, no. 18. Berkeley.

1987   *Archaeological Investigations in the Northern Maya Highland: Interaction and the Development of Maya Civilization*. University Museum Monographs, no. 59. Philadelphia: The University Museum, The University of Pennsylvania.

Thompson, J. E. S.
1962   *A Catalog of Maya Hieroglyphs*. Norman: University of Oklahoma Press.

Winfield C., F.
1988   *La Estela de La Mojarra, Veracruz, Mexico*. Research Reports on Ancient Maya Writing 16. Washington, DC: Center for Maya Research.

V

Excavating Among the Collections: A Reexamination of Three Figurines

Elin C. Danien

Department of Anthropology
University of Pennsylvania

Fieldwork occupies the major portion of most archaeological research, but for those who delve into the twice-buried treasures of museum collections, the application of new theories to previously acquired and subsequently forgotten objects can be equally productive, both in generating information about the societies that created those objects and in finding additional material confirmation of those newly formed theories. New hypotheses concerning the Maya worldview and the symbolism used in Maya art have resulted in a reexamination of polychrome pottery, which in turn has led to further hypotheses. This has been a high priority among art historians and epigraphers, who dissect the narrative scenes for their symbolic content and interpret the glyphs for their mythological and historical information (Gallenkamp and Johnson 1985; A. G. Miller 1986; Schele and Miller 1986, among others). Among the objects most neglected, perhaps because their great variability renders classification extremely difficult, are the study collections of figurines, whole and partial, that gather dust on storage shelves in institutions around the world.

I recently began an examination of a collection of figurines sent to The University Museum of The University of Pennsylvania more than 60 years ago by Robert Burkitt, an eccentric who found his life's purpose among the Maya of Guatemala (Fig. 5.1). He went to Copan in 1895 as second-in-command to George Byron Gordon, Director of the Peabody Museum's Fourth Copan Field Project. At the end of the field season, Gordon returned to this country, but his colleague never again left that part of the world. Instead, Burkitt settled into Guatemala and turned his hand to ranching, engineering, and trad-

ing, all the while pursuing an interest in the analysis of Mayan languages. In 1910, Gordon became director of The University of Pennsylvania's Free Museum of Science and Art (now known as The University Museum of Archaeology and Anthropology) and shortly thereafter hired Burkitt to purchase antiquities and excavate among the Maya ruins on behalf of the Museum (Danien 1985).

Much of Burkitt's work, which continued for over twenty years, was in the Alta Verapaz and other parts of the highlands of Guatemala. Some of the objects he collected are on view in The University Museum; among them is a figurine (Fig. 5.2) of particular interest for the subject of this paper. Some sixteen additional figurines, along with broken sections of perhaps two dozen others, are in storage. These figurines, all from the Guatemala highlands, lack the sophistication of the more famous Maya figurines from Jaina, which are found in burials on the island necropolis and represent a broad range of subjects including mythology, ritual, and daily life. Highland figurines are found, for the most part, in the debris of house mounds, as part of construction fill, sometimes in ceremonial precincts, but usually not in burials (Kidder 1965:146ff, Rands 1965:156). Borhegyi (1956:149) suggests that these highland figurines were private possessions, used in a personalized way to attract, control, and placate supernatural forces. Benson (1967:89) adds that they may have been symbols of status, or household gods, or personal amulets. Most of these figurines are whistles or flutes and may have been used as musical instruments in ritual processions or to call the gods they represent.

Figure 5.1. Robert Burkitt.

THE BURKITT FIGURINE COLLECTION

In contrast to the painted pottery and architectural reliefs of the Classic Maya, where palace scenes and mythological beings illustrate the elite view of the gods, death, and rebirth, the figurines present us with themes that seem closer to the concerns and worldview of the ordinary Maya. Any examination of the Burkitt Collection figurines must focus on subject and symbol analysis through comparison with other figurines of known provenance and context, as well as through the application of currently accepted theory, since the small number of figurines precludes any attempt at statistical analysis.

The jaguar, one of the major symbols in Maya iconography, is well represented in the Burkitt Collection. Of partial figurines, four of the heads can be identified as representations of the jaguar Sun God of the night. Head #NA 10899, of unknown

provenance, has some of the characteristics of the night jaguar listed by Joralemon (1975:63), including the trilobate plaques as eyebrows and the line under the eyes that twists into a cruller knot over the nose. Two other heads in the Burkitt Collection, #NA 11256 from Chama and #NA 10954 from Senahu, both in the Alta Verapaz, also bear markings of the night sun. Another head, #NA 10945, a gift to the museum "said to be from Cahabon district" in the Alta Verapaz, has the emaciated cheeks and large mouth of the night sun, and seems also to have its filed T-shaped upper teeth.

Veneration of the jaguar as more than merely animal has its origins certainly as early as Olmec depictions of about 1200 B.C. (Coe 1972:10; Soustelle 1981:185) and the 1000 B.C. village of San Jose Mogote in the valley of Oaxaca (Blanton et al. 1981:55). In *The Blood of Kings,* Schele and Miller (1986:51) suggest that the baby jaguar is one of several representations of GIII, the second-born of the trio of gods celebrated as divine ancestors by the kings of Palenque. GIII, always anthropomorphic in form, is nonetheless always shown with a jaguar tail. In all of his multiple manifestations, there is an element of the jaguar; among his many names is that of Jaguar Lord. The concept of the jaguar continued to be preternaturally significant throughout the development of Mesoamerican cultures, with the jaguar as night sun merely one manifestation of the powerful force perceived within the animal. In two Dumbarton Oaks conferences, one on the feline and the other on the Olmec (Benson 1968, 1972), there was much discussion about the apparent association of shamans and jaguars throughout Mesoamerican prehistory as well as about the transformation process whereby the shaman becomes the jaguar (see Furst 1968; Coe 1972; Grove 1972). This association covers a vast geographic area and has been ethnographically documented down into the rain forests of South America and up into northern Mexico, where among the Huichol this equivalency between jaguar and shaman continues today (Furst 1968:154). Three figurines from the Burkitt Collection emphasize the important iconographic theme of shaman as jaguar and offer an avenue for further exploration of Maya iconography and the use of ethnohistory, as well as ethnographic and historic analogy, to understand the Classic Maya worldview. Only by approaching this fragmentary material in such a holistic manner can its ultimate value as a description of reality be evalu-

Figure 5.2. Figurine in the form of a shaman transformed into a jaguar.

Figure 5.3. Seated figure of shaman, in the process of transforming from human into jaguar.

ated (Carlson 1981:144). These figurines, when examined in light of comparative archaeological and ethnographic materials, suggest the possibility of symbolic continuity and the perpetuation of a tradition across more than two millennia.

AN EXAMINATION OF THREE FIGURINES

The first figurine, #NA 11208/516 from the site of Chama, is on view in the Museum's Maya gallery (Fig. 5.2). The figure may be seen as either a jaguar or a man wearing a full jaguar mask, or, to use the term usually descriptive in discussing the Olmec, a were-jaguar, in the sense of a being combining both human and animal aspects. Another consideration in interpreting the symbolic meaning of the figurine is the diamond-shaped design on the costume covering his body, arms, and legs, finished at wrists and ankles with fringe. In Teotihuacan, one of the important artistic and symbolic themes is that of the netted jaguar. Although it is exceedingly dangerous to leap across time and space and expect to find similarity of symbolic meaning, it is not impossible to see a physical similarity between the netting on the Early Classic Teotihuacan jaguar and the diamond pattern on the Late Classic Maya figurine, from which one may infer a symbolic similarity. I will return to this theme below.

The second figurine, #NA 11027, also from Chama, appears at first glance to be an old man. On closer examination, however, one can see that his arms are not those of a human—they are the forelimbs of an animal, ending in paws. The tiny round ears at the top of his head are also animal rather than human. His eyes are sunken slits within their sockets (Fig. 5.3). An earlier treatment of a similar subject has been identified by Michael Coe as an Olmec transformation figure (Coe, Snow, and Benson

Figure 5.4. Figurine from Roknimaa in the form of a man holding a jaguar cub.

1986:97). Here, the animal ears are the same, but the were-jaguar features of the face are much more pronounced. The two figurines can be seen as representing shamans at different stages of the process wherein human is transformed into jaguar.

The third figurine, #NA 10977, from Roknima on the Chixoy River in the Alta Verapaz, is a man holding a jaguar cub in his right arm (Fig. 5.4). Although the cub's upper torso and head are missing, the thick jaguar tail is unmistakable. The unusual facial characteristics of the man, so powerful and monumental in impact, command attention. The line running from the nostrils back to the upper cheeks marks the upper edge of a raised, textured portion of the face. Remaining traces of paint indicate that this lower cheek was originally painted yellow. Such a raised area occurs on other figurines, where it has been identified variously as an animal pelt, stylized beard,

tattooing, or scarification (M. E. Miller 1975:40; Gallenkamp and Johnson 1985:134). It may also refer to the number nine, sometimes shown in its head-variant forms with a beard and what may be a pelt around the jaw. The beard and thickened lips may be indicators of age (Gallenkamp and Johnson 1985:105).

SIMILARITIES TO OTHER FIGURINES

The Burkitt figurine is strikingly similar to a figurine from Tamahu in the recent exhibit Maya: Treasures of an Ancient Civilization. Its description is as follows:

Stone figurine pendant from Tamahu, Alta Verapaz, Guat. Late Preclassic, 200 B.C.-A.D. 100. Fuchsite, 18 cm, in the Dieseldorff Collection of the Museo Nacional de Arqueologia y Etnologia, Guatemala 5095. A jaguar cub is held like a baby over the right shoulder of this bearded and mustached man wearing a close-fitting cap, with what may be a shaman's horn at the top of his head. The man's large head, with its heavy features, resembles those of other Late Preclassic Guatemalan sculptures, as does the presence of flanges rather than earflares. This man's close relationship with the jaguar may signify his role as chief of a highland group or lineage for whom the jaguar, king of tropical American beasts, was the supernatural associate and protector. (Gallenkamp and Johnson 1985:105, Fig. 15)

The site of Tamahu is not far from Roknima. Both Erwin Dieseldorff and Robert Burkitt collected in and around Coban and all through the Alta Verapaz, and they frequently were competitors in their search for previously untouched sites in this geographic area. In this case, they seem to have each collected similar representations of a shaman, created in villages separated by only a few kilometers in space and more than several centuries in time.

The figure of the human-jaguar, and the two pairs of figurines with almost identical iconography created at least half a millennium apart, suggest a direction for inquiry that may yield fruitful hypotheses for a further understanding of the folk religion of the Classic Maya and perhaps of the Maya today. Ethnographic research indicates that the concept of the jaguar, so basic to the Precolumbian Maya, continues to be important among the cultures of the Amazon and in Mexico among the Huichol of northern Mexico, the Tzotzil Maya of Chiapas, and the Lacandon Maya (Furst 1968:166-170).

In Heinz Walter's 1956 dissertation (cited by Furst 1968:145) an examination of the role of the jaguar, particularly among the natives of South America, reveals that while the jaguar is considered to be a supernatural entity, it is not necessarily a god. Rather, it is an institutionalized version of the Master of the Species, a concept characteristic of hunting cultures and still found in the worldview of many tropical forest cultivators. In this belief, the jaguar is, in fact, a man. As Furst points out in his examination of the were-jaguar motif (1968:148), the worldview of the hunter is rooted in the equivalence of man and wild animals. The jaguar, however, is equivalent only to those men who alone possess supernatural powers: the shamans. Shamans and jaguars are not merely equivalent; each is at the same time the other, as clearly articulated in the Yucatec Maya phrase *chilam balam,* or "priest jaguar." *Chilam* is "priest," and *balam,* "jaguar." But balam can also mean "sorcerer" or "priest," echoing the shaman-jaguar equivalency.

In a clear material example of this abstract concept, a figurine from the Bliss Collection at Dumbarton Oaks seems to have had the skin over his skull removed to reveal the jaguar beneath, as if the shaman had commanded the jaguar within to emerge. In other manifestations, the shaman transforms himself into the jaguar, with the union of the two evident through the combination of human and animal aspects in the same body, as in the were-jaguar from the Bliss Collection, which reveals its humanity through its stance and the shape of its hands.

EVIDENCE FOR SHAMANIC TRANSFORMATION

Let us now reexamine the three figurines in the Burkitt Collection to determine whether they fall within this shamanic transformation category. In light of the above discussion, the first example, the standing human figure with jaguar head (see Fig. 5.2), may be interpreted as a shaman now transformed into his more animal state, holding as-yet-unidentified objects that may be appurtenances of his art. The were-jaguar of the Olmecs is, by definition, a combination of animal and human. Kubler (1972:20) has noted that in Teotihuacan none of the jaguars is depicted with only jaguar traits. Each is a compound image with nonjaguar parts drawn from other life forms. Furst (1968: N. 166) has suggested that the netted jaguar of Teotihuacan is really the portrayal of a priest. The netting on the Teotihuacan jaguar and the diamond design on this figurine are separate developments arising from similar traditions: the netted jaguar as priest of an elite religious focus serving within major state rituals, the shaman jaguar reflecting the folk religion of the Maya. The diamond pattern or netting of this figurine's clothing would have served to corroborate his identity as jaguar shaman to the Maya peasant of the Late Classic as well as to confirm the overarching shamanic control of the more frightening, supernatural aspects of the jaguar. The netting or diamond design reflects a symbol with common origins but branching development.

The second figurine (see Fig. 5.3), a seated figure, may now be similarly identified as a shaman undergoing transformation into a jaguar. The jaguar ears atop the still human-shaped head and the forearms transformed into the paws and forelimbs of the jaguar presage the continued transformation into the form of the supernatural being. The Preclassic figurine in a similar pose appears to have been transformed much beyond the stage of the Burkitt figurine, whose face is still more human than jaguar. The face of the Preclassic figurine combines animal and human aspects in the Olmec style so quickly recognized as the were-jaguar. There are eroded markings on the sides and back of the Burkitt figurine that may indicate an animal skin as part of the costume. Such use of animal skins can be seen on one of the gigantic Olmec stone heads, Monument 5 of San Lorenzo, which has as part of its headdress the pelt of a jaguar, and in a vessel on display in The University Museum galleries, the Chama vase, in which a jaguar pelt forms a cloak for one of the two central figures. The use of animal skins by priests and shamans is attested to in both archaeological and ethnohistoric records. Bernardino de Sahagún, that extraordinary sixteenth-century ethnographer, tells us (1950-1963: Bk. 11:3) that Aztec conjurers "carried jaguar hides, tail, nose and claws, heart and fang and with these, they did daring feats and were feared by the populace." Thus the use of jaguar pelts was associated with the concept of control, of mastery, as late as the sixteenth century in central Mexico.

The figurine holding the jaguar cub (see Fig. 5.4) represents yet another aspect of the shamanic tradition. Instead of incorporating the jaguar within the human, the shaman is shown as human, in the role of Master of the Species. That concept of supernatural being, midway between man and god, is an ancient belief still adhered to by groups in Mexico and Central and South America. The shaman, Master of the Species, controls the jaguar and thereby controls the fortunes of the community (Furst 1968:148). The comparative Preclassic figurine, carved over half a millennium earlier, has the same iconography and wears a cap with what may be a shaman's horn. If the Late Classic figurine acquired by Burkitt had not been broken at the forehead, we might well have found a headdress topped with a similar horn. Note that both figures have heavily lidded, deep-set eyes, unusual in Maya iconography, perhaps a physical manifestation of the reflexive nature of concentration or meditation necessary for shamanic control. The raised, textured lower portion of the face, while frequently identified in other terms, here can be interpreted as the jaguar hide worn by the shaman (M. E. Miller 1975:40).

Preliminary examination of these figurines, then, suggests that the jaguar symbol may have had a similar but separate development for Maya elite and Maya peasant. While of equal importance to each of the classes, the detail of the iconography was different for each. At one time, king, jaguar, and shaman may have been interchangeable concepts, but through the centuries the attributes required of king and shaman separated. For the elite, the king was perceived as the personification of the Sun God, a sublime being protected by the great jaguar spirit. He was represented in architectural embellishments and on monumental sculpture (A. G. Miller 1986). During the Early Classic, when the power of the king was great, the need for separate shamanic intercession diminished, and the archaeological record reflects this through a reduction in the number of figurines recovered. A similar change occurs in the archaeological record of Oaxaca, where the small

figurines, so prevalent in the earlier periods, disappear in Monte Alban II, a phase noted for the evolution of a state religion and centralized control (Flannery et al. 1981:89).

In the Late Classic, the number of figurines shows a marked increase (Rands 1965:156; Rands and Rands 1965:539, 557). If these figurines were indeed personal amulets or household gods, such an increase in use can be understood as one of the many effects of changing political patterns. As the problems that plagued the Maya polities at the end of the Late Classic mounted, reliance on the state and the king would no longer have been seen as the most assured way to secure the favor of the gods. Instead, the concept of personal intercession with the owners of the universe through the powers of the shaman may have been rekindled. Concomitant with renewed belief in and reliance upon shamanism would have been increased veneration of his animal equivalent, the jaguar. The huge carnivore that stalked the jungle at night and at will was master of his universe and theirs, owner of the land on which they both lived. He could be called and controlled only by the shaman, the Master of the Species. Figurines created during this period should reflect such beliefs, with depictions of shamans and shaman-jaguars encountered in large numbers. Although the importance of the concept of the jaguar as night sun and king may have diminished during the Classic Maya Collapse, then disintegrated under the religious pressures of the Spaniards, the significance of the jaguar as an underlying symbol in Maya folk religion continued apparently unchanged.

CONCLUSIONS

I suggest, then, that the subjects chosen for figurine manufacture may reflect the religious focus of the ordinary Maya and his belief in shamanic intercession. The quantity of figurines noted in the archaeological record for a given era suggests the nature of folk religion during that period of time. The large numbers of Preclassic figurines reflect the importance of shamanism during that period; the dearth of such figurines in the Early Classic coincides with the rise and prominence of the king and state religion. The increase of figurines in Late Classic context indicates a resurgence in the importance of shamanism during the decline of the power of state-directed religion in the Late Classic, as well as the efficacy of shamanic ritual to enable the ordinary Maya to cope with the vicissitudes of an unstable and disintegrating society.

The archaeological record indicates that the interwoven concepts of shaman, jaguar, and transformation may have their roots at least as early as the Olmec Preclassic, and continue through the Maya Classic. Through the use of ethnographic analogy, a strong case may be made for a correlation of archaeological artifact and current behavior. Ethnohistoric documents and ethnographic analogy suggest that these beliefs survive unchanged among Maya groups that have maintained their cultural isolation. Among the Yucatec Maya, four *balams* protect not only the village but also each individual *milpa* (Thompson 1970:291). Masked Highland Maya, in ritual dance, use a head cloth to cover the edge of the face mask and add dramatic credibility to the performance (Christopher Jones, personal communication 1987), much the way the knotted head cloth in Figure 2 may cover the edge of the jaguar mask. Among the Huichol of western Mexico and among two groups of Maya—the highland Tzotzil and the lowland Lacandon—the concept of the transformation of shaman into jaguar, the theme of two Late Classic

figurines discussed in this paper, is understood and accepted as part of traditional reality (Furst 1968:169).

Perhaps these figurines, few as they are, can help us arrive at a better understanding of the underlying concepts that have guided the spiritual life of the Maya for more than two millennia. When examined along with other figurines, they enrich the resource pool and enhance our ability to extrapolate from the relatively small data base available to us. Indeed, they may represent the belief system of the ancient Maya peasant more accurately than does the ceremonial center or the richly appointed tomb.

The worldview of the Maya was expressed through their material culture in ways we are but beginning to understand. The symbolism and information incorporated in objects collected many years ago, in less than ideal circumstances, may yet be recovered. Although provenance and context may have been irretrievably lost during acquisition, a reexamination of these objects in the light of new theories and knowledge may reveal more of their original function than had been believed possible, and show them to be guideposts that lead on to further understanding of the ancient Maya.

BIBLIOGRAPHY

Benson, E. P.
1967 *The Maya World.* New York: Thomas Y. Crowell.

Benson, E. P. (editor)
1968 *Dumbarton Oaks Conference on the Olmec.* Dumbarton Oaks Research Library and Collections, Washington, DC.

1972 *The Cult of the Feline: A Conference in Pre-Columbian Iconography.* Dumbarton Oaks Research Library and Collections. Washington, DC.

Blanton, R. E., S. A. Kowalewski, G. Feinman, and J. Appel
1981 *Ancient Mesoamerica: A Comparison of Change in Three Regions.* Cambridge: Cambridge University Press.

de Borhegyi, S.
1956 The Development of Folk and Complex Cultures in the Southern Maya Area. *American Antiquity* 21(4):343-356. Reprinted in *Ancient Mesoamerica:*

Selected Readings, ed. J. A. Graham, pp. 148-161. Palo Alto: Peek Publications, 1966.

Carlson, J.
1981 A Geomantic Model for the Interrpretation of Mesoamerican Sites: An Essay in Cross-Cultural Comparison. In *Mesoamerican Sites and World-Views,* ed. E. P. Benson. Dumbarton Oaks Research Library and Collections, Washington, DC.

Coe, M. D.
1972 Olmec Jaguars and Olmec Kings. In *The Cult of the Feline,* ed. E. P. Benson, pp. 1-18. Washington, DC.: Dumbarton Oaks.

Coe, M., D. Snow, and E. Benson
1986 *Atlas of Ancient America.* New York: Facts on File.

Danien, E.
1985 Send Me Mr. Burkitt...Some Whisky and Wine! Early Archaeology in Central America. *Expedition* 27(3):26-33.

Flannery, K., J. Marcus, and S. A. Kowalewski
  1981   The Preceramic and Formative of the Valley of Oaxaca. *Handbook of Middle American Indians*, Supplement I, V. Bricker, general editor, pp. 48-93. Austin: University of Texas Press.

Furst, P.
  1968   The Olmec Were-Jaguar Motif in the Light of Ethnographic Reality. In *Dumbarton Oaks Conference on the Olmec,* ed. E. P. Benson. Washington, DC.: Dumbarton Oaks.

Gallenkamp, C. and R. E. Johnson
  1985   *Maya: Treasures of an Ancient Civilization.* New York: Harry N. Abrams in association with The Albuquerque Museum.

Grove, D. C.
  1972   Olmec Felines in Highland Central Mexico. In *Cult of the Feline,* ed. E. P. Benson, pp. 153-164. Washington, DC.: Dumbarton Oaks.

Joralemon, D.
  1975   The Night Sun and the Earth Dragon: Some Thoughts on the Jaguar God of the Underworld. In *Jaina Figures: A Study of Maya Iconography,* by M. E. Miller, Appendix II. Princeton: The Art Museum, Princeton University.

Kidder, A. V.
  1965   Preclassic Pottery Figurines of the Guatemalan Highlands. *Handbook of Middle American Indians,* vol. 2, R. Wauchope, general editor, pp. 146-155. Austin: University of Texas Press.

Kubler, G.
  1972   Jaguars in the Valley of Mexico. In *The Cult of the Feline,* ed. E. P. Benson, pp. 19-45. Washington, DC.: Dumbarton Oaks.

Miller, A. G.
  1986   *Maya Rulers of Time.* Philadelphia: The University Museum, The University of Pennsylvania.

Miller, M. E.
  1975   *Jaina Figurines: A Study of Maya Iconography.* Princeton: The Art Museum, Princeton University.

Rands, R. L.
  1965   Classic and Postclassic Pottery Figurines of the Guatemalan Highlands. *Handbook of Middle American Indians,* vol. 2, R. Wauchope, general editor, pp. 146-155. Austin: University of Texas Press.

Rands, R.L., and B. C. Rands
  1965   Pottery Figurines of the Maya Lowlands. *Handbook of Middle American Indians, vol. 2,* R. Wauchope, general editor, pp. 535-560. Austin: University of Texas Press.

Sahagún, Fr. B. de
  1950-1963   *General History of the Things of New Spain.* Translated from the Aztec by A. J. Anderson and C. E. Dibble. Sante Fe, NM: School of American Research and the University of Utah.

Schele, L., and M. E. Miller
  1986   *The Blood of Kings: Dynasty and Ritual in Maya Art.* Fort Worth, TX: Kimbell Art Museum.

Soustelle, J.
  1981   *The Olmecs: The Oldest Civilization in Mexico.* Trans. H. R. Lane. Norman: University of Oklahoma Press.

Thompson, J. E. S.
  1970   *Maya History and Religion.* Civilization of the American Indian Series No. 99. Norman: University of Oklahoma Press.

VI

Pure Language and Lapidary Prose

Clemency Chase Coggins

Department of Archaeology
Boston University

Modern Mayan languages and ancient Maya hieroglyphic writing share a predilection for playing with words, by punning and metaphor—the languages aurally and the writing both pictorially and phonetically. There is ample evidence for this practice and way of thinking in modern Mayan languages (Bricker 1973; B. Tedlock 1982a,b) as well as in extant colonial Maya literature (Brotherston 1979; Edmonson 1982; Edmonson and Bricker 1986:60; Roys 1933, 1965). Furthermore, in recent years epigraphers have noted the use of homophonous (sound-alike) punning glyphs that substitute for each other in the Classic Period inscriptions (Mathews and Justeson 1984; Houston 1984).

Playful and ambiguous usage is perhaps most obvious in the Colonial Chilam Balam literature of Yucatan, in which an example is found in the sequences of names of towns that were regularly turned into puns. For instance the account of the westward wanderings of the Itza in the *Chilam Balam of Chumayel* includes the following touristic information: "So then they reached *Tah Kab,* where the Itza stirred for honey [*Tah kab* means division of land, but *huytah kab* means to stir honey] . . . Then they reached K'ik'il, where they had dysentery [*K'ik'* means both rubber and blood, while *k'ik' nak',* bloody guts, means dysentery] . . . Then they reached *K'al,* where they closed themselves in" (Edmonson 1986a:83, 84).

Two of several meanings of *k'al* are "to imprison" or "to trap," although the name of the site, like the name of Tikal, may actually refer to a unit of twenty (Coggins 1987b).

THE LANGUAGE OF ZUYUA

Another example of Mayan word play in the *Chilam Balam of Chumayel* is found in the "Interrogation of the Chiefs." Here riddles are asked in order to ascertain the esoteric knowledge and thus the eligibility of incoming rulers. The questions are written in "the language of Zuyua"; in Yucatec Mayan this would be *Suyua than* (see Barrera Vásquez 1980 for Yucatecan words and orthography). Examples of these empowering riddles make it clear that the questions are densely metaphorical, and it is likely that the correct replies included in the Chumayel provided only one level of possible answers and of interpretation. A fairly straightforward riddle is: "Let them go and get the brains of the sky, so the head chiefs may see how large they are . . . [and the answer] This is what the brains of the sky are; it is copal gum. Zuyua language" (Roys 1933:90).

Almost every answer is identified by the tag "Zuyua language." The language of Zuyua is self-defined as presenting sacred information known only to rulers. But what is Zuyua? Roys says, "The frequent mention of the language of Zuyua, a mythical place name [associated with the seven caves of Nahua origin], suggests that this interrogatory once abounded in terms familiar to the Toltec conquerors of Yucatan but not understood by the people of the country" (Roys 1933:88, n. 1, and 98, n. 1).

Munro Edmonson in his translation of the *Chumayel* translates *Zuyua* as "bloody water" in Nahuatl, and as another name for Tula, and remarks that it was used to "draw the mantle of the Toltecs over the ritual language of the Maya examination system" (1986a:3501). While Zuyua very likely was a name for Tula (Edmonson 1971:5257, 5260; Recinos 1950:62, 63; Recinos and Goetz 1953:45, 53, 65), I believe it was also a name for Chichen Itza, and that *Zuyua* (*Suyua* in Yucatecan) referred specifically to the Sacred Cenote. *Suy ha'* means "vortex of water," or "water that draws in like a whirlpool"—a good description of this circular cenote into which sacrificial offerings were thrown—whereas the punning *suhuy haa'* is "virgin, pure, or sacred water." Once it became a religious center in the eighth century the Sacred Cenote at Chichen was probably never used as a source of drinking water (if it ever was)—instead it was a supreme source of *suhuy haa'*.[1] I propose that a punning meaning for the language of Zuyua, or *Suyua than,* was *suhuy than,* meaning "virgin, or pure, language." However, I believe the association of the language of Zuyua with Toltec ancestors is accurate, although it may refer to an earlier period than is usually suggested. In the eighth century Chichen Itza was founded at the Sacred Cenote by Maya who, by virtue of Teotihuacan ancestry, probably referred to themselves as Toltec (Coggins 1987a, 1989), and the language of Zuyua—originally a (non-Mayan) language of the ruling elite—influenced and ultimately became synonymous with the esoteric Mayan ritual language that eventually came to refer to the focal ritual of the Sacred Cenote at Chichen Itza.

PURE LANGUAGE

In his ethnographic work on the oral tradition of the Chamulas, Gary Gossen describes three basic kinds of words or language: ordinary or conversational language; language for people whose hearts are heated; and pure words or oral tradition (1974:46-55; 1986, Fig. 4-2). Pure language comprises two parts: recent words and ancient words. Recent words are concerned with the present, fourth creation. There are four kinds of ancient words: true ancient narrative (which deals with the first three creations); language for rendering holy (for speaking of life rituals); prayer; and song. According to Gossen, pure language is "closed" and it is "bound," which is to say it is traditional and predictable—and becomes hot as it approaches the ideal in style, content, form, and setting. This contrasts with the lowest, ordinary level of language, which is cold (1974:47-49; 1986, Fig. 4-1).

Using this classification one can describe the formalized Yucatecan "Interrogation of the Chiefs" as "pure language," or *suhuy than* in Yucatec Mayan, as well as with its proper name, *Suyua than,* the "language of Zuyua," since this was the pure language of Chichen Itza. *Suyua than* probably fell into the category of "language for rendering holy," the second type of Chamula ancient words. The use of

pure language could thus be traced back to these Colonial Yucatecan books, and there may be evidence of its use in the Classic period hieroglyphic inscriptions.

From what is known of the content of Classic monumental inscriptions it is likely that both recent words and ancient words would be included in them. Recent words would record dates and biographical information about the births, accessions, alliances, captures, and deaths of rulers that had occurred within the present, fourth creation, whereas ancient words were probably mostly "language for rendering holy," which described life rituals that served to secure the position of the ruler in time and in the cosmos. References to mythical earlier creations are rare in monumental inscriptions, although they are often found pictorially in Classic Maya iconography (Coggins 1988b and d). Prayer and song are found in the inscriptions on ceramics but probably not on monuments.

STELA A AT COPAN

Stela A at Copan (Maudslay 1889-1902:I, Pls. 25-30) is a Late Classic Maya monument that illustrates the use of pure language in lapidary prose. During the reign of the Copan ruler "XVIII Jog" the carving of inscriptions reached a sophistication, beauty, and erudition found nowhere else. Although it is unpleasant to think that such masterpieces were created by a committee, it is hard to believe that one man could have worked out all the artistic, stylistic, formating, semantic, and theological facets of one of these inscriptions as well as of the interrelated portraits that accompanied them. In Western culture "lapidary prose" usually refers to writing that is elegant enough to commit to stone, but for the Maya there were more considerations. Lapidary prose was precise and economical and ideally carried as much weight as possible. In this the scribes of Maya monumental prose excelled. In the finest inscriptions many words, possibly every word (even dates), carried several levels of meaning, and many phrases might be read in more than one way and were thus more poetry than prose. The choice of meaning may have been determined by the occasion or context in which it was read.

The last passage of the inscription on Stela A incorporates a prime example of some of the basic concepts and words of Mayan pure language as well as some of its forms. In order to illustrate this hypothesis a tentative free interpretation of this passage will be found below; this is based on a rough glyph-by-glyph "translation" that is included as an Appendix.[2] where it serves as an illustration of this laconic literary form with its homophonous words so characeristic of Maya lapidary prose. (By homophonous, I mean loosely homophonous, or a deliberate punning and pairing of sound-alike words, sometimes irrespective of glottal stops.) It has been suggested that the inscriptions of Copan were "written" in a Cholan language (Kelley 1976:13), although Lounsbury has identified a Cakchiquel [or Quiche] personal name (in press). Some of the words may be read phonetically in Cholan, but I suggest that the writing was legible to Cholan and Yucatecan speakers—and may have been as Yucatecan as Cholan for reasons having to do with the educated rulers, rather than with the language or languages actually spoken at Copan.

Munro Edmonson has found that couplets were a dominant formal device in Maya scripture (1971, 1982, 1986b; cf. D. Tedlock 1983: ch. 4, 12) or in what may have been called ancient words. Couplets that contrast or that restate one concept in two ways are familiar to us from our own Biblical scripture, as in Psalm 19:

The heavens are telling the glory of God;
and the firmament proclaims His handiwork.

Day to day pours forth speech,
and night to night declares knowledge.

There is no speech, nor are there words;
their voice is not heard;

Yet their voice goes out through all the earth,
and their words to the end of the world.

In them He has set a tent for the sun,
which comes forth like a bridegroom leaving his chamber,
and like a strong man runs its course with joy.

Its rising is from the end of the heavens,
and its circuit to the end of them;
and there is nothing hid from its heat.
(Psalm 19:1-6, Revised Standard Version)

This psalm even uses some of the same poetic imagery that I postulate is found in the Copan inscription and in the Chichen image to be considered next ; for instance, the heavens, speech, world directions, a dominant male identified with the sun and sunrise, and world/sky directions. Rituals involving the naming of the four directions, or five (including center), or six (including up and down) were a common part of Maya ritual and pure language (Roys 1933:170-172). The recitation of these ritual circuits commonly produces quadruplets, and two are found in this Stela A passage as well as one sextuplet (see free translation below, Appendix). Each such larger unit is actually made up of two or three antonymous couplets. (East and west, north and south are opposite, and they are complementary.) This is the kind of cumulative and repetitive formal language that Gossen describes as the most accomplished or hot pure language, since the modern Chamulas associate "stylistic *redundance* with . . . rising spiritual heat" (emphasis added 1974:48).

Here is a free translation of one way in which the inscription on the south side of Stela A at Copan might have been read aloud. The lines in brackets are hypothetical couplet elaborations (see Appendix for a straighter reading):

In the highest heaven
In the bowels of the earth
On the stony land
By the river
In the east corner
Of the four-part sky
[Where the sun is born]

[In the highest heaven]
[In the bowels of the earth]
[By the river]
[The speaking together]
At the north corner
In the four-part abode of the zenith serpent-bird
[Where the ancestors live]

[In thc highest heaven]
[In the bowels of the earth]
[By the River]
In the west corner
of the four-part celestial realm
[Where the sun dies]

[In the highest heaven]
[In the bowels of the earth]
[On the stony land]
[By the river]
At the south corner
The fourth corner of the firmament
[Where the sun is hidden]

[In the highest heaven]
[In the bowels of the earth]
[On the stony land]
[By the river]
At sovereign Copan
The precious seed is cast
[In the east]
[Where the cycle is born]

[In the highest heaven]
[In the bowels of the earth]
[On the stony land]
[By the river]
At sovereign Tikal
The precious seed is cast
[In the west]
[Where the burden of the cycle is set down]

[In the highest heaven]
[In the bowels of the earth]
[On the stony land]
[By the river]
At ancestral El Peru
The precious seed is cast
[In the north sky]
[Where the ancestors live]

[In the highest heaven]
[In the bowels of the earth]
[On the stony land]
[By the river]
At sovereign Palenque
The precious seed is cast
[In the underworld (south)]
[Where the ancestors are buried]

The corn is scattered
[The seed cast]
[Divination]

Mirror of the sky
Mirror of the earth

In the east
[Where the cycle is complete]
In the west
[Where the sun is swallowed]
In the underworld
[Inside the earth]
In the sky
[At the serpent heaven]

On the Stony land
By the river
At the tower of fire-making
[The new fire is drilled]
[The new cycle begins]

The prophecy is auspicious
[Abundance the tidings]
The prophecy
At the completion of the katun
[The prophecy
Of the new katun 2 Ahaw]

This inscription employs ritual sets that have symmetries and closures at many levels—formal, iconographic, semantic, and phonetic—and if this hypothetical reading seems redundant, it was probably many times longer and more tautological in the performance. The written text supplied the necessary (if skeletal) structure, while the priest or ruler who read it aloud would have transformed it into couplets, triplets, and repetitions that were constrained only by his personal heat—his authentic religious correctness and inspiration.

The encapsulation of many extraneous couplets within a few glyphs is only one likely stylistic device employed here in response to the demands of lapidary form. A more obvious one is the interplay of various forms and meanings of the words *kan, k'an, k'aan,* and *ka'an* (see Houston 1984). The choice of words for this inscription exemplified both pure language itself and the historic and religious role of Copan in the Maya lands. The various meanings of these four sound-alike words (see Table 6.1) were particularly interrelated within religious and cultural constructs probably brought by the founder of Copan late in the fourth century A.D. (Coggins 1988a, 1991, n.d.)

In this inscription *kan* means both "four" and "serpent," and may also signify "speech," thus referring to the speaker who transformed the written record. Stela A was dedicated to the Katun Four Ahau, or *Kan* Ahau, that ended at 9.15.0.0.0. (A.D. 731); the number four here also describes the corners of the cosmos, the limits of the Maya world, and the form of this Copan, or any Maya, ritual circuit. In the Quiche *Popol Vuh* this four-fold symbolism also involves measuring the "sky-earth" (D. Tedlock 1985:72); in Yucatecan measuring, *k'aan* makes a pun with *kan*, "four." The concept of four dominates this final passage of the stela inscription.

Kan also means "serpent." In the Maya scriptures this is usually the Venus serpent, or *K'uk'ulkan*. I have postulated that Copan was founded by a man of Teotihuacan affiliation whose name could be read *Yax K'uk'um*, which may mean "Venus Quetzal," or *K'uk'ulkan* (Coggins 1988a, n.d.) as well as the phonetically analogous *Yax-K'uk-Mo'*, or "Quetzal Macaw" (Stuart and Schele 1986). Several Copan rulers had variations on the *K'uk'ulkan* name, including this first one and the last, *Yax Pak* (Lounsbury n.d.), "First or Venus Dawn." The only serpent appearance in this part of the inscription is found in the emblem glyph of El Peru (D5R), where it is loosely homophonous with the word for sky (and north), *Ka'an* (see Bricker 1983:350-352). This may be of particular historical significance at Copan, because the sky was the home of the ancestors and El Peru is apparently described here as a paternal or ancestral place (see Coggins 1988a:102).

The conventional Yucatecan word for sky, *ka'an*, is a third word that is related phonetically to *kan;* it appears, appropriately enough, four *(kan)* times in this section of the inscription (D2R; D3R; D4L; D7L), while the "heaven" phrase "four sky" (D2R-D4I) was itself repeated four times. "Four Sky" would have been read *kan ka'an* in Yucatecan.

The fourth *kan*-related word, *k'an*, adds a new symbolic dimension. In this inscription *k'an* signifies "drilled precious stone," "*Spondylus* shell," and the "kan cross"; one of these serves as the first element of the first emblem glyph prefix. Copan of the east and El Peru of the north have *kan* cross elements in the prefix, whereas Tikal of the west has a *Spondylus* shell, and Palenque of the south, a drilled precious stone (see Maudslay 1889-1902: I Pl. 30). This common compound is known as the "water group" prefix (T36-40; Thompson 1960:276, 277), which I suggest may have been read *k'anhel*, "precious seed." If, however, this prefix were read as the pun-

Kan	Four, square (kan cross)
	Serpent
	Speech
	Forceful
Ah Kan	Speaker
K'aan	Measure with cord
Ka'an	Sky
K'an	Precious stone (worked, drilled)
	Precious yellow (colored) shell, *Spondylus* shell (worked, drilled)
	Yellow (golden) kan cross (golden pyrite mirror)

Table 6.1. Some meanings of four loosely homophonous Yucatec Mayan words.

ning *kanhel,* it would mean "serpent succession," and it would also refer to the four ritual directions and to the ceremonial circuit that was followed at the places denoted by the "water-group" prefix (Coggins 1987b, 1988c, 1989).

These place names, the emblem glyphs, are each implicitly, by their location in the text, and as standard metaphors, symbolic of a direction; this directional significance was originally determined by the history and cultural roles assumed by each place. The four emblem glyphs are organized in contrasting couplet order and not in the order of the standard counterclockwise ceremonial circuit as the preceding sky glyphs probably are. Ceremonial circuit order is usually east, north, west, and south (beginning where the sun rises), whereas the place names are arranged east/west, north/south—if we may assume that the sky serpent name of El Peru places it in the north, or sky, position and that the skeletal bone significance of the Palenque name places it in the south, or underworld.

The four emblem glyphs are followed by a recitation of the six directions in contrasting couplet order, but at the end, south precedes north in a reversal of the order of the last two emblem glyphs and of the first two glyphs in the inscription. This serves to close the directional recitation. Although we cannot be sure why these directions change in relation to one another, one practical effect would have been to keep the circumambulating celebrants "on their toes" as they followed the speaker or "caller"; errors in sacred ceremony could seriously affect the outcome.

The last complete glyph in the inscription on Stela A (D12R) is *lamay*, meaning "four-cornered" or "completed" cycle (Coggins 1988b); it here refers to the katun 9.15.0.0.0. However, *lamay* is prefixed here by two affixes, ti' (T59) and *ma'* (T74). Together these modify the cycle glyph to read *ti' ma'lamay* (if read *ti' mahlamay* this might translate "at the great cycle"; Justeson 1984:321). However, I suggest that it might possibly read "at the incomplete cycle," and refer to a time before the end of the cycle or to the Initial Series date that begins the stela inscription at 9.14.19.8.0, which is twelve uinals, or 240 days, before the end of the katun—although it seems more logical that the described ceremony of circumambulating, casting seed, and drilling new fire, followed by giving the prophecy of the new katun, would have taken place at the turn of the katun.

This analysis has considered two inferred characteristics of this inscription: the form and redundancy of pure language as well as the punning and metaphors of lapidary prose, without comment on the many glyphic details that complicate the text and that doubtless indicated ways to recite variations and elaborations on the themes at much greater length.

CHICHEN ITZA

Another kind of lapidary prose or poetry was carved at Chichen Itza two or three katuns after the erection of Stela A at Copan. At Chichen the image of a ruler, probably the founder of that northern site, was cut into the west vault of the Lower Temple of the Jaguars. This man is Toltec by my definition, which includes any person of Teotihuacan ancestry or cultural affiliation, no matter how far from Teotihuacan he may have lived in distance or in time (Coggins 1987a, 1989, n.d.). "Toltec" ancestry was significant at Chichen Itza as it was at Copan, and in both places homonymns and puns on the word *kan* figured in inscriptions, whether as words or images.

No inscription identifies him, but this apotheosized Chichen ruler is seated on a throne within the disc of the sun, and from his mouth there issues a "speech scroll" in the form of a serpent head. This head, with upturned snout, is the Venus serpent, known as *k'uk'ulkan* in Yucatecan. The beaded perforated precious disc on the snout may be read as *k'an*, thus identifying the speech-scroll serpent with the sky *(ka'an)* serpent. This device also may be read as "star"; an identical motif just outside and above the sun disk may be read *k'anek'*, "precious star," or *kanek'*, a name for Venus. Venus is thus shown as close companion to the sun as it actually is a heliacal rise. Although his official name was probably *K'uk'ulkan*, in this portrait this ruler was also designated *Ah Kan*.

Ah Kan may mean both "(Lord) Serpent" and "The Speaker." Since speech is *kan* and serpent is *kan*, the serpent speech scroll is *kan kan*; In addition *kan* means "forcefully," so this image might be read as depicting both serpent speech and forceful or powerful speech. Furthermore, since this ancestor has entered or merged with the golden yellow *(k'an)* sun, at the top of the sky *(ka'an)*, we know that he has achieved the highest, the most perfect, indeed the hottest form of pure language. This was the language of Zuyua, or *Suyua than,* the pure language of Chichen Itza.

ACKNOWLEDGMENTS

I am grateful to Berthold Riese, who supplied me with his analysis of the inscription and transcription of the dates on Copan Stela A and with the drawing of the inscription by Barbara Fash, for which I also thank the Instituto Hondureño de Antropología e Historia. However, Riese is not responsible for my interpretation of side D of Stela A.

NOTES

1. There is no clear evidence that the Sacred Cenote was ever used for domestic water procurement. No sherds from Early or Preclassic vessels were found in it, although such early sherds were found in the Hacienda Cenote not far away (Brainerd 1958:34-45). The cenote may always have been considered sacred.

2. A transcript and analysis of the Stela A text was kindly supplied me by Berthold Riese. Most of his commentary is confined to the first three parts of the inscription (A-C) and to the associated calendrics; in part D he mainly notes the "four-fold parallelism."

Translations in this paper go beyond and differ from Riese's in so many small ways that I do not know how to indicate them; in view of their "literary" pur-pose, I will simply express my gratitude to Riese and assure readers that the errors are all mine.

APPENDIX

A proposed reading of the inscription on the south side of Stela A, Copan.

114:566:23; **xa-ma-na**, north (Closs 1988). [Zenith].

74:110:74; **ma-k'o-ma, (mam-k'o)**, [belly of earth]. (**ko**, Stuart and Grube 1987).

59?.1040; **ta? tsek'**, on rocky earth. (identified as locative by D. Stuart and S. Houston, see Schele 1990, p. 42.)

694.501; **talk? nab**, by the water [river]. (Stuart and Houston as above)

4:87:561a:23; **kan-te KA'AN(na)**, fourth firmament.

4:118.746:23; **kan-kan-K'UK'(an)**, four celestial cycle bird-serpent.

4:116:561e:23: **kan-ne-KA'AN(na)**, four(?) sky.

4:294:561:23; **kan-(a)may KA'AN(na)**, four-cor-nered heaven, [*may* = hoof].

36.168:756; **K'AN HEL ah-aw SOTS'**, precious seed Lord Copan.

38.168:569:130; **K'AN HEL ah-aw K'AL**, precious seed Lord Tikal.

25:36.168:764:130; **K'AN HEL k(a)-ah-aw KAN**, pre-cious seed Father El Peru.

36.168:570:130; **K'AN HEL ah-aw BAK**, precious seed Lord Palenque.

1000b.116:130/178?; **WAH-(wa)-nah?**, spill corn, [divination]. (see Taube n.d.).

121.561e:23; **NEN KA'AN(na)**, mirror of heaven (F. G. Lounsbury, B. Riese, pers. comm.).

121:1000[526]; **NEN KABAN**, mirror of earth (Lounsbury, B. Reise, pers. comm.).

546:544:116; **lah-k'in-(ni)**, east [complete solar cycle].

666[544]:544:116; **chi'(k'in)-k'in-(ni)**, west [swal-lowed sun].

74:134.210:178; **mah-(xV)-XIKIN-al**, south [great shell, underworld].

114:566:23; **xa-ma-na** (Closs 1988), north [zenith].

59?.1040; **ta? tse'k**, on the rocky earth.

?:542?.501:142; **tak? nab**, by the water.

602:630; **pa' k'ak'**, fire tower [to drill new fire].

134.595.134.74; **(xV)-tama(ma)-xV**, [**taman**, cotton] 769:126; **chi'(hi)**, mouth, jaws; time hence (Justeson 1984:325): **tamax chi'** =s prophecy, **hi** suffix =s time future.

502[533]:142.25; **ma'-k(a)**, auspicious.

134.595.134:74; **(xV)-tama(ma)-xV**, 769:126; **chi'(hi) tamax chi'**, prophecy.

59:74:173[606], **ti' mah LA(h)-MAY**, at the comple-tion of the great cycle.

BIBLIOGRAPHY

Barrera Vásquez, A. (editor)
1980   *Diccionario Maya Cordemex*: Mérida: Ediciones Cordemex.

Brainerd, G. W.
1958   *The Archaeological Ceramics of Yucatan.* University of California Anthropological Records No. 19. Berkeley and Los Angeles.

Bricker, V. R.
1973   *Ritual Humor in Highland Chiapas.* Austin: University of Texas Press.
1983   Directional Glyphs in Maya Inscription and Codices. *American Antiquity* 48(2):347-353.

Brotherston, G.
1979   Continuity in Maya Writing: New Readings of Two Passages in the *Book of Chilam Balam of Chumayel.* In *Maya Archaeology and Ethnohistory,* eds. N. Hammond and G. R. Willey, pp. 241-258. Austin: University of Texas Press.

Closs, M. P.
1988   A Phonetic Version of the Maya Glyph for North. *American Antiquity* 53(2):386-393.

Coggins, C. C.
1987a   New Fire at Chichen Itza. *Memorias del Primer Coloquio Internacional de Mayistas, 5-10 Agosto, 1985,* pp. 427-484. Universidad Nacional Autonoma de Mexico.
1987b   The Names of Tikal. *Primer Simposio Mundial Sobre Epigrafia Maya,* pp. 23-45. Instituto de Antropología e Historia, Asociación Tikal, Guatemala. *Memorias.*
1988a   On the Historical Significance of Decorated Ceramics at Copan and Quirigua and Related Classic Maya Sites. *In The Southeast Classic Maya Zone,* eds. E. H. Boone and G. R. Willey, pp. 95-123. Washington, DC: Dumbarton Oaks.
1988b   Classic Maya Metaphors of Death and Life. *Res* 16:64-84.
1988c   The Manikin Scepter: Emblem of Lineage. *Estudios de Cultura Maya* 17:123-158.
1988d   The Observatory at Dzibilchaltun. *In New Directions in American Archaeoastronomy,* ed. A. D. Aveni, pp. 17-56. BAR International Series 454. Oxford.
1989   New Sun at Chichen Itza. *World Archaeoastronomy,* ed. A. F. Aveni, pp. 260-275. Cambridge: Cambridge University Press.

1991   Tikal and Seibal and the Birth of the Baktun, *In Vision and Revision in Maya Studies,* eds. F. Clancy and P. Harrison. Albuquerque: University of New Mexico Press.
n.d.   Names of Quetzalcoatl at Teotihuacan and among the Classic Maya. Paper presented in a Teotihuacan symposium. Society for American Archaeology Meetings, Toronto, 1987.

Edmonson, M. S. (translator)
1971   *The Book of Counsel: The Popol Vuh of the Quiche Maya of Guatemala.* Middle American Research Institute, Publication 35. New Orleans: Tulane University.
1982   *The Ancient Future of the Itza: The Book of Chilam Balam of Tizimin.* Austin: University of Texas Press.
1986a   *Heaven Born Merida and Its Destiny: The Book of Chilam Balam of Chumayel.* Austin: University of Texas Press.
1986b   Quiche Literature. In *Handbook of Middle American Indians,* ed. M. S. Edmonson. Supplement 3, *Literatures,* pp. 107-132.

Edmonson, M. S., and V. R. Bricker
1986   Yucatecan Mayan Literature. In *Handbook of Middle American Indians,* ed. M. S. Edmonson. Supplement 3, *Literatures,* pp. 44-63.

Gossen, G. H.
1974   *Chamulas in the World of the Suni: Time and Space in a Maya Oral Tradition.* Cambridge, MA: Harvard University Press.
1986   Tzotzil Literature. In *Literatures,* ed. M. S. Edmonson. *Handbook of Middle American Indians Supplement* 3:64-106.

Houston, S. D.
1984   An Example of Homophony in Maya Script. *American Antiquity* 49:790-805.

Justeson, J. S.
1984   Appendix B: Interpretations of Mayan Hieroglyphs. In *Phoneticism in Mayan Hieroglyphic Writing,* eds. J. S. Justeson and L. Campbell. Institute of Mesoamerican Studies, Publication 9. Albany: State University of New York.

Kelley, D. H.
1976   *Deciphering the Maya Script.* Austin: University of Texas Press.

Lounsbury, F. G.
n.d.   The Names of a King: Hieroglyphic Variants as a Key to Decipherment.

Mathews, P., and J. S. Justeson
1984   Patterns of Sign Substitution in Maya Hieroglyphic Writing: The "Affix Cluster." In *Phoneticism in Mayan Hieroglyphic Writing*, eds. J. S. Justeson and L. Campbell. Institute for Mesoamerican Studies, Publication 9. Albany: State University of New York.

Maudslay, A. P.
1889-1902   *Biologia Centrali-Americana: Archaeology.* London: R. H. Porter and Dulau.

Recinos, A. (translator)
1950   *Popol Vuh: The Sacred Book of the Ancient Quiche Maya.* English trans. D. Goetz and S. G. Morley. Norman: University of Oklahoma Press.

Recinos, A., and D. Goetz (translators)
1953   *The Annals of the Cakchiquels.* Norman: University of Oklahoma Press.

Roys, R. L. (translator and editor)
1933   *The Book of Chilam Balam of Chumayel.* Carnegie Institution of Washington, Publication 438. Washington, DC.
1965   *Ritual of the Bacabs.* Norman: University of Oklahoma Press.

Schele, L.
1990   *Notebook for the 14th Maya Hieroglyphic Writing Workshop at Texas.* Austin: University of Texas.

Stuart, D., and N. Grube
1987   Observations on T110 as the Syllable *ko. Research Reports on Maya Hieroglyphic Writing,* no. 8. Washington DC: Center for Maya Research.

Stuart, D., and L. Schele
1986   Yax-K'uk-Mo', the Founder of the Copan Dynasty. *Copan Note* no. 6. Austin: Kinko's Copies.

Taube, K. A.
n.d.   "The Maize Tamale, *wah,* in Classic Maya Epigraphy and Art."

Tedlock, B.
1982a   *Time and the Highland Maya.* Albuquerque: University of New Mexico Press.
1982b   Sound Texture and Metaphor in Quiche Maya Ritual Language. *Current Anthropology* 23:269-272.

Tedlock, D.
1983   *The Spoken Word and the Work of Interpretation.* Philadelphia: University of Pennsylvania Press.
1985   *Popol Vuh: The Definitive Edition of the Mayan Book of the Dawn of Life and the Glories of Gods and Kings.* New York: Simon and Schuster.

Thompson, J. E. S.
1960   *Maya Hieroglyphic Writing: An Introduction.* Norman: University of Oklahoma Press.

Tozzer, A. M.
1957   *Chichen Itza and the Cenote of Sacrifice.* Peabody Museum Memoirs XI, XII. Cambridge, MA: Harvard University Press.

VII

The Myth of the Popol Vuh as an Instrument of Power

Justin Kerr

Kerr Associates

The purpose of this paper is to demonstrate the manner in which Maya rulers exploited their myth, known as the Popol Vuh, to prove their right to rule. Along with long dynastic informational texts, they portrayed themselves in the images of gods and demigods. The most powerful and popular of the characters they cloaked themselves with were the famous Hero Twins, Hunahpu and Xbalanque.

Among the many images of the Hero Twins are many characteristics by which they can be identified. Michael Coe called them the "Headband Twins" (Coe 1973). Their classic portrayal can be seen on a vase (Fig. 7.1) they wear a headband, which is a scarf knotted at the back of the head with the ends flaring away.

Lounsbury (1985) shows us that God G1 of the Palenque Triad and Hunahpu are often interchangeable. Hunahpu is generally marked with dark spots on his body and wears the attributes of G1: a diadem marked with crossed bands, a shell over his ear, and fish barbels on his cheek. He wears a knot pendant on his chest and at his waist, and he often carries, or wears, an upside-down vase marked with the glyph *akbal,* meaning "darkness." He may also carry an ax or a handstone (Fig. 7.2; Spero 1990) Another important facet of Hunahpu's costume is a kilt or skirt that is made of knotted ropes, and in this costume he is generally shown with his blowgun and wearing his hunter's hat (Fig. 7.3)

Xbalanque may wear an *ahau* glyph in his headdress, which is sometimes replaced with a long-lipped deity head, but more often he has as his identifier a patch of jaguar skin that may be shown as three spots attached to his cheek (Fig. 7.4). The jaguar skin patches may be attached to other parts of his body as well. He sometimes wears a jaguar ear or tail. Xbalanque is interchangeable with G3 of the Palenque triad (Lounsbury 1985). The Twins wear

ball game yokes, establishing their roles as ballplayers. The various aspects of the Twins are sometimes interchangeable, and one figure may represent both of them.

On the Metropolitan Vase (see Fig. 7.2), G1, also known as Chac Xib Chac (his glyphic name), brandishes an ax over the body of his brother, Xbalanque, here represented as a baby jaguar. Michael Coe in a recent paper has challenged this identification (1989). However, I believe that at least in one sense this scene is an allegory from the story in the Popol Vuh in which the Hero Twins perform before the Lords of the Underworld (in this case, God A, one of the death gods). As part of a magical act in which they confuse and confound the Lords of the Underworld, they cut themselves up and put each other back together again. Also on this vase are other parts of the story. The firefly has aided the Twins in deceiving the Lords of the Underworld by keeping his body aglow throughout the night while the Twins pretend to smoke cigars. The dog is part of the magic, and the Twins cut him up and return him whole. The purpose of these magical acts is to trick the Lords of the Underworld into demanding that they be included in the magic. When this happens, the Twins cut up the Lords of the Underworld but decline to make them whole again. Thus Hunahpu and Xbalanque triumph over the Lords of the Underworld and bring about their demise.

Although the written version of the Popol Vuh did not appear until the sixteenth century, there are images which show us that the basic story was in place in Izapan times. On Stela 25 from Izapa (Fig. 7.5) the essence of the story is shown. The crossbars represent the nance tree where the vain bird, Vucub Caquix, comes to eat, and it is there that the Twins station themselves so as to be able to ambush and kill the bird. The first pellet from Hunahpu's blow-

Figure 7.1. The Hero Twins in their classic dress. From a Rollout photograph of a Maya vase. Kerr Number 1183.

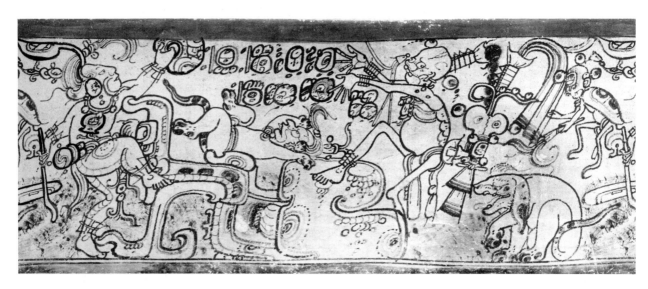

Figure 7.2. The God G1 from the Metropolitan Vase. From a Rollout photograph of a Maya vase. Kerr Number 521.

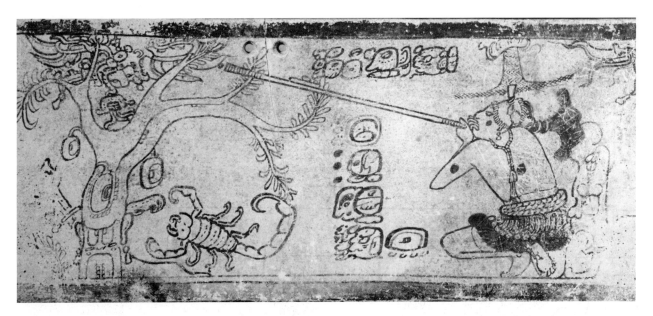

Figure 7.3. Hunahpu the hunter and killer of Vucub Caquix. From a Rollout photograph of a Maya vase. Kerr Number 1226.

Figure 7.4. Xbalanque carrying a cache vessel. From a Rollout photograph of a Maya vase. Kerr Number 1004.

gun misses and only wounds the bird in the jaw. They struggle, and the bird tears off Hunahpu's arm. On the stela, the blood flowing from the arm is shown as three streams. The saurian in the scene is Zipacna, one of the sons of Vucub Caquix, who will also be killed by the Hero Twins.

The image of Vucub Caquix is seen on early classic vessels (Cortez 1986) and is ubiquitous at Izapa. I believe that this portion of the story is a marker which says that the Maya are in revolt against another people (perhaps Olmec, or some other non-Mayans), and through their mythology the Maya have created the Hero Twins, who are the personification of these forces of change.

Rulers routinely reaffirm their divinity by taking on the form of the Hero Twins, thereby incorporating their supernatural powers. On a slate scepter in the form of an ax (Fig. 7.6) is a portrayal of a ruler

Figure 7.5. Hunahpu with the bleeding stump of his arm after fighting with Vucub Caquix. From Izapa, Stela Number 25. Drawing by Constance Cortez.

Figure 7.6. Slate scepter showing a ruler and Hunahpu. Private collection. Kerr Number 3408.

dressed in all his finery. On the reverse (Fig. 7.7) we see the same individual in the costume of the Hero Twin Hunahpu. Here the ruler wears the costume of the hunter, with blowgun, hunter's hat, and knotted skirt. This is the costume of the killer of Vucub Caquix. The ruler is telling us in this portrait that he not only rules but that he has risked his being for his people.

Another ruler shows himself as a Hero Twin on a jade celt that dates from the fifth century A.D. This celt may have been part¹ of his own costume. Generally there are sets of three celts that form a unit hanging from the belt. The dots on the ruler's body proclaim his identity as that of Hunahpu. This act of showing himself as a Hero Twin aligns the ruler with the forces that hold nature in balance and endows

him with the magical ability to control the Gods of the Underworld.

The Maya were not the only people who used their myths to enforce kingship. The kings of Europe and Asia loudly proclaimed a divine right to rule. The Maya rulers may have taken this process one step further. Not only do they claim the divine right but also descent directly from the gods. The Palenque rulers, Pacal and his son Chan Bahlum, declare that their lineage descends directly from the Mother of the Gods, and Chan Bahlum goes on to say that he and the Mother of the Gods are one and the same (Schele 1987).

Since the story of the Popol Vuh deals with the conflict between the Hero Twins and the Lords of the Underworld, another aspect of the competition is

Figure 7.7. Slate scepter reverse. Private collection. Kerr Number 3409.

Figure 7.8. Ball court marker from Copan, Honduras. The Ruler 18 Rabbit as a ball player. Drawing by Barbara Fash.

the ball game. Briefly, the Twins, as ballplayers, are summoned to Xibalba (the underworld) to confront the Lords of the Underworld in a cosmic ball game (Miller and Houston 1982).

The story of the ball game is utilized as an instrument of authority, as in the case of 18 Rabbit of Copan. On this ball court marker (Fig. 7.8) we see him as a ballplayer in a game against one of the underworld denizens (Schele and Miller 1986). The text tells us (in a paraphrase) that 18 Rabbit, as Hunahpu, is the player, and as such is the intermediary between the underworld and the real world. He literally "carries the ball" for his people. Chan Bahlum uses the title Ah Pitz, Bac le balam-ahau, or "He of the Ballgame" (Schele 1987:82), a reference to the Hero Twins as ballplayers. On monuments and

buildings, ball court markers, and portable objects, the rulers continually proclaim their connection to the gods as well as their ability to enter the underworld and interact with them.

On the Dumbarton Oaks Tablet (Fig. 7.9) Kan Xul, the brother of Chan Bahlum, is seen dancing as G1, in the same manner as we see Chac Xib Chac dancing on another codex-style vase (Fig. 7.10). He shows himself as G1 in order to prove his connection to the gods and his ability to move in this world and in the other world. On Tablet XIV, from Palenque, Chan Bahlum dances dressed as G3, again stating his otherworld connections (Fig. 7.11)

Another device that the rulers used to prove their connection to the Hero Twins was the use of the ceremonial bar. As we see on Stela 16 from Dos Pilas (Fig. 7.12) the ruler holds this ceremonial bar across his chest as supernaturals emerge from either end. On a codex-style vase (Fig. 7.13) we see the same type of ceremonial bar held in the arms of a Hero Twin. In this case the serpent of Xibalba entwines through the bar. The Popol Vuh tells us that after going through various trials forced on them by the Lords of the Underworld, the Heroes take refuge inside their blowguns. Since we are dealing with

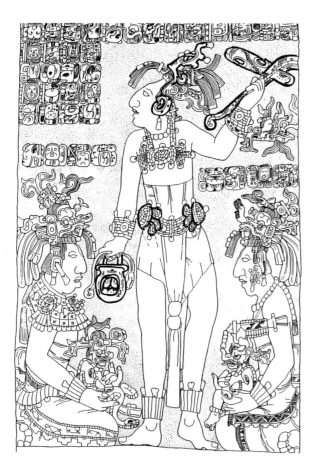

Figure 7.9. Kan Xul of Palenque portraying himself as G1. The Dumbarton Oaks tablet. Drawing by Linda Schele.

supernaturals, it would not be illogical for them to increase the size of the blowgun so that they may take refuge there. In the case of the Naranjo Stela and others like it, the ceremonial bar is often shown as the mythological blowgun. Here again, the ruler shows his control of the universe by carrying the weapon of the Hero Twins.

A model of how a ruler presents himself as a powerful mortal with the supernatural capability of interacting with the underworld is clearly shown in the Palenque Cross Group, built by the ruler Chan Bahlum (his accession 9.12.11.12.10 8 Oc 3 Kayab, or January 10, A.D. 684). Chan Bahlum finished the Temple of Inscriptions, his father's tomb, and then proceeded to erect the Cross Group. On the piers of the Temple of Inscriptions, he portrays himself in his father's arms, as a supernatural. One of his legs has

turned into a snake, identifying him as Chac Xib Chac (Fig. 7.14; Green Robertson 1983)

Inside each of the three buildings of the Cross Group there are tablets on which Chan Bahlum writes his history. He starts at the beginning of time, telling of the birth of the Mother of the Gods, the birth of the Palenque Triad (the Gods G1 G2 G3) and his ancestors both mythological and real. The tablets contain pictorial representations as well as text, and it is in the iconography of the scenes that he uses the mythology of the Popol Vuh to prove his right to rule.

The entrance to the Temple of the Cross, where the text begins, is guarded by two figures, Chan Bahlum on one side and God L on the other. Chan Bahlum is wearing his costume of royalty and tells us briefly that he is the legitimate heir of the blood-line of Palenque. He faces God L, suggesting the conflict with the underworld which is to follow. The inner panel shows Chan Bahlum preparing to receive the trappings of royalty from his father in the midst of images of the underworld (Fig. 7.15).

In the Temple of the Sun, the inner panel contains the next part of the story (Fig. 7.16) Chan Bahlum holds the symbols of office; groveling at his feet and supporting his jaguar throne are two Lords of the Underworld. On the left is God L, whom we saw in the Temple of the Cross, and on the right is God D, another of the Lords of the Underworld. The gods are now in the traditional pose of prisoners. Tedlock's translation of the Popol Vuh tells it this way:

And when they arrived,
  they all bent down low in surrender,
  they arrived meek and tearful.
(Tedlock 1985:155)

A scene on a codex-style vase (Fig. 7.17) illustrates the subjection of the gods. The Maize God (Hun Hunahpu, the father of the Twins) has been resurrected, and acts out the final scene. The Popol Vuh describes the Lords in defeat this way:

Their ancient day was not a great one,
  these ancient people only wanted conflict,
  their ancient names are not really divine,
  but fearful is the ancient evil of their faces.
They are the makers of enemies, users of owls,
  they are inciters to wrongs and violence,

Figure 7.10. G1 dancing in the underworld. From a Rollout photograph of a Maya vase. Kerr Number 1370.

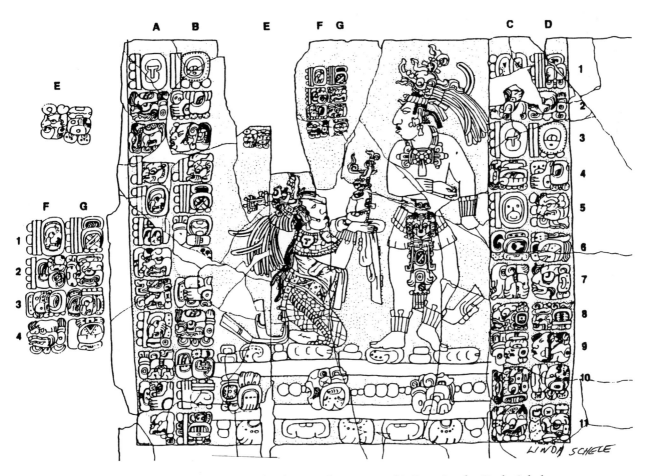

Figure 7.11. Chan Bahlum of Palenque dancing as G1. Drawing by Linda Schele.

Figure 7.12. A ruler of Naranjo holding a ceremonial bar. Stela 12 of Naranjo. From a rubbing by Merle Green Robertson.

they are the masters of hidden intentions as well,
they are the black and white,
masters of stupidity, masters of perplexity,
as it is said.
By putting on appearances they cause dismay,
Such was the loss of their greatness and brillance.
Their domain did not return to greatness.
This was accomplished by Hunaphu and
Xbalanque.
(Tedlock 1985:158)

On the panel of the Temple of the Foliated Cross (Fig. 7.18) is the final act in the story. Here Chan Bahlum is again receiving the symbols of royalty, but the underworld imagery has changed. He has made himself into the image of the Maize God. He wears the apron of the Maize God decorated with jeweled ornaments. On a codex-style vase (Fig. 7.19) are images of women dressing the Maize God. The adornments they carry are the same as those worn by Chan Bahlum (Taube 1983).

Chan Bahlum is not the only ruler to adopt this scene. On a carved bone excavated at Copan (Fig. 7.20) the ruler, Yax Pac, is shown in the typical scene of being dressed as the Maize God (Schele and Miller 1986:152). This scene of women dressing the young corn god appears on a number of poly-chrome vessels as well.

The transformation is apparent. Freidel and Schele (1985) have shown that Chan Bahlum on this panel is "First Father," another name for Hun Hunahpu, the Maize God, the father of the Hero Twins. The Popol Vuh tells us that after the defeat of the Lords of the Underworld, the Twins, Hunahpu and Xbalanque, resurrect their father. Tedlock (1985:159) translates the passage this way:

And the first to die, a long time before, had been their fathers, One Hunaphu and Seven Hunaphu. And they saw the face of their father again, there in Xibalba. Their father spoke to them again when they had defeated Xibalba. And here their father is put back together by them.

On a codex-style plate (Fig. 7.21) the image of the resurrection is shown. The Maize God, or Hun Hunahpu, is emerging from a turtle carapace, a symbol of the earth. He is flanked by his two sons, Hunahpu, written here as Hun Ahau, and Xbalanque, written here as Yax Balam.

By assuming the guise of the Hero Twins, Chan Bahlum has said that as Hunahpu and the resurrected Hun Hunahpu, he has gone to the underworld, gambled his existence in a ball game, and eventually, through magic and artifice, defeated the Lords of the Underworld, and holds them powerless. He is the guardian of his people, and with his blood lineage, is secure in his right to rule.

Figure 7.13. Hero Twin holding a mythological blowgun. From a Rollout photograph of a Maya vase. Kerr Number 2715.

Figure 7.14. Pacal of Palenque holding his son Chan Bahlum, as the baby G1. Drawing by Merle Green Robertson.

Figure 7.15. Panel from the Temple of the Cross, Palenque. Drawing by Linda Schele.

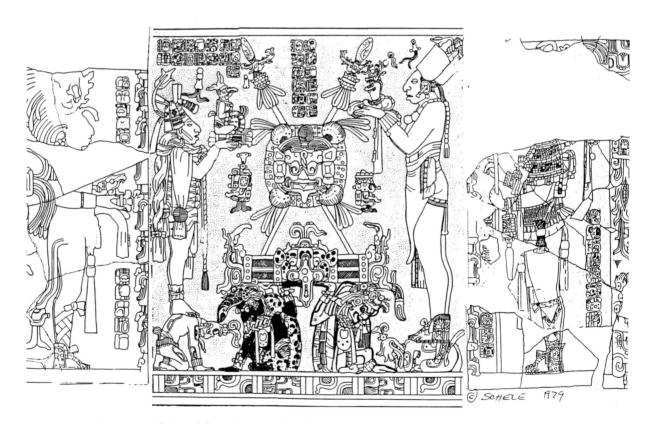

Figure 7.16. Panel from the Temple of the Sun, Palenque. Drawing by Linda Schele.

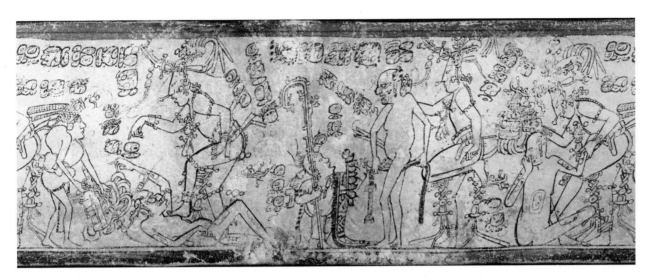

Figure 7.17. The Lords of the Underworld being humiliated by Hun Hunahpu. From a Rollout photograph of a Maya vase. Kerr Number 1560.

Figure 7.18. Panel from the Temple of the Foliated Cross, Palenque. Drawing by Linda Schele.

Figure 7.19. Hun Hunahpu being dressed by ladies. From a Rollout photograph of a Maya vase. Kerr Number 1202.

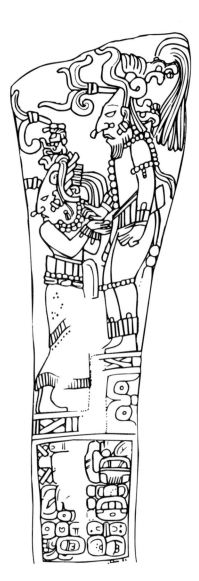

Figure 7.20. Yax Pac of Copan being dressed by a lady. Drawing by Barbara Kerr.

Figure 7.21. Scene of the resurrection of Hun Hunahpu. Photograph by J. Kerr. Kerr Number 1892.

BIBLIOGRAPHY

Coe, M. D.
1973   *The Maya Scribe and His World*. New York: The Grolier Club.
1989   The Hero Twins: Myth and Image. In *The Maya Vase Book*, vol. 1, pp. 161-184, ed. J. Kerr. New York: Kerr Associates.

Cortez, C.
1986   The Principal Bird Deity in Pre-Classic and Early Classic Maya Art. Master's thesis, University of Texas at Austin.

Freidel, D., and L. Schele
1985   Knot Skull the Shining Seed. Death Rebirth and Heroic Amplification in the Lowland Maya Ballgame. International Symposium on the Mesoamerican Ballgame and Ballcourts, Tucson, AZ.

Greene Robertson, M.
1983   *The Sculpture of Palenque*, vol. 1. Princeton: Princeton University Press.

Lounsbury, F.
1985   The Identities of the Mythological Figures in the "Cross Group" of Inscriptions at Palenque. In *Fourth Round Table of Palenque 1980*, vol. 6, M. Greene Robertson, general editor. Pre-Columbian Research Institute, San Francisco.

Miller, M., and S. Houston
1982   *Stairways and Ballcourt Glyphs: New Perspectives on the Classic Maya Ballgame*. New Haven: Yale University Press.

Schele, L.
1987   *Workbook for the Maya Hieroglyphic Writing Workshop at Texas*. Austin: University of Texas.

Schele, L., and M. Miller
1986   *The Blood of Kings: Dynasty and Ritual in Maya Art*. Photographs by J. Kerr. Fort Worth, TX: Kimbell Art Museum.

Spero, J. M.
1990   Beyond Rainstorms: The KAWAK as an Ancestor, Warrior and Patron of Witchcraft. In *Sexta Mesa Redonda de Palenque*, vol. 8. M. Greene Robertson, general editor. San Francisco: Pre-Columbian Art Institute.

Taube, K.
1985   The Classic Maya Maize God: A Reappraisal. In *The Fifth Palenque Round Table, 1983*, vol. 7, pp. 171-181. M. Greene Robertson, general editor. San Francisco: Pre-Columbian Art Research Institute.

Tedlock, D.
1985   *Popul Vuh, The Definitive Edition of The Mayan Book of the Dawn of Life and the Glories of Gods and Kings*. New York: Simon and Schuster

VIII

New Ceremonial and Settlement Evidence at La Venta, and its Relation to Preclassic Maya Cultures

William F. Rust, III

Department of Anthropology
University of Pennsylvania

PAST MODELS OF LA VENTA

Since its rediscovery in the 1920s (Blom and LaFarge 1926-1927), La Venta has both promised and withheld, in its swampy rain-forest setting, essential keys to understanding the origins of civilization in Mesoamerica. First excavations in the site's central portion during the 1940s and 1950s (Drucker 1952; Drucker et al. 1959) revealed large scale, sophisticated artistic work and ceremonial deposits, showing that the Gulf coast Olmec (ca. 1150-500 B.C.) were a focus of primary civilization in Middle America as well as a likely precursor to later, better-known Classic Maya cultures. Conspicuously lacking, however, from early investigations at La Venta and other Olmec sites was a full body of evidence on settlement, subsistence, population size, and the actual range of social groups that made up this early complex society. Lack of such explanatory evidence has been particularly acute in the case of the Olmec, whose rise as a primary civilization in a swampy lowland setting has, to many, always seemed anomalous (Sanders and Price 1968; Coe and Diehl 1980).

To help provide such needed evidence on Olmec social structure and subsistence, my own survey at La Venta during 1986-1987 focused on the location and testing of areas of houses, workshops, burials, and other primary remains of settlement, domestic life, and economic activities. The resultant findings (Rust and Sharer 1988), summarized below, show clear evidence of an unexpectedly dense and complex riverine settlement pattern developing at and around La Venta from the Early Preclassic (ca. 2250-1150 B.C.) through the Middle Preclassic (1150-500 B.C.) periods. During a peak phase of 800-500 B.C., La Venta and surrounding villages were occupied by a diverse and stratified range of groups including artisans, traders, subsistence workers such as fishers and farmers, religious specialists, and chiefly or elite families.

These findings show a social structure too complex to be accurately mirrored by previous, traditional models of La Venta as a vacant ceremonial center (Drucker et al. 1959; Sanders 1971; Lamberg-Karlovsky and Sabloff 1979), and are consistent with a series of recent Lowland Maya studies that, since the 1960s, have gradually replaced this older hypothesis (Becker 1979; Ashmore 1978; Willey et al. 1965). The vacant center model, partly derived from ethnographic study of the Highland Maya peasant groups in Chiapas and Guatemala (Vogt 1961), has proposed low-density, slash-and-burn agriculture as the support base of Lowland Maya ceremonial centers, whose society was seen as a simple priest-peasant dichotomy. This model, which has been proved generally inaccurate in the case of Classic Lowland Maya centers by findings of dense nonnucleated settlement and intensive agriculture, now seems inappropriate for the much earlier Olmec site of La Venta as well (Turner 1974; Rust and Sharer 1988).

Although the vacant-center model was almost routinely applied to La Venta during the early analysis of the 1940s and 1950s, examination of these reports shows that the actual, empirical basis for interpreting the site as a vacant center was scanty (Drucker 1952; Drucker et al. 1959). While emphasis was placed on low ceramic counts at a few test excavations, which were then used as a kind of self-fulfilling prophecy to discount the need for further settlement studies. As a result, no additional systematic sampling of the areas around the La Venta ceremonial zone was attempted until the present studies of 1986-1987.

Meanwhile, the opinion has generally prevailed that La Venta's Middle Preclassic enviroment (1150-500 B.C.) was, just as today, a swampy terrain with little potential for concentrated permanent settlement. This static view of the local enviroment, in turn, reinforced the notion that a swampy, inhospitable location was chosen deliberately by Preclassic founders of the La Venta center, for its very isolation (Tamayo and West 1964:95). Because of ongoing lack of positive evidence, this vacant-center perspective on La Venta's enviroment has remained in general use until the present, with La Venta typically portrayed as a site without promise of settlement evidence (Lamberg-Karlovsky and Sabloff 1979; Swanson, Bray, and Farrington 1989).

LA VENTA ENVIRONMENT

The actual picture emerging from present investigations of enviroment, settlement, and social groupings at ancient La Venta is quite different from that of a remote religious sanctuary with little permanent settlement. Current findings show, instead, that La Venta evolved in the midst of a changing estuarine and riverine enviroment which saw significant rises in Preclassic population densities and social complexity occuring in conjunction with alterations in overall riverine regimes (Rust and Sharer 1988).

A central finding, derived from study of aerial photographs, shows the existence of intensive Preclassic settlement along a now extinct river course, the Río Bari (Rust 1987; Rust and Sharer 1988). This ancient river, which passed right by La Venta's northern end (Fig. 8.1), extended from the eastern limits of Olmec territory to the Gulf of Mexico, a distance of greater than 50 km. Between 2250 and 500 B.C., spanning the Early and Middle Preclassic eras, settlement along the Río Bari evolved from small-scale populations relying on cultivated

maize as well as fish, molluscs, and other aquatic resources to a relatively complex range of site types including both local ceremonial center villages and lower-status village sites. By the Late La Venta period (800-500 B.C.), when local population was at a maximum, differences in social status at various sites were clearly reflected in both subsistence and ceremonial practices.

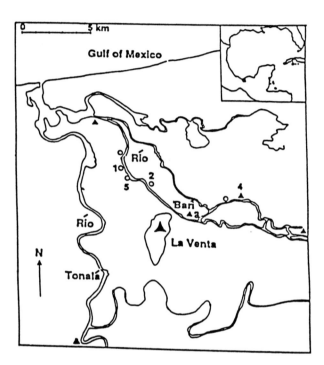

Figure 8.1. Map of the La Venta region showing levee occupational sites along the abandoned Río Bari channels.

NEW LA VENTA FINDINGS

Recent findings on La Venta itself have provided another key basis for redefining local patterns of Preclassic cultural change and chronology. Testing from 100 to 500 m north and east of the Great Mound revealed a series of large occupation zones, beginning in the Middle and Late Bari periods (ca. 1750-1150 B.C.), when La Venta "island" (actually a salt dome about 4 km long) was first permanently settled (Rust and Sharer 1988). Occupation in these zones continued to grow during the subsequent,

Early La Venta period (1150-800 B.C.), when La Venta first arose as an important ceremonial focus for local riverine populations and when neighboring San Lorenzo was at its peak as a religious and artistic center (Coe and Diehl 1980).

During the Late La Venta period (800-500 B.C.), the site reached a maximum of both local settlement density and wide-ranging influence in trade and ceremonial control. At this time, the ridgetop containing La Venta's main ceremonial precinct also contained clusters of houses and storage pits; lithic workshop areas for serpentine, an exotic green stone transported in vast quantities into La Venta, probably by river; and burial and offering zones for varying statuses of people, some clearly distinct from the elite offerings or caches found previously in Complex A (Drucker 1952; Drucker et al. 1959). Radiocarbon dates from several of these settlement features cluster around 700-800 B.C., and show that, during this time, La Venta's central core contained numerous residential and artisan areas as well as ceremonial zones representing at least two strata of Olmec society.

Relatively large and well-preserved ceramic and utilitarian artifact samples recovered during this survey from La Venta's Complexes E and G have also contradicted prior notions, derived from early testing in the 1940s, that the site contains only small, poorly preserved settlement remains (Drucker 1952). These new La Venta findings, in turn, now allow detailed comparisons with recently discovered, adjacent Río Bari sites, whose ceramics, figurines, and other artifacts are closely similar and often identical to La Venta's.

Four major ceramic wares were consistently used during the Late La Venta period (800-500 B.C.). These wares include fine paste vessels, usually a ceremonial or elite ware with black-and-white, differentially fired surfaces and frequent symbolic decoration; medium sandy paste, slipped and unslipped wares, both often decorated with incised design motifs; and coarse paste ware, usually undecorated and serving as everyday, utilitarian vessels such as tecomates (neckless cooking jars), cantaros (narrow-necked water storage jars), and ollas (wide-necked cooking jars).

In general, Late La Venta period ceramics and figurines strongly resemble those of the same time in the Grijalva valley of Chiapas, the Pacific coast of Guatemala, the Tehuacan valley in Puebla, and at San Lorenzo in Veracruz (Coe 1961; MacNeish et al. 1970; Coe and Diehl 1980; Lowe 1989). Frequent designs incised on fine- and medium-paste vessels include the well-known double-line-break motif, probably a shorthand, symbolic rendering of an Olmec deity (Joralemon 1971); hatched triangles, often found on fine-paste ceremonial bowls, also with probable symbolic meaning; and zoned punctate or rocker-stamped designs made with hollow reeds or shells. Also typical of the Late La Venta period ceramic complex, and found at all site types, is the use of red and white slips or painted surfaces, which show long-term localized development (Rust 1987). Some red- or cream-slipped vessels with a waxy, soapstonelike ingredient also show ties to late Middle Preclassic, Mamom period ceramics such as Joventud Red from the Maya lowlands (Smith 1955; Gifford 1965; Andrews 1986).

Typical Late La Venta figurines include slender nude females, some of which may be adolescents; males with helmets, some representing ballplayers with yokelike belts, and others possibly portraits (see Grove and Gillespie 1984); chubby, turbaned figures with upraised arms, sometimes wearing mirror or medallion necklaces; and seated, infantlike figures from burial and ceramic offering contexts (Rust 1987). The high frequency of ceramic figurines found in various domestic features at La Venta is repeated at outlying mound sites on the Río Bari (Rust and Sharer 1988), suggesting broad-based status associations for these, unlike jade figurines whose main provenience is so far limited to elite offerings in La Venta's main ceremonial zone (Drucker 1952; Drucker et al. 1959).

RIO BARI SITES

Findings at Río Bari sites closely resemble artifact and feature types already indicated for La Venta, with the added proviso that here, at levee sites such as San Andres and Isla Alor (see Fig. 1), occupation began earlier. Deepest excavated levels at San Andres, 5-6 m below the present surface, reveal that an early village settlement based on maize cultivation, and with simple coarse-ware ceramics, had begun by 2250-1750 B.C. in the Early Bari period. Here, pollen, faunal, and stratigraphic analysis show an ancient estuarine, or tidal river, setting with dominant mangrove vegetation that was cleared for maize growing (Rust and Leyden 1990). Brackish water molluscs such as *Rangia cuneata* were also heavily exploited for food, along with fish and wild plant foods such as palm nuts (Rust and Sharer 1988). At that time, in a mangrove setting related to, but distinct from, the fresh water swamp which today surrounds La Venta (West et al. 1969), the material culture of La Venta sites seems to have been relatively simple and egalitarian, with subsistence tied to both maize and immediate marine and riverine resources.

This pattern continued during the Middle and Late Bari periods (ca. 1750-1150 B.C.), which saw heavy alluvial deposition in the lowlands north of La Venta. Now, however, widespread permanent settlement occured for the first time on elevated Río Bari levees as well as on La Venta itself. Utilitarian materials now include an increase in manos and metates (corn-grinding implements) of imported basalt, with population rise coincident with growing use of domesticated maize (Rust and Leyden 1990).

During the ensuring Early and Late La Venta periods (1150-500 B.C.), settlement expanded throughout the entire Río Bari and adjacent riverine zones, with overall population between La Venta and San Miguel, 40 km to the east, probably as high as 10,000 during the Late La Venta peak. By this time, two basic site types evolved in the La Venta riverine periphery, sites with and without central mounds. Both site types show continued use of early dietary staples of maize, fish, and turtle, but a contrast in the presence or absence of central mounds, ceremonial apparatus, elite ceramics, figurines, and large-vertebrate food remains (Rust and Sharer 1988). Río Bari sites with central mounds, echoing La Venta, show local ceremonial control and higher-status activities, while sites without mounds, like some settlement areas on La Venta itself, seem to have been basically utilitarian, lower-status villages.

Dietary differences observed in the two La Venta site types seem especially promising in leading to a clearer understanding of Olmec social structure (Rust 1989). Presumably lower-status, Río Bari sites without mounds show more strict continuity with earlier subsistence patterns, including maize and a faunal assemblage dominated by local, easily accessible turtle and fish. Río Bari sites with central mounds and ceremonial apparatus consistently have, in addition to these traditional resources, large-vertebrate food remains, including crocodilians as well as deer and domesticated dogs.

Although such vertebrates have long been recognized as an important part of Preclassic Gulf Coast diet (Wing 1987), faunal studies up to now concentrated mainly on larger sites with mounds. Current work at newly discovered mound and nonmound sites along Río Bari levees shows that large-vertebrate food remains are mostly restricted to sites with central mounds (Rust 1989). In addition to material advantages held by higher-status villagers, which probably included some control over trade of subsistence items, food restrictions or taboos may also have occurred. Differential presence of crocodilian faunal remains at La Venta sites, meanwhile, raises new possibilities for linking subsistence findings to iconographic studies of both Olmec and Maya symbolism, as well as for improved focus on distinctions in Olmec social groupings (Joralemon 1971; Stocker et al. 1980).

Present evidence, in summary, suggests at least three social strata in La Venta Olmec society: (1) chiefs or elite families, represented by Complex A offerings as well as some Río Bari deposits; (2) craftsworkers and merchants, occupying both La Venta's center in areas such as Complexes E and G, and the Río Bari sites; and (3) primary subsistence workers such as fishers and farmers, occupying nonmound village sites both off and on La Venta. The corresponding overall social structure seems to be that of an advanced chiefdom in the process of evolving into an early stratified society, with La Venta identifiable as a temple town both administrating and surrounded by complex social groupings (Redman 1978; Rust 1988; Rust and Sharer 1988). At the evolutionary base of La Venta and its support zone sites lay the fertile riverine setting of the Río Bari, whose yearly-flooded levees could be continually farmed, allowing permanent settlement and population growth. A dual subsistence base of maize and other domesticates, combined with local aquatic foods such as fish and turtles, provided long-term stability, which underlay the development of complex society at both La Venta and other Olmec sites such as San Lorenzo (Wing 1978; Coe and Diehl 1980; Rust 1989). Although the causes of emergent stratification in Olmec society are not yet understood, they may well have included competition over prime riverine lands and trade control (Adams 1966; Carneiro 1970).

Figure 8.2. Portion of Late Preclassic carved and incised ceramic vessel from San Miguel, ca. 500-200 B.C.

RELATION TO EARLY MAYA CULTURES

During the Middle Preclassic, Late La Venta period (800-500 B.C.), certain developments at La Venta and its neighboring riverine sites closely parallel traits found in contemporary lowland Maya sites. These include the basic estuarine and riverine subsistence traditions just described, with settlements and ceremonial areas following rivers in dispersed clusters (Ashmore 1978; Willey et al. 1965; Bullard 1960). Other similar traits include the practice of urn burials (Andrews 1981), the status-related use of polished greenstones, and the use of some ceramic and figurine types resembling Mamom types (Smith 1955).

Evidence of changing riverine courses by the Late Preclassic era (500 B.C.-A.D. 200) fits an overall picture of basic shifts in settlement and the relocation of major centers. Ties between the late Olmec and early Maya cultures are especially notable in centers such as San Miguel, located 40 km east of La Venta. San Miguel began in the Late La Venta period as a relatively small village cluster in the Río Bari zone. During the first half of the Late Preclassic, after La Venta's demise as a major center, San Miguel grew considerably in size and importance; several earthern mounds ranging up to 12 m in height were constructed in a central plaza, where stone sculpture occurs in styles closely allied to Late Preclassic examples from Pacific coastal Chiapas (Parsons

1986; Stirling 1957).

During the Early San Miguel period (500-200 B.C.), the site shows increasingly clear evidence of links between this portion of the Gulf coast and the developing complex society in the Maya regions of the east and south. One recently excavated deposit in San Miguel's central mound group, radiocarbon dated at about 300 B.C., produced elaborately carved and incised ceramics that closely resemble contemporary "Post-Olmec" or Izapan-style carvings at Kaminaljuyu and other Late Preclassic centers (Rust 1987; see Fig. 8.2). Complex, curvilinear motifs of dragons, crocodilians, or other earth monsters on this pottery are intermediate between earlier motifs associated with La Venta and forms found in later Maya symbolism (Parsons 1986). Other traits of the Late Preclassic San Miguel ceramic complex, including a predominance of incised, wide-everted rim bowls, are also closely comparable to Chicanel period ceramics from the Maya lowlands (Smith 1955; Gifford 1965) as well as to contemporary materials at Tehuacan Valley sites (MacNeish et al. 1970).

By the Late Preclassic period, when the focus of regional ceremonial and political power shifts from La Venta to sites in the sphere of highland Kaminaljuyu, transformations of trade and ideological networks leading to Classic Maya culture are well under way. In the meantime, the original riverine subsistence and settlement complex that had supported the development of La Venta, San Lorenzo, and other Gulf Coast Olmec centers, basically continues at emergent centers such as San Miguel in the context of new political and trade alliances. Such new centers typically occur in strategic riverine or interriverine zones, a pattern suggesting trade control practices that continues in Lowland Maya centers.

These new findings from La Venta—revealing the long-term development of complex settlement within a changing riverine environment—offer a much-improved focus on specific trends in Preclassic Gulf coast subsistence, social structure, and ceremony. Most importantly, the assured presence of such evidence at La Venta, often doubted previously, now shows new possibilities of a more general understanding of the evolution of primary civilizations in tropical lowland settings, through processes observable in the archaeological record of Olmec society. While some old myths about La Venta have been necessarily overturned, this only clears the way for a closer view of this important early civilization and its apparent relation to subsequent Maya culture.

ACKNOWLEDGMENTS

A preliminary version of this paper was read on April 9, 1987, at the 5th Annual Maya Weekend, held

at The University Museum, University of Pennsylvania, Philadelphia, PA. The La Venta settlement research was supported by the Francis Boyer Fund of The University Museum and NSF Grant #BNS-8518557, and it was conducted in collaboration with the Proyecto Arqueológico La Venta of the Mexican Instituto Nacional de Antropología e Historia.

BIBLIOGRAPHY

Adams, R. McC.
1966   *The Evolution of Urban Society*. New York: Aldine.

Andrews, E. W., V
1981   Dzibilchaltun. In *Handbook of Middle American Indians*, Supplement 1, ed. J. A. Sabloff, pp. 313-241. Austin: University of Texas Press.
1986   Olmec Jades from Chacsinkin, Yucatan, and Maya Ceramics from La Venta, Tabasco. *Middle American Research Institute* 57:11-49. New Orleans: Tulane University Press.

Ashmore, W. (editor)
1978   *Lowland Maya Settlement Patterns*. School of American Research. Albuquerque: University of New Mexico Press.

Becker, M. J.
1979   Priests, Peasants and Ceremonial Centers: The Intellectual History of a Model. In *Maya Archaeology and Ethnohistory*, eds. N. Hammond and G. Willey, pp. 3-20. Austin: University of Texas Press.

Blom, F., and O. La Farge
1926-1927 *Tribes and Temples*. New Orleans: Tulane University Press.

Bullard, W. R.
1960   Maya Settlement Patterns in Northeastern Peten, Guatemala. *American Antiquity* 2(3):1-56.

Carneiro, R. L.
1970   A Theory of the Origin of the State. *Science* 169:733-738.

Coe, M. D.
1961   *La Victoria: An Early Site on the Pacific Coast of Guatemala*. Peabody Museum Papers 53. Cambridge, MA: Harvard University Press.

Coe, M. D., and R. A. Diehl
1980   *In the Land of the Olmec*. 2 vols. Austin: University of Texas Press.

Drucker, P.
1952   *La Venta, Tabasco: A Study of Olmec Ceramics and Art*. Smithsonian Institution, Bureau of American Ethnology. Bulletin 153.

Drucker, P., R. F. Heizer, and R. J. Squier
1959   *Excavations at La Venta, Tabasco, 1955*. Smithsonian Institution, Bureau of American Ethnology, Bulletin 170. Washington, DC.

Gifford, J. C.
1965   Ceramics. In *Prehistoric Settlements in the Belize Valley*, by G. R. Willey et al. Peabody Museum Papers 54. Cambridge, MA: Harvard University Press.

Grove, D. C., and S. D. Gillespie
1984   Chalcatzingo's Portrait Figurines and the Cult of the Ruler. *Archaeology* 37(4):27-33.

Joralemon, P. D.
1971   A Study of Olmec Iconography. In *Studies in Pre-Columbian Art and Archaeology*, no. 7. Washington, DC.: Dumbarton Oaks.

Lamberg-Karlovsky, C. C., and J. A. Sabloff
1979   *Ancient Civilizations: The Near East and Mesoamerica*. Menlo Park, CA: Benjamin/Cummings.

Lowe, G. D.
1989   The Heartland Olmec: Evolution of Material Culture. In *Regional Perspectives on the Olmec*, eds. R. J. Sharer and D. C. Grove. pp. 33-67. School of American Research: Cambridge, Cambridge University Press.

MacNeish, R. S., F. Peterson, and K. V. Flannery
1970   *The Prehistory of the Tehuacan Valley*, Vol. 3: *Ceramics*. Austin: University of Texas Press.

Parsons, L. A.
1986   The Origins of Maya Art. *Studies in Pre-Columbian Art and Archaeology*, no. 28. Washington, DC.: Dumbarton Oaks.

Redman, C. L.
1978   *The Rise of Civilizations.* San Francisco: Freeman.

Rust, W. F.
1987   *1986 Preliminary Report: A Settlement Survey of La Venta and Its Riverine Periphery.* 2 vols. Proyecto Arqueologico La Venta, Instituto Nacional de Antropología e Historia, Mexico.

1988   New Settlement Evidence at La Venta. Paper read November 20, 1988, at 87th Annual Meeting, American Anthropological Association, Phoenix.

1989   Diet and Emergent Social Stratification in Olmec Civilization. Paper read January 9, 1989, at the First Joint Archaeological Congress, Baltimore.

Rust, W. F., and B. W. Leyden
1990   Evidence of Maize Use at Early and Middle Preclassic La Venta Olmec Sites. Paper read May 11, 1990, at the symposium "Corn and Culture in the Prehistoric New World," University of Minnesota, Minneapolis.

Rust, W. F., and R. J. Sharer
1988   Olmec Settlement Data from La Venta, Tabasco, Mexico. *Science* 242:102-104

Sanders, W. T.
1971   Settlement Patterns of the Gulf Coast. In *Handbook of Middle American Indians*, vol. 11, eds. G. F. Eckholm and I. Bernal. Austin: University of Texas Press.

Sanders, W. T., and B. J. Price
1968   *Mesoamerica: The Evolution of a Civilization.* New York: Random House.

Smith, R. E.
1955   *Ceramic Sequence at Uaxactun, Guatemala.* 2 vols. Middle American Research Institute, Publication 20. New Orleans: Tulane University Press.

Stirling, M. W.
1957   *An Archaeological Reconnaissance in Southwestern Tabasco.* Smithsonian Institution. *Bureau of American Ethnology Bulletin* 164:213-240.

Stocker, T., S. Meltzoff, and S. Armsey
1980   Crocodilians and Olmecs: Further Interpretations in Formative Period Iconography. *American Antiquity* 45(4):740-758.

Swanson, E. H., W. Bray, and I. Farrington
1989   *The Ancient Americas.* London: Peter Bedrick.

Tamayo, J. L., and R. C. West
1964   The Hydrography of Middle America. In *Handbook of Middle American Indians*, vol. 1, ed. R. C. West. Austin: University of Texas Press.

Turner, B. L.
1974   Prehistoric Intensive Agriculture in the Maya Lowlands. *Science* 185:118-124.

Vogt, E. Z.
1961   Some Aspects of Zinacantan Settlement Patterns and Ceremonial Organization. *Estudios de Cultura Maya* 1:131-146. Universidad Autónoma de México.

West, R. C., N. P. Psuty, and B. G. Thom
1969   *The Tabasco Lowlands of Southern Mexico.* Technical Report 70, Coastal Studies Institute. Baton Rouge: Louisiana State University.

Willey, G., W. R. Bullard, J. B. Glass, and J. C. Gifford
1965   *Prehistoric Maya Settlements in the Belize Valley.* Peabody Museum Papers 74. Cambridge, MA: Harvard University press.

Wing, E.
1978   The Use of Dogs for Food. In *Prehistoric Coastal Adaptations*, eds. B. L. Stark and B. Voorhies. New York: Academic.

IX

The Preclassic Origin of Lowland Maya States

Robert J. Sharer

Department of Anthropology
University of Pennsylvania

The genesis of Maya civilization, long a major concern of archaeological research, has been the subject of several well-known theories that, for the most part, have been based on simple unilineal models. The best known of these include the indigenous Maya lowland theory, the Maya highland transplant theory, and, of course, the *cultura madre,* or Olmec, theory. Suffice it to say that, at the present time, none of these unilineal theories accounts adequately for the complexity of the evolutionary process that led to civilization, either in the Maya area or elsewhere in Mesoamerica (Sharer and Grove 1989).

Although it is still too early to claim that we have the solution to this problem, it is now clear that Maya civilization was the product of a complex, multilinear process within a broad temporal and spatial framework. The relevant time frame includes the entire Preclassic era, (ca. 2000 B.C.-A.D. 250), but the latter half of this period—Middle and Late Preclassic—was undoubtedly the most crucial. The relevant area comprises a broad array of environmental zones, including both the lowland heartland of Classic Maya civilization, the highlands to the south, and a far more vast "periphery" (see Urban and Schortman 1986).

Although a great deal of recent work has substantiated the importance of the highlands, Pacific coast, and southeastern periphery in this process (Sharer and Sedat 1987), a like amount of recent evidence bearing on the issue of the origins of Maya civilization comes from the lowland heartland area itself. Recent excavations have revealed important Preclassic developments at sites such as Cerros (Freidel 1979), Cuello (Hammond 1977), and Lamanai (Pendergast 1981), all located in the eastern lowlands of Belize (see Hammond 1986). The most dramatic findings, however, come from the lowland core, at the immense site of El Mirador (Matheny 1986), and more recently at the nearby site of Nakbe (Hansen 1988). This evidence indicates that the levels of Preclassic populations and organizational complexity were far greater than previously suspected, especially when combined with data from Preclassic sites in Belize and other lowland areas.

It is now apparent that a hierarchy of sites, scaled by size, had emerged in the lowlands by the Late Preclassic. El Mirador would occupy the uppermost position in such a hierarchy, sites such as Tikal and Lamanai might be second-order centers, sites such as Cerros might be third-order centers, and sites such as Kichpanha, fourth-order centers. Although we cannot yet describe the structure of this hierarchy in any detail, it seems reasonable to assume that the Late Preclassic polities were similar to the small-scale independent states of the Classic era (Mathews and Willey 1986; Houston this volume).

The success of any given polity (measured by duration and size of architecture and settlement) derived from a variety of factors, including location, environmental potential, economic conditions, organizational efficiency, prestige, and intersite competition. We can glimpse the reflections of the operation of these factors in the obvious distinctions between centers (size, architectural complexity, etc.) and differences in their evolutionary careers (the timing of the rise and fall of individual centers, duration and size of occupation, etc.). We are just beginning to address questions as to the organizational diversity among these polities that helps explain the less-than-random pattern visible in several episodes of growth and decline. In the central Maya lowlands we can see two or three cycles of this synchronized process—an expansion in the Late Preclassic and contraction by the Early Classic, renewed expansion in the Late Classic and a most far-reaching decline in the Terminal Classic. Of course our understanding of the Classic political order is heavily dependent upon historical data from decipherment of Classic texts, but we can see the beginnings of the lowland state system in the archaeological and iconographic record of the Late Preclassic. For the remainder of this paper I will summarize the data bearing on this issue from Nakbe and El Mirador.

Nakbe is located in northern Guatemala, in the department of El Peten, about 13 km southeast of the larger center of El Mirador (see below). Nakbe and El Mirador are connected by a causeway, and both sites were discovered in 1930 by an aerial survey of the Maya Lowlands sponsored by The University Museum (Madeira 1931). Nakbe was surveyed by Ian Graham in 1962 (Graham 1967:49). Since 1987 the site has been investigated by a project from UCLA led by Richard Hansen (1988).

Like El Mirador, Nakbe's civic-ceremonial core is divided into an eastern and western group, although this area of monumental construction covers a smaller area (ca. 0.9 km east-west) than El Mirador (see Graham 1967:48). The largest platform of Nakbe's eastern group is 32 m high, whereas the largest in the western group is 45 m high (Hansen 1989). Fragments of a new carved monument, Stela 1, were discovered in the main plaza of the western group, in front of a small platform, Structure 52. This monument has been reconstructed, revealing an outstanding example of Preclassic sculpture depicting two facing figures (Hansen 1988, 1989).

Excavations are continuing, but the results thus far have indicated that the major period of construction and occupation at Nakbe date to the Middle Preclassic. This conclusion is based on both radiocarbon dates and ceramics. Four uncorrected radiocarbon assessments date between 1000 and 450 B.C., while the overwhelming majority of pottery sherds associated with construction and occupation belong to the Middle Preclassic Mamom complex (Hansen 1989). If borne out by additional evidence—and there is every indication that this will happen—the Nakbe findings will surely revolutionize our understanding of the origins of Maya civilization. Nakbe is the first Middle Preclassic lowland Maya site with evidence of such monumental construction. Given its apparently unique architectural development in the Middle Preclassic, Nakbe is the closest thing we have to being the prototype for all subsequent low-

land Maya civic-ceremonial centers. And given its physical connection via a causeway to El Mirador, it seems likely that the sociopolitical developments reflected by Nakbe's precocious architecture were directly transferred to its larger neighbor during the Late Preclassic.

El Mirador is located north of Tikal, some 7 km south of the Mexican border. Like Nakbe, El Mirador was first surveyed by Ian Graham (1967), who, on the basis of observed sherd material and sculpture fragments, tentatively dated the site to the Late Preclassic era. Few, if any, Maya scholars accepted this evaluation at the time, because the size of constructions at the site contradicted the prevailing assessments of lowland Maya development prior to the Classic period. But Graham's estimate has been verified by a series of more recent investigations, including those directed by Dahlin (1984), Matheny (1980, 1986), and Demarest and myself (Demarest and Sharer 1982; Demarest and Fowler 1984; Sharer 1985).

El Mirador is situated at the hub of a series of causeways that radiate from the site, connecting it to an extensive hinterland, including its apparent predecessor, Nakbe. The known extent of the civic and ceremonial core covers an area some 2 km from east to west, or about the same as central Tikal. But within this area are a series of architectural complexes and individual constructions that dwarf anything built by the Maya in later times. The most distinctive of these monumental structures is the triadic pyramid (a central platform flanked by two smaller constructions integrated on a single basal platform). The largest mapped and investigated triadic pyramid, El Tigre, covers a surface area six times larger than Temple IV at Tikal (Dahlin 1984), the greatest building at that site.

El Tigre dominates a complex of structures on the western edge of the main, or western, group of monumental architecture at El Mirador. Test excavations within the Tigre pyramid itself indicate construction during the Late Preclassic, although even earlier building phases may underlie the bulk of the untested platform (Matheny 1986). Our 1982 test excavations in the plaza fronting the Tigre pyramid to its east revealed a series of superimposed floors all dating to the Late Preclassic (Demarest et al. 1984). One Sierra Red sherd recovered from the redeposited trash sealed beneath these floors was incised with a design very similar to carved motifs from Late Preclassic monuments in the southern Maya area (Abaj Takalik, Kaminaljuyu, El Porton). Terminal activity at this locus may be represented by the filling of a *chultun* in the El Tigre plaza; the trash from this feature dates to the Protoclassic era (Hansen 1985).

A small triadic platform on the south side of the Tigre complex, Structure 34, is the most thoroughly investigated building at El Mirador (Hansen 1984). Debris from roof collapse sealed Late Preclassic material on the floor of the central superstructure. A pit in the top step of the central staircase, intruded after the partial collapse of the superstructure walls, provided a carbon sample dated at 115 ± 90 B.C. (or 130 B.C., MASCA corrected; Hansen 1984:320). The principal staircase was flanked by the remains of monumental stucco deity masks, equivalent to those found on Late Preclassic platforms at other lowland sites, including Cerros, Tikal, and Uaxactun (Freidel 1977; Freidel and Schele 1983).

Test excavations were conducted within the Central Acropolis, immediately east of the Tigre complex, and south of the plaza containing the shattered remains of a few sculpted stelae possessing apparent stylistic affinities to Terminal Preclassic monuments of the southern Maya area (Graham 1967). The Central Acropolis contains a series of buildings, including at least one large complex identified as an elite residence and dated to the Late Preclassic (Matheny 1986). Overall, construction of the Central Acropolis appears to have begun during the Middle Preclassic, although the bulk of it was constructed in the Late Preclassic. As in many other areas of the site, there is evidence here of superficial construction and occupation during the Classic era (Matheny 1986).

The eastern platform complex known as Danta is the largest at the site, although its bulk includes the modification (by terracing) of a low natural hill. It supports two monumental triadic pyramids, the Pava pyramid on its southwest quadrant and the larger Danta pyramid at its eastern apex. The latter is about the same size as Tigre in basal area, but its summit is some 15 m higher, rising about 70 m above the forest floor. Excavations in the Pava pyramid (Howell 1983) indicate construction during the Late Preclassic; charcoal from burning at the base of its principal staircase—apparently representing terminal use of the structure—furnished a date of A.D. 180 (MASCA corrected). Although the Danta pyramid has

not been adequately tested by excavation, its triadic plan and method of construction are consistent with the other monumental Late Preclassic platforms at the site (Tigre, Pava, Monos, and Structure 34).

The archaeological evidence from the monumental core of El Mirador strongly favors a Late Preclassic date for most of its construction activity. In order to test the assessment of El Mirador's Preclassic date further, Demarest and I conducted a pilot settlement research program at the site in 1982 (Demarest and Sharer 1982; Demarest and Fowler 1984), aimed at locating, mapping, testing, and dating domestic remains. Prior to this work, there was simply no information about the location, size, or antiquity of such evidence. Quite obviously, the determination of the age of occupational remains at El Mirador would be instrumental in verifying the date of the site.

Our program succeeded in locating a series of residential groups in areas immediately peripheral to the civic and ceremonial core. These remains possessed the usual characteristics of lowland Maya "house platforms"—typically low, elongated mounds arranged in orthogonal patterns, usually enclosing central plaza spaces on three or four sides. Test excavations were conducted in a sample of these groups to secure occupational debris from both constructional and midden contexts.

Both contexts produced evidence of domestic occupation dating to the Late Preclassic. The midden material comprised typical debris from household activities. Of particular interest were Late Preclassic sherds reflecting direct contacts with the southern Maya area, including Usulutan decorated trade wares and local wares with probable imported highland volcanic ash temper (Bishop 1984). Earlier pottery dating to the Middle Preclassic was found in smaller quantities, usually mixed with later materials in construction fills, indicating that the origins of occupation at the site date at least this early. Excavations also documented subsequent residential activity in the Late Classic, but this settlement seems clearly to represent a reoccupation after a period of severe decline or near-abandonment (such remains are often perched on top of Preclassic monumental platforms such as the Danta complex).

It seems clear, therefore, that El Mirador represents a significant Late Preclassic development—the largest known site for its time in the Maya area. Beyond this, El Mirador is also part of a widespread emergence of sociopolitical complexity in the Maya area during the Late Preclassic. Although neither El Mirador nor any other coeval lowland site possessed all the distinctive material traits that characterize the elite subculture of the Classic period, there can be little doubt that the scale of architectural planning and execution at El Mirador signals the presence of a powerful elite that controlled its destiny. At the same time, the disparity in sheer size between El Mirador and other Late Preclassic sites may be a clue to organizational diversity within the elite segment of society; at minimum it would seem to reflect relative differences in power derived from control over human and natural resources among lowland sites. The traditional theories of the evolution of Classic Maya civilization cannot account for the El Mirador evidence, especially given the rapid growth and unprecedented size of its constructions. It is obvious, therefore, that to better understand the origins of Maya civilization we need to know more about El Mirador (along with its neighbor, Nakbe).

It is safe to assume that there was an evolutionary relationship between the Preclassic elite and the far-better-documented ruling class of the Classic era, although the details of this connection remain little known. But intervening factors undoubtedly complicated the link between Preclassic and Classic elites. These include the still poorly understood collapse of many Preclassic centers at the onset of the Classic period, especially the apparently rather swift decline of El Mirador itself. It would seem that this process was due to a transformation of the lowland elite and the political system under their control at the onset of the Classic period (Freidel and Schele 1983), although the degree to which this change was due to internal versus external factors—specifically influences from the southern Maya area (Freidel 1979, 1981; Sharer and Sedat 1987)—remains to be explicated. With more complete art-historical and historical evidence from the Classic period, the role of external intervention in the political affairs of lowland centers such as Tikal can be discerned (Coggins 1975, 1976). It is probable that similar events had significant impacts on Preclassic political evolution—at El Mirador and elsewhere in the lowlands—but lacking adequate art-historical and historical evidence these may remain invisible in the archaeological record.

In the emergent Maya polities of the Preclassic era, political authority appears to have been less centralized than in later times. Although the institution of the hereditary ruler may have emerged by this time, Preclassic political authority seems to have been based on the mediation between gods and men. This is reflected in the archaeological record by huge expenditures on monumental public ritual architecture dedicated to the gods rather than individual rulers. The earliest known examples of such architecture appear to be at Nakbe, dating to the Middle Preclassic. Following the apparent decline of Nakbe, the even larger temple platforms of El Mirador became the most dramatic examples of monumental architecture produced by the Maya, but similar buildings were constructed at Tikal, Cerros, and several other Late Preclassic sites. At the same time there was little investment on behalf of individual members of the elite—a relative lack of emphasis on palace architecture or funerary embellishments.

During the Classic era, with the development of political authority vested in rulers who increasingly assumed supernatural identities, we see nearly the opposite pattern. By the Late Classic the greatest architectural investments were made on behalf of individual rulers in the construction of great funerary temples (together with their tombs) and palaces. But although many of the Preclassic polities dramatically declined or were completely abandoned at the onset of the Classic period (the greatest, El Mirador, never recovered and never gained the status of a Classic polity), no one has been compelled to label this process a collapse of Maya civilization. Rather, it seems reasonable to view it as an evolutionary transformation—one centered on the kind of changes in the elite political order described above—within the overall trajectory of Maya lowland development.

BIBLIOGRAPHY

Bishop, R. L.
1984   Análisis por activacion de neutrones de la cerámica de El Mirador. *Mesoamérica* 5(7):103-111.

Coggins, C. C.
1975   Painting and Drawing Styles at Tikal: An Historical and Iconographic Reconstruction. Unpublished Ph.D. dissertation, Harvard University.
1976   Teotihuacan at Tikal in the Early Classic Period. *Actes de XLIIe Congres International des Américanistes* 8:251-269.

Dahlin, B. H.
1984   A Colossus in Guatemala: The Preclassic City of El Mirador. *Archaeology* 37(5):18-25.

Demarest, A. A., and W. R. Fowler (editors)
1984   Proyecto El Mirador de la Harvard University, 1982-1983. *Mesoamerica* 5(7):1-160.

Demarest, A. A., and R. J. Sharer
1982   The 1982 Ceramic Excavation Program at El Mirador, Guatemala. Paper presented at the 44th International Congress of Americanists, Manchester, England.

Demarest, A. A., R. J. Sharer, W. L. Fowler, E. King, and J. Fowler
1984   Las excavaciones. In *Proyecto El Mirador de la Harvard University, 1982-1983*, eds. A. A. Demarest and W. R. Fowler. *Mesoamerica* 5(7):14-52.

Freidel, D. A.
1977   A Late Preclassic Monumental Mayan Mask at Cerros, Northern Belize. *Journal of Field Archaeology* 4:488-491.
1979   Culture Areas and Interaction Spheres: Contrasting Approaches to the Emergence of Civilization in the Maya Lowlands. *American Antiquity* 44:36-54.
1981   The Political Economics of Residential Dispersion among the Lowland Maya. In *Lowland Maya Settlement Patterns*, ed. W. Ashmore. School of American Research. Albuquerque: University of New Mexico Press.

Freidel, D. A., and L. Schele
1983   Symbol and Power: A History of the Lowland Maya Cosmogram. Paper presented at the Conference on the Origins of Classic Maya Iconography, Princeton University.

Graham, I.
1967   Archaeological Explorations in El Peten, Guatemala. *Middle American Research Institute Publication 33*. New Orleans: Tulane University Press.

Hammond, N.
1977   The Earliest Maya. *Scientific American* 236(3):116-133.
1986   The Emergence of Maya Civilization. *Scientific American* 255(2):106-115.

Hansen, R. D.
1984   Excavation on Structure 34 and the Tigre Area, El Mirador, Peten, Guatemala: A New Look at the Preclassic Lowland Maya. Unpublished Master's thesis, Brigham Young University.
1985   A Protoclassic Deposit at El Mirador, El Peten, Guatemala. Paper presented at the 1985 Maya Ceramic Conference. Washington, D.C.
1988   Resultados preliminares de las investigaciones arqueologicas en el sitio Nakbe, Peten, Guatemala. Paper presented at the II Simposio sobre Investigaciones Arqueológicas de Guatemala, Guatemala City.
1989   *Archaeological Investigations at Nakbe, Peten, Guatemala: The 1989 Season.* Institute of Archaeology, University of California, Los Angeles.

Howell, W. K.
1983   Excavations in the Danta Complex, El Mirador, Peten, Guatemala. Unpublished Master's thesis, Brigham Young University.

Madeira, P. C., Jr.
1931   An Aerial Expedition to Central America. *The Museum Journal* 32(2):93-155. The University Museum, University of Pennsylvania, Philadelphia.

Matheny, R. T. (editor)
1980   El Mirador, Peten, Guatemala, An Interim Report. *New World Archaeological Foundation Paper 45.* Provo: Brigham Young University.

1986 Investigations at El Mirador, Peten, Guatemala. *National Geographic Research* 2:322-353.

Mathews, P. and G. R. Willey
1986 Prehistoric Polities of the Pasion Region: Hieroglyphic Texts and their Archaeological Settings. Paper presented at the School of American Research Advanced Seminar on Maya Elites, Santa Fe.

Pendergast, D. M.
1981 Lamanai, Belize: Summary of Excavation Results 1974-1980. *Journal of Field Archaeology* 8:29-53.

Sharer, R. J.
1985 New Perspectives on the Origins of Maya Civilization. Paper presented at the III Seminario Arqueologia Hondure:a. Tela, Honduras.

Sharer, R. J., and D. C. Grove (editors)
1989 *Regional Perspectives on the Olmec.* School of American Research. Cambridge: Cambridge University Press.

Sharer, R. J., and D. W. Sedat
1987 Archaeological Investigations in the Northern Highlands, Guatemala: Interaction and the Development of Maya Civilization. *University Museum Monograph 59.* Philadelphia: The University Museum, The University of Pennsylvania.

Urban, P. A. and E. M. Schortman (editors)
1986 *The Southeast Maya Periphery.* Austin: University of Texas Press.

X

Preclassic Maya Civilization

Norman Hammond

Department of Archaeology
Boston University

Six centuries before Hernán Cortés destroyed the Aztec empire in Central Mexico, the earlier and perhaps greater civilization of the Maya collapsed in the tropical forests to the east. The Maya realm, centered in the Peten province of northern Guatemala, covered the entire Yucatan Peninsula as well as modern Belize and the western portion of Honduras and El Salvador; its Classic period had lasted for more than six centuries, from about A.D. 250 to 900. It is known to the world through the great ruined cities that have been uncovered over the past century: sites such as Tikal, with its towering temple-pyramids rising above the jungle; Palenque, with the history of its rulers depicted in fine carved panels and delicate stucco reliefs; and Quirigua, where the ruler Cauac Sky raised a forest of tall sandstone stelae carved in his likeness as monuments to his reign of more than a half a century between A.D. 725 and 784.

These stelae bear dates in the Maya calendar, a linear progression of time similar to the Christian calendar, but starting from the last creation of the world, in 3114 B.C., and divided into *baktunob* of 400 years and *katunob* of 20 years instead of centuries and decades. Precise to a single day, the correlation of the Maya and Christian calendars worked out earlier this century indicates that the earliest dated monuments known so far are of the second and third centuries A.D., and the latest were carved about the year 900.

This Maya calendar was the most precise calibration of time in the entire New World, and the prehistoric culture sequence in Mexico and Central America was geared to trade or artistic connections with the Maya Area. Maya influence was even seen as far away as Ecuador in South America.

When, in 1958, Gordon R. Willey and Philip Phillips of Harvard University developed a continental perspective on New World chronology as part of a theoretical scheme of development for the Prehispanic cultures of North, Middle, and South America, this one solid correlation of time with culture took a prominent position. In *Method and Theory in American Archaeology,* Willey and Phillips (1958) defined a central Classic stage that centered on this period during that the Maya had erected dated monuments and that was extensible to other areas of the Americas as the time when Precolumbian cultural development had reached its height.

The Classic was followed by a Postclassic, or Decadent, period, which lasted until the Spanish Conquest in the sixteenth century, and with equal logic it was preceded by a Preclassic period, sometimes called the Formative. The Preclassic was conceived of as an age of village farming societies that had succeeded the hunter-gatherers of the Archaic with the beginning of agriculture and that preceded the rather sudden emergence of the Classic civilizations.

Over the three decades since the original formulation of Willey and Phillip's scheme, its smooth Gaussian curve of rise and decline has been greatly modified in some areas of Mesoamerica (the term used to define the area of advanced cultures in central and southern Mexico through to central Honduras and El Salvador, which share a number of specific traits). The most dramatic development has been in the Gulf Coast area of Mexico and the adjacent highlands, where work at the sites of La Venta and San Lorenzo has shown that the Olmec culture, with its famed giant stone heads carved from volcanic boulders, had begun as early as the late second millennium B.C. and lasted until perhaps 400 B.C. Here was a society on the brink of civilization but developed early in the Preclassic period, rather than in the Classic, alongside the Maya and their neighbors of Oaxaca and the valley of Mexico.

Although the notion of a simple village farming Preclassic remained intact among Maya scholars for some years longer, there has now emerged a consensus that this is inaccurate: the Maya had developed a complex society at a much earlier date than had originally been indicated by the evidence for Preclassic and earlier habitation.

The Maya area embraces a wide range of environments, from the volcanic highlands of Guatemala and Chiapas and the steep Pacific slope, north through the tropical-forested lowlands of the Peten and Belize, to the flat, low-lying peninsula of Yucatan with its low rainfall and scrub vegetation. Mayan-speaking peoples are found throughout the area to this day, occupying almost the same area as the civilization of their forebears, although the once-populous heartland of the Peten and its surrounding regions is now peopled only by pioneer farmers and inhabitants of small towns. The tropical forest zone was the focus of the most spectacular cultural developments in the earlier part of the Classic period (A.D. 250-900), but in the late and Terminal Classic, after about A.D. 700, there were also major developments in Yucatan at cities such as Uxmal and Chichen Itza, which flourished for some time after the ninth-century collapse of the southern cities (see Morley et al. 1983).

The new discoveries that have led to a revision of our notions on the origin and development of Maya civilization have occurred in both Yucatan and the Peten-Belize tropical forest zone, as well as in the Guatemalan highlands to the south. In all three regions there is evidence that the first human settlement occurred soon after the end of the last Ice Age, perhaps as much as 10,000 years ago. At Loltun Cave, in the Puuc Hills of Yucatan, a long preceramic sequence of deposits with flaked chert fragments indicating human activity has been documented; the lowest layers are said to contain bones of animal species, such as the native horse, which became extinct in the Americas shortly after the end of the Pleistocene Ice Age. Unfortunately there is only one radiocarbon date for the Loltun sequence so far, placing the end of the preceramic occupation in the region of 2300 B.C.

In Belize, there have been a number of surface finds of projectile points of forms related to those used by big-game hunters in the Clovis culture of the U.S. Great Plains between 12,000 and 10,000 years ago. The best known of these finds is the Ladyville

Point near Belize City, found by a team from the University of Texas at San Antonio. Many other finds have been made by Richard S. MacNeish of Boston University, who has suggested that they can be fitted into a six-stage sequence running from 9000 to 2000 b.c. In the highlands, the site of Los Tapiales has yielded tools, including Clovis-related points, and radiocarbon dates around 10,000 years ago. In the surrounding region of El Quiche a survey by Kenneth Brown of the University of Houston showed that there were numerous sites of the preceramic period before 2000 b.c.

The overall evidence is that people were occupying all parts of the Maya area for perhaps 10,000 years before the emergence of Classic Maya civilization, and it must be a strong possibility that these early inhabitants were the direct ancestors of the Classic and present Maya population (see Hammond 1986 for references to Archaic and Formative period developments).

Not only the initial human penetration of the Maya area has been pushed to an earlier date by recent research: the beginning of settled farming communities, as recently as 1975 thought to date back no earlier than about 900 b.c. is now known to have begun between 1000 and 2000 b.c. Radiocarbon dates associated with maize-farming, pottery-making people at the site of Cuello in northern Belize suggest that the first sedentary occupation may have been about 1200 B.C. (Andrews and Hammond 1990). The presence of a clearly Maya cultural tradition before 1000 B.C. makes it plain that the Maya were not the poor cousins of the Olmec, flourishing coevally to the west. They were the producers of their own history, creators rather than borrowers from more advanced societies, which they had been labeled by archaeologists working in the central Mexican highlands. The extended time span for the development of Maya culture had in turn made it easier to accept an earlier development of complex society than the beginning of the Classic period in the third century A.D.

Some of the building blocks for that society were present long before the beginning of the Late Preclassic period, about 400 b.c., and some had already existed early in the Middle Preclassic, about 1000 b.c. Maize-based agriculture, the economic underpinning of all New World civilizations, is documented at the Cuello site before 1000 B.C., and by then these corn farmers were already building plaster-surfaced house platforms set around patios, constructing thatched wood-framed houses on them, and making competent pottery in a range of colors and vessel forms of varying function. In the Middle Preclassic, interregional exchange networks became established: obsidian from the highland source of San Martin Jilotepeque, near Guatemala City, and jade from sources around the Motagua Valley of central Guatemala were traded north to communities in the lowlands. One burial at the Cuello site has a blue jade pendant of a form most closely matched at the great Olmec site of La Venta, to the west as the crow flies.

In spite of a gradually increasing amount of evidence from Middle Preclassic sites, ranging from Komchen in far northern Yucatan to the Pacific coastal slope of Guatemala, and including centers of later importance such as Tikal and Seibal in the rain forest zone, the centuries between about 700 and 400 B.C. remain obscure. While Archaic and Classical Greece flourished, and Zhou Dynasty China slid into a mass of warring states, the foundations were laid for the emergence of a complex society in the Maya lowlands. What occurred, and why, is one of the most crucial research topics in New World archaeology today, but the evidence is in many feet of later construction and occupation deposits.

By the beginning of the Late Preclassic in 400 B.C. we do, however, start to see a totally different society from that envisaged in the village farming model extant a decade and a half ago. In the next six or seven centuries through to the formal beginning of the Classic period, a true civilization emerges.

We can see something of this even at the small site of Cuello, which, by the Late Preclassic, was still only a large village with a population probably not exceeding 2,000. About 400 B.C. the inhabitants converted the small courtyard surrounded by wooden buildings on raised platforms, which had been the ceremonial core of the Middle Preclassic community, into a broad open platform capable of holding a large audience or congregation, with a small pyramid at its western end. We found that the conversion had been carried out by filling in the courtyard with rubble to the tops of the surrounding platforms. The wooden temples were burned and the facades of their substructures ripped apart in ceremonial deconsecration. A saucer-shaped depression was left in the top of the rubble over the center of the courtyard, and in it were deposited the butchered bodies

of some 32 persons. Analysis of the skeletal remains by Frank and Julie Saul at the Medical College of Ohio at Toledo has shown that almost all were young, and possibly all were male. Accompanying the hacked bodies were a number of pottery vessels and six carved bone tubes. These last are of unknown function—they may have been handles for blood-letting implements such as were used in Classic Maya ritual or for ceremonial feather fans—but what is important is that four of them bore an interlace design clearly identifiable as the Maya pop, or woven mat. Rulers used these mats, and the mat had the equivalent meaning to "throne" in our iconography. Here at this small site we have the icon of royal power displayed; were there already rulers by 400 B.C. who had established both the reality of power and its symbolic expression?

The mounting evidence from other Late Preclassic Maya sites suggests that real power had indeed been forged by at least midway through the period. Growing population is indicated by much larger numbers of Late than of Middle Preclassic sites, and these tend to be themselves larger and more densely packed in the landscape. A survey of northern Belize that we carried out in 1973-1974 suggested that as many as four times the number of sites were present after 400 B.C. as before.

The inhabitants had to be fed, on a scale similar to that of the large Classic period populations of which we have been aware since extensive site-mapping began at Tikal a generation ago. For the Classic period, we now know that simple slash-and-burn farming in annual *milpa* fields was supplemented by more intensive forms of agriculture. The landscape was modeled into hillside terraces that prevented erosion, trapped soil as it washed downhill, and made uncultivable areas useful. Some quite shallow slopes were thus divided, and the permanent land division that resulted suggests allocation and cultivation on a more than casual basis. In the wetlands of the river valleys and in slow-draining basins such as that of Pulltrouser Swamp in northern Belize, or the Bajo de Morocoy in Quintana Roo, Mexico, canals were cut to create drained or raised fields, turning the damp margins into seasonally or perennially cultivable land with a support potential of 19 persons per hectare or more.

Although so far few of these landscape modifications for intensive agriculture have been dated to the Preclassic, the investigation of Pulltrouser Swamp by

B. L. Turner II and Peter D. Harrison (1983) produced radiocarbon dates that did suggest initial use
in the latter half of the Late Preclassic. On the Río
Hondo, not far to the west, another set of canal-
drained fields may date to the Middle Preclassic and
may have been abandoned by the Late Preclassic.
The Late Preclassic city of Nohmul lies just west of
Pulltrouser Swamp and probably controlled the output from its fields; Nohmul is also girdled by field-
by-field complexes in the swamps along the Río
Hondo's western margin, although those investigated so far are of Classic date (Hammond et al.
1988).

One site at which we know Preclassic drained
fields were created is Cerros, which lies on a small
peninsula on the coast of Belize. The ceremonial
heart of the site was cut off from the mainland by a
canal some 1,200 m long up to 6 m wide and 2 m
deep in places. Running into the main canal, which
investigation by Vernon Scarborough (1983) has
shown to date to between 200 and 50 b.c., was a
feeder channel draining a set of five to nine fields
that had been cut from a scrub-filled depression. The
largest was 40 m by 22 m, comparable in size to
those at Nohmul and Pulltrouser Swamp, although
the economic contribution of the fields cannot have
been great.

At Edzna, a city in the coastal plain of Campeche,
waterworks several orders of magnitude greater
have been dated to the Late Preclassic period
(Matheny et al. 1983). Edzna lies at the north end of
a long, flat valley with the headwaters of the Río
Champoton at its southern end. A canal more than
12 km long has been traced running south from the
city toward the river, with a moated "fortress" at its
northern end. The moat, still water-filled today, is up
to 100 m wide, and over 253,000 m3 of soil and limestone were quarried away to create it. Most of this
was used within the island fortress, which was constructed between 200 B.C. and A.D. 100 and which
may have been a sacred as well as a defensive
precinct.

Seven shorter canals, up to 1,500 m long, fan out
on the north side of the city center, feeding reservoirs and providing canoe transportation. The largest
had a capacity of 123,000 m³, and the total 22 km of
canals, a capacity of 1,480,000 m³. When reservoirs
and waterholes are added in, the people of Later
Preclassic Edzna had made for themselves in a dry
country some 2,225,000 m³ of water storage, at an

estimated cost of 1.68 million man-days of labor.

Another massive undertaking, although the ditch
may never have held water, was the deep trench and
rampart around the center of Becan, in the center of
the Yucatan Peninsula southeast of Edzna.
Apparently defensive in function, the Becan fortifica-
tions are about 1,900 m in circumference, crossed by
seven causeways, and would have taken 400,000
man-days to excavate and construct, according to
the calculations of David Webster (1976).

It seems certain from the size and density of Late
Preclassic communities that Maya society had an
organized subsistence economy that involved intensive food production, including the construction of
artificial microenvironments, which turned useless
swamps and hillsides into productive farmland capable of yielding several crops a year. Evidence from
the extensive chert-tool workshops at Colha, a site
southeast of Nohmul and Cerros and their major sup-
plier, shows that there was also an organized production economy tied to a regional distribution
network. Colha lies in the coastal swamp belt of
eastern Belize on a massive seam of flintlike chert
nodules: our initial excavations in 1973-1975 proved
its importance as a factory site, and from 1979 on the
project, directed by Thomas R. Hester and Harry J.
Shafer, has demonstrated the massive scale of the
artifact-manufacturing activities carried out there
(Shafer and Hester 1983).

Within the 6 square kilometers of the site our two
projects have recorded nearly a thousand mounds,
many of them house platforms. Hester and Shafer
have already identified 89 of them as chert workshops, and of these at least 32 were operating in the
Late Preclassic period. The scale of production can
be gauged from the thick beds of waste flakes, up to
1.5 m deep and containing hundreds of thousands of
flakes per cubic meter. There was a limited range of
tools made: the most common were large oval axes
and hoes—general-purpose tools for clearing brush
and working the land—and adzes made by the
"tranchet" technique, whereby the sharp edge was
produced by detachment of a final curved flake from
the bit end of the tool. These curved flakes, nicknamed "orange peels" because they look like segments of discarded rind, were waste products left on
site: from their sample, Hester and Shafer calculate
that over 2 million tranchet adzes were made at
Colha. Even if the workshops were operating
throughout the 650 years of the Late Preclassic, out-

put would still have been more than 3,000 adzes a year, far more than the local population would have needed. If we add to this even larger numbers of oval axes (less easy to quantify because they do not leave a single striking discard like the "orange peels"), and many thousands of triangular-bladed "daggers" made from large chert flakes, the total output of the Colha workshops is very impressive.

Distribution of Colha chert goods was wide: they have been found throughout northern Belize and as far away as El Mirador and Uaxactun in the Maya heartland of Peten. Although many Maya communities had a local chert-tool industry, the standardized products of the Colha factories captured a large part of the market within a radius of 40 km and were in demand from communities more than 160 km away.

Economic organization of Maya society is also in evidence most dramatically in the public buildings of Late Preclassic civic centers: at Komchen in northern Yucatan five large platforms with more than 60,000 m3 of construction between them lie around a plaza some 80 m by 150 m, larger than a football field. Two are long, narrow, high structures approached by two stairways each; the others are broad, covering 3,000-3,900 m^2 in area now standing up to 7.5 m high. Two are linked by a raised causeway 250 m long. This complex of buildings came into being in the first century of the Late Preclassic, between 400 and 300 b.c. (although additions were probably made to all the platforms in succeeding centuries of the era, and earlier structures of about 500 b.c. lay inside these Late Preclassic stages. The plaza lay at the heart of a densely nucleated community some 2 km^2 in area, which Ringle and Andrews (1988) estimate to have held some 3,000 people and to have required a supporting area of farmland up to 20 km in diameter, unless as yet undetected forms of agricultural intensification were present.

Komchen is notable in the development of Maya civilization for the early date and high density of its construction, a centralized town rather than a ceremonial center amid rural farming communities. Impressive though its central structures are, however, they are dwarfed by those at Late Preclassic sites farther south, in the rain forest zone of Peten and Belize, which developed after 300 B.C.

Among the smaller and later of these sites is Nohmul, where the Late Preclassic center (in the third century A.D.) consisted of a large plaza with buildings on the north, east, and west. The plaza was 130 m across and at least as long, flanked on east and west by large but low mounds that probably supported wooden buildings. To the north was the "acropolis," a huge platform covering some 6,000 m^2 in area and rising 10 m above the natural soil. It was built in one continuous operation of limestone blocks quarried a few hundred meters away, and contained as much construction fill as the entire group of mounds around the plaza at Komchen. The great plaza to the south contained half as much, and together with the flanking mounds the total amount of limestone quarried and laid in the center of Nohmul approaches 100,000 m^3.

One of the more interesting buildings of the Late Preclassic at Nohmul was not of stone at all, but of wood: on top of the acropolis we found the postholes of a long timber hall, with three aisles spanning a total of over 7 m and at least seven bays covering over 20 m. Too large to be a simple house, and not of temple plan, we interpret this long structure to be the perishable predecessor of the stone-built "palaces" of the Classic period, buildings that are thought to have housed the rulers of Maya cities and their administration.

Nohmul has a second major concentration of buildings lying some 540 m northwest of the acropolis, including an isolated temple-pyramid some 17 m high which we believe to be of Late Preclassic date. Similar pyramids exist at other sites, but they are much larger than the one at Nohmul. At Lamanai, a major center of this period lying about 56 km to the south on the same limestone ridge between the Río Hondo and Río Nuevo, the work of David Pendergast (1981) has shown that the massive structure N10-43, over 30 m high and with a cluster of three small temples on its top, is wholly of Late Preclassic date; and at Tikal the famous "Lost World Pyramid" (Structure 5C-54) is of similar height and date, and is surrounded by other buildings of the same period. At almost all of these sites the buildings are so large that when they were discovered they were assumed to belong to the peak of Classic period civilization about A.D. 700; only excavation has shown that they are from between four and eight centuries earlier.

One site that was suspected to be early from the beginning is El Mirador, which lies in the remote country near the Guatemala-Mexico border in northern Peten. First seen from the air in the 1920s, El Mirador was explored in 1962 by Ian Graham, who mapped some of the massive buildings there and reported that the style of stonework and lack of inscribed monuments were indicative of an early date. Just how large the site is has been confirmed by recent survey and excavations by a team from the New World Archaeological Foundation under Ray T. Matheny (1986).

The heart of the site is an area of dense construction about 1 km by 800 m, bounded by swamps on the west and by a long rampart with an outer ditch and narrow gateways on the other sides. Stone-built causeways known as sacbeob fan out beyond the western margin to cross the swamps, and others run for long distances to the south and southeast toward neighboring cities. Within the core of El Mirador are some of the largest buildings ever raised by the Maya: two pyramids close together, known as El Tigre and Monos, were both built about 150 b.c., each containing over 250,000 m³ of construction fill. El Tigre is 55 m high, the equivalent of an 18-story building, and supports a trinity of temples like those at Lamanai. Two large pyramids flanking El Tigre make a larger but identical pattern, which seems to be characteristic of Late Preclassic ritual architecture. The pyramid on the south side, Structure 34, has been excavated, revealing modeled-stucco jaguar masks taller than a man, with paws 2 m high. The claws and teeth are painted red; black and a cream background are also used.

This use of red and black, a common feature in Classic Maya art, begins in the Late Preclassic and seems to be of ritual significance. The east in Maya iconography is linked with the color red, and west with black, and this path of the sun's daily course is the dominant axis in Maya cosmography. It is my thesis that red and black are conscious transformations of each other: the Maya observed that pottery vessels fired red in an oxidizing atmosphere would turn black when refired under reducing conditions, and go red again on reoxidation. Late Preclassic pottery, which often had controlled areas of red and black surface, shows that the Maya understood this magical phenomenon from the fourth century B.C. onward.

Two km east of El Tigre lies the single largest building complex at El Mirador, and perhaps the most colossal in Maya history: known as Danta, it consists of two vast terraces leveling the landscapes, each 300 m wide, with a two-tiered temple ten stories high on top of it. The entire complex is 64 m high, rising above the rain forest like a breaching whale and visible from a great distance. As seen from the center of the city by an observer on top of El Tigre, in certain years the planets Jupiter, Mercury, Mars, and Saturn all appear to rise out of the top of the Danta pyramid at a time close to the vernal equinox. Such astronomical significance in Maya site planning has been known to date back to the end of the Late Preclassic at sites such as Uaxactun, but the layout of El Mirador suggests that Maya knowledge of the heavens had already been developed for several centuries. We begin to see, in fact, a society that was intellectually as well as economically and politically organized perhaps as early as the second century B.C.

Evidence for a shared intellectual culture has been found at numerous sites and in varying forms over the past decade: the jaguar masks at El Mirador are matched by others similarly decorating the facades of temples at Lamanai, on the famous Structure E-VII Sub at Uaxactun, and on a small temple, Structure 5C-2nd, at Cerros in northern Belize. The grotesque humanoid faces of the Cerros masks, with elaborate ear-ornaments copying in stucco the jade jewelry of human rulers, have associated glyphs from an early stage of Maya hieroglyphic writing. David Freidel, who excavated them, argues that they are evidence for a cult involving the east-west path of the sun across the sky and its return under the earth to rise again, an endless cycle of death and rebirth.

Another discovery at Cerros underlines the widespread acceptance of complex beliefs at this time: an offering in the top of Structure 6B included four jade heads of three facial types. An identical offering was found at Nohmul, 28 km to the southwest, in the foundations of another small temple. At least two of the head types have been found northward across the Yucatan Peninsula, suggesting that the whole of the northern Maya lowlands understood and embraced the iconography of what I interpret as three Maya gods (probably the same ones as are portrayed on the Pomona jade flare, discussed below).

Maya rulers were themselves shown in godlike form in the Classic period: at Tikal there was an explicit parallel drawn between the sun in splendor at the zenith and the glory of the local monarch. Ruler portraits only began to appear on public monuments at the beginning of the Classic. The stone stelae with dates in the Maya calendar and inscriptions detailing events of their reigns were long held to be a defining characteristic of Classic Maya civilization. Until a generation ago, their initial appearance in the archaeological record was set at A.D. 300, but the discovery of Tikal Stela 29, portraying perhaps the ruler Jaguar Paw, with a date equivalent to A.D. 292, suggested that a formal beginning to the Classic should be put at A.D. 250. Although we are still unable to bring any earlier Maya ruler out from anonymity, many of the characteristics of what is called the "stela cult" have been found to occur in Late Preclassic sites.

At Cuello we found a plain stela, only 80 cm high, set into the surface of Platform 34 in front of the Late Preclassic pyramid. Because it had been erected when an earlier platform floor was in use, it was probably in place in front of an earlier temple, 150 to 200 years before the end of the Preclassic, about A.D. 50-100. Several carved stelae are known, bearing figures of rulers and sometimes inscriptions, but lacking dates in the Maya calendar: those at El Mirador, a rock carving at San Diego in Peten, and a looted stela now in Seattle are all stylistically attributable to the Late Preclassic. Perhaps the earliest inscribed monument in the Maya lowlands is a fragment of an altar from Polol, in the Peten, which shows two richly clad figures on either side of a column of Maya bar-and-dot numbers. The top sign is the Initial Series Introducing Glyph, indicating a date in the Maya calendar; Although the altar is too eroded for the date to be read, John Graham of the University of California at Berkeley believes it to be in Cycle 7 of Maya time, that is, before A.D. 41, and points out the parallel composition of two stelae, Numbers 2 and 5, at the site of Abaj Takalik, which he has investigated on the Pacific coast of Guatemala. The designs are strikingly similar, in detail as well as overall conception, and the latest date for the Abaj Takalik monuments is early in the second century A.D., whereas the earliest could be up to four centuries earlier.

There is certainly corroborative evidence for both numeracy and literacy in the Maya lowlands by about A.D. 100. A tomb inside the Cuello pyramid, part of an earlier enclosed structure approximately coeval with the stela, included several seals, one of which bore a bar and four dots: the Maya number nine. Even more convincing is the great jade ear flare from Pomona, a small site in coastal Belize: the flare was found in 1949, and by examining the notes of the first scholars to see it and the pottery from the same tomb I have been able to place its date in the second part of the Late Preclassic. The jade is itself consummate lapidary work in a notably fractious medium, but the major interest lies in the four profile heads and accompanying signs that are engraved at the four quarters of its circumference. Two of the heads are those of the Maya sun god, Kinich Ahau, identified by a glyph for *kin,* "sun," in his cheek. A third is the maize god, and the fourth a long-lipped deity with the sign for *akbal,* "darkness," in his cheek. The maize god and the sun god opposite him are each also identified by the numbers of which they are patrons in Maya iconography, eight and four respectively. The other signs attached to the heads have been read by John Justeson of Vassar College and Will Norman of Tulane as a statement in the Yucatec Maya dialect involving interaction of the gods and accession of a ruler; they think that this may have been one of the early rulers of Yaxchilan (Justeson et al. 1988).

In addition it is my belief that the gods are those portrayed in the offerings of jade heads from Cerros and Nohmul—the former at least was laid out in a cruciform pattern recalling the Pomana flare—and that the two gods lacking numbers but possessing attached writing are the Sun God of the East and the God of Western Darkness. Thus the iconography and syntactic structure of the Pomona design shows us that the Late Preclassic Maya had already distinct deity portraits and personalities, had acquired hieroglyphic writing, and were using bar-and-dot numbers in a symbolic as well as a practical manner. With this collocation of craftsmanship, artistic expression, literacy, and intellectual depth, lowland Maya civilization is no longer what it once seemed, a contradiction in terms.

BIBLIOGRAPHY

Andrews, E. W., V., and N. Hammond
 1990   Redefinition of the Swasey Phase at Cuello,
             Belize. *American Antiquity* 54:570-584.

Hammond, N.
 1986   New Light on the Most Ancient Maya. *Man.*
             N.S. 21:398-412.

Hammond, N., L. J. Kosakowsky, A. Pyburn, J. Rose, J. C.
 Staneko, S. Donaghey, M. Horton, C. Clark,
 C. Gleason, D. Muyskens, and T. Addyman
 1988   The Evolution of an Ancient Maya City:
             Nohmul. *National Geographic Research*
             4:474-495.

Justeson, J. S., W. M. Norman, and N. Hammond
 1988   The Pomona Flare: A Preclassic Maya
             Hieroglyphic Text. In *Maya Iconography,*
             eds. E. P. Benson and G. G. Griffin, pp. 94-
             151. Princeton: Princeton University Press.

Matheny, R. T.
 1986   Investigations at El Mirador, Petén,
             Guatemala. *National Geographic Research*
             2:332-353.

Matheny, R. T., D. L. Gurr, D. W. Forsyth, and F. R. Hauck
 1983   *Investigations at Edzna, Campeche,
             Mexico, Vol. 1. Part 1: The Hydraulic
             System.* Papers of the New World Archae-
             ological Foundation 46, Provo, UT.

Morley S. G., G. W. Brainerd, and R. J. Sharer
 1983   *The Ancient Maya.* 4th rev. ed. Stanford:
             Stanford University Press.

Pendergast, D. M.
 1981   Lamanai, Belize: Summary of Excavation
             Results 1974-1980. *Journal of Field Archae-
             ology* 8:29-53.

Ringle, W. M., and E. W. Andrews V.
 1988   Formative Residences at Komchen,
             Yucatan, Mexico. In *Household and
             Community in the Mesoamerican Past,* eds.
             R. Wilk and W. Ashmore, pp. 171-199.
             Albuquerque: University of New Mexico
             Press.

Scarborough, V. L.
 1983   A Preclassic Maya Water System. *American
             Antiquity* 48:720-744.

Shafer, H. J., and T. R. Hester
 1983   Ancient Maya chert Workshops in Northern
             Belize, Central America. *American Antiq-
             uity* 48:519-543.

Turner, B. L., II, and P. D. Harrison (editors)
 1983   *Pulltrouser Swamp: Ancient Maya Habitat,
             Agriculture and Settlement in Northern
             Belize.* Austin: University of Texas.

Webster, D. L.
 1976   *Defensive Earthworks at Becan, Campeche,
             Mexico.* Middle American Research
             Institute, Publication 41. Tulane University.

Willey, G. R., and P. Phillips
 1958   *Method and Theory in American Archae-
             ology.* Chicago: University of Chicago
             Press.

XI

The Development of a Regional Tradition in Southern Belize

Richard M. Leventhal

Department of Anthropology
University of California, Los Angeles

The ancient occupation of the southern Belize region has been the focus of intensive research over the past several years. From this research, our understanding of the mechanisms for the occupation of this region and the interaction between sites within the region has increased dramatically. Most importantly, we can now place this little-known region within the broader context of the Maya civilization, chronologically and culturally.

The region of southern Belize (Fig. 11.1) covers an area of roughly 4,000 km^2 and generally corresponds to the modern Belize district of Toledo. Within this region, five major sites have been located, with numerous secondary centers. From west to east, these five sites are Pusilha, Uxbenka, Lubaantun, Xnaheb, and Nim Li Punit.

The main theoretical approach of the Southern Belize Archaeological Project has been to examine a single region within the Maya lowlands. We feel that the numerous similarly sized cities evident throughout the lowlands indicate the likely existence of regions with internal cohesion focused on numerous cities and not on a primary center. This regional organization is unique to the Maya lowlands and is not common in Mesoamerica. To test this hypothesis, we began to examine the entire region as a cohesive unit. One of the most important results of this study has been a settlement chronology for the region, the focus of this paper.

One of the advantages of the use of southern Belize for this initial test of regions in the Maya lowlands is that this region can be defined geographically. To the east, it is bounded by the Caribbean Sea, to the north and west by the Maya Mountains, and to the south by the wide swampland between the Sarstoon and Temash River drainages (see Fig. 11.1). Although bounded, it should not be considered to have been closed to external contacts and ties. Movement into and out of the region was probably focused on the Caribbean to the east and the lowland and highland areas to the west through a narrow funnel or pass in the Maya Mountains.

Within southern Belize, the Maya cultural sphere appears earliest in the western part of the region and gradually spreads eastward. As will be examined in greater detail later, I use the words "Maya Cultural Sphere" with great care as it is unclear whether people from the northeast Peten were the first to colonize the region or whether there was a local population previously living in southern Belize. The two western sites are Pusilha, located between the Poite and Pusila Rivers where they join to become the Moho River, and Uxbenka, located near the modern village of Santa Cruz (see Fig. 11.1). A detailed examination of Uxbenka followed by a rapid review of the information from other southern Belize cities will allow me to present the background for this settlement organization.

UXBENKA

The ancient city of Uxbenka (meaning "ancient place" or "old city" in the Mayan language Mopan) is located about 0.75 km to the northeast of the center of the modern village of Santa Cruz. It was first brought to the attention of the Southern Belize Archaeological Project in 1984. Following that initial discovery, only the central stela plaza has been cleared and examined. At least two additional outlying groups of this center were identified by Hammond (1975) during an earlier survey of the region.

Uxbenka is located on a section of good soil (the

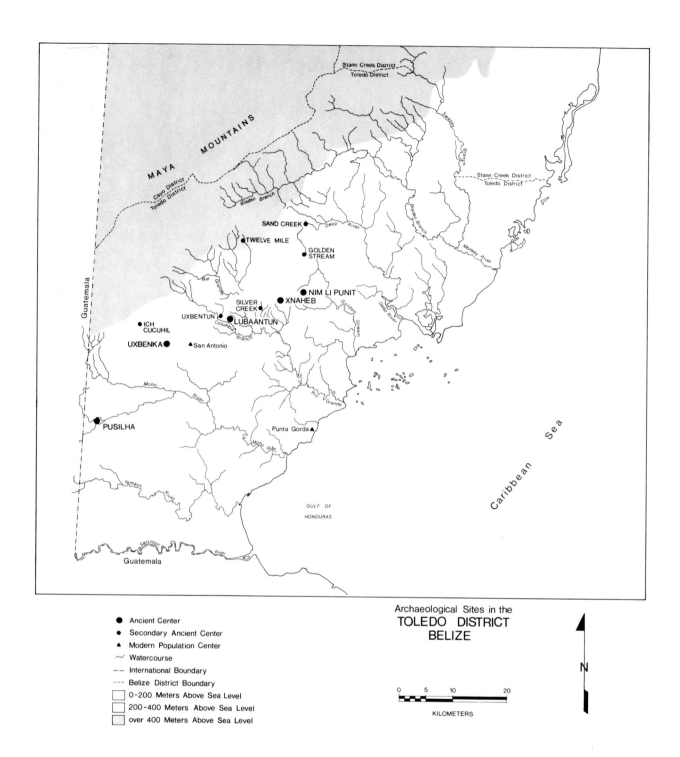

Figure 11.1. Archaeological sites of Southern Belize.

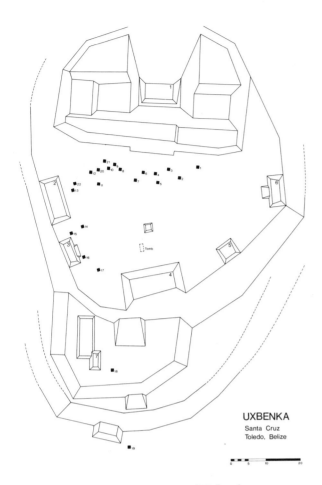

Figure 11.2. Map of Uxbenka.

Figure 11.3. Photograph of Stela 19, Uxbenka.

Toledo Beds) within the upper foothills of the Maya Mountains (Wright et al. 1959). The central part of the ancient city seems to be dispersed over several small hilltops. At least three large architectural groups, which probably make up the elite residential core of the city, have been identified. This use of natural terrain, resulting in the dispersal of normal architectural units, is a common occurrence at all the ancient sites in southern Belize.

The stela plaza of Uxbenka sits on top of a small, natural hill that has been modified in several ways. First, the top has been flattened, probably by moving some of the dirt from the central part of the top to be used as fill along the sides. Second, the front or southern edge of the hill has been faced with a retaining wall–a facade and a large central staircase (Fig. 11.2). The sides and back of the hill/structure were not faced or apparently modified. This type of "Hollywood set" construction is common within this

region. The front of the hill/structure consists of a central staircase, with Stela 19 located axially in front of the building. Halfway up the stairway is an irregularly shaped medial terrace with a small structure and terrace (Structure 7) located on the western side. Stela 18 sits in front of this building.

A central staircase continues to rise behind the medial terrace and onto Structure 4, which is located on the south side of the plaza. This central plaza consists of six structures irregularly grouped around the central plaza area. The two structures on the west side are fairly small, low, long structures, perhaps similar to palace structures at other Maya sites. The two structures on the east are smaller buildings of unknown function. The largest building, Structure 1, is located on the northern side of the plaza and rises 8 m above the plaza floor. It consists of a main central structure with two flanking terraces and a

Figure 11.4. Photograph of Stela 15, Uxbenka.

front medial terrace. It slopes directly down to the north, eventually merging with the natural slope of the hill.

Twenty-two stelae have thus far been identified at the site. Fourteen monuments appear to have been placed in a line in front of this northern Structure 1. Two other stelae were placed in apparent association with Structure 2, and four seem to be associated with Structure 3. As mentioned, Stelae 18 and 19 are located on the front medial terrace and in front of the building respectively. There is fragmentary evidence of carving on at least seven of these stelae. Only three, however, have enough of the carving still visible for interpretation (Leventhal and Schele ms).

Two of the monuments have been dated to the Late Classic. Stela 19 (Fig. 11.3) at the base of the entire plaza substructure, and Stela 15 (Fig. 11.4) near Structure 3, have been dated by Linda Schele to

9.17.10.0.0 (A.D. 780). They are both purely hieroglyphic texts. However, there are two other monuments that can be stylistically dated to the Early Classic and have been tentatively assigned the date of 8.18.0.0.0 (A.D. 395). These are Stelae 11 and 21, both part of the line of monuments in front of Structure 1.

Only Stela 11 is in good enough condition to have thus far been examined in great detail; unfortunately, this monument was vandalized after its discovery. A brief examination of the iconography on this monument, however, clearly indicates its Early Classic date and raises some interesting questions about Uxbenka's tie to the northeast Peten. An examination of this monument and the site of Uxbenka is presently in preparation by Leventhal and Schele (ms). Stela 11 (Fig. 11.5a, b) presents what appears to be a local ruler in a typical Early Classic pose. The upper part of the monument has been lost, and the figure is visible only from below the shoulders. A double-headed serpent is draped over his left and right shoulders, and only a fragment of the serpent head behind his left shoulder remains visible. Schele identifies two primary pieces of clothing: a loincloth and an elaborate belt assemblage.

The belt assemblage includes a front and rear head which identifies the ruler as an ahau k'in–"sun lord" or "lord of the mirror." In addition, there is a dangling god suspended on a chain from the belt. Schele has identified such a god at several other Early Classic sites in the lowlands. This seems to indicate that Uxbenka is part of the full Early Classic cultural sphere. It is the front head on the belt on which Schele sees possible Tikal connections. The front section of this head turns into a jaguar paw and seems to make this a head variant of the Jaguar Paw title from Tikal.

Schele therefore strongly argues for a late Cycle 8 date for the monument, about 8.18.0.0.0 (A.D. 395). This Cycle 8 monument is the earliest within this southern Belize region, probably indicating that the initial occupation or tie to the "Maya cultural sphere" was here at Uxbenka. However, what was the form of this contact?

MAYA CULTURAL EXPANSION

Peter Mathews's recent examination of the Early Classic monuments within the lowlands (1985)

Figure 11.5a. Photograph of Stela 11, Uxbenka.

Figure 11.5b. Drawing of Stela 11, Uxbenka. Drawing by Linda Schele.

Site	Monument	Dedicatory Date
Tikal	Stela 29	8.12.14.8.15
Loltun	Cliff Carving	(style 8.14.0.0.0 ± ?)
Tikal	Leyden Plaque	8.14.3.1.12
Uaxactun	Stela 9	8.14.10.13.15?
Tikal	Stela 33	(style 8.15.0.0.0 ± 2KT)
Xultun	Stela 12	(style 8.15.0.0.0 ± 2KT)
Uaxactun	Stela 10	(style 8.15.0.0.0 ± ?)
Uaxactun	Stela 19	8.16.0.0.0
Uaxactun	Stela 18	8.16.0.0.0?
Yaxha	Stela 5	(style 8.16.0.0.0 ± 2KT)
Uaxactun	Stela 5	8.17.1.4.12?
Tikal	Stela 4	8.17.2.16.17?
Tikal	Altar 1	8.17.2.16.17?
Bejucal	Stela 2	8.17.17.0.0
Tikal	Stela 18	8.18.0.0.0?
Uaxactun	Stela 4	8.18.0.0.0?
Uxbenka	**Stela 11**	**(style 8.18.0.0.0 ± ?)**
Uxbenka	**Stela 21**	**(style 8.18.0.0.0 ± ?)**
Balakbal	Stela 5	8.18.10.0.0
El Peru	Stela 15	8.19.0.0.0
Collections	Belmopan Stela	8.19.0.0.0
Uaxactun	Stela 17	8.19.0.0.0???
Tikal	Stela 28	(style 8.19.0.0.0 ± 3KT)
El Zapote	Stela 5	9.0.0.0.0
Tikal	Stela 1	(style 9.0.0.0.0 ± 2KT)

Table 11.1. List of Early Classic monuments with dedicatory dates between 8.12.0.0.0 and 9.0.0.0.0 (adapted from Mathews 1985: Table 3).

clearly indicates that almost all the Cycle 8 monuments are centered within the northeast Peten, around and in the vicinity of Tikal (Table 11.1) If correctly dated, this Uxbenka monument marks the possible beginning of an outward expansion of this Maya cultural sphere.

This outward expansion seems to have picked up momentum. In the southeastern lowlands, both Copan and Quirigua are first tied into this cultural sphere about 9.0.0.0.0 (A.D. 435). The earliest monument at Copan is Stela 35, found within the fill of Structure 4 (William L. Fash and Claude Baudez, personal communication). It is dated to 9.0.0.0.0 on stylistic grounds. Similarly, the earliest monument from Quirigua, monument 26, dates to 9.2.18.0.0

(A.D. 493; Jones 1983). The iconography on both of these monuments clearly indicates, as with the Uxbenka stela, that these sites and many others, such as Yaxchilan and Piedras Negras, are beginning to participate in the broad Maya cultural sphere. There is a continuation of this expansion with the proliferation of what has become known as the "stela cult" throughout the lowlands. Many sites seem to first participate within this sphere at the beginning of Cycle 9 through 9.4.0.0.0 (Mathews 1985). Uxbenka, however, appears to have been one of the earliest outlying sites to be tied into the sphere.

What may have been the mechanism for tying into this cultural sphere? Several possibilities are outlined in a recent examination of the material from Copan (Leventhal, Demarest, and Willey 1987). The first model focuses on whether a local population and settlement of Maya speakers existed prior to the arrival of this cultural sphere. I believe that the evidence on two fronts speaks strongly for the existence of such a local population. First, at Copan, we found a strong indication of a differentiation between the material culture of the central elite of the city and the outlying population. This contrast, evident at A.D. 800, was probably the result of the existence of an earlier local population.

The second argument focuses on the regional model being examined and tested within southern Belize. We argue that Maya culture is actually a broad fa(ade that ties together and covers local regional cultures. Such a regional organization results in regional art styles that can be identified when one contrasts the iconography at Copan, Tikal, and Palenque; or regional architectural styles, for example, the Puuc, Chenes, and Río Bec styles, which are greatly different in their form and structure but at the same time are considered to be within the mainstream of the Maya architectural tradition; or regional Mayan languages throughout the lowlands. These regional styles force us to utilize a broad definition of Maya culture rather than a narrow one. At the same time, such a broad cultural construct allows Maya civilization to encompass the whole of more than 250,000 km^2 of the lowlands. Therefore, as part of this argument, I would state that originally there was probably a local Maya people at Uxbenka without the trappings of the central Maya elite cultural sphere. Although the evidence does not as yet exist for Uxbenka, our material from Copan argues for the existence of such a local population. On this assumption, two broad models for the appearance of the stela cult and iconography can be presented. One possibility includes what has been termed "site unit intrusion" (Lathrap et al. 1956) and focuses on the actual movement of people out of northeast Peten in order to colonize or control these outlying areas. The second model, as we have stated for Copan, follows Flannery's model for the Olmec and Oaxaca areas and is based upon local development with outside influence (Flannery 1968). With this model, a local emerging elite takes on the material trappings of power and importance as part of the gradual growth of a strong hierarchical economic, political, and social system. These trappings of power are accepted and utilized by the local elite in order to demonstrate their difference from the surrounding nonpowerful local population.

To differentiate between these models archaeologically is a most difficult task. Hodder (1979) discusses the difficulty in attempting to define either model. He states that even if two material cultures are defined, the development of a local elite taking on new trappings and symbols of power might produce as sharp a contrast of material culture as the movement of a new people into a region. Perhaps one of the ways in which we can begin to differentiate between the models is by defining and examining the early local culture and attempting to follow the change in its material culture over time. If it is gradual, it might be argued that a local elite is gradually emerging. A more abrupt change of the entire material culture, however, might argue for the imposition of people from outside. It is clear at Uxbenka, as well as at Copan and Quirigua, that these early monuments show a very close tie between these outlying sites and northeast Peten. Except for the fact that these stelae are of local stone, they could easily be lost among the monuments of Tikal or of other sites within the central lowlands. The assimilation of the local culture and the development of a regional style had not yet started; it is just the beginning of the presence of the Maya cultural sphere. Future study of Uxbenka is planned in order to examine the mechanism for the appearance of this Maya cultural overlay into outlying areas like southern Belize.

SOUTHERN BELIZE

With the initial appearance at Uxbenka of material from the central Maya lowlands about 8.18.0.0.0, southern Belize becomes part of this tradition. It remains part of this tradition until the collapse within the region, about 9.18.0.0.0/9.19.0.0.0, more than 400 years. It never seems to become a central or major player within the Maya lowlands but maintains a constant secondary role.

Following the occupation of Uxbenka, the second site on the west, Pusilha, seems to begin to participate in this cultural sphere. The earliest clearly dated monument at Pusilha is Stela O, dated to 9.7.0.0.0; however, Morley (1938) speculates that there is an earlier monument, Stela Z, which he dates to the first quarter of Cycle 9. It is quite possible that both

Uxbenka and Pusilha became part of the cultural sphere at approximately the same time. It appears that the connection between either of these sites and northeast Peten was not over the Maya Mountains but through a rather narrow pass in the mountains to the west of Pusilha and this southern Belize region.

The three eastern sites, Lubaantun, Xnaheb, and Nim Li Punit, are all initially occupied at a later time. The earliest monument from these sites is Stela 15 at Nim Li Punit, dated to 9.14.10.0.0. It appears quite likely that Nim Li Punit and Lubaantun were both occupied during the second half of Cycle 9. However, Lubaantun is a problem as no stelae have been discovered at the site. It is a large site, in fact the largest of the region, yet its only carved monuments are three ball-court markers all dated between 9.17.10.0.0 and 9.18.0.0.0. Hammond's excavations at the site in 1970 (Hammond 1975) clearly indicate an occupation at about A.D. 700 and not much earlier. Therefore, I believe that both Lubaantun and Nim Li Punit were first occupied around A.D. 700. This is not a similar movement of ideas or people from the northeast Peten but rather an internal regional expansion. Southern Belize regional traditions of architecture, iconography, hieroglyphs, ceramics, and other artifacts all appear coevally at Lubaantun and Nim Li Punit.

The final major site to develop within the immediate region appears to be Xnaheb, located about 4.5 km to the west of Nim Li Punit. Although it looks impressive, it actually shows the smallest amount of construction of any site within the region. All the large construction is, in fact, a facade or facing over the natural terrain. The only carved monument, Stela 3, is dated to 9.17.10.0.0. This late date, the lack of truly monumental architecture, and a preliminary examination of the ceramics all indicate the late occupation of this site. It does appear to be the last of the major sites within the region to have been settled.

Xnaheb may have been settled for several reasons. Its close proximity to Nim Li Punit and the close ceramic ties might indicate a connection between these two sites. Might it be possible to argue that Xnaheb was settled by members of the ruling family at Nim Li Punit—perhaps a second or younger son? The existence of secondary centers tied to larger primary centers is evident throughout the lowlands and within this southern Belize region. Such secondary centers may have gradually devel-

oped in importance for economic, political, or social reasons. Xnaheb is located between Nim Li Punit and Lubaantun and may have developed initially as a midpoint between the centers. Some of these hypotheses are being examined by Peter Dunham, a member of the southern Belize project.

Several secondary centers within this region appear to have been located to take advantage of a favorable economic position between primary centers. They do not initially appear to be tied specifically to one primary center. The site of Silver Creek is the best example. It is located at roughly the midpoint between Xnaheb to the east and Lubaantun to the west. There is no evidence of settlement continuity between any of these three sites such as we have identified between Nim Li Punit and Xnaheb. In fact, the site of Silver Creek consists of two medium-size architectural complexes with almost no outlying settlement. It appears as though the occupation of Silver Creek occurred just prior to the collapse within this region and that there was little time to develop a sustaining population. It might be termed an emerging center with an economic basis that never completed its development.

CONCLUSIONS

The regional study of southern Belize has begun to indicate the importance of such studies for the Maya lowlands. A regional style in architecture, construction techniques, iconography, hieroglyphs, and ceramics is gradually being defined. In addition, the chronology of site settlement has been outlined in this paper.

The region first became part of the Maya cultural sphere about A.D. 400, as seen by Stela 11 at Uxbenka. A local population either tied into the Maya cultural sphere or was controlled by people from the central Peten. A thorough examination of the process and spread of the Maya cultural facade will be the focus of future research in the southern Belize region. With the occupation of Uxbenka and Pusilha about A.D. 400-450, the process of assimilating a local culture and developing a strong regional tradition began. The eastern sites were settled at a later time, probably about A.D. 650-700. In addition, we have identified what appear to be gradually developing secondary centers around and between the large primary centers of southern Belize.

BIBLIOGRAPHY

Flannery, K. V.
1968   The Olmec and the Valley of Oaxaca: A Model for Interregional Interaction in Formative Times. In *Dumbarton Oaks Conference on the Olmec*, ed. E. Benson, pp. 79-110. Washington, DC: Dumbarton Oaks.

Hammond, N.
1975   *Lubaantun: A Classic Maya Realm.* Monographs of the Peabody Museum, no. 2. Harvard University.

Hodder, I.
1979   Economic and Social Stress and Material Culture Patterning. *American Antiquity* 44:446-454.

Jones, C.
1983   Monument 26, Quirigua, Guatemala. In *Quirigua Reports Vol. II*, eds. E. M. Schortman and P. A. Urban, no. 13, pp. 118-128. Philadelphia: The University Museum, The University of Pennsylvania.

Lathrap, D. W., G. R. Willey, C. C. Di Peso, W. A. Ritchie, I. Rouse, and J. H. Rowe
1956   *An Archaeological Classification of Culture Contact Situations.* Salt Lake City: Society for American Archaeology.

Leventhal, R. M., A. A. Demarest, and G. R. Willey
1987   The Cultural and Social Components of Copan. In *Polities and Partitions: Human Boundaries and the Growth of Complex Societies*, ed. K. M. Trinkaus, pp. 179-205. Anthropological Research Papers 37. Arizona State University.

Leventhal, R. M., and L. Schele
ms   Uxbenka, an Ancient Maya City of Southern Belize.

Mathews, P.
1985   Maya Early Classic Monuments and Inscriptions. In *A Consideration of the Early Classic Period in the Maya Lowlands*, eds. G. R. Willey and P. Mathews, vol. 10, pp. 5-54. Albany: Institute for Mesoamerican Studies, State University of New York at Albany.

Morley, S. G.
1938   *The Inscriptions of Peten, Vol. IV,* Publication 437. Washington DC: Carnegie Institution of Washington.

Wright, A. C. S., D. H. Romney, R. H. Arbuckle, and W. E. Vial
1959   *Land in British Honduras,* Colonial Research Publication 24, London

XII

Beyond Temples and Palaces: Recent Settlement Pattern Research at the Ancient Maya City of Sayil (1983-1985)

Jeremy A. Sabloff

Department of Anthropology, University of Pittsburgh

and

Gair Tourtellot

Department of Anthropology, Northwestern University

The rise and fall of the ancient Maya civilization in the New World tropics has long been a fascinating topic.[1] Attention has been focused mainly on the Maya who settled the lush wet forest at the base of the Yucatan peninsula. Less attention has been paid to the Maya of the north, who occupied a drier, spiny scrub forest landscape with little surface water and only shallow soils. In the Puuc Hills region situated in the northwestern part of the peninsula, the end of the first millennium A.D. witnessed an amazing, brief florescence of regional Maya civilization at the very time that of other regions, particularly in the south, were experiencing vast upheavals, reorganizations, and even collapse.

The Terminal Classic period (A.D. 800-1000) in the Maya lowlands is a critical time for archaeological understanding of several of the most important developments in the growth of ancient Maya civilization. Clearly, there were significant demographic and economic changes taking place in the Maya lowlands at this time. While much recent attention has been paid to the so-called collapse in the south, such attention has been relatively lacking in the north. However, in order to understand these critical developments in Maya civilization, it is crucial that we study the growth of settlement in the relatively little-known Puuc region (Fig. 12.1).

What were the population sizes of the major Puuc region sites? How did the populations change from Late Classic to Postclassic times? Did the settlements of the Puuc zone differ from earlier Classic settlements, given the changing economic patterns of the Terminal Classic Period? Is an influx of peoples from the southern lowlands into the north visible in the settlement record? Are "foreign" influences present in Puuc region settlements? Can we validate and then explain the "boom and bust" experience of the large Terminal Classic sites and populations? What is the relationship between peoples in the Puuc region and those at Chichen Itza?

We cannot begin to answer these questions without intensive settlement pattern and household studies at Puuc region sites, nor can general hypotheses about the growth of Maya civilization be tested. Although Puuc sites represent possibly the peak of New World architectural development (see Andrews 1975; Pollock 1980), we have lamentably little information on the people who built and sustained them, how they lived, and how they disposed themselves across their dry and hilly landscape.

Unlike the situation for most other Maya regions, there has never been a settlement pattern study at any Puuc site that has been both intensive and comprehensive. The recent pioneering settlement survey of a part of Uxmal by Alfredo Barrera Rubio (1980), the salvage studies at various Puuc sites by the Centro Regional de Yucatan, and the publication of the Archaeological Atlas (Garza T. de Gonzalez and Kurjack 1980) have all provided important new information about aspects of settlement in the

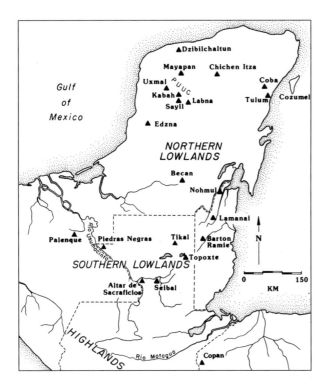

Figure 12.1. The Maya lowlands showing the location of the Puuc region and the site of Sayil.

region, but without large scale and systematic settlement pattern studies at and between Puuc region sites, knowledge of these sites and the region as a whole will remain surprisingly limited.

In 1983, Sabloff initiated the three-season-long mapping phase (Phase I) of a long-term project at the site of Sayil that is for the first time investigating the archaeology, environment, adaptation, organization, and history of an entire Maya city in the Puuc Hills. He was joined in 1984 by Tourtellot (see Sabloff et al. 1984, 1985; Sabloff and Tourtellot 1984; Tourtellot et al. 1988). The second, or intensive, surface collection/excavation phase (Phase II) of the project was completed in 1987-1988 under our joint direction.

Let us briefly summarize some of the principal findings from Phase I of our research. During the three field seasons of this phase, we nearly completed the first mapping of the architecture and settlement distribution of an entire Puuc community (the final piece of reconnaissance/mapping was finished in Phase II). We found that the "urban" part of Sayil, with stone-walled platforms and chultuns

(underground cisterns), extends over a clearly delimited area of approximately 4.5 km². An incredibly broad and detailed compilation of data, based almost entirely on visible surface characteristics alone, is currently being analyzed. We have recorded over 2,500 individual features of archaeological interest, ranging from mounds or piles of stone cobbles (called chich by the local Maya) to three-story buildings (see Sabloff and Tourtellot in press).

Among the 2,500+ features are a wide variety of buildings that run the gamut from well-preserved stone palaces to foundation braces for perishable structures (Fig. 12.2), plain platforms, basal platforms, a few slope terraces and artificial levelings, a ball court, ring-shaped structures, causeways and walkways, hundreds of chich mounds, chultuns, quarries, and several historic features, including apsidal houses and house-lot walls.

The center of Sayil is located on the floor of the northern end of a long valley. Settlement of predominantly residential appearance usually extends outward to the valley margins, but only slightly beyond. More-distant outliers are known, but settlement is not continuous out to them. No sign of a causeway linking Sayil to any other site has yet been seen. Fairly distinct and characteristic limits have been established in all directions for the type of settlement on platforms that is found in the main valley. Feature clusters with dressed stone platforms, buildings, and chultuns virtually disappear between 600 and 1,000 m from the central causeway yielding to large numbers of shapeless chich cobble mounds. The principal exceptions to this picture lie in the southeastern and southwestern corners, where ruins extend out along the valley margin to well beyond a kilometer. But even in these two lobes of settlement, reconnaissance by N. P. Dunning has shown that clear borders to the urban zone can be delineated.

Good land, a term containing subtleties at different scales of reference, appears to have been the primary locational consideration. Some definite, albeit preliminary, impressions of the major factors controlling gross settlement location within the community of ancient Sayil have emerged from our mapping of contiguous areas in the valley and along radial transects, as follows:

1. Utterly flat land with few outcrops and red kankab soil is favored as the location for the major architectural complexes and big structures: this is the center of the valley. Conversely, very few small

Figure 12.2. The remains of a perishable structure at Sayil. The door jambs of the middle room of a three-room structure (Feature N7645/E5515-4) are visible in the center of the photograph. The floor plans of perishable buildings at Sayil are often relatively well preserved.

structures of residential appearance occur there.

2. Probable residential locations are concentrated on limestone outcrops of low relief bearing brown tzekel soils: these outcrops occur toward the margins of the valley as it rises gradually to the encircling lines of cone karst hills.

3. Locations on the outcrops closer to the site center were more densely occupied than the more distant outcrops presumably because of their greater access to control, services, and all types of soil, and perhaps due to greater duration of occupation as a result. Proximity to the center usually overrode tendencies to disperse onto available, suitable outcrops out in the more distant countryside, except in the southeast and southwest.

4. These low outcrops were also probably the

best locations in which to find suitable and cheap places to dig chultuns to provide the vitally necessary year-round supply of water.

5. Low outcrops also made it easier to build the basal platforms that kept house floors and activities up out of the wet season mud, the outcrops providing a ready source of building materials as well as "preformed" cores for the platforms. Most of the chultuns and their rainfall catchments are located on these basal platforms.

6. Pockets of mapped house-lot space are much larger than the architecturally improved spaces, ranging from one-quarter to a full hectare in area. These lots are not defined by walls, yet were clearly essential. Future excavation is intended to test just how "vacant" these lots really were.

Within its borders Sayil appears to be roughly divisible into two concentric zones. The inner zone consists of the narrow, 1.2-km-long site-core on the flat valley floor, comprising the central causeway and its various appendages like the Great Palace, Mirador, South Palace, and ball court plus a high percentage of the stone buildings and sculptured stone and all the multistory buildings. The outer ring, or site-periphery, is located on the outcrops and includes a high percentage and high density of the perishable buildings and chultuns.

Within the central site-core the series of building complexes linked by the causeway may be heuristically and tentatively subdivided into two sectors. The first is an elite residential area at the north, perhaps for the ruling families. This area consists of gradually expanded multistory and "palace" complexes with some 11 chultuns, numerous pilas or metates for food preparation, and a possible reservoir. The second sector, a civic-ceremonial area at the south, consists of the formal South Palace, used perhaps for bureaucratic office space, an adjacent vast and empty platform, a stela platform, and the ball court, but only three chultuns and one pila.

In the site-periphery zone there appear to be two high-density elite sectors comprised of numerous vaulted but single-story stone buildings and many chultuns. One is an elite sector west of the South Palace adjacent to the site-core; the other sector of stone buildings lies along an axis 1.5 km long on the first outcrops east of the site-core. Additionally, three or four sectors of dense habitation in perishable buildings also occur in the site periphery, along with most of the chultuns and a few small stone buildings. These high-density sectors may have held a higher proportion of the "commoners." The eastern and southern outer borders of this site-periphery appear to coincide with the occurrence of several rubble pyramids, one of them circular. Perhaps these were ritual entry markers placed at the cardinal points.

Also, in the site-periphery are found large numbers of chich mounds that may have served as platforms for tiny structures. These chiches increase in frequency toward the borders and are virtually the only potentially artificial features found beyond the site-periphery. The distant chiches represent a great change in the character of Sayil settlement, if they are not actually beyond the residential nucleus. It is possible that these distant chiches may really be field rather than domestic structures.

Because the major site of Kabah, just 7 km to the north, lies out of the cone karst region in the adjacent flatter and richer Puuc upland, a transect between the two offers the possibilities of detecting direct settlement response to improving edaphic and topographic changes. Conversely, a transect southward toward little Xcalopec offers a similar possibility to investigate the apparent lack of big sites and public architecture in that direction.

Since we cannot discuss all the other fascinating patterns we are discovering, we shall focus on just two more particularly interesting features and patterns: water and commodity supply.

Devices for storing water were needed by the ancient inhabitants of the Puuc region in order to capture and store sufficient rainwater during the annual wet season to survive the long dry season during the winter and spring. There are no natural sinkholes, or cenotes, near Sayil like those at Chichen Itza or Dzibilchaltun. The nearest permanent water source is not local but lies 3.6 km distant, deep in a cave at the Gruta de Chac.

Chultuns are the principal artificial water storage devices observed at Sayil. They are hollowed out, underground cisterns with constricted necks and mouths that drained specially constructed rainwater catchment surfaces. Chultuns occur only in areas of limestone outcrops, and usually are found beneath platforms. The absence of outcrops in much of the valley bottom is believed to account for the observed dip in settlement density in the site core.

Only 17 percent of chultuns are not in a basal platform, but they are always located very close to a structure of some type. Surprisingly, about three-quarters of the off-platform chultuns are associated with basal platforms that already have a chultun; off-platform chultuns probably were no more than supplements to the regular on-platform chultuns, not substitutes. Some of these off-platform chultuns may actually have been used for dry storage rather than water.

The reasons that the ancient Maya carved chultuns from rotten bedrock, rather than constructing them from masonry as needed, may well be due to the much greater ease, cheapness, and indeed safety to be gained from using the naturally occurring hard caprock as a roof. The actual size of chultun catchment areas, where these are still clear, is very small. The reason for this must be the limited capacity of

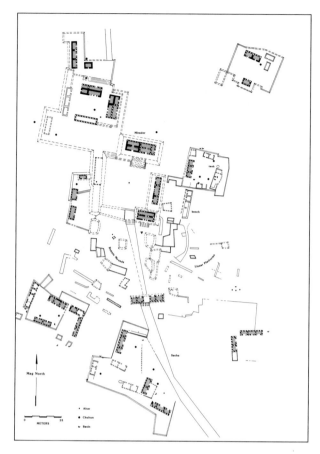

Figure 12.3. At the heart of Sayil, the Mirador Complex and nearby basal platform units bracket an unusual area that might have been the central marketplace.

the chultuns. Brainerd (1958) estimated that the average capacity of a sample of chultuns was about 28,000 liters. Since rainfall in the Puuc area is about 1 m per year (1,000 liters per square meter), it only takes about 28 m^2 of collection surface (a circular catchment less than 7 m across) to fill a chultun.

Two negative associations may be significant. No small cobble or chich mound that is off a platform ever has a chultun on it or anywhere nearby. This is one material expectation of the hypothesis that chich mounds were not permanent dwellings but ancillary structures, since water was otherwise vital to everyday family life. A strong alternate possibility is, of course, that they were the dwellings, either permanent or seasonal, of lower-class individuals who were dependent on others for water. The chich

mounds also may have been multifunctional. This large class of remains will be examined carefully in the ongoing analyses of the Sayil settlement and compared to similar remains from Northern Lowland sites such as Komchen (see Ringle 1985).

The other provocative negative association of chultuns is with the large South Palace building, which has no chultuns, and indeed with its adjacent huge complex of buildings where only three have been found.

The second interesting set of features and patterns involves discoveries made while mapping on the flat just south of the Mirador Complex. An ordered array comprised chiefly of long linear platforms and low rubble mounds lies between the Mirador Group and two spacious basal platform units farther south (Fig. 12.3) There also are some stone alignments and bare platforms. Most features here are oriented with a more extreme deviation from the cardinal points than is usual. Terraces extending off the north sides of the two big basal platforms to the south are also parallel to the other features and appear to be part of the unusual feature complex here.

At present, we think that the most likely use of this unexcavated area was as a concourse for a market or fair. Among our reasons are that this flat area is centrally located and easily approached by the main causeway; the permanence of the structures here also suggests a regular activity; the linear platforms and stone alignments are more or less aligned with each other, forming aisles, as are commonly seen in native markets; these linear platforms could have been bases for market stalls, while the few rubble mounds and bare platforms may be foundations for workshops or more important stalls, or for the storage of surplus products; unusually, several stone buildings face into this area rather than onto their courts, as if for administrators or judges of the market; at the eastern end of the area with linear platforms is a stela with a unique phallic image, perhaps representing a commoner or vulgar use of the area; and finally, strong evidence against the former domestic use of this area consists of a complete lack in it of chultuns and pilas or any of the common foundation brace dwellings. Additionally, soil cores taken by N. P. Dunning of the University of Minnesota recovered many sherds and evidence of a floor across the entire flat. This entire zone was intensively studied in 1988, and analyses currently being undertaken by Susan Wurtzburg will be discussed in forthcoming publications.

Although this putative marketplace has only limited formal similarities to other alleged marketplaces at Chichen Itza, Tikal, Ixtutz, Yaxha, and Seibal, the similarities among the latter are no greater, either. Clearly, more research is needed on how to monitor market activities in the archaeological record and on the significance of the observed differences.

In the second phase of research at Sayil, the recently completed map of Sayil provided us with a splendid platform from which to delve into a sample of a wide series of architectural types in order to test a variety of functional hypotheses. In particular, we undertook, through both intensive surface collection and excavation, large-scale horizontal exposures encompassing both domestic architecture and the areas between them. The thin deposits and the relatively short occupation at the site clearly aided us in this endeavor. Again, future publications will report on the results of the Phase II research.

Hopefully, the investigation of Sayil will ultimately help us to understand where its builders came from, how their community was organized within its environmental setting, the role chultuns

played in Sayil's rise and fall, and the nature of the interaction between Sayil and the larger sweep of Maya civilization.

NOTE

1. This article is a revised version of a paper presented at the 51st Annual Meeting of the Society for American Archaeology, New Orleans, LA (April 1986). The 1983-1985 research at Sayil has been supported by the National Science Foundation (Grant #BNS 8302016). We are grateful for the assistance provided by our many colleagues and friends in Mexico City and Merida, by our students, by the administrations at the University of New Mexico and the University of Pittsburgh, by the Uc family at Sayil, and by our field and laboratory crews that were recruited from the local towns and villages of the Puuc region in Yucatan.

BIBLIOGRAPHY

Andrews, G. F.
1975   *Maya Cities: Placemaking and Urbanization.* Norman: University of Oklahoma Press.

Barrera Rubio, A.
1980   Patron de asentamiento en el area de Uxmal, Yucatan. *XVI Mesa Redonda de la Sociedad Mexicana de Antropologia* (Saltillo, 1979) 2:389-398. Mexico, D.F.

Brainerd, G. W.
1958   *The Archaeological Ceramics of Yucatan.* Anthropological Records, University of California, vol. 19, Berkeley and Los Angeles.

Garza T. de Gonzalez, S., and E. B. Kurjack
1980   *Atlas Arqueologico del Estado de Yucatan.* Instituto Nacional de Antropología e Historia, México, D.F.

Pollock, H. E. D.
1980   *The Puuc: An Architectural Survey of the Hill Country of Yucatan and Northern Campeche, Mexico.* Memoirs of the Peabody Museum, vol. 19. Cambridge, MA: Harvard University Press

Ringle, W. M.
1985   *The Settlement Patterns of Komchen, Yucatan, Mexico.* Unpublished Ph.D. dissertation, Department of Anthropology, Tulane University, New Orleans.

Sabloff, J. A., P. A. McAnany, B. F. Beyer, T. Gallareta N., S. L. Larralde, and L. Wandsnider
1984   *Ancient Maya Settlement Patterns at the Site of Sayil, Puuc Region, Yucatan, Mexico: Initial Reconnaissance (1983).* Latin American Research Institute, Research Series 14. University of New Mexico, Albuquerque.

Sabloff, J. A., and G. Tourtellot
1984   The Sayil Settlement Survey: Some Preliminary Observations. *Mexicon:*84-85.
in press *The Ancient Maya City of Sayil: The Mapping of a Puuc Region Center.* Publication 60. Middle American Research Institute, Tulane University.

Sabloff, J. A., G. Tourtellot, B. F. Beyer, P. A. McAnany, D. Christensen, S. Boucher, and T. R. Killion
1985   *Settlement and Community Patterns at Sayil, Yucatan, Mexico: The 1984 Season.* Latin American Institute Research Series 17. University of New Mexico, Albuquerque.

Tourtellot, G., J. A. Sabloff, M. P. Smyth, L. V. Whitley, S. L. Walling, T. Gallareta Negron, C. Perez Alvarez, G. F. Andrews, and N. P. Dunning
1988   Mapping Community Patterns at Sayil, Yucatan, Mexico: The 1985 Season. *Journal of New World Archaeology* 7 (2/3):1-24.

XIII

Variations on a Theme: A Frontier View of Maya Civilization

John S. Henderson

Department of Anthropology
Cornell University

The territory to the south and east of the area traditionally defined as the Maya world (Fig. 13.1) provides a distinctive perspective on the ancient Maya. This "Southeast Periphery," embracing western and central Honduras and most or all of El Salvador, is usually considered to be a frontier zone in which the cultural patterns that are taken to be typical of Mesoamerica and the Maya cultural traditions give way to others thought to typify differently structured societies. Inevitably, excavation of Maya centers, with their public architecture, monumental art, and hieroglyphic texts, took priority over investigation of the less impressive ancient communities of the periphery. The resulting sketchiness of the archaeological record in the Southeast Periphery has exacerbated the temptation to characterize the region negatively, in terms of the absence of "Maya features" and the corollary tendency to phrase interpretation in terms of interaction with the Maya world. Schortman and Urban (1986:8) provide an apt summation in the introduction to their recent collection of essays on the region:

> The Southeast Periphery . . . is uniquely situated to address questions of the nature and effects of intercultural interaction. Located on the fringes of two major cultural zones, Mesoamerica and Lower Central America, between which contact was maintained prehistorically, local socio-cultural developments were probably always influenced to a great extent by outside contacts and cannot be understood apart from those contacts.

They go on (Schortman and Urban 1986:8-14) to emphasize the importance of developing a thorough descriptive picture of the culture history of the region along with a conceptual framework that will permit interpretations to do justice to the complexity of these processes of "influence" and to assess their impact on local and regional developments. Their rejection of the prejudgment implicit in the term periphery and their insistence on the need to document patterns of variability and to understand local societies in organizational and behavioral terms—echoed in much recent work in the area (Hirth 1988; Robinson 1987; Urban and Schortman 1986)—represent a far more sophisticated approach to interaction than has been traditional. Nonetheless, for them, and for most archaeologists working in the region today, the central question remains the same: "the extent of contact with Maya and Mesoamerican societies in general, and the degree to which that contact influenced local developments" (Schortman and Urban 1986:9).

Phrasing the issue in this way highlights the importance of a prior question: What are the essential distinctive characteristics of Maya societies, and how shall we recognize them archaeologically? Traditional definitions have focused on lists of material traits, derived mainly from the relatively well documented Classic period centers of the southern Maya lowlands. Public architecture with corbeled vaults, stelae with hieroglyphic texts and Long Count dates, and certain styles of elaborately painted pottery have been particularly popular. The drawbacks in such definitions are obvious (Brown 1987; Henderson 1987). At best, they embody a static view of southeastern Mesoamerica and its societies that is at odds with the dynamic view we now have of the culture history of the region. Traditional approaches to defining a Maya cultural tradition do not accommodate change in basic Maya cultural patterns or shifts in the geographic distributions of the societies

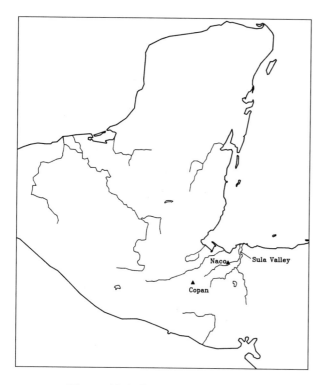

Figure 13.1. Eastern Mesoamerica.

	Sula Valley	Copan	Lago Yojoa	Chalchuapa
1500	Naco			Ahal
	Botija	Ejar	Rio Blanco	Matzin
1000	Santiago			
	Ulua	Coner	Yojoa	Payu
500		Acbi		Xocco
	Chamelecon	Bijac	Eden 2	Vec
				Caynac
AD/BC		Chabij		
			Eden 1	Chul
500	Playa	Uir	Jaral	Kal
	de los			Colos
	Muertos			
1000		Rayo		Tok

Figure 13.2. Sula Valley and Southeast Periphery chronology.

they are meant to characterize. Moreover, these standard definitions reflect a very narrow, elite-focused conception of the Maya cultural tradition that does not begin to take account of the emerging picture of variability even within the Classic period in the southern lowlands; whole sectors of what we normally think of as the Maya world—notably the highlands of Guatemala and Chiapas—are entirely beyond the pale.

It has become an archaeological commonplace to acknowledge that distribution of elements of material culture may crosscut language distributions, and few Maya archaeologists would now defend the proposition that any roster of material traits corresponds perfectly to Mayan-speaking groups. Nonetheless, many (perhaps most) current approaches to the archaeology of southeastern Mesoamerica still incorporate the assumption, usually unstated, that there is a reasonably coherent, if not entirely homogeneous, Maya cultural tradition: that is, a series of distinctive cultural patterns shared by speakers of Mayan languages. The continuing popularity of the rich body of information on Conquest period and modern Highland Maya soci-

eties as a source of analogies and models for interpreting earlier Lowland Maya societies reflects this implicit reliance on the reality of Maya cultural tradition. Recent attempts to understand the symbolic dimensions of Classic period art in terms of six-teenth-century Quiche myths recorded in the Popol Vuh (Coe 1973, 1978; Robicsek and Hales 1981; Schele and Miller 1986) provide the most obvious example.

A somewhat different interpretive strategy treats "standard" Maya features as the archaeological signature of the particular kind of sociopolitical organization that first crystallized in the Peten region of the southern Maya lowlands. The imprecision of continuing to refer to these traits as markers of Maya-ness is more than a semantic quibble, for it is not clear in what subtle, perhaps unconscious, ways this terminology may condition the argument that the spread of these features into the southeastern sector of the Maya world represents the imposition, by Peten-oriented Maya elites, of a new form of political organization and its associated ideology on culturally different, perhaps non-Maya, peoples (e.g., Schortman 1986; Willey 1986).

Figure 13.3. Olmec greenstone figurine (scale 10 cm).

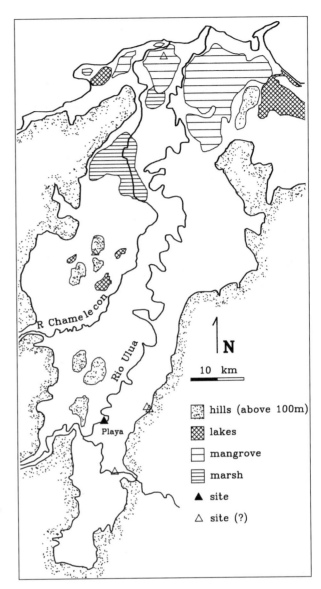

Figure 13.4. Sula Valley: Middle Preclassic and Playa phase settlements.

The attempt to understand the ancient societies of the Southeast Periphery in terms of relationships with Maya peoples to the north and west poses precisely the same risk of implicit bias. Systematic investigation of this issue clearly requires not only a definition of the material traits considered to be archaeological signatures of Maya-ness but also an explicit statement of their presumed relationship to Maya cultural identity. Language is not the only way to define cultural identity, but the issue must be addressed, for language is certainly a central dimension of interaction. It may not be possible to deal with the nature of interaction without adopting some model, stated or unstated, of the role of language, at least in terms of the degree of mutual intelligibility of the native tongues of the parties involved.

A more emic conceptualization of cultural identity—recognizing that the social definition of identity (the composition of the group with which affiliation is claimed) varies enormously with social context—would require quite a different approach to the archaeological record. Under this kind of definition, the linguistically and culturally cosmopolitan communities of the frontier zone would present a kaleidoscopic picture of continually shifting reference groups. The material reflections of these myriad facets of identity will inevitably be very confusing, and sorting them into comprehensible archaeological signatures will demand a very detailed picture of material variability within and among regions, but

Figure 13.5. Playa de los Muertos figurines (scale 10 cm).

the potential interpretive improvement is substantial. Even the opportunistic definition of cultural identity in terms of features easily detected archaeologically can be defended as long as the arbitrary nature of the traits and their lack of specifiable relationships with language or society is explicitly acknowledged.

The Sula Valley of northwestern Honduras (see Figs. 13.1, 13.4), often characterized as part of the cultural frontier along the southeastern fringe of the Maya world (Henderson 1977, 1978), is a region in which the issue of relationships with the Maya world is of particular concern. The very size of the Sula Valley—some 2,400 km^2 of territory, embracing a substantial range of environmental conditions— immediately highlights the critical dimension of regional variability. The differences among the ancient communities within the valley itself are, at least in some periods, as great as those between many regions in southeastern Mesoamerica. Beyond the essential task of creating a chronological framework in this previously very sketchily known area (Fig. 13.2), recent archaeological investigations (Henderson 1984) have focused largely on documenting this variability. A systematic approach to understanding the archaeological record in terms of interaction and cultural relationships is necessarily a later phase of an analysis still only in its initial stages, but a brief summary of the basic historical sequence will illustrate the complexity of the interpretive problems.

Apart from scattered traces of preceramic groups, the earliest known occupation of the valley appears to correspond to the early part of the Middle Preclassic period. A few Olmec-style objects (Fig. 13.3) without archaeological context, may lend themselves to traditional interpretations—that the valley was already under the "influence" of a more complex society centered to the west and north in Mesoamerica proper—but existing archaeological data do not permit a plausible reconstruction of the interaction involved.

In the later part of the Middle Preclassic and the earlier Late Preclassic period (Fig. 13.4) Sula Valley ceramic vessels and figurines (Fig. 13.5) represent the famous "Playa de los Muertos" style (Kennedy 1986). These objects, too, have been the basis for much speculation about far-flung currents of external interaction, but beyond the fact that some local villagers used them as grave goods, we have no real information about their significance.

By the beginning of the Chamelecon phase (ca. 200 B.C.), some villages had grown to substantial size (Fig. 13.6) and some of them featured structures much larger than ordinary house platforms (Pope 1986, 1987; Robinson 1987; Wonderley 1985). These developments seem to signal the beginnings of a process of increasing social, political, and economic complexity in the valley, although we cannot be certain that these characteristics had not emerged earlier. An obsidian-blade industry utilizing raw

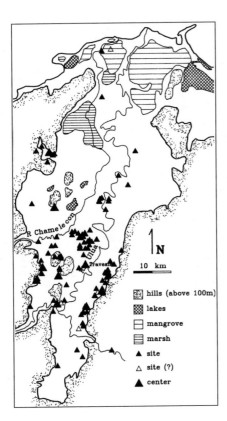

Figure 13.6. Sula Valley: Early Chamelecon phase settlements.

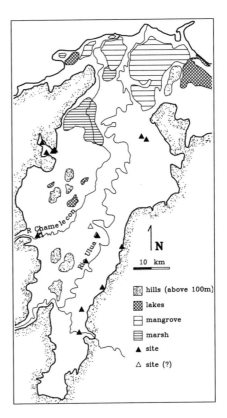

Figure 13.7. Sula Valley: Middle and Late Chamelecon phase settlements.

materials imported from highland Guatemalan sources was well established. At the same time, the appearance of Usulutan decoration and related features of ceramic manufacture indicate that Sula Valley potters shared ideas of how to make and decorate pots with their counterparts in communities throughout southeastern Mesoamerica.

Again, we have no good idea of the nature of the networks of communication that produced this situation. Through the first part of the Chamelecon phase, before the standard features of Maya civilization had appeared in the southern lowlands, the notion of "Maya influence" on a peripheral southeastern zone makes little sense. A classificatory approach would include the Sula Valley along with the rest of the Southeast Periphery and the highlands of Guatemala in a single archaeological culture area (Demarest and Sharer 1986). A simple characterization of trajectories of influence would in fact emphasize the impact of the southeastern zone on the southern Maya lowlands rather than the reverse.

Middle and Late Chamelecon phase (A.D. 100-500) communities in the Sula Valley (Fig. 13.7) were generally very much like their predecessors, reflecting a continuation of the gradual processes of community growth and increasing complexity (Pope 1986, 1987; Robinson 1987). These processes included a gradual elaboration of repertoires of pottery form and decoration, while ceramic assemblages in the valley continued to reflect a general affinity with the rest of the Southeast Periphery and the southeastern fringe of the Maya lowlands. Apart from scattered ceramic vessels that may represent imports, there are no indications of particularly close connections with more distant sectors of the Maya lowlands.

In the Ulua phase, equivalent to the Late Classic period in the Maya world (A.D. 500-850), long-standing growth processes culminated in a period of maximal complexity in the Sula Valley (Hasemann et al. 1978; Joyce 1985, 1986, 1987; Pope 1986, 1987; Robinson 1986, 1987; Sheptak 1987; Stone 1941).

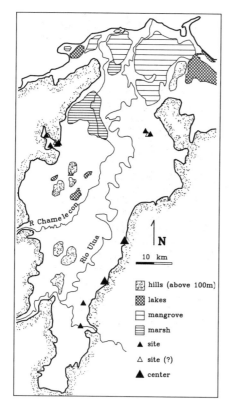

Figure 13.8. Sula Valley: Ulua phase settlements.

Figure 13.9. Ulua polychrome vessel (scale 10 cm).

Communities were more closely spaced and more differentiated than ever before (Fig. 13.8). Some grew to great size, with substantial public architecture in their civic cores. Arts and crafts reflect a process of florescence with the emergence of the elaborate Ulua Polychrome style of pottery decoration (Fig. 13.9) and the associated carved Ulua "marble" vessels, both widely distributed in the Southeast Periphery and beyond. Many aspects of Ulua phase communities suggest connections with the Maya world, and the traditional interpretation has been that the valley was the seat of "Mayoid" societies: non-Maya peoples imitating their more sophisticated neighbors to the west and north without fully participating in the essential patterns of Maya civilization. The nature of the interaction is certainly critical to an understanding of the Sula Valley and of wider processes of interaction in the Southeastern Periphery; plausible interpretations require a much more carefully reasoned approach to the issue of cultural identity.

One facet of the interaction is economic exchange, and the Sula Valley communities certainly continued to import obsidian from sources in the Guatemalan highlands, though we can neither reconstruct the full range of materials exchanged nor characterize the exchange relationships themselves in any detailed way. Ulua Polychrome and marble vessels found in Maya sites might represent economic ties as well, although the evidence from Copan—the only case in which there is reasonably detailed contextual information—suggests that the situation was rather more complicated (Gerstle 1987). Ulua Polychrome pottery and mold-made figurine whistles, at least some of which appear to have been manufactured in the Sula Valley, have been found in concentration as part of the basic domestic equipment of one sector of an aristocratic residential compound at Copan. Ulua Polychrome vessels also served as mortuary and cache offerings here as well as in elite tombs elsewhere in the center. Gerstle's interpretation, positing the presence of Lenca resi-

Figure 13.10. "Stela" from Calabazas (note stylized outline face near top).

dents among Maya aristocrats, may very well be correct, but it depends upon an undemonstrated characterization of the Sula Valley potters as non-Maya.

In the Sula Valley itself, scattered ceramic vessels may represent imports from the Maya lowlands, and skeletal remains featuring Maya-style jade dental inlays may represent foreign individuals who happened to die away from home. However, other aspects of Ulua phase communities—ranging from very general features of settlement organization to very specific elements of ceramic manufacture and decoration—certainly represent local patterns shared with the Maya world. Large centers feature ball courts, temples, and other civic structures, sometimes with dressed-stone construction and sculptural ornamentation. Several centers erected vertical stone shafts among public buildings; these "stelae" (Fig. 13.10) do not have hieroglyphic texts or portraits of nobles carved in relief, but at least one, from Travesía, was originally plastered and painted. Caches in low shrines include offerings of Spondylus shells accompanied by red pigment and jade ornaments. At least one center built internal causeways.

Some domestic architectural groupings have a familiar plazuela layout. Ceramic assemblages associated with both civic and domestic structures reflect several patterns of similarity with pottery from the Maya world. Some relatively simple Ulua-phase decorated serving vessels are essentially Sula Valley equivalents of types manufactured at communities in several parts of the southern Maya lowlands. Ulua Polychrome pottery (see Figs. 13.9, 13.11) is quite varied and shows a more complex array of similarities with Maya polychrome ceramics, ranging from a comparable overall style, through shared features of design organization, to identical vessel forms and design elements. To what degree Ulua Polychrome iconography represents a variant of the symbol systems of the Maya lowlands—as opposed to a redefinition of Maya symbols in the context of a very different cultural system—is an open question that can be resolved only through a thorough comparative analysis, which remains to be accomplished. I believe that this kind of analysis, with its potential to provide a systematic measure of the degree to which local peoples shared belief systems with the Maya

Figure 13.11. Ulua polychrome vessel; figure seated in stylized building (scale 10 cm).

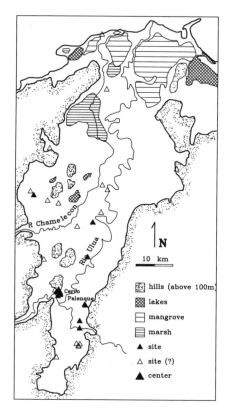

Figure 13.12. Sula Valley: Santiago phase settlements.

world, represents an important approach to the issue of cultural identity.

In the Santiago phase (A.D. 850-1050), equivalent to the Terminal Classic period, Sula Valley societies experienced the same process of cultural disruption that afflicted the southern Maya lowlands. Most communities in the valley were abandoned, and only Cerro Palenque survived as a preeminent civic center (Fig. 13.12) The manufacture of Ulua Polychrome pottery ceased as Sula Valley potters began to produce a local version of the fine-paste ceramics associated with the collapse in the Pasion region of the southern Maya lowlands. Cerro Palenque, too, was abandoned in the subsequent Botija phase, and the valley was apparently very sparsely settled during the Early Postclassic period (Fig. 13.13)

By the time of the European invasion, the valley was much more densely settled, although the extensive destruction and rebuilding of larger Conquest-period communities by the Spanish have largely obscured the archaeological record of the Late

Postclassic Naco phase. Sula Valley communities (Fig. 13.14) were closely allied with the nearby town of Naco, on the Río Chamelecon, and may actually have been subordinate to it politically (Henderson 1977; Wonderley 1981, 1984a, 1984b, 1986a, 1986b, 1987). Ceramics, architecture, and settlement organization all point to renewed interaction with the Maya lowlands. Documentary sources leave no doubt that both areas participated in a thriving commercial network that forged intimate economic links with Maya communities to the north and west, but they do not provide clear indications of the linguistic affiliation of the native populations of either the Sula Valley or the Naco Valley.

The basic outline of Sula Valley culture history, sketchy though it is in many respects, affords clear evidence of continued relationships between local societies and the Maya world. Economically, the areas were always linked. To judge by similarities in material items, interaction was particularly intense in the Late Classic period, and from this time on the

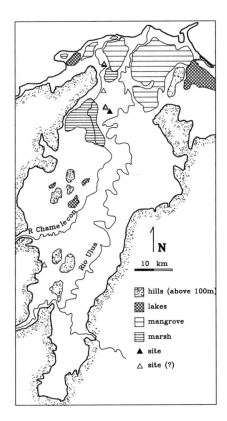

Figure 13.13. Sula Valley: Botija phase settelements.

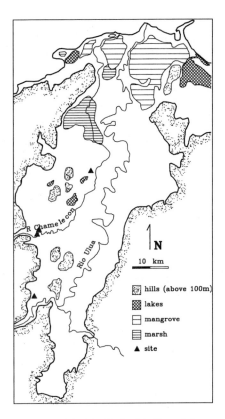

Figure 13.14. Sula Valley: Naco phase settlements.

basic trajectory of change in settlement organization, and in at least some facets of sociopolitical organization, were the same as in the Maya world. These features can only be understood in the context of patterns of variability within and beyond the valley, which remain incompletely determined (Henderson 1987; Schortman and Urban 1986). Even when the archaeological context is much more fully documented, however, it will not necessarily be self-evident which, if any, of these similarities reflect "foreign influence" and which might be better interpreted as indications that Sula Valley societies shared basic cultural patterns indicative of a common cultural identity with their neighbors in the Maya world.

A serious reconsideration of the problem of defining a Maya cultural tradition—however normative and old-fashioned it may seem in the context of recent trends in archaeological theory—is clearly in order. A proper definition will not emerge quickly, for a thorough documentation of regional patterns of similarity and availability throughout the Maya world and the Southeast Periphery—the delineation of archaeological "culture areas" (Demarest and Sharer 1986)—is only the first step that will allow us to recognize interaction and to begin to characterize it in terms of cultural processes. It is equally critical, and far more difficult, to deal with the more general theoretical issues surrounding cultural identity: In what cultural realms does it lie, and how may it be expressed materially and thereby detected in the archaeological record? Meanwhile, explicit statements of the working models of the Maya cultural tradition that inform our analyses and interpretations will sharpen and strengthen our arguments.

BIBLIOGRAPHY

Brown, K. L.
1987   Core or Periphery: The 'Highland Maya'
            Question. In *Interaction on the Southeast
            Mesoamerican Frontier: Prehistoric and
            Historic Honduras and El Salvador*, ed. E.
            J. Robinson, pp. 421-434. BAR International
            Series 327. Oxford.

Coe, M. D.
1973   *The Maya Scribe and His World*. New
            York: Grolier Club.
1978   *Lords of the Underworld: Masterpieces of
            Classic Maya Ceramics*. Princeton: The Art
            Museum, Princeton University.

Demarest, A. A., and R. J. Sharer
1986   Late Preclassic Ceramic Spheres, Culture
            Areas, and Cultural Evolution in the
            Southeastern Highlands of Mesoamerica. In
            The Southeast Maya Periphery, eds. P. A.
            Urban and E. M. Schortman, pp. 194-223.
            Austin: University of Texas Press.

Gerstle, A.
1987   Ethnic Diversity and Interaction at Copan,
            Honduras. In *Interaction on the Southeast
            Mesoamerican Frontier: Prehistoric and
            Historic Honduras and El Salvador*, ed. E.
            J. Robinson, pp. 328-356. BAR International
            Series 327. Oxford.

Hasemann, G., V. Veliz, and L. Van Gerpen
1978   Informe Preliminar, Currusté: Fase I. Ms.
            om file, Instituto Hondureño de Antro-
            pología e Historia.

Henderson, J. S.
1977   The Valle de Naco: Ethnohistory and
            Archaeology in Northwestern Honduras.
            Ethnohistory 24(4):363-377.
1978   El noroeste de Honduras y la frontera ori-
            ental maya. *Yaxkin* 2(4):241-253.
1987   Frontier at the Crossroads. In *Interaction
            on the Southeast Mesoamerican Frontier:
            Prehistoric and Historic Honduras and El
            Salvador*, ed. E. J. Robinson, pp. 455-462.
            BAR International Series 327. Oxford.

Henderson, J. S. (editor)
1984   *Archaeology in Northwestern Honduras:
            Interim Reports of the Proyecto Arque-
            ológico Sula*, vol. I. Occasional Papers,
            Latin American Studies and Archaeology
            Programs, Cornell University.

Hirth, K. G.
1988   Beyond the Maya Frontier: Cultural
            Interaction and Syncretism along the
            Central Honduran Corridor. In *The
            Southeast Classic Maya Zone*, eds. E. H.
            Boone and G. R. Willey, pp. 297-334.
            Washington, DC: Dumbarton Oaks.

Joyce, R. A.
1985   Cerro Palenque, Valle del Ulua, Honduras:
            Terminal Classic Interaction on the
            Southern Mesoamerican Periphery. Ph.D.
            dissertation, University of Illinois.
1986   Terminal Classic Interaction on the
            Southeastern Maya Periphery. *American
            Antiquity* 51(2):313-329.
1987   Intraregional Ceramic Variation and Social
            Class: Developmental Trajectories of
            Classic Period Ceramic Complexes from
            the Ulua Valley. In *Interaction on the
            Southeast Mesoamerican Frontier:
            Prehistoric and Historic Honduras and El
            Salvador*, ed. E. J. Robinson, pp. 280-303.
            BAR International Series 327. Oxford.

Kennedy, N.
1986   The Periphery Problem and Playa de los
            Muertos: A Test Case. In *The Southeast
            Maya Periphery*, eds. P. A. Urban and E. M.
            Schortman, pp. 179-193. Austin: University
            of Texas Press.

Pope, K. O.
1986   Palaeoecology of the Ulua Valley,
            Honduras: An Archaeological Perspective.
            Ph.D. dissertation, Stanford University.
1987   The Ecology and Economy of the
            Formative-Classic Transition along the Ulua
            River, Honduras. In *Interaction on the
            Southeast Mesoamerican Frontier:
            Prehistoric and Historic Honduras and El
            Salvador*, ed. E. J. Robinson, pp. 95-128.
            BAR International Series 327. Oxford.

Robicsek, F., and D. M. Hales
1981   *The Maya Book of the Dead: The Ceramic
            Codex*. Charlottesville: University of
            Virginia Art Museum.

Robinson, E. J.
1986   A Typological Study of Prehistoric
            Settlement of the Eastern Alluvial Fans,
            Sula Valley, Honduras: Comparison to
            Maya Settlement Forms. In *The Southeast*

Maya Periphery, eds. P. A. Urban and E. M. Schortman, pp. 239-261. Austin: University of Texas Press.

1987 Sula Valley Diachronic Regional and Interregional Interaction: A View from the East Side Alluvial Fans. In *Interaction on the Southeast Mesoamerican Frontier: Prehistoric and Historic Honduras and El Salvador*, ed. E. J. Robinson, pp. 154-195. BAR International Series 327. Oxford.

Robinson, E. J. (editor)
1987 *Interaction on the Southeast Mesoamerican Frontier: Prehistoric and Historic Honduras and El Salvador*. BAR International Series 327. Oxford.

Schele, L., and M. E. Miller
1986 *The Blood of Kings: Dynasty and Ritual in Maya Art*. Fort Worth, TX: Kimbell Art Museum.

Schortman, E. M.
1986 Interaction between the Maya and Non-Maya along the Late Classic Southeast Maya Periphery: The View from the Lower Motagua Valley, Guatemala. In *The Southeast Maya Periphery*, eds. P. A. Urban and E. M. Schortman, pp. 114-137. Austin: University of Texas Press.

Schortman, E. M., and P. A. Urban
1986 Introduction. In *The Southeast Maya Periphery*, eds. P. A. Urban and E. M. Schortman, pp. 1-14. Austin: University of Texas Press.

Sheptak, R. N.
1987 Interaction between Belize and the Ulua Valley. In *Interaction on the Southeast Mesoamerican Frontier: Prehistoric and Historic Honduras and El Salvador*, ed. E. J. Robinson, pp. 247-266. BAR International Series 327. Oxford.

Stone, D. Z.
1941 *The Archaeology of the North Coast of Honduras*. Harvard University, Peabody Museum Memoirs, vol. 9, no. 1. Harvard University.

Willey, G. R.
1986 Copan, Quirigua, and the Southeast Maya Zone: A Summary View. In *The Southeast Maya Periphery*, eds. P. A. Urban and E. M. Schortman, pp. 168-175. Austin: University of Texas Press.

Wonderley, A. W.
1981 Late Postclassic Excavations at Naco, Honduras. Ph.D. dissertation, Cornell University.
1984a The Land of Ulua at Conquest. In *Archaeology in Northwestern Honduras: Interim Reports of the Proyecto Arqueologico Sula*, ed. J. S. Henderson, vol. 1, pp. 4-25. Occasional Papers, Latin American Studies and Archaeology Programs, Cornell University.
1984b Naco Phase (Late Postclassic) Test Excavations. In *Archaeology in Northwestern Honduras: Interim Reports of the Proyecto Arqueologico Sula*, ed. J. S. Henderson, vol. 1, pp. 26-66. Occasional Papers, Latin American Studies and Archaeology Programs, Cornell University.
1985 Investigaciones arqueológicas en R2o Pelo, Valle de Sula: Preclásico Tardío. Paper presented at Tercer Seminario de Arqueología Hondureña, Tela, Honduras.
1986a Materials Symbolic in Pre-Columbian Households: The Painted Pottery of Naco, Honduras. *Journal of Anthropological Research* 42(4):497-534.
1986b Naco, Honduras: Some Aspects of a Late Pre-Columbian Community on the Eastern Maya Frontier. In *The Southeast Maya Periphery*, eds. P. A. Urban and E. M. Schortman, pp. 313-332. Austin: University of Texas Press.
1987 Imagery in Household Pottery from 'La Gran Provincia de Naco.' In *Interaction on the Southeast Mesoamerican Frontier: Prehistoric and Historic Honduras and El Salvador*, ed. E. J. Robinson, pp. 304-327. BAR International Series 327. Oxford.

XIV
Deciphering Maya Architectural Plans

Wendy Ashmore

Department of Anthropology
Douglas College, Rutgers University

Many city plans have been created deliberately to serve as maps of the proper structure of the cosmos as conceived in the cultures of which the individual cities are parts. These layouts do more than provide information and a guide, however. As Nancy Shatzman Steinhardt (1986) has recently reminded us, such city plans are sometimes used by new sovereigns to legitimate their political authority, almost as badges of kingship, as was the case with Mongol Chinese capitals built by Khubilai Khan and his successors. Certainly the mere existence of monumental architecture as the material expression of an ability to commission construction of imposing buildings bespeaks some degree of potency in a centralized authority (Price 1978). Indeed, ancient Mesopotamian cities with their ziggurats, Machu Picchu and other imperial Inca sites with their cyclopean masonry, and North America's Cahokia with its huge focal Monks Mound all continue to impress observers by the grand scale of their remains. These same constructions, however, often contain more pointed and specific messages of power, for their plans generally place the working and/or living quarters of those in power in symbolically paramount locations (Fritz 1986; Fritz and Michell 1987), thereby asserting that maintenance of order in the universe is bound to perpetuation of the political and social status quo. Ancient Maya cities were certainly no exceptions in any of these regards, and Maya rulers used monumental architecture—as they did elaborate sculpture, hieroglyphic inscriptions, ostentatious personal regalia, and public ceremonies—to make pointed statements reinforcing the strength of their sovereignty in the minds of both peers and subordinates.

The present paper explores some particular forms in site planning from several parts of the Maya areas of Mexico, Guatemala, Belize, and Honduras as well as adjacent non-Maya regions in the latter country

(Fig. 14.1). As will be described, the specific architectural patterning is most strongly manifest in Maya remains from the Classic period (ca. A.D. 250-900), although it derived, at least in part, from more general Mesoamerican roots in the Preclassic period (before A.D. 250). The pattern spoke of the divine mandate for authority and invoked elements of creation myths to underscore the primordial and immutable nature of that authority. By Classic times, Maya builders were drawing from a standard grammar but flexible vocabulary of spatial expression that allowed them to make statements of varying degrees of grandeur and pretension, from the scale of individual buildings or building groups to that of architectural complexes embracing entire civic cores.

As many authors have reminded us (e.g., Schele and Miller 1986), these architectural features had dynamic aspects as well as static ones, serving as stages for performance of rites and ceremonies by priests and kings, with these activities likewise designed to reinforce the messages of divinely mandated power. Abundant and dramatic new data and interpretations bearing on the nature of these rites have emerged in recent years, perhaps most broadly disseminated through a spectacular museum exhibition and accompanying volume, both entitled *The Blood of Kings* (Schele and Miller 1986). While I agree that the activities performed *within* the architectural settings were crucial to communication of the intended messages, the settings themselves still need intensive study. The focus here will therefore remain on description of the architectural arrangements themselves and inference of political contexts in which they were created. Recognition and interpretation of aspects of the arrangements have been discussed by others (e.g., Coggins 1967, 1980; Guillemin 1968), and discussion here is part of a continuing and evolving consideration on my own part (Ashmore 1986, 1987a, 1987b, 1989). The fol-

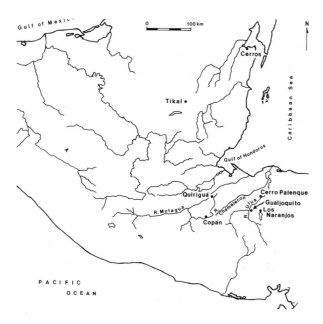

Figure 14.1. Map showing locations of sites mentioned.

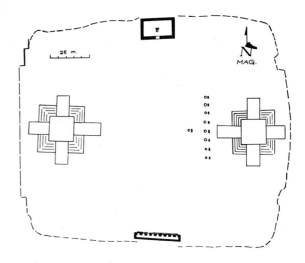

Figure 14.2. Reconstruction drawing of Tikal Twin Pyramid group 4E-4. Courtesy of Tikal Project, The University Museum, The University of Pennsylvania.

lowing paragraphs constitute therefore an interim statement, not a definitive one.

DESCRIPTION AND INTERPRETATION: EXAMPLES FROM TIKAL

The five principal components of the pattern are (1) a strongly marked north-south axis; (2) mutually complementary, paired functions for construction and spaces at north and south ends of that axis, in which north stands for the celestial supernatural sphere, and south, for the underworld or worldly; (3) the appendage of subsidiary eastern and western units to form a triangle with the north; (4) the common but not invariant presence of a ball court as mediator between north and south; and (5) the frequent use of causeways, or paved roadways, to underscore the linkage between various elements and thereby stress the symbolic coherence of the whole.

The inferred cosmological bases for the pattern include several tenets shared broadly by indigenous cultures across Mexico and Central America, and even in other areas, but with strongly Maya-flavored expressions within southern Mesoamerica. These tenets include (1) conceptions of a multilayered universe, with a many-tiered heaven above, wherein the ancestors reside, and a similarly stratified underworld, home of various other supernaturals and the scene of primordial ordeals involving the legendary Hero Twins; (2) unification of these layers *in time* via cyclical movement of the sun, moon, Venus, and other deified entities through the upper- and underworlds; (3) explicit vertical connectors in *space* between the earth and other cosmic domains, such as the four *bacab* deities holding up the corners of the sky, mountains mediating between sky and earth, and caves linking earth with the world below; and (4) a horizontal division of the world into four cardinal quarters (plus a center), each with color and life-form associations.

The relation between these conceptions and the architectural patterning can be seen most easily at Tikal, and there, most readily in the famous Twin Pyramid groups (Fig. 14.2). The earliest known of these groups probably pertains to the sixth century A.D. (Jones 1969:93-96, and personal communication, 1987; see also Coggins 1983:53), and all have been interpreted as arenas for celebration of rituals associated with the completion of 20-year calendric periods called *katuns* (Jones 1969:128-137). Physically, each group (where complete) consists of a pair of multitiered pyramids to the east and west of

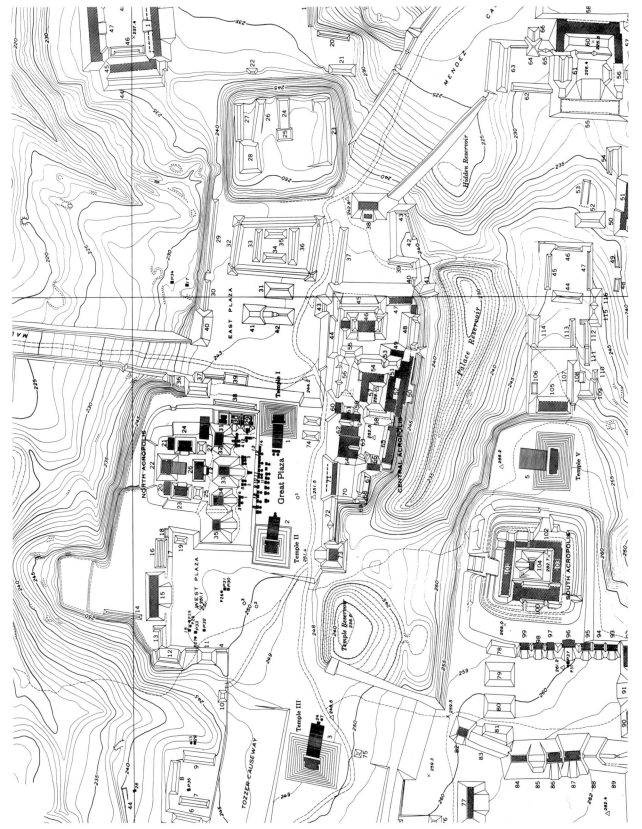

Figure 14.3. Map of Great Plaza area of Tikal. Courtesy of Tikal Project, The University Museum, The University of Pennsylvania.

a large plaza, with a small enclosure to the north and a single structure to the south. The eastern pyramid has from three to eight uncarved stone slabs, or stelae, on its plaza side. The northern enclosure is unroofed and houses a single carved stela and altar pair, in most cases depicting the current ruler (not always the same individual who commissioned construction of the group; Ashmore and Sharer 1975), and the southern structure has nine doorways. Although the northern and southern enclosed spaces are small and do not invite entry by large numbers of people, the plaza between them would allow quite sizable congregations, and the stela and altar are easily visible to any individuals passing the northern enclosure doorway. In fact, Christopher Jones, who excavated and first analyzed these complexes, suggests that the north stela was the intended focus for the group (Jones 1969:136).

Clemency Coggins (1980) has argued convincingly that the Twin Pyramid group depicts the Maya cosmos in miniature, turned 90°, on its side. That is, the pyramids are each, like the universe itself, cardinally quartered in plan and vertically layered in profile, and together the pair mark the rise and set points of the sun's daily passage into, across, and out of the heavens. The nine-doorwayed southern building stands for the underworld and the Nine Lords the Maya believe rule there. The northern enclosure, open to the sky, represents the zenith of the celestial world, an equation of "north" and "up" supported by modern Maya belief and custom (e.g., Bricker 1983; Gossen 1974). Not only is the microcosmic arrangement of the Twin Pyramid groups appropriate for celebration of rituals marking the completion of a 20-year time cycle, but it also serves as perpetual reminder of the validity of the political status quo: one's attention is drawn to the king, visibly and materially apotheosized by prominent placement of his portrait monument in the symbolic heavens, where he joins his divine ancestors. His power and authority are reiterated for every observer who enters the Twin Pyramid precinct.

Beginning with Guillemin (1968), numerous scholars have noted the similarities between these Twin Pyramid groups and the Late Classic plan of Tikal's North and Central Acropolis complexes (Fig. 14.3). There, the northern position again is marked by the presence of Tikal's dynasts, this time by the tombs, funerary shrines, and sculpted monuments of Early Classic rulers; again, the location stands for the heavens, where the venerated royal ancestors now reside. To the south, across the Great Plaza, is a nine-doorwayed building, Structure 5D-120, built about the same time as, or slightly earlier than, the first known Twin Pyramid group (Jones 1969:94). This nine-doorwayed building does not now stand alone, however. Instead, it is an early element in what was to become the large residential-administrative complex we call the Central Acropolis. East and west edges of the Great Plaza are marked by pyramids, but in this instance each has only one stairway and its summit is crowned with a building. Each of this pair is also a funerary or memorial monument.

Surely it is more than coincidence that the king buried beneath Temple I, Ah Cacau, was the same one who reinvigorated the tradition of building Twin Pyramid groups. That is, by the time the eastern temple, Temple I, was raised in the late seventh or early eighth century A.D., the North Acropolis had become extremely crowded with tombs and temples. Symbolic apotheosis in the stela enclosure of the Twin Pyramid groups may thus be interpretable as an acceptable alternative to actual northern interment (see Ashmore and Sharer 1975; Coggins 1975; A. G. Miller 1986), and certainly occupation of an eastern position—in this case, by interment there—carries connotations of power in Maya thinking (Gossen 1974; see also M. E. Miller 1985 for specific interpretation of the relative placements of all the Great Temples of Tikal).

The layouts of the Twin Pyramid groups and the North-Central Acropolis combination thus seem to be variants of the same cosmic map. In the latter expression, however, there are two important additions. One is the Central Acropolis complex backing Structure 5D-120, and the other is the ball court on the southeast corner of the Great Plaza, just south of Temple I. Both, I would argue, imply the commanding authority held by the occupants of the Central Acropolis—if not the sovereign and his family, then certainly individuals and groups under his direct control. First, the ball court is the legendary arena where, as recounted in the Popol Vuh, the great creation story of the Quiche Maya (e.g., Tedlock 1985), the legendary Hero Twins defeated the evil Lords of the Underworld in the quintessential battle for power and survival. The court thus stands for the supernatural realm itself. Ball courts also served as boundary markers, points of transition or of integration, including the juxtaposition between the world

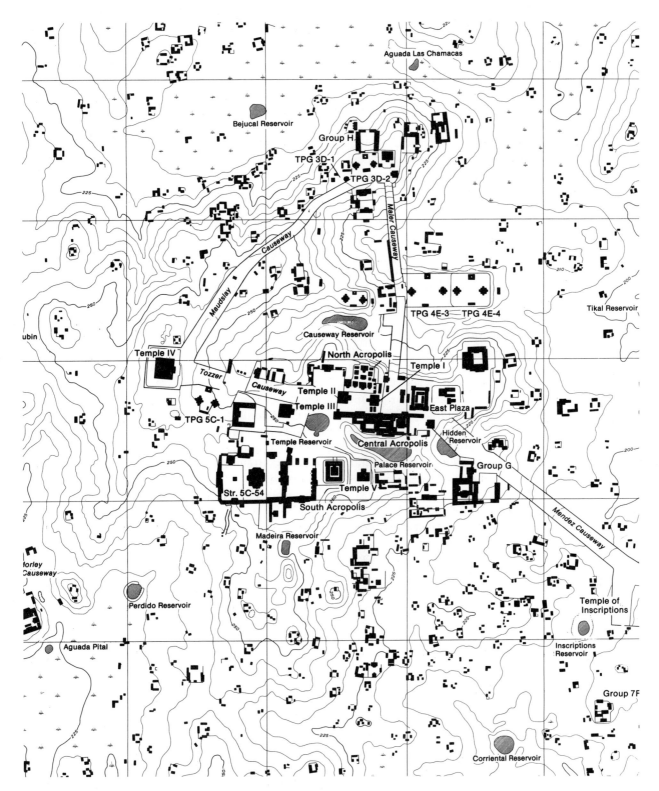

Figure 14.4. Map of the central portion of Tikal, Guatemala, with Twin Pyramid groups highlighted (courtesy of Tikal Project, The University Museum, The University of Pennsylvania).

of humans and the dark supernatural world (Gillespie 1985). Finally and most concretely, each ball court seems to have been an arena where the primordial power struggles were ritually reenacted by living men, to demonstrate repeatedly the supremacy of the king among his contemporaries (Schele and Miller 1986). Kings could stage "fixed" games, defeating peers already captured in battle, and there deal them the final mortal defeat. Thus the south side of Tikal's Great Plaza combines references to the underworld itself and to passage into and out of it: that is, the southern location here may mark simultaneously both the underworld, symbolized by Structure 5D-120 and the ball court, and, in the latter construction, the earth's surface as transition point to the supernatural world below. This dual connotation of south implies that whoever occupies that position controls access to supernaturals, at least those other than direct ancestors.

There is yet another expression of the cosmic template at Tikal, this one, like the one just described, pivoting on the ball court in the Great Plaza but dramatically dwarfing the earlier version in grandeur (Fig. 14.4). Ah Cacau's constructions clearly emphasized the microcosmic layout of both the Great Plaza complex and the Twin Pyramid groups. He may also, however, have begun to trace a larger layout in which the ball court retained the southern position but where the other points were marked by Twin Pyramid groups. Whether such intention underlay locations for his Twin Pyramid groups 3D-1 and 5C-1, that plan does seem evident in the positioning of major constructions commissioned by his successors. Certainly they continued to build Twin Pyramid groups, and these were larger in scale than Ah Cacau's. But Ah Cacau's son, Yax Kin Caan Chac, executed the template on a gigantic scale, in some places partly obliterating the work of his father.

In this grandest expression, Temples IV and VI mark the west and east points, Twin Pyramid group 3D-2 occupies the north, the ball court/Central Acropolis the south, and a series of paved causeways, either newly built or newly refurbished, unite the whole. Actually, it is not clear whether the previously cited ball court pivot was used for this version, for the East Plaza ball court, built in the mid-seventh century (Christopher Jones, personal communication, 1987), defines an alternative pivot point, east of Temple I at—importantly—the junction of the Maler and Mendez causeways. It would also seem signifi-

cant, a physical as well as metaphorical juxtaposition of symbols, that this court was built directly over the earliest of the known Twin Pyramid groups, Group 5E-Sub.1 (Jones 1969:31-32).

The role of the causeways in the grand cosmic map deserves further attention. Because the complete composition is not visible simultaneously except on a map or from the air, the causeways would have served not only to link the key positions by routes of literal physical access but also to remind those passing along them that the points so linked were few and special, and all parts of a larger whole. Presumably some portion of causeway traffic involved progress from one ritual observance to another, where the role and importance of the specific architectural complex at a road's end would have been pointed out. But the causeways themselves are the key to perception and continuous active integration of the otherwise invisible whole. And lest the passerby lose sight that the message conveyed by this whole is one of power and authority, at least the Maler Causeway, connecting the north and south/center points of the design, is flanked at its midpoint by three Twin Pyramid groups and, nearer its north terminus, incorporates a well-known sculpted outcrop with a bound-captive motif. Certainly the same kinds of messages were being conveyed in other sculptural, textual, and ritual media, but this complex architectural expression is remarkably coherent and emphatic.

ANTECEDENTS, CONTEMPORARIES, AND DERIVATIVES

Elsewhere (Ashmore 1987a, 1987b, 1989), I have suggested that the origins of the template here described can be found in some site layouts of the Preclassic. Not all antecedents are Maya, as seems to be illustrated, for example, by the Main Group of Preclassic/Early Classic Los Naranjos in west-central Honduras (Baudez and Becquelin 1973). By the Late Preclassic, however, about 50 B.C.-A.D. 50, most elements of the template were in place in the Maya area, as can be seen in the plan of Cerros (Fig. 14.5), a small but precocious center on Chetumal Bay in northern Belize. As explained elsewhere (Ashmore 1986; Freidel 1985, 1986a, 1986b; Schele and Miller 1986), the role of north as up, celestial, and eminence is embodied in the famous mask-adorned

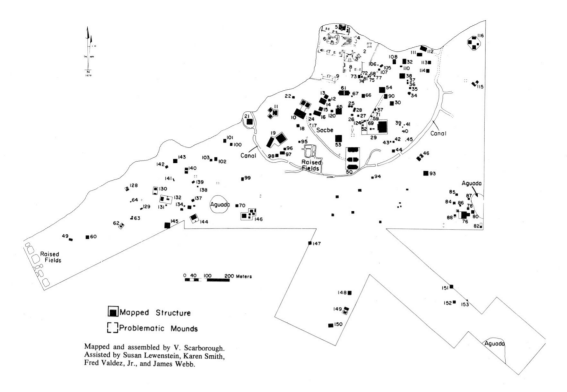

Figure 14.5. Map of Cerros, Belize, with ball courts highlighted (after Freidel 1986b; courtesy of David A. Freidel).

Structure 5C-2nd there. The dual significance of the ball court as transition and as south is apparently attested to in the position of the two ball courts, Structure 61 and the Structure 50 group (Scarborough et al. 1982), as well as within the arrangement and probable functional differentiation (David Freidel, personal communication, 1986; Lewenstein 1987) of the Structure 50 group.

The onset of the Classic period, about A.D. 250, is marked by a dramatic shift in the identity of the sovereign from mediator between this world and the divine to divinity incarnate (Freidel 1981; A. G. Miller 1986; see also Sahlins 1983). This shift is heralded by an explosive proliferation of media and icons for expressing kingly power, as outlined eloquently elsewhere by other scholars (e.g., Schele and Miller 1986). One variant still little studied, however, is precisely the architectural template under discussion here (cf. Schele and Miller 1986:34-35).

Although the distribution of Early Classic manifestations of this template still needs much investigation, the patterning is abundantly (if not ubiquitously) evident in Late Classic times. Indeed,

some years ago Coggins (1967) noted that the juxtaposition of a northern ritual group and a southern residential-administrative group is a pattern common in Classic sites of northeast Guatemala, frequently with a ball court between. It also occurs in the southeast Maya centers of Copan (see Fash 1983, Fig. 9.7, pp. 284-285) and Quirigua (Fig. 14.6). In these sites, too, the south-lying acropolis complexes have been strongly asserted to represent controlled-access domains of the sovereigns, for combined ritual and residential activities (e.g., for Copan, M. E. Miller 1984, 1988; for Quirigua, Ashmore 1984; Jones and Sharer 1986; Sharer 1978). The argument here is that the relative southern placement of these compounds is not coincidental: rather it was a deliberate reiteration by the sovereign of his authority.

In places like these, the presence of this template seems to correlate, in fact, with new and/or intrusive power. Perhaps analogy with Khubilai Khan's strategy is appropriate: as Steinhardt (1986) has recently remarked, that ruler's cities were deliberately built according to a time-honored cosmic plan, serving to legitimate the outsider's claim to authority by placing

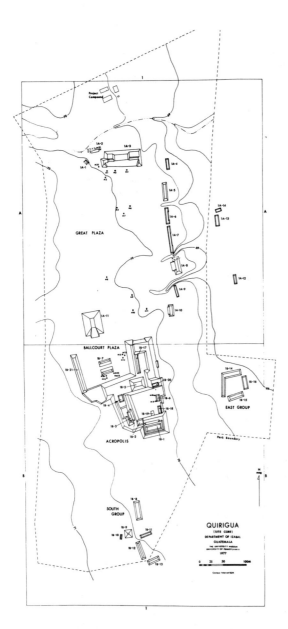

Figure 14.6. Map of site core of Quirigua, Guatemala (courtesy of Quirigua Project, The University Museum, The University of Pennsylvania).

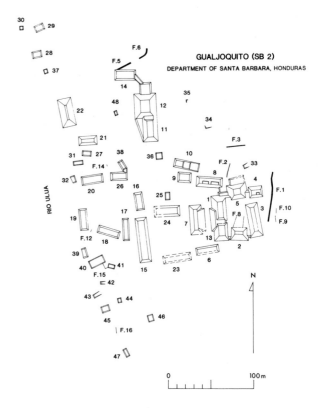

Figure 14.7. Map of Gualjoquito, Honduras (Santa Barbara Project).

him and his court in positions and contexts traditionally defined as the seats of power. Among the Maya, Quirigua seems to represent the same situation, in which a group of Early Classic Maya intruded their rule over the local populace, from whom they were perhaps ethnically distinct (Schortman 1980, 1984, 1986); the new rulers then proceeded to use a battery of means to proclaim their right to rule. Among

other media—as varied as sculpture, hieroglyphic inscriptions, and painted pottery—they certainly adopted power-imbued cosmic templates for site planning (Ashmore 1984, 1986), as seen most clearly in the final Late Classic plan of the Quirigua site core. But whereas this plan is most often compared with that of Quirigua's southern neighbor, Copan, its true source is probably northeast Guatemala (Ashmore 1984, 1986). Indeed, the ruling echelon of Copan, itself, may have derived from Guatemala, likewise as an Early Classic intrusion (Leventhal, Demarest, and Willey 1987).

By the Late Classic, the form of Copan's widely known core area had assumed a variant of the now-familiar cosmic layout. What is less immediately obvious, however, is that Copan shares with Tikal a truly grand expression of the template, in which the north, west, and east positions are—as at Tikal—approximately a kilometer distant from the ball court that provides a pivot for the whole (Ashmore 1987a; Fash 1983: Fig. 9.7). And, again resembling the Tikal version, causeways provide at least partial linkage between the key points (Fash 1983). Copan, in turn, seems to have served as a model for rulers and their architects in at least two other, smaller centers in non-Maya areas of Honduras.

One of these is Gualjoquito, which sits athwart an important ancient crossroads in the middle Ulua drainage of Honduras (Fig. 14.7). Evidence suggests that the advent of the hierarchically organized society at Gualjoquito in the Early Classic was linked to the rise in volume of long-distance traffic using the crossroads and, more specifically, to a rapid growth in demand for commodities and information for and from a suddenly ascendant Copan (Ashmore et al. 1987; Schortman et al. 1986). The nouveau riche elite who controlled this strategic location had no tradition of rulership, so they adopted and adapted at least some of the symbols of power worn so elegantly by their Copanec patrons, including the cosmic template. The published maps of both Copan and Gualjoquito illustrate their final, Late Classic form. In both, open plazas, presumably created for public ritual gatherings invoking celestial beings (ancestral or othewise), lie to the north of elaborate enclosed compounds, with ball courts in between. Evidence from excavations strongly suggests, however, that at least some aspects of the layout in question were in place in the Early Classic, at or near the beginning of each center's expansion (Ashmore 1987a; see also Cheek 1983). Once again, the use of this layout seems to mark assertion of power.

The same can be said with respect to the final illustration, Cerro Palenque (Joyce 1982, 1985, 1986), another non-Maya site that seems to have drawn on Copan for architectural and other inspiration. In this instance, too, the local rise to power seems to have been rapid, but this time as partial heir rather than contemporary beneficiary of Copanec power. That is, while Gualjoquito found its strength in the prosperity radiating from Copan, the form and timing of ascendance at Cerro Palenque suggests that it successfully filled at least part of the vacuum created by collapse of kingship at the larger, Maya center at the beginning of the ninth century A.D. Cerro Palenque occupies a strategic position at the south end of the rich lower Ulua (Sula) Valley of northern Honduras, and although part of the site complex (CR-144) was occupied earlier in the Late Classic, the final elite core (CR-157) was a new creation, built rather suddenly about A.D. 830. The excavator, Rosemary Joyce (1986), suggests that it quickly developed trade connections with the Maya to the far north and

west, links largely unprecedented in the Sula Valley before that time. I would suggest that this new center represents response to a need to counter the loss of the long-established power center in the southeast—Copan—and that one of the ways in which the occupants of the new Cerro Palenque center identified themselves as legitimate heirs to power was to provide a setting that placed them unequivocally in the Copan Maya tradition. The expression of the cosmic template at Cerro Palenque is small but recognizable (Joyce 1982: Fig. 4). And once again, it is an assertion of authority.

FINAL REMARKS

This has been, admittedly, a rapid survey, some of it, likewise admittedly, speculative. Other examples could be cited, but what is clearest is that more investigation is still needed, in more places and across the fullest range of time. If the preceding arguments indicate the potential fruitfulness of amplifying this kind of analysis of pre-Columbian architectural remains, and if they help stimulate more such analyses, the aims of this interim statement will have been well met.

ACKNOWLEDGMENTS

This paper is part of an evolving consideration of ideological underpinnings of ancient settlement patterns of the Maya and their neighbors. Slightly modified versions were presented elsewhere for comment during 1987, in a colloquium before the Anthropology Section of the New York Academy of Sciences and in a symposium, "Pre-Columbian Architecture" (Jeff Karl Kowalski, organizer), held at the 40th Annual Meeting of the Society of Architectural Historians, San Francisco. I am grateful to those who have read (or listened to) and commented on these ruminations, and—for both inspiration and tolerance—I want especially to thank Clemency Coggins, Susan Gillespie, David Freidel, Robert Sharer, Barbara and Dennis Tedlock, Edward Schortman, Patricia Urban, William Fash, Christopher Jones, Jeff Kowalski, Richard Leventhal, Marshall Becker, David Sedat, and Don Rice.

BIBLIOGRAPHY

Ashmore, W.
1984   Quirigua Archaeology and History Revisited. *Journal of Field Archaeology* 11:365-386.

1986   Peten Cosmology in the Maya Southeast: An Analysis of Architecture and Settlement Patterns at Classic Quirigua. In *The Southeast Maya Periphery*, eds. P. A. Urban and E. M. Schortman, pp. 35-49. Austin: University of Texas Press.

1987a   Cobble Crossroads: Gualjoquito Architecture and External Elite Ties. In *Prehistoric Interaction on the Southeast Mesoamerican Periphery: Honduras and El Salvador*, ed. E. J. Robinson, pp. 28-48. BAR International Series 327, Oxford.

1987b   La dirección norte en la arquitectura precolombina del sureste de Mesoamérica. Paper presented at the Fourth Seminar in Honduran Archaeology, La Ceiba, Atlántida, Honduras.

1989   Construction and Cosmology: Politics and Ideology in Lowland Maya Settlement Patterns. In *Word and Image in Maya Culture: Explorations in Language, Writing, and Representation*, eds. W. F. Hanks and D. S. Rice, pp. 272-286. Salt Lake City: University Of Utah Press.

Ashmore, W., E. M. Schortman, P. A. Urban, J. C. Benyo, J. M. Weeks, and S. M. Smith
1987   Ancient Society in Santa Bárbara, Honduras. *National Geographic Research* 3(2):232-254.

Ashmore, W., and R. J. Sharer
1975   A Revitalization Movement at Late Classic Tikal. Paper presented at West Chester State College Area Seminar in Ongoing Research.

Baudez, C. F., and P. Becquelin
1973   *Archéologie de Los Naranjos, Honduras*. Collection Etudes Mesoamericaines 2. Mexico: Mission Archéologique et Ethnologique Française au Mexique.

Bricker, V. R.
1983   Directional Glyphs in Maya Inscriptions and Codices. *American Antiquity* 48:347-353.Cheek, C. D.

1983   Excavaciones en la Plaza Principal. In *Introducción a la Arqueología de Copan, Honduras*, ed. C. F. Baudez, pp. 191-289. Tegucigalpa: SECTUR.

Coe, W. R.
1967   *Tikal: A Handbook of the Ancient Maya Ruins.* Philadelphia: The University Museum, The University of Pennsylvania.

Coggins, C. C.
1967   Palaces and the Planning of Ceremonial Centers in the Maya Lowlands. Unpublished manuscript, Tozzer Library, Peabody Museum, Harvard University.

1975   Painting and Drawing Styles at Tikal: An Historical and Iconographic Reconstruction. Unpublished Ph.D. dissertation, Department of Fine Arts, Harvard University.

1980   The Shape of Time: Some Political Implications of a Four-Part Figure. *American Antiquity* 45:727-739.

1983   *The Stucco Decoration and Architectural Assemblage of Structure 1-sub, Dzibilchaltún, Yucatán, México. Middle American Research Institute, Publication* 49. New Orleans: Tulane University.

Fash, W. L.
1983   Deducing Social Organization from Classic Maya Settlement Patterns: A Case Study from the Copán Valley. In *Civilization in the Ancient Americas: Essays in Honor of Gordon R. Willey*, eds. R. M. Leventhal and A. L. Kolata, pp. 261-288. Albuquerque: University of New Mexico Press.

Freidel, D. A.
1981   Civilization as a State of Mind: The Cultural Transformation of the Lowland Maya. In *The Transition to Statehood in the New World*, eds. G. D. Jones and R. R. Kautz, pp. 188-227. Cambridge: Cambridge University Press.

1985   Polychrome Facades of the Lowland Maya Preclassic. In *Painted Architecture and Polychrome Monumental Sculpture in Mesoamerica*, ed. E. H. Boone, pp. 5-30. Washington, DC: Dumbarton Oaks.

1986a   Introduction. In *Archaeology at Cerros, Belize, Central America*, eds. R. A. Robertson and D. A. Freidel, pp. xiii-xxi. Dallas: Southern Methodist University Press.

1986b   The Monumental Architecture. In *Archaeology at Cerros, Belize, Central America*, eds. R. A. Robertson and D. A. Freidel, pp. 1-22. Dallas: Southern Methodist University Press.

Fritz, J. M.
1986   Vijayanagara: Authority and Meaning of a
             South Indian Imperial Capital. *American
             Anthropologist* 88:44-55.

Fritz, J. M., and G. Michell
1987   Interpreting the Plan of a Medieval Hindu
             Capital, Vijayanagara. *World Archaeology*
             19:105-129.

Gillespie, S. D.
1985   Ballgames and Boundaries. Paper pre-
             sented at the International Symposium on
             the Mesoamerican Ballgame and
             Ballcourts, Tucson, AZ.

Gossen, G. H.
1974   *Chamulas in the World of the Sun: Time
             and Space in a Maya Oral Tradition.*
             Cambridge, MA: Harvard University Press.

Guillemin, G. F.
1968   Development and Function of the Tikal
             Ceremonial Center. *Ethnos* 33:1-35.

Jones, C.
1969   The Twin Pyramid Group Pattern: A Classic
             Maya Architectural Assemblage at Tikal,
             Guatemala. Unpublished Ph.D. disserta-
             tion, Department of Anthropology, The
             University of Pennsylvania.

Jones, C., and R. J. Sharer
1986   Archaeological Investigations in the Site
             Core of Quirigua. In *The Southeast Maya
             Periphery*, eds. P. A. Urban and E. M.
             Schortman, pp. 27-34. Austin: University of
             Texas Press.

Joyce, R. A.
1982   La zona arqueológica de Cerro Palenque.
             Yaxkin 5(2):95-101.
1985   Cerro Palenque, Valle del Ulua, Honduras:
             Terminal Classic Interaction on the
             Southern Mesoamerican Periphery.
             Unpublished   Ph.D.   dissertation,
             Department of Anthropology, University of
             Illinois, Champaign-Urbana.
1986   Terminal Classic Interaction on the
             Southeastern Maya Periphery. *American
             Antiquity* 51:313-329.

Leventhal, R. M., A. A. Demarest, and G. R. Willey
1987   The Cultural and Social Components of
             Copán. In *Polities and Partitions*, ed. K. M.
             Trinkaus. Tempe, AZ: Anthropological
             Research Papers.

Lewenstein, S. G.
1987   Stone Tool Use at Cerros: the Ethno-
             archaeological and Use Wear Evidence.
             Austin: University of Texas Press.

Miller, A. G.
1986   *Maya Rulers of Time: A Study of
             Architectural Sculpture at Tikal,
             Guatemala.* Philadelphia: The University
             Museum, The University of Pennsylvania.

Miller, M. E.
1984   The Main Acropolis at Copán and
             Quiriguá: Its Meaning and Function. Paper
             presented at Dumbarton Oaks Symposium
             on the Southeastern Classic Maya Zone,
             Washington, DC.
1985   Tikal, Guatemala: A rationale for the
             Placement of the Funerary Pyramids.
             Expedition 27(3):6-15.
1988   The Meaning and Function of the Main
             Acropolis, Copán. In *The Southeast Classic
             Maya Zone*, eds. E. H. Boone and G. R.
             Willey, pp. 149-194. Washington, DC:
             Dumbarton Oaks.

Price, B. J.
1978   Secondary State Formation: An Explanatory
             Model. In *Origins of the State: The
             Anthropology of Political Evolution*, eds. R.
             Cohen and E. R. Service, pp. 161-186.
             Philadelphia: Institute for the Study of
             Human Issues.

Sahlins, M. D.
1983   Other Times, Other Customs: The
             Anthropology of History. *American
             Anthropologist* 85:517-544.

Scarborough, V., B. Mitchum, S. Carr, and D. Freidel
1982   Two Late Preclassic Ballcourts at the
             Lowland Maya Center of Cerros, Northern
             Belize. *Journal of Field Archaeology* 9:21-
             34.

Schele, L., and M. E. Miller
1986   *The Blood of Kings: Dynasty and Ritual in
             Maya Art.* Fort Worth, TX: Kimbell Art
             Museum.

Schortman, E. M.
1980   Archaeological Investigations in the Lower
             Motagua Valley. *Expedition* 23(1):23-34.
1984   Archaeological Investigations in the Lower
             Motagua Valley, Department of Izabal,
             Guatemala: A Study in Monumental Site
             Function and Interaction. Unpublished
             Ph.D. dissertation, Department of
             Anthropology, The University of
             Pennsylvania.

1986   Maya/Non-Maya Interaction along the Late Classic Southeast Maya Periphery. In *The Southeast Maya Periphery*, eds. P. A. Urban and E. M. Schortman, pp. 114-137. Austin: University of Texas Press.

Schortman, E. M., P. A. Urban, W. Ashmore, and J. C. Benyo
1986   Interregional Interaction in the Southeast Maya Periphery: The Santa Bárbara Archaeological Project, 1983-1984 Seasons. *Journal of Field Archaeology* 13:259-272.

Sharer, R. J.
1978   Archaeology and History at Quiriguá, Guatemala. *Journal of Field Archaeology* 5:51-70.

Steinhardt, N. S.
1986   Why Were Chang'an and Beijing So Different? *Journal of the Society of Architectural Historians* 45:339-357.

Tedlock, D. (translator)
1985   *Popol Vuh: The Mayan Book of the Dawn of Life*. New York: Simon and Schuster

XV

Burials as Caches; Caches as Burials: A New Interpretation of the Meaning of Ritual Deposits Among the Classic Period Lowland Maya[1]

Marshall J. Becker

Department of Anthropology and Sociology
West Chester University

Archaeology is concerned with the examination of material and data on the lives of ancient people, including a concern for those ritual behaviors which allow us to understand how the ancients viewed the world. The reconstruction of Maya ritual (see Pohl 1981) is a particularly interesting undertaking because we have recovered so much information that reflects this aspect of their ancient social behaviors. Despite our extensive knowledge of Maya burials surprisingly little attention has been paid to the interpretation of these mortuary behaviors. This is particularly notable now that the archaeology of death (see Chapman et al. 1981) is of major interest to archaeologists throughout the world. The lack of distinct cemetery areas or necropolises among the ancient Maya means that burials generally are recovered in a random, if not chance, manner.[2] Thus, studies of cemeteries, such as are conducted in other areas of the world, cannot be a special focus of a research project in the Maya area (see Welsh 1988b). These factors may explain why no formal burial typology has emerged from any Maya site, despite the excavation of well over 300 burials from Tikal alone. Examination of burials at Tikal, Guatemala, has been further complicated by the evidence from caches at that site, and the relationship between Maya burials and caches is the subject of this paper.

TYPOLOGIES

Our initial concern with burials should be that of making a general purpose typology (as distinct from a problem-oriented typology; see Kejn 1982). Using the data as we see them to construct a formal typology as we see it (etic) should enable us to understand how the Maya themselves saw these categories (emic). Gathering a wide range of data and subjecting them to multivariate analysis (O'Shea 1984) is one way of studying Maya burials, but it does not reveal possible relationships between Maya burials and caches. In any case, burials are clearly a means by which the members of a society embody their beliefs about the transition between life and death, thereby affording us a view of both realms.

Mortuary problems have been the concern of many scholars such as Binford (1971), Chapman et al. (1981), O'Shea (1984), Peebles and Kus (1977), and Tainter (1975, 1978). Although much of their effort has been directed toward the demonstration that burials reflect social status and that the hierarchy of statuses can be used to reconstruct the complexity of a society, the basis for each reconstruction depends upon the development of a mortuary typology that accurately depicts the culture whose dead are being examined. This fundamental chore of establishing a typology that accurately reflects the cognitive structure of the society in question, including variations in meaning, is the problem addressed here.

Focused studies of Maya burial customs began with Ricketson's work (1925) and was continued by Ruz Lhuillier (1959, 1968), but burial typologies for the Maya area remain on the level of field classification (see Sprague 1968:482). That is, when considerable numbers of human bones, or sometimes just a grave chamber, are found, a burial is defined. Smaller quantities of human bone may be defined as "Problematical Deposits" (P.D.), and sometimes small or random scatters of bone from disturbed contexts are simply noted. In situations where "ritual" objects are found without human bone, the field classification used generally is "cache," with the presumption of ritual origins unless the ritual objects are those typically found in association with a burial (see Haviland et al. 1985: Burial 21).[3] Thus A. L. Smith (1950) was able to describe the caches recovered at Uaxactun, Altar de Sacrificios (1972), and Seibal (1982) using this simplest of archaeological field classifications: cache or burial. W. R. Coe used this simple typology at Piedras Negras (1959), and the same approach was employed for many years at Tikal. As Chase (1988) has noted, Coe's definition (1965: 462) has done little to demonstrate the relationship between these two "extremes":

> The term 'cache', prefaced by 'dedicatory' or 'votive,' customarily designates a limited but significant variety of offerings found apart from human interments though not necessarily devoid of human skeletal remains.

Our basic question remains, did the ancient Maya conceptualize these deposits that we call caches and burials as being part of a single concept? Our concern must be whether these terms (field categories) represent distinct units, or what Klejn (1982: 58) would call "the boundaries of a type." Quite obviously, many of the burials at Tikal were "making a ritual statement" while others were simply disposing of the remains of a deceased "person" using a less complex but still prescribed ritual. What we call burials also may have been the means by which the Maya eliminated bodies of "nonpersons," such as those of infants who had not yet been inducted into the society as a "person" (see Becker in press). The

following discussion treats the possible relationship between caches and burials at Maya sites, a study begun some years ago (Becker 1963:83-94).

The conceptual continuum that appears to exist between caches and burials among the Classic Maya reflects a cognitive concern not unique to these complex people. Many cultures have a generalized category of "earth offerings," a category within which there may be various conditions that distinguish aspects (or stages) of the whole.

Maya caches and burials, at least at Tikal during the Classic period, may not have been two different things, but rather two subsets of a single category called "earth offerings" (see Becker 1963). The problem of distinguishing between certain caches and certain burials was noted thirty years ago at Piedras Negras, where, Coe (1959:120) commented, there were instances here "burial and cache features tended to merge." Despite Coe's recognition that some burials which he presumed to be dedicatory and some dedicatory caches he said could have had identical ends for the Maya, he concluded that "that objective is utterly obscure to us" (Coe 1959:120). Coe's basic typical errors, including his failure to recognize that cache pits need not be distinct from grave pits and that the cache vessels themselves often were the analogues to complex built tombs, stem from his use of an archaeological-material perspective.

The recognition that caches and burials may have had similar cognitive meaning for the Maya, perhaps relating to the death-planting-rebirth cycle, clearly parallels Maya thoughts regarding various categories (names used) for parts of the human body (see Danien 1989) or for the meaning of an entire human corpse in the cosmic scheme. The details of these relationships are now being considered by various scholars. Welsh (1988a) suggests that those burials which resemble dedicatory caches are one category of evidence for human sacrifices. While I do not believe that these people were themselves sacrificed, the notable cognitive element here is the use of the body itself as an offering.

What needs to be made clear at this point is that the Classic Period among the Lowland Maya spans some 700 or more years and that the concepts under discussion may have varied through the temporal as well as the spatial dimension (C. Coggins, personal communication, April 17, 1987). In addition, variations may appear at the same point in time but at different points within a single Maya city, correlated with factors of social class (Becker 1986b) or even ethnicity (Moholy-Nagy 1988). As regards variations in the contents of burials between social classes, one might consider Adams' (1977a:263,328; 1977b:98) suggestion that a Maya Royal cult involved "burials" of which the tomb and the temple erected over it, as well as any associated building caches and monuments, all composed a single unit (Moholy-Nagy 1985:155-156). However, these behaviors all appear to be part of normal mortuary ritual, but with the elite more able to translate cultural ideals into material goods. Even in burials of much less wealthy individuals, similar traits appear but much less lavishly expressed. One may infer that the lower classes expressed the same cultural rules but used perishable goods, which leave no archaeological traces.

Our goal here is to understand the Maya rules involved in making the deposits that traditionally have been called caches and burials. The areas where these "categories" overlap may enable us to recognize what the Maya had in mind when they did these things.

MAYA BURIALS

Certainly one of the best manifestations of social behavior at Tikal, possibly on a par with the social aspects revealed by the architecture, derives from the data and material remains recovered from burials. As the burials excavated at Tikal now number in the hundreds, and the variety of situations from whence they derive is incredibly diverse, the possibility of formulating a working typology has become rather simple.

Whereas many archaeologists consider any or all the remains of one or more individuals to indicate a "burial," the term generally has been held to have more restricted definition by members of the Tikal project. Careful data recovery at Tikal, Guatemala, has produced an enormous number of human bone fragments scattered at random throughout the site, an occurance that is duplicated in any archaeological context where soil conditions foster bone preservation and where burials commonly were made within the habitation area rather than in special areas (cemeteries) beyond the residential area. I assume that the vast majority of finds of the human remains at Tikal derive from disturbed graves. However,

even where ancient cemeteries are far removed from living areas, the quantities of bone from disturbed burials also can be impressive in volume. Haviland (1985:14) points out that most Maya burials may have been in middens, the subsequent reuse of which resulted in much of the human bone found scattered thought the city.

Generally speaking, a "burial" involves the original interment of one or more individuals in a prepared repository, however simple, together with any furniture or associated material, which may be absent (see Shook and Coe 1961; see also Becker 1963; Navarrete and Martinez 1977). The matter of identifying an original interment, also referred to as a "primary" burial, has been a matter that leads directly to the problem at hand. This problem is to distinguish between the complete or partial interment of an individual as a "burial" or to recognize whether the human remains actually represent a ritually deposited "cache." Archaeological evidence may not be able to determine if the intent was to cache (make an offering) or to bury (dispose of the dead). If this cannot be determined from an archaeological reconstruction of the evidence, then the process may not have been differentiated by those who made the burial/cache. Thus the difficulty may be an epistomological problem of projecting our categories onto a situation in which the participants may not have made the distinctions that the archaeologists would make.

Whether dealing with burials (bones, chamber, offerings, etc.) or simply the human remains, we must try to infer the function of the burial with regard to the concept of death and afterlife as understood by the participants in the funeral; the meaning of the funeral; and the relationship of the living to the dead in the culture that conducted these activities. The burial of an individual or individuals is conducted in a manner that fulfills all the postmortem requirements of both the deceased and the people with whom the deceased was involved during his or her life. One may assume that the death of a *milpero* did not have the far-reaching effect that would be felt at the death of a royal person or some other important individual. Correspondingly, all ranks or grades or social levels would tend to have funerals somewhat in accordance with their "social persona" (Binford 1971) including their social class (see Landa 1941:130).

The requirements of the soul or spirit of a

deceased Maya are important for us to understand because of the continued relationship which the dead had with the world of the living (death-burial-rebirth; see Landa 1941:129-130, Fn. 604; Closs 1988). Perhaps the deceased's position, either formally or informally determined, dictated the nature of the steps taken to provide for his or her afterlife as well as to protect those still living from the wrath or woes of an ill-provisioned ancestral spirit. The construction and contents of graves often reveal data concerning concepts and feelings about the transitions from life to death, or from one life to another. Thus the archaeologist may be provided with insights into both of these worlds through the excavation of burials.

Burials found dug into middens at Tikal reflect what might be considered to be the cross-cultural norm for body disposal. The body was simply buried. Haviland et al. (1985:142) discusses simple interments at Tikal, but at Tikal we also must examine those more formal burials that have elements in common with the ritual deposits at Tikal called caches.

Returning to the problem of the relationship between caches and burials, note should be made that there generally exists a concern of living peoples for the remains of their dead. This concern relates to the problem of categorizing human remains when sufficient time has passed (one generation, more or less) for the concerns of survivors to be altered. Persons encountering an "old" grave may have very different concerns from those of the people who were responsible for the deposition of the human remains. Those concepts which applied at the time of death may have had little relevance twenty years later. As in the case of determining what constitutes a burial, there exists a need to provide a theoretical reconstruction of the intentions of the people representing the living culture as regards their interactions with people representing the "dead" or past culture.

THE PROBLEM AT TIKAL

At Tikal, as throughout the Maya area, a profusion of different types of assemblages that are apparently offeratory come to light in the course of excavation (see Laporte 1988: ch. 8). These are generally considered as having been ritually proffered on all occasions other than those relating to burials or funerals. However, there exist a number of circumstances in which the Maya began construction subsequent to and directly over a burial (such as Burial 160) or a cache, using the building (temple or platform, etc.) to "seal" the grave or cache. Such an interment or cache might be considered to be "dedicatory" to the structure immediately covering it; or the structure may be seen as commemorative to the burial beneath. If the burial or cache pit intrudes through a surface and that surface is subsequently restored (plastered over or patched) so that the former surface continues in use, we can assume that this neatly sealed "deposit" was not dedicatory (see Coe 1959:78) unless, as William Haviland suggests (personal communication 1989), the burial or cache were dedicatory to a more removed modification of the building. I would suggest that a physical association with the addition or modification is a direct and necessary linkage required of dedicatory offerings. Because one cannot be certain whether the individual interred beneath a structure or other architectural feature had been sacrificed, as Thompson (1939:220) suggests at San Jose, one cannot determine beyond any doubt whether this kind of "burial" represents a case of an offering being made of a human (or its spirit) to the structure or if other circumstances may have led to this particular type of relationship between the individual and the structure.

Identification of the age and gender of skeletal remains having such a dedicatory relationship to a structure reveals no clear regularity and therefore precludes the possibility of a specific class of sacrificial victims of a required gender and age. Older males tend to predominate, suggesting the possibility that the death of an individual of some importance such as a priest or an elder motivated the construction of a building, must be considered from both the negative and the positive aspects, as in the case of Burial 160. On the positive side are the elaborate tombs, richly furnished, that apear to have been built specifically to receive the remains of a single individual, plus any human offerings that are simply grave goods. Considerations of whether the structures covering such burials can be considered mausoleums of a sort, housing the remains of an individual, or whether the individual and his burial furnishings are dedicatory to the structure further complicate the problem. One possible variation along these lines is that the individual may be considered as only a ritual item who must be "sacrificed" and interred together with other ritual goods that we interpret to be burial furniture. The negative side of the problem concerning the possible dedicatory nature of certain burials involves two factors of time relating to construction. The first is that time or part of the year during which construction would be most likely to begin, assuming that this might be a constant; the second being the specific year in any period encompassing the occupation span of a group of buildings during which construction on a structure with a dedicatory burial may be undertaken. Quite possibly the data involving decisions regarding the initiation of tomb construction might be seriated (see Rouse 1967), which might enable us to determine whether a death (and burial) initiated the construction of such structures or if they were built according to some other agenda, with the necessary burial being taken from wherever a reasonably important individual's body was available.

At Tikal all those structures that have either dedicatory burials or caches (which are the cognitive equivalent) had nonresidential "ritual" functions (Becker 1971, 1987; see Note 3). Such burials are diagnostic of the ritual functions, as in the case of some range-type structures appearing within residential groups (Haviland et al. 1985: see Structure 4E-31). The construction of such a structure within a residential cluster may be of significance in the development of that group or in the religious life of the people or family responsible for the construction of the group. This might mean that a sacrificial victim was involved (see Welsh 1988a:146-147), but it could equally suggest that anyone dying immediately prior to the time when construction was scheduled to begin might be entombed beneath the structure. Quite possibly the death of the head of a residential family (the occupants of a group of buildings around a plaza) required more than a simple interment. Excavations at Tikal, however, indicate that a burial could be made at a time considerably before the construction of the covering structure. This might indicate that the death of a specific person could relate to, if not initiate, the construction of such a structure. The funeral could take place any time of the year in such cases, and the construction could begin at a time more favorable to building activity, such as after the harvest season or at the beginning of the dry season. We do not know, for example, the reason for the apparent long delay in constructing

the temple over Tikal Burial 48. However, Burial 48 was a "seated," bundled, headless, elite individual. All of these characteristics are shared with Tikal Burial 85, which also may have been interred after some delay—at least enough time having elapsed to allow the bones to be cleaned without cutting the flesh from them.

Dedicatory burials, in many cases, suggest a retrospective orientation to the related activities. This is implied by the nature of the grave (chamber) provided for these burials that appear to "dedicate" a shrine. In cases in which the grave chamber has been cut through the floor of a platform, or through a plaster floor which is inside a room, the act may be interpreted as signifying the ritual "killing" or defacement of the existing architectural feature. This is most clear when a new building or major renovation completely covers the one just "killed." In cases in which a building appears to continue in use after such an "interment" we might do well to determine how such burials differ from those in which the old structure "must" be replaced by a new construction.

The Maya act of cutting into the floor of an old structure and down into its deepest fills, like entering into bedrock, has a quality similar to that which is associated with ritual offerings, which at Tikal would be considered to be caches. Ritual defacement, or "killing," is well documented for carved stelae at Tikal (e.g., Stela 31) and is suggested to have occurred prior to the burial of certain large vessels with flat bottoms and nearly vertical sides. Each vessel had a single, large, appliqued face on it, and the vessels may have served as censers. Two examples of these are known from Tikal: one in Burial 35 (see Becker 1963: Fig. 15c; Haviland et al. 1985: Fig. 48b) and another in Burial 162 (Haviland 1981: 107-110). Note that both of these burials had been placed in chambers cut into the bedrock.

Ritual defacement of buildings, such as the destruction of decorative masks on their facades, also may have been associated with the process by which structures were "buried" by being covered with a later building. Thus the act of cutting a grave through the floor of a structure may have served a similar ritual purpose to those mentioned above. The function of a structure or platform would thus be formally ended, and subsequent construction at the same locus would not only fill in the grave but would literally bury the earlier structure. The intrusion of a burial into bedrock prior to erecting the initial structure at a given locus may relate to the sanctification of the ground over which the structure is to lie, or may otherwise relate to the concept of defacement by intrusion.

If Coggins' (1988) "impregnation" model (which appears to hold only for the Early Classic period) is considered, a greater sense of cultural continuity can be seen in this act of penetrating the bedrock (or structure) in order to place a grave. The impregnation (or fertilization) created by excavation for a grave provides the basis for rebirth and new life, as was implied by Holland (1964) for the modern Tzotzil Maya and reaffirmed by Vogt (1969) and Lowe (1982: Fig.15.2). Thus the act of burial achieves both a forward and a backward temporal orientation (see Becker 1988a:123). The dual relationship created by the interment might reflect a life-from-death motif, but duality also can be seen in the grave digging serving to deface ("kill") the earlier structure, with the subsequent construction built as a monument to the occupant of the grave (also dedicated to his reborn self). The relationship among duality, creation, and procreation appears as a strong theme throughout this area (see Lowe 1982:291-292; see also Closs 1988).

Before turning to a situation from Tikal in which a burial actually served as a cache, note should be given to the important work of H. Moholy-Nagy (1987) in the identification of Teotihuacan-related burials at Tikal. Her studies demonstrate that some of the interpretive difficulties that may confront excavators of urban sites such as Tikal could derive from the discovery of anomalous situations reflecting the presence of or contact with foreign populations. These studies may point the way toward the recognition of variations in the cultural elements existing within the Maya area, as between individual cities or towns. Variations in architectural patterns between relatively proximal sites in the Maya lowlands (e.g., Plaza Plan 1 at Tikal and its mirror image at Yaxha, Becker 1982:112) have been noted, and similar variations should be expected in burials and caches among these many sites. However, as in the case of this architectural variation, the basic cognitive elements may be expected to be relatively uniform, with their material or behavioral expression manifesting local differences.

A BURIAL THAT IS A CACHE, OR A CACHE COMBINED WITH A BURIAL

The discussion thus far touches only on the problem of distinguishing between what are to be called burials and what are to be considered in the category of caches and whether both of these are cognitively "earth offerings."[4] Is a dedicatory burial, such as described above, an offering or a variety of offerings? More complex situations, however, call for a greater probing of the relationships that affect burials and offerings, and perhaps the best example we have from Tikal derives from Burial 132, which also was excavated from the locus of Structure 7F-30.[5] Vessel no. 3 from Burial 132 is the uppermost of a pair of cache vessels that were placed under the head of the deceased. This large vessel has an elaborate decorative panel carved into the "upper" surface and five smaller panels carved into the sloping "rim." The lower member of this otherwise matched pair of vessels is unadorned.

At Tikal the discovery of this enormous substairway cache combined with a burial (Burial 132: Ik) provides the best evidence that these two categories may include elements that are cognitively related, or can be transposed. The body in Burial 132 is flexed, with the head resting on the upper member of a very large pair of cache vessels, which were filled with marine offerings and other goods. Similar vessels appear to be known from Tikal (Coggins 1975:243-247), suggesting that the Burial 132 example is not unique and that the context also may not be different. Note should be made that there are similar clues relating burials and caches from other sites in the Maya lowlands (see Ashmore 1980:43). At least one other burial at Tikal (Burial 160: Manik 3B) included "eccentric" flints, which are the equipment "normally" found in caches.[6] Children often are found as part of the goods included in caches, but this may be a function of size rather than of religious belief.

Trophy heads placed in cache vessels as "offerings" (see Becker 1988a) are common at Tikal. Such caches are an important characteristic of Tikal Plaza Plan 4, which appear to date from the Terminal Classic period (see Becker 1962, 1971, 1987). Diagnostic of this Plaza Plan 4 residential group arrangement is the appearance of a small platform in the center of the plaza. One or more such "trophy heads" (their origin remains uncertain) are cached within each of these small structures diagnostic of Plaza Plan 4 (e.g., Tikal Groups 6E-III, and 6F-I; see Becker 1982). What became of the headless corpses remains unknown, but here we have an important part of the body being offered (buried) in a specific context that appears ritual.

Also of interest within the burial-cache continuum are the numerous Problematical Deposits (P.D.) at Tikal, which have elements of both burials and caches within them. Excavations in the area of Tikal Group 6D-V conducted under the auspices of the Proyecto Nacional Tikal (PNT) encountered several extremely interesting P.D.s (Iglesias 1986). One was located behind Structure 6D-18, but the more significant is PNT P.D.21, found behind Structure 6D-20. This deposit appears to be a huge trash heap filled with cache materials as well as two primary (?; see Iglesias 1986) burials all dating to Manik IIIa times. The combination of materials suggests that both the caches and the burials had been together, or that they were being disposed of through the same pattern of deposition.

The great importance of these data is the light shed on the relationships between "temples" and the burials that they so often cover. The information reviewed here suggests that many Maya burials may have been viewed by the makers as offerings to the temples covering them, rather than that the temples served as monuments to the people interred beneath them.

SIGNIFICANCE

The problem of reconstructing the origin and significance of certain burials now considered dedicatory, or serving to dedicate a specific construction, should be taken up again. Generally such a structure would have a function other than residential. If the persons interred in such graves had been sacrificed, the remains might be regarded as more offertory in nature than funereal; but if the individual died a natural death, the reverse might be a more logical judgment. Further, there exists the possibility that either alternative might be correct in any given instance. Obviously what begins to form is a picture of a transitional area in which the remains do not derive from simple interments made according to spectific rituals that serve to dispose of a deceased individual.

Neither can one assume that these remains were definitely deposited as a ritual offering, which might be the case with a piece of furniture of even a household slave.

Burials conforming to a standard pattern, located in association with small structures that appear to be residential in nature present little or no problem. These, however, may grade into the problem of dedicatory burials, or burials associated with construction in temples and other buildings that may have been religiously oriented. The ultimate problem in classification appears when materials which clearly signal a grave are found to include material which alone would clearly be identified as a cache (e.g., Tikal Burial 132). When human remains are the principal features, these assemblages are classed as burials. Where only the furniture, without skeletal remains of gravelike repository, occurs, the situation is more likely to be considered an offering. This category, which is transitional in nature, grades into the final category of "offerings." When human remains occurred with secreted offerings, or caches, in situations normally containing offering without human remains, the remains are dealt with simply as objects belonging to the assemblage comprising the offering. In the case of some bundle burials, the remains deposited in the grave may not represent the entire individual. Some portions might have been removed for ritual purposes or might have passed directly into a cache of nonburial repository.

It is possible that the interment of an individual along with cached objects may not have differed in intent as regards the deceased from any other form of interment. Dedicatory burials may also be of this nature, having attributes of a cache while fulfilling the main purpose of a burial. However, the intentional deposition of bodies in repositories other than those which contain only burials, such as in cache pits, must be assumed to have a different basic character or significance. The establishment of a Lowland Maya typology would be most useful. Resolving the definition of *burial* and related assemblages must precede the work on subsequent problems that already has begun. Typologies of this sort should result from the discovery of regularities and patterns that may demonstrate progressive changes in the thoughts and concepts of the people who dealt with these patterns in terms of their own folkways and mores. Archaeological typologies have been established for ceremonies, and tentative sequences have been worked out for architectural features. Thus one should expect that concepts relating to death and burial changed during the course of Maya history. The rate of change may not have been as rapid as the change in ceramic traditions. At Tikal, by the time the data (bones and grave goods) from the first 150 excavated burials were available to work with, clear patterns began to emerge. These patterns relate to and complement the chronological sequence that had been described for ceramics for Classical times as well as for the latter part of the Preclassic period.

Ultimately, of course, a working burial typology will be established for individual sites, if not for the Maya area as a whole. The typology will do more than provide the assignment of a number-letter designation to a burial, to serve as an adequate identifier of the interment as an archaeological unit; it should at least indicate the regularity in gross features which have meaning for social and chronological relationships peculiar to the site (see O'Shea 1984). Moholy-Nagy's (1986) paper focusing on the Early Classic burials at Tikal, demonstrates variation by social class and makes useful suggestions regarding the possibility of recognizing ethnic differences from these data. Her work is extremely important for archaeological studies of urban populations (complex societies). Because the list of minimally necessary data exceeds the scope of information usually provided by excavators, a check list has been provided (Becker 1988a:128-130; see also Ruz Lhuillier 1959, 1968; Moholy-Nagy 1986; Coggins 1988). The data usually collected from the excavation of caches (see Becker 1988a:130) generally is quite different. Obviously, parallel data on caches are necessary to demonstrate the points made regarding their relationships to burials. Since the complexities provided by skeletal remains generally are absent from caches, the range of variation generally is less than found in burials (see Nagao [1985] on Mexica [Aztec] caches). Laporte's (1988) discoveries of caches in his excavations of Tikal Group 6C-XVI are extremely important and should be noted, particularly since this Group 6C-XVI (Structures 6C-51/53) conforms to PLaza Plan 2 group (Becker 1971, 1982:127). The question of how these characteristics merge or overlap with those sought when recording a burial remain the focus of our attention.

DISCUSSION

The difficult task of formulating a typology of Maya mortuary behaviors that will accurately reflect the cognitive structure of these ancient people must begin by understanding what kind of typology we are seeking. A multivariate technique, using all the possible data available, may be too complex. A technique by which we identify specific traits may err in the selection of the factors that observers select for study. Although we cannot focus on a single technique which will guarantee that Maya meanings will be revealed to us, our hope is that field recording will be sufficiently broad as to allow a typology to emerge from the data which we *have* gathered (inductive). Obviously we must recognize that *what* it is that we choose to record may color what it is that we *believe* that we see. The following observations are believed to be of importance in the study of urban Maya mortuary programs:

1. Every aspect of the situation within the building clusters at Tikal, from refuse distribution to the arrangement of the various structures within the individual clusters, implies that *most* of the architectural groups at Tikal served as residential compounds.

2. At Tikal the artifact inventory, distribution of refuse, and details about the construction of various buildings are among the many features about which our knowledge of the Lowland Maya has been increased, and new understandinggs have developed.

3. Patterns of architectural construction related to mortuary programs, the size and shape of related buildings, burial procedures, and other commonplace activities of the Maya began to be clarified through excavations in the early 1960s. The map of Tikal plus excavations of selected buildings have been of great use in directing subsequent excavations at Tikal as well as at other Lowland Maya sites (e.g., Quirigua: see Becker 1972). These data also should help, eventually, in dating or chronologically relating various aspects of a site prior to initiating excavations. The synthesis of a working typology for structures, groups, and burials would appear to be a logical result.

4. Small structure excavations at Tikal (e.g., Haviland et al. 1985; Iglesias 1986) have provided a great range of information about burial types previ-

ously unknown at the site. A maximum description of each burial will serve eventually to develop a typology covering the entire range of interments at that site. By deriving a typology from these data, rather than forcing the data into preconceived categories, a functioning system can be achieved for Tikal "earth offerings" that should be of use in comparisons with data from other sites.

CONCLUSIONS

The problem of understanding the burial-cache continuum aas it operated during the Classic Period in the Maya lowlands (and perhaps throughout ancient Central America) requires a far more realistic approach to the data base than has yet been considered. The dichotomous categories originally established, and derived from previous archaeological research, fail to serve in all situations at Tikal. New insights and attitudes afford a more flexible interpretation, which supercedes the former categories. Perhaps the most important observation from the Maya realm is the lack of formal cemeteries that remove the dead from the world of the living. The use of "burials" as "caches" (offerings) may reflect Maya cosmological concerns with using human remains to feed the gods (or to impregnate the "earth"; see Coggins 1988), in order to bring forth renewed life and to continue the cycle of being (rather than to dispose of the unwanted corpse of the dead, as if a life had come to an end). Such concerns appear to have been developed by the Middle Formative period throughout Mesoamerica and to have reached sophisticated levels of implementation around the beginning of the Classic period, probably as a result of emerging socioeconomic organization.

The consideration of Maya burials and caches as existing along a continuum would appear to be in order, and might provide improvements in the ability to understand the cultural situation as it existed at Tikal and perhaps throughout the Lowland Maya realm.

NOTES

1. Thanks are due Dr. Clemency Coggins, Elin Danien, Dr. Olivier de Montmollin, Prof. Birgitte Ginge, Prof. Juan Pedro Laporte, Dr. Merle Greene Robertson, Dr. John M. Weeks, and, in particular, Hattula Moholy-Nagy, for their careful reading of earlier versions of this manuscript and for offering numerous valuable suggestions regarding both the text and related information. Special thanks are due Prof. Wendy Ashmore for rekindling my interest in this subject, to William A. Haviland for his many useful suggestions regarding these matters, and to Prof. Robert Sharer for his kind aid in locating data relevant to this research. The ideas presented as well as any errors of fact or of interpretation are solely the responsibility of the author.

Funding for the initial fieldwork at Tikal was provided by The University Museum of The University of Pennsylvania. Thanks also are due Prof. Colin Renfrew (Department of Archaeology, University of Cambridge) for aid in the production of an earlier version of this paper (Becker 1988a), prepared for the Archaeology Symposium of the Society for Latin-American Studies, Cambridge University (1987).

2. This is not to imply that we cannot predict the locations of burials, but cemeteries as we know them simply do not appear at Maya sites. The North Acropolis at Tikal, with considerable numbers of elite burials associated with the temples, might be considered a necropolis (H. Moholy-Nagy, personal communication 1989), but I see it as more like the burials beneath the floor of a European church. At Tikal large numbers of interments often are found clustered within what appear to be ordinary house platforms (e.g., Structure 4F-7 of Operation 20; Haviland et al. 1985:82) and in some of the household shrines associated with Plaza Plan 2 (e.g., Structure 4H-4; Becker 1971:62 and tables). Each shrine in a Plaza Plan 2 group has at least several burials, and interments can be found at several other predictable locations throughout Tikal. However, these are not cemeteries in the sense of areas where tombs of most of the inhabitants of the site are concentrated.

3. William A. Haviland notes that the funerary temples, such as those on the North Acropolis at Tikal as well as the many "shrines" located in household groups conforming to Tikal Plaza Plan 2 (see Becker 1971), commonly have caches that appear to have been placed at various stages in their construction. If the temples or shrine buildings themselves are

directly associated with (dependent for their existence on) the structure itself, then are not the offerings that appear to have been made to the structure actually associated with the burial (or the funeral ritual) even though these offerings are not placed within the grave? The logic of this argument appears clear, but the complexities of degrees of relationiships are not always so simple in a religious cosmology. Haviland notes (personal communication) that the only "houses" at Tikal in which caches were made were residences of the ruling elite (e.g., Caches 197 and 198 in Structure 5D-46).

4. Every building stage and alteration of Structure 7F-30 was accompanied by an axial burial or a cached offering. Haviland (personal communication) suggests that both a cache and a burial were associated with each phase of this particular structure.

5. Note should be made of Welsh's (1988b: Tables 36, 37) "burials" of severed heads, placed within,

under, or between bowls as well as "burials" of infants placed between two plates. Others would see many of these as "caches," but Welsh's classification reflects an amibiguity that might be solved by calling them "earth offerings." The very few examples (ca. 20) of such severed head "earth offerings" tabulated by Welsh are a reflection of the small numbers that have been reported in the literature, not their rarity in the Maya realm.

6. Moholy-Nagy points out, however, that Burials 132 and 160 at Tikal, found at the same locus, are the *only* known examples at the site where flint and obsidian eccentrics normally found in caches were placed *inside* the repositories. She suggests that this characteristic may have been peculiar to the occupants of Group 7F-I. Moholy-Nagy also is studying cache vessels of the types found in Burial 132 and has data correlating the presence of associated artifacts.

BIBLIOGRAPHY

Adams, R. E. W.
1977a   Prehistoric Mesoamerica. Boston: Little Brown.
1977b   Rio Bec Archaeology and the Rise of Maya Civilization. In *The Origins of Maya Civilization*, ed. R.E.W. Adams, pp. 77-99. Albuquerque: University of New Mexico Press.

Ashmore, Wendy
1980   Discovering Early Classic Quiriqua. *Expedition* 23(1):35-44.

Becker, M. J.
1962   Small Structure Excavations at Tikal Guatemala: A Fourth Season. Paper presented at the American Anthropological Association, Annual Meeting, Chicago, November 18.
1963   *Small Structure Excavation at Tikal.* Master's thesis, Department of Anthropology, The University of Pennsylvania. Philadelphia: The University of Pennsylvania Press.
1971   *The Identification of a Second Plaza Plan at Tikal, Guatemala, and Its Implications for Ancient Maya Social Complexity.* Ph.D. dissertation, The University of Pennsylvania. Ann Arbor: University Microfilms.

1972   Plaza Plans at Quirigua, Guatemala: The Use of a Specific Theory Regarding Cultural Behavior in Predicting the Configuaration of Group Arrangements and Burial Patterns in a Yet Untested Community Settlement pattern. *Katunob* 8(2):47-62.
1982   Ancient Maya Houses and Their Identification: An Evaluation of Architectural Groups at Tikal and Inferences Regarding Their Functions. *Revista Española de Antropología Americana* 12:111-129.
1986a   An Ethnographical and Archaeological Survey of Unusual Mortuary Procedures as a Reflection of Cultural Diversity. *La Parola del Pasato: Rivista di Studi Antichi* 226:31-56.
1986b   Household Shrines at Tikal, Guatemala: Size as a Reflection of Economic Status. *Revista Española de Antropología Americana* 16:81-85.
1987   Understanding Complex Society in the Lowland Maya Realm: The Identification of Plaza Plans at Tikal, Guatemala and other Sites. Paper prepared for the Easter Term Series of the Centre for Latin-American Studies of the University of Cambridge (May 13).

1988a   Caches as Burials; Burials as Caches: The Meaning of Ritual Deposits Among the Classic Period Lowland Maya. In *Recent Studies in Precolumbian Archaeology*, ed. N. J. Saunders and O. de Montmollin, pp. 117-142, BAR International Series 421. Oxford.

1988b   The Contents of Funerary Vessels as Clues to Mortuary Customs: Identifying the *os exceptum*. In *Proceedings of the 3rd Symposium on Ancient Greek and Related Pottery* [Copenhagen 1987], eds. J. Christiansen and T. Melander, pp. 25-32. Copenhagen: Nationalmuseet.

in press   Human Skeletal Remains Recovered from the Ficana (Italy) Excavations: Their Analysis and Importance in the Evaluation of the Site. *Scavi di Ficana* 8, Part 1:1-40. Rome: Poligrafico dello Stato.

Binford, L. R.
1971   Mortuary Practices: Their Study and Potential. In *Approaches to the Social Dimensions of Mortuary Practices*. Memoir 25. Society for American Archaeology.

Chapman, R., I. Kinnes, and K. Randsborg (editors)
1981   *The Archaeology of Death*. New York: Cambridge University Press.

Chase, D. Z.
1988   Caches and Censerwares: Meaning from Maya Pottery. In *A Pot For All Reasons: Ceramic Ecology Revisited*, eds. C. C. Kolb and L. M. Lackey, with M. Kirkpatrick, Chap. 4: "Ceramica de Cultura Maya." Special Publication. Philadelphia: Temple University.

Closs, M. P.
1988   The Penis-Headed Manikin Glyph. *American Antiquity* 53:804-811.

Coe, W. R.
1959   *Piedras Negras Archaeology: Artifacts, Caches, and Burials*. The University Museum Monographs. Philadelphia: The University Museum.

1965   Caches and Offertory Practices of the Maya Lowlands. In *Handbook of Middle American Indians, Vol. 2: The Archaeology of Southern Mesoamerica*, eds. R. Wauchope and G. R. Willey. Part 1: 462-469. Austin: University of Texas Press.

Coggins, C.
1975   Painting and Drawing Styles at Tikal: An Historical and Iconographic Reconstruction. Ph.D. dissertation, Yale University. Ann Arbor: University Microfilms.

1988   Classic Maya Metaphores of Death and Life. *RES* (Anthropology and Aesthetics) 16:65-84.

Danien, E.
1989   Looking Down a Long Time Line: Ixil Vocabulary and Maya Iconography. In *In Love and War: Hummingbird Lore and Other Selected Papers of Laila/Alila's 1988 Symposium*, ed. M. H. Preuss, pp. 23-27. Culver City, CA: Labyrinthos.

Haviland, W. A.
1981   Dower Houses and Minor Centers at Tikal, Guatemala: An Investigation into the Identification of Valid Units in Settlement Hierarchies. In *Lowland Maya Settlement Patterns*, ed. W. Ashmore, pp. 89-117. Albuquerque: University of New Mexico Press.

Haviland, W. A., with M. J. Becker, A. Chowning, K. A. Dixon, and K. Heider
1985   *Excavations in Small Residential Groups of Tikal: Groups 4F-1 and 4F-2*. Tikal Report No. 19. The University Museum Monograph 58. Philadelphia: The University Museum.

Holland, W.
1964   Conceptos cosmológicos Tzotziles como una base para interpretar la civilazación Maya Prehispánica. *America Indigena* 24:11-28.

Iglesias Ponce de Leon, J.
1986   *Excavations at Group 6D-V at Tikal, Guatemala*. Master's thesis, Universidad Complutense, Madrid.

1989   Analisis de un deposito problematico de Tikal, Guatemala. *Journal de la Société des Américanistes*. Pages 25-47.

Klejn, L. S.
1982   *Archaeological Typology*. Translated by Penelope Dole. BAR International Series 153. Oxford.

Kubler, G.
1977   *Aspects of Classic Maya Rulership on Two Inscribed Vessels*. Studies in Pre-Columbian Art and Archaeology 18. Washington, DC: Dumbarton Oaks.

Landa, D. de
1941   *Landa'a Relación de las cosas de Yucatán, a Translation*, ed. A. M. Tozzer. Peabody Museum Papers 18. Harvard University.

Laporte, J. P.
1988   *Alternativas del Clasico Temprano en la relacion Tikal-Teotihuacan: Grupo 6C-XVI, Tikal, Petén, Guatemala*. Ph.D. dissertation. UNAM, Mexico.

Lowe, G. W.
1982   Izapa Religion, Cosmology, and Ritual. In *Izapa: An Introduction to the Ruins and Monuments*, by G.W. Lowe, T. A. Lee, Jr. and E. Martinez Espinosa, pp. 269-305. Papers of the New World Archaeological Foundation, no. 31.

Moholy-Nagy, H.
1985   The Social and Ceremonial Uses of Marine Molluscs at Tikal. In *Prehistoric Lowland Maya Environment and Subsistence Economy*, ed. M. Pohl. Peabody Museum Papers Number 77. Harvard University.
1986   Variability in Early Classic Burials at Tikal, Guatemala. Manuscript (10 August).
1987   Early Classic Problematical Deposits: A Preliminary Report on Teotihuacan-related Burials at Tikal, Guatemala. Revision of a paper presented at the 52d Annual Meeting of the Society for American Archaeology (Toronto, May 7).

Nagao, D.
1985   *Mexica Buried Offerings: A Historical and Contextual Analysis*. BAR International Series 235. Oxford.

Navarrete, C., and E. Martinez E.
1977   *Exploraciones arqueologicas en la Cueva de los Andosolos*. Universidad Autonoma de Chiapas.

O'Shea, J. M.
1984   *Mortuary Variability: An archaeological investigation*. Orlando, FL: Academic.

Peebles, C. and S. Kus
1977   Some Archaeological Correlates of Ranked Societies. *American Antiquity* 42:421-448.

Pohl, M.
1981   Ritual Continuity and Transformation in Mesoamerica: Reconstructing the Ancient Maya *Cuch* Ritual. *American Antiquity* 46:513-529.

Ricketson, O. G.
1925   Burials in the Maya Area. *American Anthropologist* 27:381-401.

Rouse, I.
1967   Seriation in Archaeology. In *American Historical Anthropology*, eds. C. L. Riley and W. W. Taylor, pp. 153-195. Carbondale, IL: Southern Illinois University Press.

Ruz Lhuillier, A.
1959   Estudio preliminar de los tipos de enterramientos en el área Maya. 33d International Congress of Americanists (San Jose, 1958). *Acta* 2:183-199.
1968   *Costumbres funerarias de los antiquos mayas*. Seminario de Cultura Maya. Mexico: Universidad Autonoma de Mexico.

Shook, E. M. and W. R. Coe
1961   *Tikal: Numeration, Terminology, and Objectives*. Tikal Reports Nos. 5-10. Philadelphia: The University Museum.

Smith, A. L.
1950   *Uaxactun, Guatemala: Excavations of 1931-1937*. Publication 588. Carnegie Institution of Washington.

Sprague, R.
1968   A Suggested Terminology and Classification for Burial Description. *American Antiquity* 33:479-485.

Tainter, J. A.
1975   Social Inference and Mortuary Practices: An Experiment in Numerical Classification. *World Archaeology* 7:1-15.
1978   Mortuary Practices and the Study of Prehistoric Social Systems. In *Advances in Archaeological Method and Theory*, vol. 1, ed. M. B. Schiffer, pp. 105-141. New York: Academic.

Thompson, J. E. S.
1939   *Excavations at San Jose, British Honduras*. Publication 506. Carnegie Institution of Washington.

Vogt, E. Z.
1969   *Zinacantan; A Maya Community in the Highlands of Chiapas*. Cambridge, MA: Harvard University Press.

Welsh, W. B. M.
1988a   A Case for the Practice of Human Sacrifice Among the Classic Lowland Maya. In *Recent Studies in Precolumbian Archaeology*, eds. N. J. Saunders and O. de Montmollin. BAR International Series 421. Oxford.
1988b   *An Analysis of Classic Lowland Maya Burials*. BAR International Series 409. Oxford.

Wilkerson, S. J. K.
1984   In Search of the Mountain of Foam. In *Ritual Human Sacrifice in Mesoamerica*, ed. E. H. Boone, pp. 101-132. Washington, DC: Dumbarton Oaks

XVI
Rebellious Prophets

Grant D. Jones

Department of Anthropology and Sociology
Davidson College

The past decade has witnessed a renewed interest in the documentary history of the Maya as they adapted to and often resisted Spanish colonialism. Extensive new documentation from Spanish sources has been discovered, and previously known sources have been reevaluated in light of these new findings (Carmack 1981; Farriss 1984; Jones 1983, 1986, 1987b, 1989; MacLeod and Wasserstrom 1983; de Vos 1980; Wasserstrom 1983). This work has in some cases gone hand in hand with new research in the archaeology of historically documented sites, as has been the case in the study of Lamanai and Tipu, two Spanish-period Maya sites in Belize, and in the study of Tancah and Ecab, sites dating from the same period on the eastern coast of the Yucatan peninsula (Benavides Castillo and Andrews 1979; Graham, Jones, and Kautz 1985; Graham, Pendergast, and Jones 1989; Jones, Kautz, and Graham 1986; Miller 1982; Pendergast 1985). Spanish-period documentation is for some areas particularly rich, and it gives us new insights into the archaeological record, stimulating in particular the investigation of the archaeologically little-known transition from precolonial to postcolonial Maya life. In turn, the archaeological findings from these sites challenge the ethnohistorian who studies the documents to reread them and to interpret them in new ways.

Perhaps the most important outcome of this new joint research is the discovery from both sources of information—archaeological as well as documentary—that in areas fairly remote from centers of Spanish control many forms of Maya ritual and ideology remained central in public Maya life long after the Spanish Conquest. Although these forms often coexisted with imposed Christian ones, they were by no means always confined to hidden activities in caves and distant agricultural fields. Rather, they played, as they had before the arrival of the Spanish,

a central role in public political activities. In fact, certain features of public ideology were at the root of major conflicts between Spanish and Maya political and religious leaders.

One of the most important aspects of Maya culture that survived long after the Conquest and retained a central place in Maya-Spanish relations was the belief in the cyclical nature of time and the association of this belief with changing political policies and fortunes. This conception of time was useful to Maya priests and other Maya leaders, as it provided a millenarian, or prophetic, rationale for their own policies of armed as well as passive resistance against Spanish control.

At the core of the colonial period Maya calendar was the ancient concept of the *katun,* which, in its traditional form, was composed of 7,200 days, or twenty times the Maya *tun* of 360 days. Thirteen such katuns, or about 256 years, made up a full katun cycle. During the Spanish period, beginning in 1539, a particular katun was identified by the name and number of its first day, beginning in 1539 with Katun 11 Ahau. The next katun began in 1559 and was called Katun 9 Ahau. The numerical coefficients of the following katuns, then, were 7, 5, 3, 1, 12, 10, and so on. The Maya believed that each katun cycle was essentially a reenactment of those cycles that it followed, so that the characteristics of a particular katun of the previous cycle might be anticipated in the same katun of the current one. Although we seldom know just how a particular katun was interpreted historically during the colonial period, we have discovered that these periods of time were of decisive importance in Spanish-Maya history. In the best-known case, Tah Itza or Tayasal, the Itza capital on Lake Peten Itza, fell undefended to Spanish forces around the beginning of Katun 8 Ahau in 1697 (see interpretation of colonial period katun dates in

Edmonson 1982). I shall return to the issue of prophecy shortly, but something more of the historical context must be presented to make it possible to understand the issues.

By and large, the Spanish political and economic conquest of Yucatan was confined to the northern third of the peninsula and to portions of the western and eastern coasts. In these areas the Spaniards created one small city and three administrative towns, or *villas* complete with European administrative machinery and a Spanish town plan. Around the one capital city (Merida) and the three *villas*—Campeche, the west coast seaport with strong trade ties to Veracruz; Valladolid, an interior town in the midst of a particularly recalcitrant indigenous population; and Salamanca de Bacalar, a tiny settlement on the southeastern frontier—were scattered several hundred Maya communities. The Maya lived both in their own *pueblos* and in the *barrios* of the *villas*, and they were forced to serve the Spanish both by paying *encomienda* tribute and by performing various forms of forced and semiforced labor and production activities. They were also expected to give up all indigenous religious activities—called by the generic term *idolatry* by the Spanish—and to accept the practice and message of Christianity from the missionary priests with completely open hearts.

The Spanish colonial world of Yucatan was, however, an imperfect place. The accommodation between Spaniard and Maya was a complex and dynamic one fraught with discontent and unhappiness on both sides, for to the Spaniards Yucatan was a pathetically poor colony with few resources beyond the agricultural labor of its native inhabitants, while to the Maya the colonialists were troublesome, greedy, meddling foreigners intent on milking them of whatever small surpluses they had. Historian Nancy M. Farriss has emphasized the remarkable strength of Maya cultural identity despite the difficult circumstances of colonial existence (1984).

Over the past several years I have been engaged in a documentary study of the little-known Yucatec-speaking Maya who shunned the life of the colonial centers of the northern part of the peninsula. Like the nineteenth-century Santa Cruz Maya, who set up an independent political and social universe in the forests of southern Quintana Roo during the Caste War of Yucatan (Bricker 1981; Reed 1964), these earlier Maya resisted white European domination with a

virtuosic display of organizational ability and ideological commitment. Tens of thousands of them lived beyond the southern frontier of Spanish control in Yucatan, in communities extending from just south of Campeche in the west to the greater part of the east coast of the peninsula and southward to incorporate most of the Peten and Belize. (References to primary sources have been largely omitted for reasons of space; see Jones 1987a and 1989 for a fuller set of citations.)

European contact in this region was initiated by Hernán Cortés, who made an ambitious *entrada* through the Peten in 1525. Cortes discovered that the political and economic heartland of much of this vast southern territory was Tah Itza itself, and that its ruler, Can Ek, controlled a trade network all the way from Manche Chol territory in southern Belize to Lake Peten Itza. He visited Can Ek at Tah Itza, vowing to return one day and leaving his lame horse under the care of the Itza (Bricker 1981:21; Jones 1983:72-73).

Cortés, of course, never returned to Tah Itza, and it would be nearly a century before official Spanish contact with the Can Ek dynasty would be reattempted. From Cortés's time on, Spanish conquest and pacification strategies would focus on the east coast and on riverine access to the Peten through Belize. The first of these efforts took place in 1528 under the leadership of the *adelantado* Francisco de Montejo and his lieutenant, Alonso Dávila. However, their plans to establish a Spanish settlement in the Chetumal area were postponed until 1531, when Dávila and his troops attempted unsuccessfully to pacify the Uaymil and Chetumal provinces and to establish a *villa* at Chetumal itself (see discussion of this early period in Chamberlain 1948; Jones 1984).

Twelve years later, in late 1543 or early 1544, after the establishment of the city of Merida and the northern *villas* of Campeche and Valladolid, Melchor and Alonso Pacheco set out to conquer the provinces of Uaymil, Chetumal, and Dzuluinicob, establishing the new *villa* of Salamanca de Bacalar near the mouth of the Río Hondo. This was the most notoriously cruel and vicious conquest in the history of Yucatan, and we now know that it was far more ambitious in scope than was previously supposed. The Pachecos probably reached southernmost Belize, and it is likely that they conquered and reduced the area around Tipu and Lamanai. The few, scattered cacao-producing *encomiendas* that these early conquerors established were never easy to administer, and rebellions broke out in the region as early as 1547 and continued on and off for the next twenty years. Tipu appears to have been the center of these rebellions, probably because it was the capital town of a major province, known as Dzuluinicob, "The Foreign People" (Jones 1984, 1989).

Only one Spanish *villa,* Salamanca de Bacalar, was to be found in all of this vast hinterland. Located on a picturesque lake adjacent to the Río Hondo near the ruined Maya town of Chetumal, it was nothing more than a small, poor village of Spanish and *mestizo* families and an adjacent neighborhood of Maya servants. From the *villa* extended outward a couple of dozen *visita,* or mission villages, some of which were in an old area long known for its rich *cacao* or chocolate groves. The Spanish Bacalareños were regarded even by their Spanish contemporaries as a band of rogues who attempted to dominate the Maya population by extracting tributes. Their attempts to enrich themselves from the labor of the indigenous people were hampered, however, by the inhospitality of the wet, malaria-ridden countryside, by the uncooperative nature of their Maya subjects, and by the distant, scattered nature of the Maya settlements.

From the standpoint of the faraway colonial administration in Merida, the only rationale for the existence of the tiny community of Bacalar was the possibility that it could help to stem the steady tide of Maya runaways from the northern *encomiendas* to the "free" regions of the frontier. The colonial image of the frontier was a simple one, and not altogether inaccurate. In the Spanish view, the entire region south of the Sierra (the area encompassing the Maya towns of Oxkutzcab, Tekax, and Mani) was literally "out of control." The area was running over with Maya priest-leaders who challenged Catholic authority and attracted runaways from the northern towns and villages, promising them freedom from taxation and tribute, on the one hand, and from the financial and spiritual demands of the Franciscan and secular missionaries on the other. Worst of all, deep in the heartland of this "satanic" land was the pagan headquarters of the last major, completely independent Maya political and religious center: Tah Itza and its outlying settlements on Lake Peten Itza. This center, steeped in mystery and fear, provided military and other supports to towns throughout the frontier, aid-

ing them in their magnetic draw of uncounted numbers of Maya refugees from Spanish colonialism.

Although the Itza myth was to some extent an exaggeration, it does appear that Tah Itza was indeed a spiritual headquarters for independent-minded Maya, much as Santa Cruz remained such a headquarters for the Caste War rebels throughout the second half of the nineteenth century. The Spanish knew that until this town was conquered the northern towns would be drained of their human resources just as a fast-dripping faucet would drain a shallow well. In fact, all Maya-Spanish interaction on the southern frontiers must be seen, I believe, as a struggle for control over the power and attraction of Tah Itza.

We have discovered, then, that the "free" Maya zones of the southern frontier were organized around localized "centers" of political activity, populated principally by runaways from *encomiendas* to the north and often under the leadership of apostate, charismatic figures who actively recruited their followings. The continued existence of these centers was dependent upon a variety of factors, the most important of which included a highly exploitive tribute economy that stimulated flight to the frontier; an underground Maya-controlled network of information about the location and activities of the frontier settlements; regularized Maya trade throughout the frontier zones; the strong influence of Tah Itza on Lake Peten Itza as a center for the fomenting of rebellions; and finally the use of katun-based prophecies by Maya leaders in order to legitimize their authority.

This last factor, that of prophecy, is of particular interest, as there is evidence that prophecy formulation was in the hands of high priests and other leaders of the Itza confederacy around Lake Peten Itza, in opposition to efforts by Can Ek, their nominal ruler, to accept Christianity and other political accommodations with the Spanish. The Franciscan priests who attempted to penetrate the region were apparently well aware of the political uses of millenarian prophecy and attempted themselves to manipulate the Maya calendar in order to further Spanish interests. Their first goal was to convince the leaders of Tah Itza that the ancient prophecies predicted the collapse of the Itza leadership during a Katun 3 Ahau, which began in 1618. When this strategy failed, further efforts had to wait until 1696-1697, the beginning of the fateful Katun 8 Ahau when Tah

Itza's leadership finally fell to Spanish military control (Bricker 1981:22-24).

Throughout the seventeenth century the Spanish envisioned the opening of a road, both physical and spiritual, to Tah Itza through the refugee zone of southeastern Quintana Roo and from there through western Belize and Tipu. Tipu was seen by the Spanish as a gateway to the Itza, as its leaders were on good terms with the Itza hierarchy and were at least nominally Christian. The failure of this effort, which resulted in 1638 in massive resistance and Spanish expulsion from virtually all of Belize, was a major setback in Spanish designs on the Peten, which would remain unconquered until the end of the century.

In 1616 or 1617 a remarkable event occurred on the eve of Katun 3 Ahau, which was to begin in 1618. A Franciscan, Fray Juan de Orbita, who had arrived in Yucatan in 1615, set out with a companion to Tah Itza with the apparent intention of convincing the Itza ruler, Can Ek, that the time was at hand to succumb to Spanish rule. His success was such that the two priests reportedly took back to Merida some 150 inhabitants of Tah Itza. These offered their submission to the Crown, and some of them were appointed as Indian officials by the Spanish governor (Lizana 1893, López de Cogolludo 1688: Bk. 9, Ch. 2).

This party of Itzas returned shortly thereafter to Tah Itza. In 1618—the first year of the new katun—Orbita set out with another companion, Fray Bartolomé de Fuensalida, to visit Tah Itza again. This time they went through Tipu, the last nominally Christian Maya town on the way from Bacalar to Tah Itza. This second visit was clearly timed to convince Can Ek and other leaders yet again that they should accept Christianity and Spanish rule as a prophetic fait accompli. However, Can Ek and the other leaders answered Fuensalida's impassioned sermon on the power of the gospel to the effect "that it was not time to be Christians (they had their own beliefs as to what that time should be) and that they should go back where they had come from; they could come back another time, but right then they did not want to be Christians" (López de Cogolludo 1688: Bk. 9, Ch. 9).

At this point the friars were taken on a tour of the island town, which was arranged with about 200 houses along the shore and about twelve large temples in the upper and middle sections. It was on this tour that Orbita "lost his cool" upon seeing a statuary replica of Cortés's poor horse, who had died nearly a century earlier because the Itza had fed it only flowers and meat. Orbita mounted the statue—which Fuensalida said they called Tzimin Chac, or "horse of thunder and lightning"—and broke it to pieces with a stone.

This action apparently dampened the Itzas' enthusiasm for permanent priests in their midst, and Can Ek repeated that "the time had not arrived in which their ancient priests had prophesied they would need to give up the worship of their gods, for the present age was one called Ox Ahau (which means "third age") and the one that he had indicated to them was not arriving so soon" (López de Cogolludo 1688: Bk. 9, Ch. 10).

Undaunted, Fuensalida and Orbita returned to Tah Itza in 1619 and found Can Ek receptive to new overtures. Can Ek even agreed to the naming of a *cabildo* (town council) among his leaders, over whom he would serve as hereditary *cacique*. He also allowed a new cross to be erected in front of his house, which would have replaced the one left in 1525 by Cortés. In short order, however, factions opposed to Can Ek's overtures to the Spanish and supported by his wife spoke out against such activities, and the priests were forced out of town. These factions were probably also supported by leaders of Tipu, who were found in 1619 engaged in various "idolatrous" activities that were attributed to Itza influence (López de Cogolludo 1688: Bk. 9, Ch. 12-13).

During Orbita's first visit to Tah Itza Can Ek himself had apparently agreed to spearhead a Christianization movement and to accept nominal Spanish rule with himself as *cacique* of a bitterly divided Itza confederacy. Can Ek's control over his fractious leaders was apparently weakened by rival prophetic interpretations of the impending Katun 3 Ahau. That katun had apparently already begun when Fuensalida and Orbita arrived at Tah Itza in 1618, and the friars surely knew of the calendrical and political situation before they decided to make the journey. Katun 3 Ahau was to be characterized, however, by intensely anti-Spanish sentiments throughout the frontier zones, setting the stage for the widespread rebellion that finally broke out at the beginning of Katun 1 Ahau in 1638. Orbita's destruction of Tzimin Chac was likely the key event in giving popular Itza support to the anti-Can Ek faction.

On about January 29, 1624, only five years after

Orbita and Fuensalida had left Tah Itza on their second unsuccessful mission, ten or eleven Spaniards were hanged and beheaded by rebel Maya at the frontier town of Sacalum, only a short distance west of Bacalar. Their military captain, Francisco de Mirones, had his chest ripped open and his heart removed. An unrecorded number of Maya who accompanied the military party were also executed. Mirones's party was part of a beleaguered group of soldiers and fellow travelers on an overly ambitious mission to conquer Tah Itza and to pacify the entire region between there and the Sierra towns—a region peppered with localized charismatic religious movements under Maya leaders (López de Cogolludo 1688: Bk. 10, Ch. 2-3; Scholes and Adams 1936-1937).

Mirones, an ambitious man who hoped to profit handsomely from his bravery, took with him another impetuous Franciscan priest, Fray Diego Delgado, who soon became outraged and angered by the soldiers' profiteering excesses with the frontier Maya whom they forced to resettle from their scattered towns to the armed camp at Sacalum. Delgado had deserted Mirones and gone on ahead to Tah Itza via Tipu. At Tah Itza he and his entire party, including eighty Tipuans and twelve Spanish soldiers sent by Mirones to protect Delgado, were killed.

Following these events rumors abounded that the perpetrators of the Sacalum massacre, together with inhabitants of the towns of the Sierra, were plotting an attack against the Spanish on Holy Thursday. Over the next two months Spanish troops were stationed in Oxkutzcab, Mani, and Tekax. Rewards were offered for anyone who could capture one Ah Kin Pol, who was reputed to have been the principal leader behind the massacre and to have had a wide following throughout the Sierra towns. Eventually Pol and his followers were apprehended by a group of loyal Maya and later hanged, dragged through the streets, and drawn and quartered. Like the victims of the massacres at Tah Itza and Sacalum, their heads were displayed on poles in the town plazas.

All of these events—from the 1616 or 1617 visit of Tah Itza representatives to Merida to the Sacalum and Tayasal massacres—appear to have been closely interconnected and coordinated by conservative Itza factions that had always opposed Can Ek's peaceful overtures to the Spanish on the basis of his interpretation of prophecies of capitulation implicit in Katun 3 Ahau.

The year 1638 ushered in Katun 1 Ahau, whose prophecies in the extant Books of Chilam Balam of Tizimin and Chumayel foretold a time of natural disaster and rebellion (Edmonson 1982:113-115; 1986:167, 213). The events of the period were focused around Tipu, but there is considerable evidence that, again, the source of the plots was at Tah Itza. Tipu was caught between two forces: Spanish rent collectors, missionaries, and military men bent on using the town in their designs on the Itza, on the one hand, and the aggressive, anti-Spanish Itza on the other. It is hardly surprising, given the harsh treatment to which we learn they were subjected by the Spaniards at Salamanca de Bacalar, that they opted for an ideologically appealing anti-Spanish movement masterminded at Tah Itza. Leaders at Tipu spread the prophetic message of this movement throughout the Belize encomienda towns and for a time consolidated much of the territory's Maya population around Tipu itself.

The first signs of rebellion appeared in 1630, when the Maya of two Belize towns deserted their homes, fleeing to the forest with the bells and ornaments of their churches. In mid-1638 there were reports of mass desertions from the interior towns, particularly at Tipu. By September the inhabitants of several coastal villages had also fled to the forests, claiming that the Tipuans had sent prophetic messages to them:

> that they were to give obedience to their king and wished them to abandon their town, saying that if they did not do so all would die and be finished, because at such a time the Itzas would come to kill them and there would be great mortalities and hurricanes that would flood the land (AGI, México 1638).

A few runaways were captured and resettled around Bacalar, but most of them fled to the environs of Tipu. One contemporary writer claimed that they had been "encouraged and deceived by those barbarous infidels of the Tah Itzaes, becoming one with them, as a result of which Bacalar will become more deserted and short of people" (Cárdenas Valencia 1937:97). The most striking result of the rebellion was the virtual collapse of Spanish control throughout what is today the northern half of Belize.

In 1641, Fray Bartolomé de Fuensalida and three other Franciscans went to Bacalar in order to attempt the reconversion of the rebels. The centerpiece of their activities was a futile attempt by Fuensalida and two of his companions to recontact Tipu. The friars found towns burned and deserted from Lamanai to the Belize River. Approaching the Belize River they saw

> statues of men dressed like Spaniards scattered about . . . These idols guarded the way and would stop and enchant anyone who tried to pass by them (López de Cogolludo 1688: Bk. 11, Ch. 13).

The rebels whom they saw were armed and had painted their bodies, and their hair was long in the style of non-Christian Indians; some of them were living in towns in the interior. They witnessed what they considered idolatry and were humiliated by the destruction of the saints' images and their crucifix. Later they were tied up and subjected to humiliating insults:

> They said, "Let the governor come. Let the king come. Let the Spanish come. We are ready to fight them. Now go and tell them . . . Others threatened to kill him because he and Father Orbita had destroyed the Itzas' idol Tzimin Chac and thereby killed their god (López de Cogolludo 1688: Bk. 11, Ch. 14).

Earlier indications of Itza inspirations for this rebellion were, then, fully confirmed. Although they were spared martyrdom, the friars and their Maya companions from Bacalar were hounded out of the Maya village with screams, whistles, and obscene gestures.

On November 22, 1642, Bacalar was sacked by the pirate Diego Lucifer de los Reyes, el Mulato, whose men desecrated the church and made off with goods valued at 12,000 to 14,000 pesos. Pirates became an increasingly troublesome scourge along this coast, and before 1654 the inhabitants of Salamanca de Bacalar had moved the *villa* to a new location at Pacha along the road to Valladolid (AGI, México 1658).

There can be no doubt that the conditions that made it possible for pirates to destroy Salamanca de

Bacalar were the same as those that made it so easy for British colonists gradually to assume control over so much of this territory during the next century. Through complex, prophecy-based strategies of violence and intimidation, the Maya had left the Spanish colonial structure in the Bacalar province in shambles; this situation simply invited foreign intervention. Like the poor local Spaniards, however, they were no match for the seafaring foreigners, and they were forced to retreat before the axes of the expanding British logging works.

Although the apparent relationships among katun reckoning and colonial period Maya political activity are intriguing, we in fact know far less about them than we wish we did. These are exceedingly complex ideas and events, and the sources that pertain to them are voluminous and difficult to interpret. This historic period provides a good lesson, perhaps, for the archaeologist who might be tempted to accept the political aspects of ritualized Maya cosmology literally or at face value. Katun prophecies were political statements to be argued over and manipulated for worldly reasons.

As we see these prophecies in use during the seventeenth century, we discover the Spanish attempting to manipulate the Itza by offering worldly returns to the Can Eks—at auspicious timely junctures—in exchange for submission. In return, the friends and enemies of the Can Eks deceived and embarrassed the Spanish by challenging their prophetic interpretations. Duplicity was compounded upon duplicity in a political milieu of artifice. Although the conditions of the seventeenth century were far from those of, say, the eighth century, they do give us a rare glimpse into the realpolitik of Maya statecraft.

ACKNOWLEDGMENTS

This research was supported by fellowships provided by the American Council of Learned Societies and Hamilton College and by funding provided by the Social Sciences and Humanities Research Council of Canada. Davidson College has provided support for documentary analysis. The author is grateful for all of this assistance.

BIBLIOGRAPHY

AGI (Archivo General de Indias), México
1638   Letter from Luís Sánchez de Aguilar et al. to Governor of Yucatan, September 20, 1638.
1658   Méritos y Servicios del Capitán Francisco Pérez, 1661.

Benavides Castillo, A., and A. P. Andrews
1979   *Ecab: Poblado y Provincia del Siglo XVI en Yucatán.* Cuadernos de los Centros Regionales. Centro Regional del Sureste. Instituto Nacional de Antropología e Historia, México D.F.

Bricker, V. R.
1981   *The Indian Christ, the Indian King: The Historical Substrate of Maya Myth and Ritual.* Austin: University of Texas Press.

Cárdenas Valencias, F., de
1937   *Relación historial eclesiástica de la provincia de Yucatán de la Nueva España escrita en el año de 1639.* Editorial Porréa, México D.F.

Carmack, R. M.
1981   *The Quiché Mayas of Utatlán: The Evolution of a Highland Guatemala Kingdom.* Norman: University of Oklahoma Press.

Chamberlain, R. S.
1948   *The Conquest and Colonization of Yucatan, 1517-1550.* Publication 509. Washington, DC: Carnegie Institution of Washington.

Edmonson, M. S.
1982   *The Ancient Future of the Itza: The Book of Chilam Balam of Tizimin.* Austin: University of Texas Press.
1986   *Heaven Born Mérida and Its Destiny.* Austin: University of Texas Press.

Farriss, N. M.
1984   *Maya Society Under Colonial Rule: The Collective Enterprise of Survival.* Princeton: Princeton University Press.

Graham, E., G. D. Jones, and R. R. Kautz
1985   Archaeology and Ethnohistory on a Spanish Colonial Frontier: The Macal-Tipu Project in Western Belize. In *The Lowland Maya Postclassic,* eds. A. F. Chase and P. M. Rice, pp. 206-214. Austin: University of Texas Press.

Graham, E., D. M. Pendergast, and G. D. Jones
1989   On the Fringes of Conquest: Maya-Spanish Contact in Colonial Belize. *Science* 246 (4935):1254-1259.

Jones, G. D.
1983   The Last Maya Frontiers of Colonial Yucatan. In *Spaniards and Indians in Southeastern Mesoamerica,* eds. M. J. MacLeod and R. Wasserstrom, pp. 64-91. Lincoln: University of Nebraska Press.
1984   Maya-Spanish Relations in Sixteenth Century Belize. *BELCAST Journal of Belizean Affairs* 1(1):28-40.
1986   The Southern Maya Lowlands during Spanish Colonial Times. In *Handbook of Middle American Indians,* Supplement Volume on Ethnohistory, ed. R. Spores, pp. 71-87. Austin: University of Texas Press.
1987a   Prophets and Idol Speculators: Forces of History in the Lowland Maya Rebellion of 1638. Paper presented at the symposium "Vision and Revision in Maya Studies," January 16-17, 1987, Albuquerque.
1987b   Recent Ethnohistorical Works on Southeastern Mesoamerica. *Latin American Research Review* 22(1):214-224.
1989   *Maya Resistance to Spanish Rule: Time and History on a Colonial Frontier.* Albuquerque: University of New Mexico Press.

Jones, G. D., R. R. Kautz, and E. Graham
1986   Tipu: A Maya Town on the Spanish Colonial Frontier. *Archaeology* 39(1):40-47.

Lizana, Bernardo de
1893   *Historia de Yucatán: Devocionario de Nuestra Señora de Izamal y Conquista Espiritual.* Museo Nacional, México. (Originally published 1654.)

López de Cogolludo, Diego
1688   *Historia de Yucatán.* Madrid: J. García Infanzón.

MacLeod, M. J., and R. Wasserstrom (editors)
1983   *Spaniards and Indians in Southeastern Mesoamerica: Essays on the History of Ethnic Relations.* Lincoln: University of Nebraska Press.

Miller, A. G.
1982   *On the Edge of the Sea: Mural Painting at Tancab-Tulum, Quintana Roo, Mexico.* Washington, DC: Dumbarton Oaks.

Pendergast, D. M.
1985   Lamanai, Belize: An Updated View. In *The Lowland Maya Postclassic,* eds. A. F. Chase and P. M. Rice, pp. 91-103. Austin: University of Texas Press.

Reed, N.
1964   *The Caste War of Yucatan*. Stanford: Stanford University Press.

Scholes, F. V., and E. Adams
1936-1937   Documents Relating to the Mirones Expedition to the Interior of Yucatan, 1621-24. *Maya Research* 3:153-176 (Part 1), 251-276 (Part 2).

de Vos, J.
1980   *La Paz de Dios y del Rey: La Conquista de la Selva Lacandona*. Chiapas, Mexico: Gobierno del Estado de Chiapas.

Wasserstrom, R.
1983   *Class and Society in Central Chiapas*. Berkeley: University of California Press.

XVII
Divination and Prophecy in Yucatan

Bruce Love

Archaeological Research Unit
University of California, Riverside

This paper explores two related themes in Maya studies. One is the long-recognized connection between the Books of Chilam Balam of colonial Yucatan and the Prehispanic hieroglyphic codices; the other is the workings of Maya divination and prophecy. These two themes find common ground in the Maya ideology underlying them. The deep-seated understanding of prophecy and divination exercised by the users of the hieroglyphic codices was not destroyed during the Spanish Conquest; instead, in the post-Contact period, when it was forbidden on penalty of death to write or even own hieroglyphic books, the Maya scribes of Yucatan produced books in the Spanish alphabet. The change was essentially exterior. These colonial period writings, which have now become known collectively as the Books of Chilam Balam, reflect the same fundamental belief system that produced the hieroglyphic books. To help understand this system, several examples of correspondences between the two kinds of books are presented here along with a modern-day illustration of Maya prophecy.

CONTEMPORARY PROPHECY IN YUCATAN[1]

There is a method of weather prediction, variants of which are used throughout present-day Yucatan, known as the *xoc k'in,* "count of the days." Although the *xoc k'in* may have European antecedents (Rubel 1965), it nevertheless serves as a useful model to help understand Maya divination. The procedure allows the *h-men,* the Maya ritual specialist, to foretell the weather for the coming year based on observations during the 31 days of January.

As described in Chan Kom, Yucatan, in the 1930s (Redfield and Villa Rojas 1934:132-133), it works as follows: the weather conditions on the first of January correspond to the weather for the rest of the month of January; the weather on the second of January corresponds to what the weather will be like in February, the third of January matches March, and the fourth, April. This continues through the first 12 days of January so that the weather on the twelfth of January matches what the weather will be like in December. Then the cycle is reversed. The thirteenth of January again matches the weather for December, the fourteenth for November, the fifteenth for October, and so on, until returning to January on the twenty-fourth. Now the *h-men* has two sets of observations with which to predict the weather for the coming year. For example, the *h-men's* observations of the weather on the third of January and the twenty-second of January are combined to form a prediction for the month of March; April is predicted by both the fourth and the twenty-first.

Then the next six days, January twenty-fifth to the thirtieth, are used to predict the weather for coming *pairs* of months; the twenty-fifth for January-February, the twenty-sixth for March-April, and so on to the thirtieth of January, which matches November and December. But there is still one more day in January, the thirty-first, and it is used as follows: each of the 12 hours from 6:00 A.M. to 6:00 P.M. is equated to the successive 12 months of the year.

In all, the *h-men* has four observations for each month of the coming year. What if the observations conflict? There is no conflict in the view of the *h-men;* instead, the differences add depth and complexity to the reading, combining to produce a more learned prognosis. Likewise, the days and numbers in the ancient Maya calendars carried their own auguries; through the expertise and art of the practitioner several such omens could be brought together

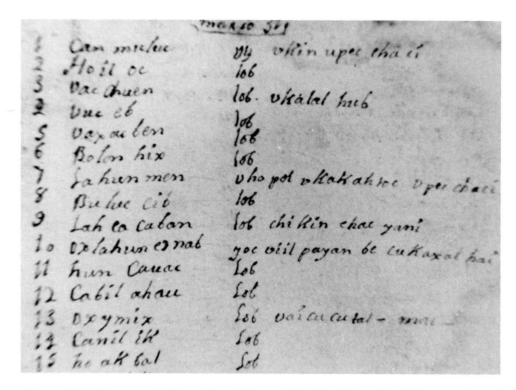

Figure 17.1. Days marked utz ("good") and lob ("bad") in the Chilam Balam of Tizimin (Akademische Druck-u. 1980).

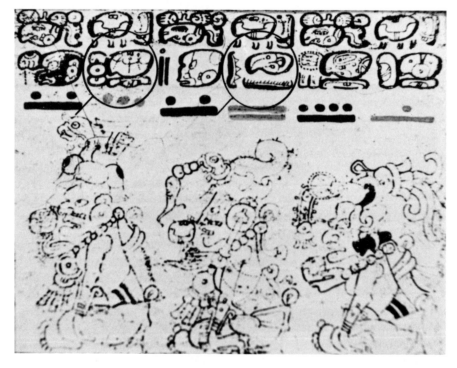

Figure 17.2. Days marked "good" (second compound in second column) and "bad" (second compound in fourth column) in the Dresden Codex (Thompson 1972).

to form a reading. The skillful intertwining of separate observations in the modern *xoc k'in* allows us, as students of the Maya, to understand the Maya penchant for bringing together and interweaving divergent number series in historic and prehistoric Maya texts.

CORRESPONDENCES BETWEEN THE BOOKS OF CHILAM BALAM AND THE HIEROGLYPHIC CODICES

The following section illustrates some of the ways in which the expertise of the Prehispanic calendar specialists endured the disruptions of the Spanish Conquest. Although the Maya colonial-period books were written in alphabetic script instead of hieroglyphs and incorporated the European calendar, the underlying Maya understanding of prophecy and divination is reflected in the following similarities.

One of the more straightforward systems of prophecy is to list the days of the 260-day calendar as "good" or "bad." In one example, from the Chilam Balam of Tizimin (Fig. 17.1), this appears as *utz* ("good") and *lob* ("bad"). In this example, the first 15 days of March are listed. In the left-hand column are the days in the European calendar, 1 through 15; next to them are the corresponding days in the Maya 260-day calendar, *can* ("four") Muluc, *hoil* ("five") Oc, *uac* ("six") Chuen, and so on. Next to these is written either *utz* or *lob*. There is also supplementary information entered beside some of the entries, such as *u kin upec chaci'*, "day of thunder" (translation by Taube, personal communication; Barrera Vasquez 1980:643). Parallel usage of good and bad auguries is found throughout the hieroglyphic codices. One example (Fig. 17.2) is from the Dresden Codex, where the fourth glyph compound in the first set of four compounds is "good" and the fourth compound in the second group is "bad" (Thompson 1972:40).

A sequence of days in the 260-day calendar, like *Can* Muluc, *Hoil* Oc, *Uac* Chuen, cited above, occurs along the tops of pages 77 and 78 of the Madrid Codex (Fig. 17.3) in which the first 13 days of the complete cycle are recorded. The vertical columns below each of these days provides information (only some of which is deciphered) for understanding or interpreting the meanings of the days. There is another case in which the entire 260-day cycle is written out, only without the numerical coefficients. A portion of this is shown (Fig. 17.4), again from the Madrid Codex.

Besides recording sequences of days from the 260-day calendar, the Maya, in both the codices and the Chilam Balams, recorded several other ritual cycles of time. Among these, three which will now be discussed are *katuns, tuns,* and *uinals*. A *uinal* is a cycle of 20 days, that is, one complete round of the 20 days from *Imix* to *Ahau*. *Tuns* are periods of 18 uinals (360 days), and katuns consist of 20 tuns (7,200 days). All three of these cycles end on the day Ahau, because Ahau is the twentieth day of the 20-day uinal, and tuns and katuns are all even multiples of uinals.

In order for the Maya to identify and talk about these different time periods, they referred to them by the particular Ahau day on which they ended. For example, if a uinal ends on 1 Ahau, it can be referred to as Uinal 1 Ahau, that is, the uinal that ends on 1 Ahau. The next uinal, 20 days later, will end on 8 Ahau and can be called Uinal 8 Ahau. The fact that 8 Ahau follows 1 Ahau is a function of the numerical coefficients, 1 through 13, cycling every 13 days alongside the 20 days of the uinal. (In Fig. 17.1, there is a good illustration of this: *Oxlahun*, or "thirteen," Ets'nab followed by *Hun*, or "one," Cauac.) The next uinal will end on 2 Ahau, the next, 9, the next, 3, and the next, 10. So if a list is given reading 1 Ahau, 8 Ahau, 2 Ahau, 9 Ahau, the reader knows by the number coefficients that the list refers to uinals. If it were tuns or katuns, they would have different numbers. A series of tuns would read 1 Ahau, 10 Ahau, 6 Ahau, 2 Ahau, 11 Ahau, and so on. Katuns, on the other hand, are sequentially 1 Ahau, 12 Ahau, 10 Ahau, 8 Ahau, 6 Ahau, and so on.

I will now give examples of these three number series—katuns, tuns, and uinals—from both the Chilam Balams and the Paris Codex. There are several katun counts in various Chilam Balams (Barrera Vasquez and Morley 1949; Barrera Vasquez and Rendon [1948]1974; Brinton 1882; Roys 1949b, 1954), one of which, from the Book of Chilam Balam of Tizimi'n (1980:21r), is shown in Figure 17.5. In this example, three paragraphlike sections are headed by Buluc Ahau, Bolon Ahau, and Uuc Ahau, "Eleven," "Nine," and "Seven" respectively. These numbered Ahaus name the katuns in sequence. After each katun is named, several lines of writing follow which, in this case, give essentially historical infor-

Figure 17.3. A series of 13 consecutive days from 1 Imix to 13 Ben in the Madrid Codex (Akademische Druck-u. 1967).

Figure 17.4. A portion of a 260-day series in the Madrid Codex (Akademische Druck-u. 1967:14).

mation, events that happened during that katun (Edmonson 1982:54, 59, 63).

In the Paris Codex, there is a katun series that is still visible on 10 (of originally 13?) pages. Figure 17.6 shows three of these pages, which correspond to Katuns 13 Ahau, 11 Ahau and 9 Ahau. The katuns are so named by Ahau day signs with bar-and-dot numbers, visible in the central scenes of each page. Figures 17.7, 17.8, and 17.9 give closer views of the numbered Ahaus. I believe that the texts around the central image convey, like the Chilam Balam of Tizimi'n, historical information, although this is not yet proven and there is no space here to present the arguments for it. Let it suffice to note that a katun sequence, for which we have many examples in the Chilam Balams, can also be found in the hieroglyphic codices.

Like the katuns, there are several tun sequences in the different Chilam Balams (Roys 1949b). One example is in the Chilam Balam of Kaua (Fig. 17.10; Wilkinson n.d.), which shows an attempt by a colonial-period Maya scribe to correlate Christian years with the traditional Maya calendar. Although there are some apparent discrepancies in the number series, perhaps caused by the difficulty in reconciling 360-day tuns to 365.25-day years, there is a good sequence running from 1798 to 1804, here labeled in Mayan, Ox ("Three") Ahau, Laca ("Twelve") Ahau, Uaxac ("Eight") Ahau, Can ("Four") Ahau, Oxlahun ("Thirteen") Ahau, Bolon ("Nine") Ahau, and Ho ("Five") Ahau.

A similar tun sequence, from pre-Conquest times, is found in the upper register of the previously mentioned katun pages of the Paris Codex (see Fig. 17.6). In this example, in the upper sections, the lower ahau dates read horizontally across the three pages, 12 Ahau, 8 Ahau, and 4 Ahau. Twelve-eight-four is a tun sequence, so the Ahau dates here must be referring to tuns; the tun signs on which the accompanying figures are seated lend support to this supposition.

In addition to the katun and tun series just described, there are also uinal series found in the Chilam Balams and, I am fairly convinced, in the Paris Codex. One uinal sequence is found in the unpublished Chilam Balam of Ixil (Fig. 17.11; Wilkinson n.d.). This sequence, running vertically on the left side of the page, is written in both Arabic numerals and colonial Yucatecan Mayan. It runs 1, 8, 2, 9, 3, 10, 4, 11, and so on.

In the Paris Codex there exist what may be the remnants of another uinal series. In the upper register of the katun pages, where the numbered Ahaus run horizontally to form a tun sequence, there are also vertical columns of Ahau signs. Although the pages are badly eroded, on two pages there is enough of the original plaster and paint left to reveal the bar-and-dot numbers of the upper as well as the lower Ahaus. On these two pages (Figs. 17.12 and 17.13) there is a 10 Ahau over a 4 Ahau and an 11 Ahau over a 5 Ahau. If these columns were read vertically from top to bottom, these pairs of numbers, 10 to 4 and 11 to 5, would be the right coefficients for uinal counts.

SUMMARY

Having now established several correspondences between the two types of books, I return to the theme of how divination and prophecy work. There is an often-cited ethnohistorical source which describes something of this process as it was found by the Roman Catholic missionary, Fray Andrés de Avendaño y Loyola, among the Maya of Tayasal, Guatemala, in the seventeenth century. He reported that the books were:

> painted on both sides with a variety of figures and characters . . . which show not only the count of the said days, months and years, but also the ages and prophecies which their idols and images announced to them. (Means 1917:1412; Roys 1933:184)

In the hieroglyphic codices, the scenes accompanying the hieroglyphic texts do appear to reflect what Avendaño described as "their idols and images." If the vertical column of Ahaus at the top of the Paris katun pages do indeed represent uinal series, then these pages show a skillful interweaving of uinals, tuns, and katuns, corresponding to Avendaño's months, years, and ages. Thus the ritual practitioners, using the Paris Codex, could integrate disparate images associated with distinct calendar cycles to reach a prophecy. The persistence of these skills into and through the colonial period is demonstrated by the intermingling of cycles found in the Chilam Balam books and the merging of dissimilar readings to produce a coherent weather forecast by

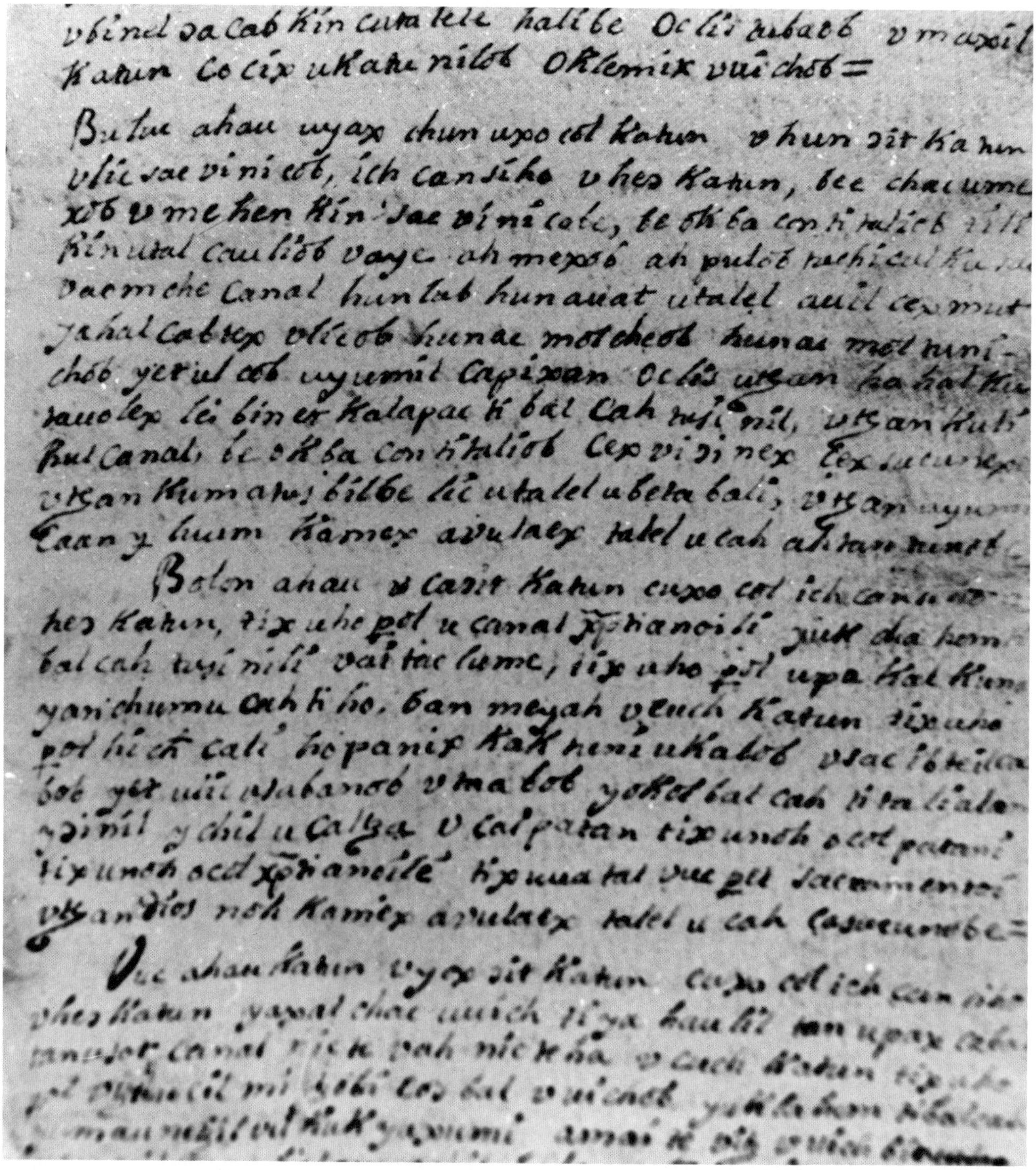

Figure 17.5. A portion of a katun series from the Chilam Balam of Tizimin (Akademische Druck-u. 1980:folio 21r).

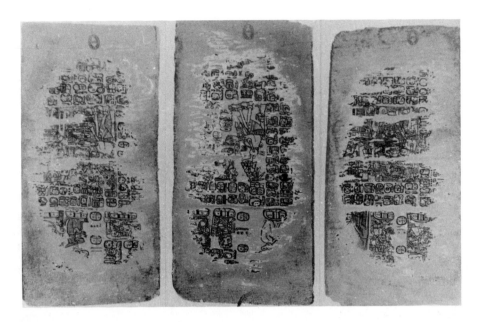

Figure 17.6. Three katun pages from the Paris Codex (Akademische Druck-u. 1968:3-5).

Figure 17.7. Katun 13 Ahau from the Paris Codex (Akademische Druck-u. 1968:3).

the present-day specialists of Yucatan using the *xoc k'in*.

inatory cycle. For a review of this practice, see Tedlock 1982 and Earle 1983.

NOTE

1. There is no recorded evidence for survival of the ancient calendar among the modern Maya of Yucatan, but the Maya of highland Guatemala and Chiapas do continue to use the ancient 260-day div-

ACKNOWLEDGMENT

Most of the research for this paper was done while I was serving as a Junior Fellow, in 1986-1987, in Pre-Columbian Studies at Dumbarton Oaks, Washington, DC.

Figure 17.8. Katun 11 Ahau from the Paris Codex (Akademische Druck-u. 1968:4).

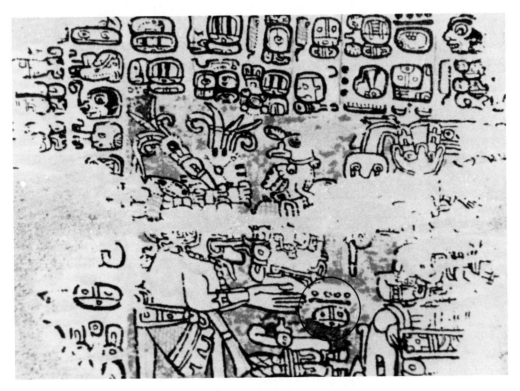

Figure 17.9. Katun 9 Ahau from the Paris Codex (Akademische Druck-u 1968:5).

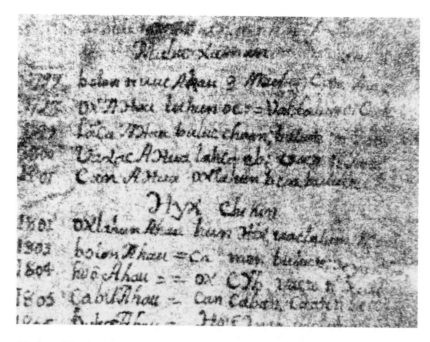

Figure 17.10. A tun sequence from the Chilam Balam of Kaua (Paul Wilkinson Indian Languages Collection: Container 25 n.d.).

Figure 17.11. A uinal sequence from the Chilam Balam of Ixil (Paul Wilkinson Indian Languages Collection: Container 25 n.d.).

Figure 17.12. Ten Ahau to Four Ahau; a possible uinal sequence from the Paris Codex (Akademische Druck-u 1968:5).

Figure 17.13. Eleven Ahau to Five Ahau; a possible uinal sequence from the Paris Codex (Akademische Druck-u. 1968:8).

BIBLIOGRAPHY

Barrera Vásquez, A.
1980   *Diccionario Maya Cordemex, Maya-Español Español-Maya.* Mérida: Ediciones Cordemex.

Barrera Vásquez, A., and S. Morley
1949   *The Maya Chronicles.* Carnegie Institution of Washington, Publication 585, Contribution 48. Washington, DC.

Barrera Vásquez, A., and S. Rendon
1974 [1948] *El Libro de los Libros de Chilam Balam. Traducción de sus Textos Paralelos.* México D.F.: Fondo de Cultura Económica.

Book of Chilam Balam of Tizimin
1980   *El Libro de Chilam Balam de Tizimin.* Reproduction. Fontes Rerum Mexicanarum, vol. 6, introduction by K. H. Mayer. Graz, Austria: Akademische Druck-u.

Brinton, D. G.
1882   *The Maya Chronicles.* Brinton's Library of Aboriginal American Literature, no. 1. Philadelphia, PA.

Codex Peresianus (Codex Paris).
1968   Reproduction, with Commentary and Summary by F. Anders. Codices Selecti, vol 9. Graz, Austria: Akademische Druck-u.

Codex Tro-Cortesianus (Codex Madrid)
1967   Introduction and Summary by F. Anders. Graz, Austria: Akademische Druck-u.

Earle, D. M.
1983   The Metaphor of the Day in Quiche: Notes on the Nature of Everyday Life. In *Symbol and Meaning Beyond the Closed Community: Essays in Mesoamerican Ideas,* ed. G. H. Gossen. Institute for Mesoamerican Studies, State University of New York at Albany.

Edmonson, M. S.
1982   *The Ancient Future of the Itza. The Book of Chilam Balam of Tizimin.* Translated and annotated. Austin: University of Texas Press.

Means, P. A.
1917   *History of the Spanish Conquest of Yucatan and of the Itzas.* Peabody Museum Papers. Cambridge, MA: Peabody Museum Press.

Redfield, R., and A. Villa Rojas
1934   *Chan Kom, a Maya Village.* Carnegie Institution of Washington, Publication 448. Washington, DC.

Roys, R. L.
1933   *The Book of Chilam Balam of Chumayel.* Carnegie Institution of Washington, Publication 438. Washington, DC.
1949a   *Guide to the Codex Perez.* Carnegie Institution of Washington, Publication 585, Contribution 49. Washington, DC.
1949b   *The Prophecies for the Maya Tuns or Years in the Books of Chilam Balam of Tizimin and Mani.* Carnegie Institution of Washington, Publication 585, Contribution 51. Washington, DC.
1954   *The Maya Katun Prophecies of the Books of Chilam Balam, Series Id.* Carnegie Institution of Washington, Publication 606, Contribution 57. Washington, DC.

Rubel, A. J.
1965   Un Vistazo al Xoc Kin de los Mayas de Hoy. *Estudios de Cultura Maya* 5:391-398. Mexico, D.F.

Tedlock, B.
1982   *Time and the Highland Maya.* Albuquerque: University of New Mexico Press.

Thompson, J. E. S.
1972   *A Commentary on the Dresden Codex, a Maya Hieroglyphic Book.* Philadelphia: American Philosophical Society.

Wilkinson, P.
n.d.   The Paul Wilkinson Indian Languages Collection, Manuscript Division, Library of Congress, Washington, DC.

XVIII

Mayan Calendars, Cosmology, and Astronomical Commensuration

Barbara Tedlock

Department of Anthropology
SUNY Buffalo

Ancient Maya astronomy, cosmology, and calendrics have engaged many scholars during the past one hundred years, and there exists an enormous published literature on the topic. On the other hand, ethnographic studies of these same topics among the nearly 5 million Maya living today in Mexico, Belize, and Guatemala have concerned but a handful of scholars who have produced only a small literature during the past forty years.[1] The question of the commensuration of astronomical cycles in Precolumbian written Maya calendars continues to engage scholars, but the investigation of ongoing indigenous methods of commensuration has been largely ignored.[2]

For Maya peoples the sun is, and always has been, the ruler of the cosmos. The term *k'in* or *q'ij,* meaning "sun" or "day" in virtually all Mayan languages, is the basic unit of timekeeping and calendrical practice used both in the past and in the present.[3] The primary directions east and west are established by observing the intersection of the daily path of the sun with the horizon. Both Lowland and Highland Maya describe the sun as a human or god-like figure with a brilliant round face rising each day on the eastern horizon and facing his universe with north on his right hand and south on his left.[4] After he reaches his meridian, he pauses briefly, then continues across the sky, entering the earth in the west and reaching a point opposite his meridian at midnight. He remains below until he begins his eastern rise once again. The terms indicating east and west, in all Mayan languages, refer to a line or vector along which the sun rises and sets, depending on the season of the year.[5] The biannual passage of the sun across the zenith, a phenomenon that occurs only in tropical latitudes, is used to fix dates in the agricultural calendar. These zenith passages, which are equally spaced on either side of the summer solstice, occur when the sun travels northward along the ecliptic and when it returns southward.

CALENDRICAL SYSTEMS

Maya calendrical and computational numerology is based on the perceived geometry and periodicity of space, the human body, and various astronomical cycles. Important cycles in many contemporary Maya communities include a 260-day almanac consisting of four 65-day periods, a lunar agricultural almanac, and a 365-day solar year.

Although some scholars have described the 260-day cycle as the effect of combining two preexisting ritual cycles consisting of 13 numerals and 20 day names (Thompson 1950:99; Justeson 1989:78), others see it as relating to a celestial cycle such as the interval between zenithal transits of the sun near the latitude 150°N (Larsen 1936; Malmstrom 1973, 1978; Coggins 1982). Still others think that this cycle is more closely related to earthly affairs, including numerology found in divinatory rituals and in agricultural and midwifery practices (Brotherston 1982:3; B. Tedlock 1982b; 1985:83-87). This almanac, called the Sacred Round by students of the Classic Maya, is a succession of day designations created by the combination of 20 names with a number from 1 to 13. As 13 and 20 lack a common factor, the total possible combinations of numbers and days are 13 x 20, or 260. Not until each of the 13 numbers appears attached to each of the 20 days will the same number and name (e.g., 1 B'atz') reappear. The lunar almanac, which is not as well understood by Maya scholars as the 260-day almanac, is based on synodic reckoning. Lunar synodic cycles, which are counted from full moon to full moon, are used in midwifery as well as in agricultural practice. The 365-day year, consisting of 18 "mesomonths" (Mesoamerican months) of 20 days each with 5 "extra" days at the end, is used in timing important community-wide political events and religious rituals in a number of contemporary Maya communities.

To illustrate current astronomical and calendrical theory and practice, I will center my discussion on the Maya with whom I am best acquainted, namely, those living in the Quiche-speaking municipality of Momostenango.[6] This community, currently consisting of approximately 72,000 persons (of whom 98% are indigenous), is located in the department of Totonicapan, Guatemala, at 15° 04' 38" latitude north of the equator, 91° 24' 30" longitude. It is known to travelers mainly for its fine woolen blankets, but it is known to archaeologists and ethnographers for its celebration of 8 B'atz', the largest ongoing Mesoamerican religious ritual scheduled according to the 260-day almanac.

Today there are many individuals in Momostenango who reckon time by combining observations of the sun, moon, and stars with Precolumbian Maya calendars. These men and women are known as *ajq'ij,* "daykeepers," and their astronomical observations are called *kajib'al ch'umil,* "descent of the stars." Daykeepers make pragmatic use of their observations and calendar keeping in many areas of their social life, including agriculture, commerce, curing, dream interpretation, divination, and midwifery. This knowledge is considered valuable and is open to individuals only through formal apprenticeship (B. Tedlock 1982b).

The 365-day solar calendar, called *masewal q'ij,* "common days," lacks a leap year; thus, Momostecans use "vague" rather than "tropical" years. The first day of the new year moves back one position each four years, or 99 positions each 400 years, when measured against the Gregorian calendar. At the end of each solar year the five days between the last occurrence of the old Mam, "grandfather" or "yearbearer," and the entrance of the new Mam are dangerous times, when people curtail social and business activity. At noon on the eve of the day on which the midnight arrival of the Mam will be awaited, many people tie a red thread around their own and their children's left wrists and

right ankles. From this time until the new Mam is seated, 20 days later, human beings are considered weak. In order to counteract this lack of strength Momostecans prepare and eat special tamales known as *ub'en* in Quiche or *tayuya* in Spanish. They consist of equal parts of double-boiled ground black-bean paste and corn dough from the previous year's harvest.

Each solar year begins with one of four possible yearbearers—Kej, E, No'j, or Iq'—which are equivalent to the Classic and Early Postclassic Yucatec yearbearers Manik', Eb, Kaban, and Ik'. They are ranked, with Kej considered the most important, followed by E, No'j, and finally Iq'. A new Mam is received once a year at midnight, or *nik'aj aq'äb',* literally "center of darkness." This is done on a mountaintop by the traditional religious and political leaders of the community, who note which stars are directly overhead. Momostecan religious and political leaders, including key members of the hierarchy of calendar experts, welcome the new Mam with prayers, food, incense, bonfires, fireworks, drum-and-flute music, marimbas, chanting, and dancing. In a Kej year the Mam is received on Kilaja, the mountain located *chiröleb'al q'ij,* "at sun's rising place," located due east of a sacred hill in the town center. When Mam Kej finishes his year of service, Mam E enters and is received on Tamancu, a mountain located due south of the town. The third yearbearer, Mam No'j, is greeted on Joyan, also in the south, just west of Tamancu. Mam Iq' is received on Socop, located *chukajib'al q'ij,* "at sun's falling place," in the west. The eighteen 20-day months of the ancient calendar are marked, each time the day of the current Mam comes around, by setting off firecrackers, burning copal, and making special prayers in the town center and rural cantons.

In Momostenango, the 260-day almanac is called both *rajilab'al q'ij,* "counting of days (or suns)," and *chol q'ij,* "ordering of days (or suns)." The nine-month growing period of high-altitude maize and/or the human gestation period may help account for its length. The 20 day names are B'atz', E, Aj, Ix, Tz'ikin, Ajmak, No'j, Tijax, Kawuq, Junajpu, Imöx, Iq', Aq'ab'al, K'at, Kan, Kame, Kej, Q'anil, Toj, and Tz'i'. Each day name has a mnemonic phrase or term indicating its nature, and most of these mnemonics are built on words that are morphologically or phonologically related to the name (B. Tedlock 1982a). The accompanying numbers change the nature of the day name; thus, low numbers such as 1, 2, and 3 are "gentle," the high numbers 11, 12, and 13 are "violent," and the middle numbers 7, 8, and 9 are neither gentle nor violent. The day numbers also designate shrines to be visited; for example, on a 1-day a person might visit *junab'al,* "one-place" shrine, at Paja'. A 6-day indicates a visit to the *waqib'al,* "six-place" shrine, on the sacred hill in the town center; an 8-day indicates the *wajxaqib'al,* "eight-place" shrine, on Ch'uti Sab'al; and a 9-day corresponds to *b'elejeb'al,* the "nine-place" shrine, on Nima Sab'al.

The 9-lunation agricultural cycle, called *junab' ik',* "moon year," is also computed. Although this cycle runs closer to seasonal time than the free-rolling 260-day almanac, the beginning date varies not only according to shifting positions of lunar cycles within the seasons but according to meteorological phenomena and hawk migrations as well (B. Tedlock 1985). Close connections between Maya agronomy and astronomy have been assumed by many scholars, but there has been precious little agreement concerning precisely which celestial phenomena are connected to specific agricultural almanacs and activities. Thus, for example, N. Cordy (1933) described the period of plant growth from the vernal equinox (March 21-22) to the winter solstice (December 21-22) as approximating the 260-day calendar. Helga Larsen (1936) argued that given the climactic conditions of a site like Copan, Honduras (located at 15°N), the spring passage of the sun through the zenith (April 30) announced the time to prepare the fields for planting, while the fall zenith passage (August 12) announced that the rain would diminish and the crop was beyond damage. She concluded that the zenith passages must have been the most important astronomical indicators of season, and that they probably meant as much to Mesoamericans as the summer and winter solstices did to the inhabitants of the extreme north.

Rafael Girard (1962, 1966), however, reported the presence and equal importance of both solstitial and zenithal principles among the Chorti of Guatemala, who are located not far from Copan. He noted that the first passage of the sun across the zenith was heralded on the evening of April 30 by the position of Orion's Belt, the Southern Cross, and the Pleiades. Further, he claimed the existence of a fixed 260-day agricultural calendar among the present-day Chorti and Quiche and hypothesized that it must have existed for the ancient Maya. A number of authors,

such as Fritchett (1974), have taken note of the interval of 105 days between the zenithal passages at 15°N and its connection to agriculture, suggesting (as does Girard) that the 260-day divinatory almanac might have originated at this latitude. However, Coe (1975:9) finds tenuous Girard's argument that the divinatory almanac resulted from turning the agricultural one into a perpetual cycle. More recently, Tichy (1983) examined Girard's data and found that the 260-day agricultural almanac was divided into an 80-day festival section followed by a 180-day rainy season. He reasoned that, since this almanac was dependent on the relationship among five astronomically significant days (the summer solstice, the two zenith passages, and the two equinoxes) at 15°N, it must have been invented in this area.

INTRODUCTION TO MAYA ASTRONOMY

There are more than 3,000 stars and planets an observer can pick out with the naked eye at any one moment on a clear night. It might be expected that at least the planets and the Milky Way, as well as all the first- and second-magnitude stars visible in the latitudes of the Maya world, would have been of considerable interest to the ancient Maya. Unfortunately, they left us no star or constellation catalogs, no treatises on astronomical theories or methods, and no measuring instruments. We also lack records of their astronomical observations, which would help us interpret the various tables and almanacs we find in the codices. What we do have are the end products of the application of ancient theories and methods. It is left to us to decipher both the problems Maya astronomers addressed and the methods they employed to arrive at the textual solutions that survive.

In order to reach some understanding of Precolumbian Maya astronomical concepts and practices, one must study inscribed stone monuments and architectural alignments; incised bones, shells, and pots; painted ceramics and murals; and the four extant hieroglyphic codices, together with colonial manuscripts written by the Maya in the roman alphabet. One must also study colonial dictionaries, Spanish chronicles, and the current astronomical and cosmological ideas and practices found in the oral and written literature and the religious practices of the living Maya.

Archaeological and architectural studies have already illuminated some facts about ancient Maya positional astronomy by demonstrating stellar alignments of buildings. For example, Aveni and Hartung (1986:22) have reported that at the Puuc site of Uxmal the orientation of the Governor's Palace is 15° clockwise from the common axis of the other buildings at the site, so that it faces 28° south of east. From the central doorway, perpendicular to the 320-foot-long facade, one can see a pyramid at the site of Nohpat, which is 6 km away. Transit measurements, taken on the perpendicular from the center of the doorway, indicate that it points to the exact position on the eastern horizon where Venus would have risen at the time of its maximum southerly eight-year journey during the era when the Palace of the Governor was constructed, around 800 A.D. Furthermore, the sculpted frieze around the building includes more than 350 Venus symbols.

CURRENT ASTRONOMICAL THEORY AND PRACTICE

In Momostenango, all the celestial bodies—including the sun, moon, planets, comets, meteors, stars, asterisms, constellations, and the Milky Way—constitute a single category labeled ch'umilal kaj, "starry sky." The diurnal, monthly, and seasonal paths and positions of these celestial bodies along the horizon and across the night sky are observed and discussed by Momostecan naked-eye astronomers. The daily path of the sun, known as ub'e saq, ub'e q'ij, "road of light, road of day," is described in Quiche as oxib' utzuk', oxib' uxukut chupam saqil, "three sides, three corners in the light." It is visualized as a triangle whose angles are the three transition points in diurnal time. This solar triangle stretches from the sun's rising position to its noon position, and on to its setting position. By analogy, heavenly bodies that rise, cross the night sky, and set in opposition to the sun, in reasonable proximity to its path, are said to form oxib' utzuk', oxib' uxukut chupam q'equm, "three sides, three corners in the dark."

Stars are used to tell the time of night and to herald the time of year for both ritual and agricultural purposes. Both the winter and summer solstice sunrise and sunset positions are called xolkat b'e,

"change of path or road." This term, unlike our own Latin-derived term solstice, or "sun stand," stresses the back-and-forth movement of the sun. The most important change of road is the winter solstice, raqan q'ij, or "sun's reach," which annually marks the end of the high-altitude corn harvest in December. At the latitude of Momostenango (15° 04' 38" north of the equator), the zenith passages of the sun occur on May 1 or 2 during the sun's northward movement, and on August 11 or 12 during its southward return. The sunrise and sunset positions on both zenith passages are referred to as jalb'al, "place of change," indicating the location of a change in the nature of the sun's path rather than a change of paths.

The planets, as a group, are known as kaq ch'umil, "red stars." When Venus (or any other planet that takes the role of evening star) appears in the western sky after sunset, it is called rasq'äb, "of-the-night." Venus in its morning-star aspect is called Junajpu, a day name that is also the personal name of a mythic hero in the Popol Vuh (D. Tedlock 1985). When Venus, or any other planet, appears as a bright star in the east before dawn, it is referred to as .qo q'ij, "sun carrier," and its path is known as ub'eal ëqo q'ij, "sun carrier's road." Comets are referred to as uje ch'umil, "tail of the star," and are considered omens of massive pestilence. Comets and meteors are both called ch'ab'i q'aq', "flaming arrow." The term ch'ab'i refers to the tip or point of an arrow, dart, dagger, or spear, and q'aq' means "fire." A colonial Quiche term for meteor was ch'olanic ch'umil, "star that makes war" (Tirado 1787:208). Meteorites, arrowheads, and obsidian points found in cornfields today are considered the remains of falling stars. These objects are gathered and placed together with other sacred objects in the family meb'il, a traditional household shrine (B. Tedlock 1982b:40-41, 81-82).

Some Highland and Lowland Maya describe meteors or comets as cigar butts of the gods (Tozzer 1907:158; Girard 1966:74; B. Tedlock 1983a:12; D. Tedlock 1985:112), and it may well be that the cigars smoked by the hero twins of the Popol Vuh (D. Tedlock 1985:112) are to be understood as meteors. At the place where a meteorite lands in Yucatan, it is believed that obsidian arrowheads can be found (Tozzer 1907:157). Throughout the Maya area, meteors are thought to be evil omens forecasting sickness, war, and death (La Farge and Byers 1931:129;

Laughlin 1975:284; Vogt 1976:217; Lamb 1981:237; Koizumi 1981:141; B. Tedlock 1983a:6; Alcorn 1984:143). The cognitive connection between obsidian, war, death, and sickness is due to the past use of obsidian-tipped spears and darts in warfare and human sacrifice, together with the past and present use of obsidian blades in bleeding procedures and in surgery (Crabtree 1968; Robicsek and Hales 1984; Orellana 1987:72-75).

Individual stars named by the Quiche include Regulus, or *jun ch'umil,* "one star," and Spica, or *pix,* "spark." Certain Quiche asterisms are rather similar to Western ones; for example, *xik,* "hawk," is recognizable as Aquila, the Eagle (B. Tedlock 1985:83). Others are not at all the same. Two or more stars or asterisms may share a single name, but single stars or asterisms may have more than one name. For example, Acrux (in the southern cross) and Polaris (in the Little Dipper) together are called *xukut ch'umil,* "corner stars." Both the Pleiades and Hyades are called *mötz,* "handful," and the Big and Little Dipper are called *paq'ab',* "ladles" or "spoons." The Milky Way, on the other hand, has two separate designations depending on which end of it is intended. The undivided segment is *saqi b'e,* "white road," while the part with the dark cleft or rift is *xib'alb'a b'e,* "underworld road." The bright stars Castor and Pollux, in Gemini, have two designations: *kib' chuplinik,* "two shiny ones," and *kib' pix,* "two sparks." Within the constellation of Orion, known as *je chi q'aq',* "dispersed fire," there are two asterisms with a one-star overlap: Orion's belt, or *je oxib' chi q'aq' ajaw,* "tail of the three fire lords," and Alnitak, Saiph, and Rigel, called *oxib' nima ch'umil,* "three big stars," of which the brightest, Rigel, is called *nima q'aq',* "big fire." This asterism is also referred to as *oxib' xk'ub',* "three hearth stones." The Great Nebula M42, which is visible to the naked eye, is located between these three stars. It is described as smoke from a celestial cooking fire.[7] Among modern Yucatec Maya residing in the town of Yalcoba, near the archaeological ruin of Coba, Orion's Belt, *theta* Taurus, and the Pleiades each have *u k'áak',* "their fire," in the form of the bright stars Rigel, Betelgeuse, and Aldebaran (Sosa 1985:431).

In Momostenango, the progress of the solar year is marked by noting acronychal and cosmical risings and settings of certain key stars. Acronychal risings or settings occur at nightfall, while cosmical risings and settings occur at dawn (OED 1979:121). Thus,

an acronychal star rise takes place on the eastern horizon at the moment of sunset on the western horizon, while a cosmical star set takes place on the western horizon at the moment of sunrise on the eastern horizon. In Momostenango, during the dry half of the year between harvest and planting (November through April), acronychal and cosmical risings and settings are observed and used in timing ritual events. Each of six stellar events, spaced from 20 to 30 days apart, singles out a particular star or constellation as *retal aq'äb',* "the sign of night." For example, in mid-November the Pleiades rise near the sunrise position during sunset twilight, cross their meridian at midnight, and go down near the sunset position in the dawn twilight. Other acronychal and cosmical events occur in mid-December with Orion, in mid-January with Gemini, in the third week of February with Regulus, in mid-March with the Big Dipper, and around April 1 with Acrux.

During our fieldwork, Dennis Tedlock and I were taught to make a series of five visits to a pair of low (1-day) and middle (8-day) shrines stretching over a 27-day period, which is the nearest whole-day equivalent to one lunar sidereal month (27.32167 days). We first visited Paja', "At the Water," a low, watery shrine, on 1 Kej, and then, 7 days later on 8 Ix, we visited a high shrine called Ch'uti Sab'al, "Little Declaration Place." This was followed by another visit to Paja', now on 1 Junajpu, followed by Ch'uti Sab'al on 8 Kej, and ending on 1 Ix with a final afternoon visit to Paja'. This 27-day period is called *chakalik,* "staked, stabilized, or set," and is compared to the firm placement of a table on its four legs, or the firm placement of a roof on the four forked poles at the corners of a house. The purpose of this "stabilization" is to overcome illness and bad luck.

Patrilineage leaders, called *chuchqajawib' rech alaxik,* "motherfathers of the born ones," visit a high shrine called Nima Sab'al, "Large Declaration Place," according to the following sequence of days: 9 Kej + 13 days = 9 Junajpu + 13 days = 9 Aj + 13 = 9 Kame + 13 = 9 Kawuq + 13 = 9 E + 13 = 9 Kan + 3 = 12 Q'anil = 82 days. This total is equivalent to three lunar sidereal months (3 x 27.32167 days = 81.96501 days). The visits are made in order to bring an abundant harvest and keep the lineage healthy. Shortly after sunset on the first day of the series, the motherfather opens a particular altar that pertains to his own patrilineage. Nima Sab'al belongs to a category of shrines called *tanab'al,* "elevated, or stepped, place," which offer an extensive view of the horizon. Motherfathers remain there for some time, burning incense, praying to their deceased predecessors by name, and observing the night sky. In their prayers they mention the specific phase of the moon and its exact position in the night sky relative to certain bright stars, planets, asterisms, and constellations. They are interested in the seasonal variation in the moon's path through the stars and across the cleft, or dark rift, in the Milky Way.

There are several lineage leaders who are known for predicting rain by noting the precise position and phase of the moon on all seven days of this series. The great majority, however, only observe the night sky seriously on the opening day (9 Kej) and 82 days later (12 Q'anil), when they once again arrive at sunset to pray and burn incense before they close the shrine for a 48-day interval that stretches from 13 Toj to 9 No'j. They begin a second 82-day period with 9 No'j + 13 days = 9 Tz'i' + 13 = 9 Aq'ab'al + 13 = 9 Toj + 13 = 9 Iq' + 13 = 9 Tz'ikin + 3 = 12 Tijax, marking another 82-day cycle. Now the shrines remain closed for 49 days (from 12 Tijax to 9 Kej) until the first cycle, 9 Kej to 12 Q'anil, begins again. These 82-day ritual periods, like the 27-day single-sidereal lunar cycles, are referred to as *chakalik,* "staked, stabilized, or set." A point of astronomical interest is that wherever the moon (if visible) might have been located among the stars on a given 9 Kej or 9 No'j, it will be in nearly the same position at the same time of night 82 days later on 12 Q'anil or 12 Tijax, respectively. However, since a sidereal month (27 days 7 hours 43 minutes 11.5 seconds) is shorter than a synodic month (29 days 12 hours 44 minutes 2.8 seconds), the moon will not be in the same phase when it returns to the same position in the night sky.

Each of the fourteen territorial divisions of the community, known as a *kanton,* from Spanish, or *kalpul,* from Nahua *calpulli,* has its own religious leader.[8] These men are referred to as *chuchqajawib' rech kanton,* "motherfathers of the canton," or *chuchqajawib' rech kalpul,* "motherfathers of the calpul." Their responsibilities include greeting the Mam, or yearbearer, on each occurrence of his day name, at one of four hilltop shrines located a short distance from the town center. In a Kej year, for example, a group of calpul heads led by the one from Xequemeya will visit the hilltop shrine on Paturas once each 20 days on days named Kej. In an E year, this same group will be led on each day named E to the shrine at Chuwi Aqan by the calpul head of Los Cipreses. Their dawn and dusk visits involve not only ritual activities such as praying, burning copal incense, and setting off fireworks, but also the observation of the sun's position along the horizon. This is an important task, for as Aveni and Hartung (1986:58-59) have noted, observations of sunrise and sunset positions at 20-day intervals help in properly anticipating the zenith passages of the sun.

Above these leaders, at a still higher rank, are two *chuchqajawib' rech tinimit,* "motherfathers of the town," who, after they are selected by these calpul leaders, serve for life (B. Tedlock 1982b:35, 74-82). Once a year these 16 men make a pilgrimage together to a shrine located on a higher and more distant mountaintop in order to welcome in the new Mam. For example, when Mam E arrives in 1991 he will be greeted by this delegation on Tamancu, a mountain located in the south. In addition to this visit to the key mountaintop of the year, each town motherfather also visits all four mountaintop shrines on a cycle of days that coordinate the four 65-day periods of the 260-day almanac with four overlapping 82-day periods. This cycle of visits provides Momostecan calendar experts with an opportunity for observation and gives them a conceptual scheme for coordinating lunar time-reckoning with the 260-day cycle and the solar year in a more orderly fashion than would be possible through synodic lunar reckoning alone. Noting the motion of the moon against the backdrop of the stars at 82-day intervals offers the possibility of conceptually linking the course of the daytime sun with that of the nighttime stars. This, in turn, opens the cognitive pathway leading from observations of acronychal and cosmical risings and settings of the stars to the mapping of a sidereal solar path.

Dütting and Schramm (1988) have found evidence of an intricate network of multiples of synodic and triple-sidereal lunar cycles at Palenque, El Peru, and in the almanac on pages 23-24 of the Paris Codex. They point out that these cycles may indicate the knowledge of celestial coordinate astronomy, one in which bodies are tracked with respect to one another rather than with respect to the horizon. More recently the Brickers (1989) have been able to confirm the zodiacal character of an almanac in the

Paris Codex and to map the approximate positions of the 13 constellations to which it refers.

ASTRONOMICAL AND CALENDRICAL COMMENSURATION

Commensuration of astronomical observations with calendrical cycles is accomplished in Momostenango through the use of days with the same four names—Kej, E, No'j, and Iq'—to mark the beginnings of the 65-day quarters of the 260-day cycle, the 82-day lunar sidereal period, and the 365-day solar cycle, or vague year. But unlike the case of solar yearbearers—which occur in such sequences as 9 Kej, 10 E, 11 No'j, 12 Iq'—the prefixed number of the four days that mark the beginnings of 65-day and 82-day cycles stays constant: 9 Kej, 9 E, 9 No'j, 9 Iq'. These four days divide the 260-day cycle into segments that follow one another without gaps or overlaps. On these days a town motherfather visits Nima Sab'al, then walks to another hill closer to the town center, and finally walks out to one of the mountaintop shrines that lie some distance from town.

The 82-day periods, unlike the 65-day periods, overlap one another. Thus, after opening the shrines on Paturas and Kilaja on 9 Kej, the motherfather returns there 80 days later in order to begin a three-day closing ritual spanning 11 Kej, 12 Q'anil, and 13 Toj. The total distance from 9 Kej to 12 Q'anil is 82 days, but the next sidereal period overlaps with the first, so that on 9 E (15 days before the closing rituals begun on 11 Kej) he opens the second set of shrines on Chuwi Aqan and Tamancu, both of which are in the south. This 82-day period is completed with the closing of these same shrines on 11 E, 12 Aj, and 13 Ix. A third such period, begun 15 days before on 9 No'j (in the west at Nima Sab'al and Socop), is completed on 11 No'j, 12 Tijax, and 13 Kawuq. The fourth period, taking place in the north at Cakb'ach'uy and Pipil, having started 15 days before on 9 Iq', is completed on 11 Iq', 12 Aq'ab'al, and 13 K'at.

Simultaneously with a sidereal rhythm, these same visits contain a synodic rhythm. For any two successive mountaintop shrines, the phase of the moon observed at the opening of one will repeat itself 147 days later at the closing of the next one, and yet again when this latter shrine is opened 178 days after it was closed, a total of 325 days after the opening of the first shrine. The event on the 147th day falls half a day short of 5 synodic moons, the one on the 178th day falls less than a day beyond 6 synodic moons, and the event on the 325th day falls just a little less than four hours beyond 11 synodic moons. To state the pattern in another way, repetitions in phases of the moon move forward by one shrine each time around the full circle of shrines. Over a period of years the precise locations of the moon within its sidereal and synodic cycles during the shrine visits will shift, but the location during any given visit remains a good predictor of what will happen over the space of a year or more.

This pattern of overlapping synodic with sidereal lunar reckoning is commensurable with the 260-day cycle. Further, the selection of 4 days from the 260-day cycle that can also serve as yearbearers brings this combined synodic and sidereal lunar scheme into partial alignment with the solar calendar. Thus, in any given circuit of the four shrines, three and sometimes four of the days on which openings are performed, or closings are started, will fall on days bearing the name of the current yearbearer, which is itself marked by ceremonies throughout a given year. On 4 out of 52 years, spaced 13 years apart, the opening of a shrine will correspond to the first day of that year, or nab'e mam, "first grandfather." On another 4 years the beginning of the closing ceremony will correspond to the first day.

There is also evidence for the mixing of synodic and sidereal lunar reckoning in Precolumbian times. The period assigned by the Dresden Codex to the visibility of Venus as the morning star, 236 days, has been shortened so as to equal the duration of eight synodic moons (Aveni 1983). The actual visibility of Venus as morning star averages 263 days, or 27 days longer than eight synodic moons. Since 27 is the nearest whole-day approximation of a sidereal moon, there could have been a rule-of-thumb for following the progress of the morning-star Venus that went something like this: starting when it first appears, count eight moons (of the synodic kind) and then expect Venus to disappear when the ninth moon has made one complete circuit of the zodiac.

CONCLUSIONS

The discovery, in a contemporary Maya community, of the notation of acronychal and cosmical risings and settings of individual stars and asterisms, combined with the use of 82-day periods anchored to the 260-day and 365-day cycles, provides evidence that Precolumbian Maya society may have developed a common frame of reference for understanding the movements of the sun, moon, and stars. Although there is as yet no evidence of past or present angular calculations, it seems likely that the ancient Maya combined horizon with coordinate astronomy.

The multimetrical temporal rituals described here involve dialectical thought patterns that go far beyond the simple dialectics of polarization, as historically exemplified in Hegelian and Marxist thought, to include the dialectics of overlapping or mutual involvement. It appears that Maya peoples have, and had in their Precolumbian past, differing systems of timekeeping that they used in the separate provinces of their biological, astronomical, psychological, religious, and social realities, and that these various systems underwent a process of totalization within the overlapping, intermeshing cycles of their calendars. Given the complexity of this cosmology, which is ritually reenacted, shared, and thus maintained by contemporary Maya, their knowledge ought not be dismissed as the degenerate remains of Classic Maya glory. Rather, current cosmological theory and practice ought to be respected as a precious resource providing the conceptual tools for reconstructing the meaning of the material objects that happened to have survived from the Classic period.

NOTES

1. Maya ethnoastronomy can be found in the following sources: Lincoln (1942); Girard (1962, 1966); Villa Rojas (1978); Gossen (1972, 1974); Gelwan (1972); Remington (1975, 1977); Köhler (1977, 1982, 1989); Neuenswander (1981); Watanabe (1983); Sosa (1985, 1989); Vogt (1985); and B. Tedlock (1982b, 1983a, 1983b, 1985, 1986).

2. See for example Hochleitner (1970); Lounsbury (1978); Carlson (1981); Bricker and Bricker (1983); Aveni (1983). The only modern interest in ongoing commensuration is Walling's (1982) extension of Vogt's (1969:571-581) replication concept into calendrics.

3. Mayan words from Guatemalan languages are transcribed here using the new alphabet decided upon by Mayan linguists who are also native speakers of these languages (Academia de las lenguas mayas de Guatemala 1988). This alphabet was written into law (Decree no. 1046-87) and signed by President Cerezo on November 23, 1987. The Mayan sounds are approximately like those in Spanish, except that q is like the initial sound in the Hebrew word qoph, tz sounds like the English ts, x is like the English sh, and the apostrophe ' indicates the glottal stop, when it follows a vowel, and glottalization, when it follows a consonant.

4. See, for example, Gossen (1972:119; 1974:231); B. Tedlock (1983a:5); Sosa (1985:420).

5. For a discussion of Maya directions see Watanabe (1983) and B. Tedlock (1989).

6. The astronomical and calendrical information presented here is but a small portion of the extant Quichean knowledge. Although Maya political leadership in Momostenango underwent major changes as a result of the recent civil war in Guatemala (1979-1983), the knowledge and practice of rituals connected to the 260-day calendar were in no way diminished. Ethnographic descriptions of Momostenango can be found in Rodríguez (1971), Carmack (1979), and B. Tedlock (1982b). My own fieldwork, undertaken during 1975, 1976, and 1979, was funded by the State University of New York at Albany and Tufts University in Boston. More recent fieldwork, undertaken during 1988 and 1989 in various Highland Maya communities, was funded by research grants from the State University of New York at Buffalo. Some of the early analysis of the calendrical and astronomical materials was made possible by a Weatherhead Resident Fellowship at the School of American Research in Santa Fe, New Mexico. I am most grateful to all of the individuals and institutions, both in Guatemala and in the United States, who have made this research possible.

7. Although the Orion Nebula known as M42, like

the Andromeda Nebula M31, is clearly visible to the naked eye, M42 went unmentioned in ancient and medieval records (Harrison 1984:65-70). Its European discovery, in 1610, was credited to the naturalist archaeologist Nicholas Peiresc (Burnham 1978:1320).

8. The term kalpul, from the Nahua calpulli, is the name of the Prehispanic Mesoamerican residential land-holding unit still present today in some areas of highland Guatemala (Carrasco 1971; Carmack 1981:109-119; B. Tedlock 1982b:35, 181, 1986:125-126; Hill and Monaghan 1987:41-42).

BIBLIOGRAPHY

Academia de las lenguas mayas de Guatemala
1988   *Lenguas mayas de Guatemala: documento de referencia para la pronunciación de los nuevos alfabetos oficiales.* Guatemala: Instituto Indigenista Nacional.

Alcorn, J. B.
1984   *Huastec Mayan Ethnobotany.* Austin: University of Texas Press.

Aveni, A. F.
1983   The Moon and the Venus Table: An Example of Commensuration in the Maya Calendar. Paper delivered at the International Conference on Ethnoastronomy, National Air and Space Museum, Washington, DC.

Aveni, A., and H. Hartung
1986   *Maya City Planning and the Calendar.* Transactions of the American Philosophical Society, No. 76, Part 7.

Bricker, H. M., and V. R. Bricker
1983   Classic Maya Prediction of Solar Eclipses. *Current Anthropology* 24:1-24.
1989   Zodiacal References in the Maya Codices. Paper presented at Colgate University in the conference "Astronomy in the Maya Codices." To appear in *The Sky in Mayan Literature,* ed. A. Aveni. Oxford: Oxford University Press (in press).

Brotherston, G.
1982   *A Key to the Mesoamerican Reckoning of Time: The Chronology Recorded in Native Texts.* British Museum Occasional Paper No. 38. London: British Museum.

Burnham, R.
1978   *Burnham's Celestial Handbook,* vol. 2. New York: Dover.

Carlson, J. B.
1981   Numerology and the Astronomy of the Maya. In *Archaeoastronomy in the Americas,* ed. R. A. Williamson, pp. 205-213. Los Altos, CA: Ballena Press.

Carmack, R. M.
1979   *Historia social de los quiches.* Seminario de Integración Social Guatemalteca, Publicación No. 38. Guatemala: José de Pineda Ibarra.
1981   *The Quiché Mayas of Utatlán: The Evolution of a Highland Guatemala Kingdom.* Norman: University of Oklahoma Press.

Carrasco, P.
1971   Social Organization of Ancient Mexico. In *Handbook of Middle American Indians* 10:349-375. Austin: University of Texas Press.

Coe, M. D.
1975   Native Astronomy in Mesoamerica. In *Archaeoastronomy in Pre-Columbian America,* ed. Anthony F. Aveni, pp. 3-31. Austin: University of Texas Press.

Coggins, C. C.
1982   The Zenith, the Mountain, the Center, and the Sea. In *Ethnoastronomy and Archaeoastronomy in the American Tropics,* eds. A. Aveni and G. Urton, pp. 111-123. *Annals of the New York Academy of Sciences,* vol. 385.

Cordy, N.
1933   The Origin of the Tonalamatl. *The Masterkey* 7(3):80.

Crabtree, D. E.
1968   Mesoamerican Polyhedral Cores and Prismatic Blades. *American Antiquity* 33:446-478.

Dütting, D., and M. Schramm
1988   The Sidereal Period of the Moon in Maya Calendrical Astronomy. *Tribus* 37:139-173.

Fitchett, A. G.
1974   Origin of the 260-Day Cycle in Mesoamerica. *Science* 185:543.

Gelwan, E. M.
1972   *Some Considerations of Tzotzil-Tzeltal Ethnoastronomy.* Unpublished manuscript in the files of the Harvard Chiapas Project Summer Field Studies Program.

Girard, R.
1962   *Los mayas eternos*. México: Antigua Librería Robredo.
1966   *Los mayas*. México: Libro Mex.

Gossen, G. H.
1972   Temporal and Spatial Equivalents in Chamula Ritual Symbolism. In *Reader in Comparative Religion: An Anthropological Approach* (3d ed.), eds. W. Lessa and E. Z. Vogt, pp. 116-129. New York: Harper and Row. (4th ed. reprinted in 1979.)
1974   A Chamula Solar Calendar Board from Chiapas, Mexico. In *Mesoamerican Archaeology: New Approaches*, ed. N. Hammond, pp. 217-253. London: Duckworth.

Harrison, T. C.
1984   The Orion Nebula: Where in History Is It? *Quarterly Journal of the Royal Astronomical Society* 25:65-79.

Hill, R. M., and J. Monaghan
1987   *Continuities in Highland Maya Social Organization: Ethnohistory in Sacapulas, Guatemala*. Philadelphia: University of Pennsylvania Press.

Hochleitner, F. J.
1970   An Attempt at a Chronological-Astronomical Interpretation. *Boletín Informativo de Escritura Maya* 4:15-18.

Justeson, J. S.
1989   Ancient Mayan Ethnoastronomy. In *World Archaeoastronomy*, ed. A. F. Aveni, pp. 76-129. Cambridge: Cambridge University Press.

Köhler, U.
1977   Chonbilal Ch'ulelal: Grundformen Mesoamerikanischer Kosmologie und Religion in einem Gebetstext auf Maya-Tzotzil. *Acta Humboldtiana Series Geographica et Ethnographica*, Nr. 5. Wiesbaden.
1982   On the Significance of the Aztec Day Sign Olin. In *Space and Time in the Cosmovision of Mesoamerica, Lateinamerika Studien, Band 10*, ed. F. Tichy, pp. 111-127. München: Wilhelm Fink.
1989   Comets and Falling Stars in the Perception of Mesoamerican Indians. In *World Archaeoastronomy*, ed. A. F. Aveni, pp. 289-299. Cambridge: Cambridge University Press.

Koizumi, J.
1981   *Symbol and Context: A Study of Self and Action in a Guatemalan Culture*. Ph.D. dissertation, Stanford University. Ann Arbor: University Microfilms.

La Farge, O., and D. Byers
1931   *The Year Bearer's People*. Middle American Research Series, no. 3. New Orleans: Tulane University.

Lamb, W. W.
1981   Star Lore in the Yucatec Maya Dictionaries. In *Archaeoastronomy in the Americas*, ed. R. A. Williamson, pp. 233-248. Los Altos, CA: Ballena Press.

Larsen, H.
1936   The 260 Day Period as Related to the Agricultural Life of the Ancient Indian. *Ethnos* 1:9-12.

Laughlin, R. M.
1975   *The Great Tzotzil Dictionary of San Lorenzo Zinacantán*. Smithsonian Contributions to Anthropology, no. 19. Washington, DC: Smithsonian Institution Press.

Lincoln, S.
1942   The Maya Calendar of the Ixil of Guatemala. *Contributions to American Anthropology and History* 38:98-128.

Lounsbury, F. G.
1978   Maya Numeration, Computation, and Calendrical Astronomy. In *Dictionary of Scientific Biography*, vol. 15, suppl. 1, pp. 759-818. New York: Scribner's.

Malmstrom, V. H.
1973   Origin of the Mesoamerican 260-Day Calendar. *Science* 181:939-941.
1978   A Reconstruction of the Chronology of Mesoamerican Calendrical Systems. *Journal for the History of Astronomy* 9:105-116.

Neuenswander, H.
1981   *Glyphic Implications of Current Time Concepts of the Cubulco Achi (Maya)*. Manuscript.

Orellana, S. L.
1987   *Indian Medicine in Highland Guatemala: The Pre-Hispanic and Colonial Periods*. Albuquerque: University of New Mexico Press.

Oxford English Dictionary
1979   Oxford: Oxford University Press.

Remington, J. A.
1975 *Maya Cosmology: A Pilot Study*. Master's thesis, University of the Americas.
1977 Current Astronomical Practices among the Maya. In *Native American Astronomy*, ed. A. F. Aveni, pp. 75-88. Austin: University of Texas Press.

Robicsek, F., and D. M. Hales
1984 Maya Heart Sacrifice: Cultural Perspective and Surgical Technique. In *Ritual Human Sacrifice in Mesoamerica*, ed. E. H. Boone, pp. 49-90. Washington, DC: Dumbarton Oaks.

Rodríguez Rouanet, F.
1971 Monografía del Momostenango: Departamento de Totonicapán. *Guatemala Indígena* 5:11-99.

Sosa, J. R.
1985 *The Maya Sky, the Maya World: A Symbolic Analysis of Yucatec Maya Cosmology.* Ph.D. dissertation, State University of New York at Albany. Ann Arbor: University Microfilms.
1989 Cosmological, Symbolic and Cultural Complexity among the Contemporary Maya of Yucatan. In *World Archaeoastronomy*, ed. A. F. Aveni, pp.130-142. Cambridge: Cambridge University Press.

Tedlock, B.
1982a Sound Texture and Metaphor in Quiché Maya Ritual Language. *Current Anthropology* 23(3):269-272.
1982b *Time and the Highland Maya.* Albuquerque: University of New Mexico Press.
1983a Earth Rites and Moon Cycles: Mayan Synodic and Sidereal Lunar Reckoning. Paper delivered at the International Conference on Ethnoastronomy, National Air and Space Museum, Washington, DC.
1983b Quichean Time Philosophy. In *Calendars in Mesoamerica and Peru: Native American Computation of Time*, ed. A. F. Aveni and G. Brotherston, pp. 59-72. BAR International Series 174. Oxford.
1985 Hawks, Meteorology and Astronomy in Quiché-Maya Agriculture. *Archaeoastronomy* 8:80-88.
1986 On a Mountain in the Dark: Encounters with the Quiche Maya Culture Hero. In *Symbol and Meaning Beyond the Closed Community: Essays in Mesoamerican Ideas*, ed. G. H. Gossen, pp. 125-138. Albany: Institute for Mesoamerican Studies.

1989 The Road of Light: Theory and Practice of Maya Skywatching. Paper presented at Colgate University in the conference "Astronomy in the Maya Codices." To appear in *The Sky in Mayan Literature*, ed. A. Aveni. Oxford: Oxford University Press (in press).

Tedlock, D.
1985 *Popol Vub*. New York: Simon and Schuster.

Thompson, J. E. S.
1950 *Maya Hieroglyphic Writing: An Introduction.* Norman: University of Oklahoma Press.

Tichy, F.
1983 *Observaciones del sol y calendario agrícola en Mesoamérica.* In *Calendars in Mesoamerica and Peru: Native American Computation of Time*, ed. A. F. Aveni and G. Brotherston, pp. 135-143. BAR International Series 174. Oxford.

Tirado, F. J.
1787 *Vocabulario de lengua Kiche*. Photocopy of manuscript located in the Tozzer Library, Harvard University, Cambridge, MA.

Tozzer, A. M.
1907 *A Comparative Study of the Mayas and the Lacandones.* New York: Macmillan.

Villa Rojas, A.
1978 Los elegidos de Dios: Etnografía de los Mayas de Quintana Roo. *Colección de Antropología Social, No. 56.* México: Editorial Libros de México.

Vogt, E. Z.
1969 *Zinacantan: A Maya Community in the Highlands of Chiapas.* Cambridge, MA: Harvard University Press.
1976 *Tortillas for the Gods: A Symbolic Analysis of Zinacanteco Rituals.* Cambridge, MA: Harvard University Press.
1985 Cardinal Directions and Ceremonial Circuits in Mayan and Southwestern Cosmology. *National Geographic Society Research Reports* 21:487-496.

Walling, S. L.
1982 *Replication in Maya Culture.* Unpublished Master's thesis, Tulane University.

Watanabe, J. M.
1983 In the World of the Sun: A Cognitive Model of Mayan Cosmology. *Man* 18:710-728.

XIX

The Popol Vuh as a Hieroglyphic Book

Dennis Tedlock

Program in Folklore, Mythology and Film, Department of English
SUNY Buffalo

During the 1550s, shortly after the Spanish conquest, the Highland Maya of Guatemala used the roman alphabet to write numerous works in their own languages. The most famous of these works, written in Quiche Maya, is the Popol Vuh ("Council Book" or "Council Paper"). Like the classic Maya scribe of Naranjo whose signature has recently been identified (Stuart 1987:5), the authors of the alphabetic Popol Vuh were members of royal lineages (D. Tedlock 1985:60-61). Their book was preceded, they tell us, by a *nab'e wujil, ojer tz'ib'am puch,* an "original book and ancient writing" (folio 1r).[1] This ancient book served as an *ilb'al,* or "instrument for seeing" (folios 1r, 54r), and its reader was an ilol, or "seer," and a *b'isol,* which is difficult to translate. The Quichean stem *b'iso-* has to do with deliberation, care, and even worry in the available Quiche and Cakchiquel dictionaries, but in Kekchi it has retained a clear reference to the making of measurements (Haeserijn 1979). This last meaning fits the context of *b'isol* in the Popol Vuh, where the very next sentence describes a process of measurement (folio 1r):

Nim upeyoxik, utzijoxik puch
ta chik'is tzuk ronojel kajulew
ukaj tzuk'uxik, ukaj xukutaxik
retaxik, ukaj che'xik
umej k'amaxik, uyuq k'amaxik
upa kaj, upa ulew.

It takes a long performance and account
to complete the lighting of all the sky-earth
the fourfold siding, fourfold cornering
marking, fourfold staking
halving the cord, stretching the cord
in the sky, on the earth.

The verb stem for "lighting" here is *tzuk-,* normally referring to the placement of a light source, such as a torch, in a high place.[2] The fourfold cornering with stakes and cords refers, at the literal level, to the measuring out of a *milpa,* but the reference to the sky and earth removes the meaning to the metaphorical level, where the very cosmos is being measured out by the movements of lights. The interpretation offered by Andrés Xiloj, a contemporary Quiche *ajq'ij,* or "daykeeper," is that the four corners are the solstitial rising and setting points of the sun, with the full measures (stretched cords) running east-west and the shorter ones (halved cords) running north-south (D. Tedlock 1985:244). But there are other fourfold correspondences between time and space in Quiche tradition, notably 65-day quarters of the 260-day calendar that correspond to four hilltop shrines, and a cycle of four 365-day years that correspond to four mountaintop shrines (B. Tedlock 1982:71, 99-101).

Like the Popol Vuh, the Book of Chilam Balam of Chumayel describes the setting up of the sky and earth as an act of measurement, in this case carried out in space by footsteps and in time through 20 consecutive days from the 260-day calendar (Roys 1967:116-118). The eve of creation and its first day are respectively *13 Ok* and *1 Chuen,*[3] corresponding to *13 Tz'i'* and *1 B'atz'* on the Quiche calendar. It happens that in the interpretive system of contemporary Quiche daykeepers, the first of these two days brings uncertainty to a climax, while the second brings the very beginning of organizing processes that are likened to the spinning of a thread or cord (B. Tedlock 1982:116-117). The Chumayel book contains a passing reference to a celestial cord (Roys 1967:155), and the ethnographic record for Yucatan includes a reference to a cord, suspended in the sky, that once linked Tulum and Coba with Chichen Itza and Uxmal (Tozzer 1907:153).

It is in the act of measurement, at the cosmic level, that the Popol Vuh has its broadest and most obvious connection to the surviving hieroglyphic books. All those books are filled with temporal measurements, many of them based on the movements of celestial lights, and it could be (since they all have missing pages) that some of them once included detailed descriptions of territorial boundaries as well. Whether such boundaries were described in the same books or in different documents altogether, they receive detailed consideration in the alphabetic script for the Quiche dance drama known as *Rab'inal Achi* or *Xajoj Tun,* "Man of Rabinal" or "Dance of the Trumpet" (Brasseur de Bourbourg 1862). The principal character is Man of Quiche, a warrior who declares, *In kojol retal ulew,* "I am the measurer of the limits of the earth" (Brasseur de Bourbourg 1862:58, translation mine).[4] He describes himself as moving from point to point, naming each point in turn. For example, he says, *Mi xineta k'amara wi tzam K'amb'a,* "I have marked Water Jar point with a cord" (Brasseur de Bourbourg 1862:54), Water Jar being a place near Rabinal, and he eventually mentions such distant points as *Pan Ajachel,* or "At the Matasano Tree" (Brasseur de Bourbourg 1862:58), on the shore of Lake Atitlan. By the time he is done, he has encompassed the entire territory claimed by the Quiche kings.

There were two different ways of reading the ancient version of the Popol Vuh, one divinatory and the other narrative. The authors of the alphabetic version mention the divinatory mode in a passage that extols the powers of Quiche kings (folio 54r):

Keta'm uwe lab'al chib'anik. Q'alaj chikiwach ronojel chikilo. Uwe kamik, uwe wa'ij, uwe ch'oj chib'anik, xax keta'm wi, k'o k'ut ilb'al re, k'o wuj. Popol Wuj ub'i' kumal.

They know whether war will be waged. They see everything clearly before them. Whether death, whether hunger, whether quarrels will be caused, they simply know it, since there is an instrument for seeing it, there is a book. Council Book is their name for it.

Francisco Ximénez, who made the only surviving manuscript copy of these words, saw books such as the one they describe as late as the early eighteenth century in Guatemala. He writes of diviners who "see things in a book they have a source of predic-

tions from the time of their heathenism, where they have all the months and signs corresponding to each day, of which I have one in my possession, and each sign or signal of that day is one of the demons who figure in their stories" (Ximénez 1967:11, translation mine).

What the books of signs seen by Ximénez were like may be guessed from the alphabetic Quiche manuscript known as the *Ajilab'al Q'ij,* or "Count of Days," produced in 1722 (Carmack 1973:165-166). The days of the 260-day calendar are listed vertically in groups of five, with 52-day intervals separating the dates within any one group; to the right of each group of five days, in a separate column, is written an augury that applies to the entire group. The grouping by fives, the 52-day intervals, and even the page layout parallel a series of divinatory almanacs at the beginning of the Dresden Codex (pages 2-22),[5] with the written prognostications of the Quiche document appearing where the pictures are in the codex (La Farge 1947:180-81). Indeed, the *Ajilab'al Q'ij* is unrivaled among Mayan alphabetic documents, whether highland or lowland, in the directness of its resemblance to a codex. This is ironic, to say the least, given that it has long been customary to assign all the surviving codices (except for Grolier) to the lowlands.

According to the Annals of the Cakchiquels, the Quiche, Cakchiquel, and other highland nations were not mere importers of calendrical documents, but were rather producers of them. In their early days, the royal lineages of the highlands paid tribute at an eastern city whose emblem of lordship was a bat, which makes it sound like Copan (D. Tedlock 1989). Among the items of tribute were these (Brinton 1885: par. 6, translation mine):[6]

Xa k'a ruyon xit, pwaq,
q'uq' uraxon, k'ub'ul chaktit,
ruk'in k'a tz'ib'anik, k'otonik;
kiyanik xul, b'ix,
chol q'ij, may q'ij,
pek, kakow.

And it was nothing but jade, metal,
green quetzal feathers, reliquaries of red feathers,
along with writings, carvings;
they were giving flutes, songs,
days in a row, days by the score,
pataxte, cacao.

The words "days in a row, days by the score" refer to divinatory almanacs.

As for the book that served as a source for the authors of the alphabetic Popol Vuh, they offer us a narrative rather than a divinatory reading. No sooner do they announce the possibility of "a long performance and account" that completes "the lighting of all the sky-earth" than they launch into a long myth, occupying over half their book, that accounts for the origin of the sun, moon, and stars. This is a clear enough indication that the original Popol Vuh, like the surviving codices, had sections devoted to astronomical matters, but the alphabetic version contains no tables of mathematical or calendrical data. Even so, the text offers enough references and allusions to dates and to astronomical and seasonal phenomena to permit a partial reconstruction of its hieroglyphic predecessor. The 260-day calendar figures in the story very early, and astronomy enters later, which fits the order of presentation in the Dresden Codex.

The protagonists of the myth of the sun, moon, and stars are an elderly couple, Xpiyacoc and Xmucane, together with their sons, daughters-in-law, and grandsons. Xpiyacoc and Xmucane are the first *ajq'ij,* or "daykeepers," diviners who read the auguries of the 260-day calendar (D. Tedlock 1985:81-83, 258-259, 335). Their two sons, who bear the names of two dates from this calendar, are Jun *Junajpu* and *Wuqub' Junajpu,* or "One Hunahpu" and "Seven Hunahpu." The firstborn twin sons of One Hunahpu, *Jun B'atz'* and *Jun Chuen,* or "One Monkey" and "One Artisan," respectively bear the Quiche and Yucatec names for a single date. Later in the story, at a moment when One and Seven Hunahpu are "of one mind," they beget a second set of twins named Hunahpu (without any number) and *Xb'alanq'e,* or "Little Hidden (or Jaguar) Sun," whose name refers to the sun at night.[7] The mother of these twins is a woman we might call "Blood Moon." Her Quiche name is *Xkik',* which means "little (or precious) blood" but carries a pun on *ik',* "moon" (D. Tedlock 1985:328).

Andrés Xiloj, a contemporary Quiche daykeeper who read through the text of the Popol Vuh with me, offered an unexpected reading of the names One and Seven Hunahpu. He pointed out that combining the numbers one and seven with any given day name is a conventional way of indicating all 13 days bearing that name. The 260-day cycle is made up of all possible combinations of two smaller cycles, one consisting of a repeating sequence of 13 numbers and the other of a sequence of 20 names. If one traces a single day name through all 13 of its occurrences in a given 260-day cycle, the prefixed numbers fall out in the sequence 1, 8, 2, 9, 3, 10, 4, 11, 5, 12, 6, 13, and 7. In the present context, this means that if the names One Hunahpu and Seven Hunahpu refer to an astronomical event, it will be an event that falls on a day whose number may vary but whose name will always be Hunahpu.

The names of the characters who are responsible for the death of One Hunahpu and Seven Hunahpu also point to an event with a variable day number and constant day name: they are *Jun Kame* and *Wuqub' Kame,* or "One Death" and "Seven Death." The four names together point straight to the Venus table in the Dresden Codex (pp. 46-50), which opens with Venus in the role of the particular kind of morning star that first appears on a day named *Ahaw* (equivalent to Quiche *Junajpu*) but with a variable number. When Venus leaves this role, it makes its next appearance as the evening star, and the day assigned to that event carries the name *Kimi* (equivalent to *Kame*) but with a variable number.

If One Monkey and One Artisan were responsible for an astronomical phenomenon, it would have to be one whose date is constant, not only in name (as in the case of One and Seven Hunahpu) but in number as well, with a periodicity of 260 days or a multiple thereof. Mars is the only celestial light that fits this description, with an average synodic period of 780 (3 x 260) days. Other Martian characteristics of One Monkey and One Artisan include the fact that when they play ball with One and Seven Hunahpu, they stay behind while their father and uncle descend into the underworld (D. Tedlock 1985:110). In the same way, Mars would stay behind if it were near Venus when the latter ceased appearing as the morning star. In a later episode, when One Monkey and One Artisan have been transformed into monkeys and begin to move off through the treetops, their younger brothers try to call them back (D. Tedlock 1985:121-124). They come closer each time they are called, but their grandmother laughs when she sees them, and they finally swing up and away again, this time without turning back. In the same way, Mars would go into a period of retrograde motion (relative to the fixed stars) when it got up high, moving back toward the east for a time, but then resuming its westward motion.

Near the end of their story, One Monkey and One Artisan go up a very high tree, never to return to a life on the surface of the earth (D. Tedlock 1985:121), but if their fate is an astronomical one, as it is for many other characters in the larger myth of which their story is a part, this is not made explicit. That they did have such a fate is indicated by a myth recorded among the contemporary Mopan Maya, who borrowed it from speakers of Kekchi (a Quichean language). In this myth, the brother of the gods of the sun and Venus, having been transformed into a monkey, becomes an unspecified planet (Thompson 1970:355) that could be Mars. It is also suggestive that in the Monkey Dance of the contemporary Quiche, as performed in Momostenango, two performers with monkey masks and stars on their costumes cross the plaza from east to west on a high tightrope, doing mid-air acrobatics that could be (or might once have been) a dramatization of retrograde motion.

In the Mars table of the Dresden Codex (pp. 43b-45b), the periodicity of that planet is reckoned at 780 days, and one of the main purposes of the table was to predict retrograde motion (Bricker and Bricker 1986:52, 57). During the long period of the table's usefulness, heliacal rises of Mars fell within a range of 63 days running from *13 Chikchan (Kan in Quiche)* through *10 Manik' (Kej)*, with the date of each rise calculated according to its distance from a single *3 Lamat (Q'anil)* base date that falls 3 days after *13 Chikchan*. A Mars table could have been constructed just as easily around a date near the opposite end of this range, as the Brickers have pointed out (Bricker and Bricker 1986:73-74), and it happens that *1 Chuen (1 B'atz')* falls 4 days after *10 Manik'*. This opens the possibility that the hieroglyphic Popol Vuh contained a Mars table similar in structure to the one in the Dresden Codex, but with a *1 B'atz'* base date. If so, we may imagine that the animals dangling from the sky bands of that table were not the cloven-hoofed "Mars beasts" of the Dresden Codex, but rather monkeys.

The case for a Venus table in the hieroglyphic Popol Vuh is much stronger than the one for Mars, and the calendrical evidence goes beyond the existence of characters named One and Seven Hunahpu and One and Seven Death. The historical section of the alphabetic version, which is generally ignored by those who deal with hieroglyphic texts, has numerous references to the first rising of the *nima ch'umil*,

or "great star," called *iqo q'ij*, or "day bringer," which is Venus in its role as morning star (D. Tedlock 1985:170-181, 335). Moreover, in a passage immediately following the description of the divinatory use of the Popol Vuh (quoted earlier), the Quiche kings are said to have gone on penitential religious retreats lasting 340 days (D. Tedlock 1985:219, 319-320). This exactly matches the sum of two successive intervals in the Dresden table (90 + 250 days), embracing both the longer of Venus's two disappearance intervals and its subsequent appearances as the evening star (see Table 1). Shortly after leaving their retreat, the kings could have expected to see Venus appear once again as the morning star, and we can guess that their retreat was intended to help make that happen.

	Above after 236 days	West after 90 days	Below after 250 days	East after 8 days
Page 46	Ajmak	Kame	Ajmak	K'at
Page 47	Junajpu	Tz'i'	Junajpu	Q'anil
Page 48	K'at	Ix	K'at	E
Page 49	Q'anil	Tijax	Q'anil	Ajmak
Page 50	E	Iq'	E	Junajpu

Table 1. Quiche names of days that open stages in the Dresden Venus table (Begin at lower right, then read across each row starting at upper left.)

One of the best calendrical links between the alphabetic Popol Vuh and the Dresden Venus table is provided by an episode that takes place soon after One and Seven Hunahpu have been sacrificed by One and Seven Death (D. Tedlock 1985:114-119). The skull of One Hunahpu, acting on behalf of both brothers, spits in the hand of Blood Moon and makes her pregnant with twins. She goes to Xmucane, claiming to be her daughter-in-law, and Xmucane tests her claim by sending her to gather a whole netful of corn in a field where only a single stalk grows. When she returns with the corn, Xmucane goes to the field and sees the imprint of the net at the foot of the cornstalk. She reads this as a sign that Blood Moon is just what she claims she is: the bearer of the successors of One and Seven

Hunahpu. To understand Xmucane's reading, we must first remember that she is a daykeeper. Second, the Quiche term for the net whose imprint she sees is *k'at*, which is the same as the Quiche day name *K'at*.[8] And third, when Venus begins its term as the morning star on a day named *Junajpu* (at lower right in Table 1), its next term in that same role begins on *K'at* (at upper right). In other words, Xmucane sees the imprint of the net as a sign that Venus will one day rise again as the morning star, which is to say that One and Seven Hunahpu, who are named for its previous rise, will have successors in the unborn children of Blood Moon.

The Dresden table divides the synodic periods of Venus into five different types, stretching across five pages corresponding to the five lines of the table given here. Each period lasts a total of 584 days, divided into four stages whose opening dates are listed in four columns on a given page. In any given column, the day name is constant but the number is variable (only the names are given here). The second column on each page assigns Venus to the western sky, meaning that it is located there in the evening, while the fourth column assigns it to the eastern sky, meaning that it is located there in the morning. The other two columns account for the intervals during which Venus is invisible to an earthbound observer at any time of day, but as I interpret them they follow the pattern of the other two columns in giving the direction of Venus at a particular time. The first column assigns it to the above, meaning that it reaches its meridian during the middle part of the day, while the third column assigns it to the below, meaning that it is opposite its meridian during the middle part of the night.[9] If my interpretation is correct, it means that Maya astronomers knew that the positions of Venus were not limited to the east, west, and underworld but could also be high in the sky. Even naked-eye observation would permit this knowledge, as it is possible to see Venus during the middle of the day when the sun is sufficiently darkened by an eclipse. Just such a situation is illustrated in the Dresden eclipse table, where (on p. 58) a Venus god is shown suspended from a sky band that is marked for a solar eclipse.[10]

It is typical of Maya narrative practice (see Tedlock and Tedlock 1985:130-135) that the sequence of Venus events, as set forth in the Dresden Codex, should begin with the story already well under way. In the first column of the first page, on a day named *Ajmak* (at upper left in Table 1), Venus is already in its final days as the morning star. By now it has been present each morning for 236 days, which is to say for eight synodic moons, having first appeared in the east on a day named *Junajpu*, in the last column of the last page (at lower right). It will now remain visible for an average of 27 more days, which is to say one sidereal moon. Once it disappears it will stay out of sight for an average of 50 days, reappearing as the evening star 13 days before the date that appears in the second column on this same page.[11] So Venus spends more than half of the 90-day period that begins in the first column, roughly equivalent to three synodic moons, out of sight, but it is visible at both ends, first in the east and then in the west.

Just as the Dresden table breaks into the story of Venus while it is already in progress, so the alphabetic Popol Vuh breaks into the story of One and Seven Hunahpu. The table begins with Venus visible but soon to disappear, whereas the Popol Vuh begins with One and Seven Hunahpu in the midst of a ball game they will soon quit (D. Tedlock 1985:105-110). And just as the table begins with Venus still in the east at morning but already in the stage when it reaches an overhead position in the middle of the day, so One and Seven Hunahpu play their game in a court at the eastern edge of the world (D. Tedlock 1985:338) but then break it off and hide their ball in the attic of Xmucane's house. Many episodes (and many Venus periods) later, Hunahpu and Little Hidden Sun will get their first look at this ball, not by looking up at it but by seeing its reflection in a bowl of liquid (D. Tedlock 1985:129). Contemporary Quiches use this same technique to avoid looking directly at eclipses (Nash 1967:92-93), so it could well be that at the astronomical level the twins are setting a precedent for spotting Venus during a solar eclipse. Appropriately enough, Blood Moon is in the house with Hunahpu and Little Hidden Sun when they look at the reflection. Not only that, but the whole episode, as the narrators point out, takes place during the middle of the day.

Just as there are five kinds of Venus period in the Dresden table, so there are fivefold recurrences of events in the Popol Vuh. Most obvious among these are the episodes in which the Lords of the Underworld shut either One and Seven Hunahpu or Hunahpu and Little Hidden Sun inside houses of horror to spend the night (D. Tedlock 1985:112, 137-

143, 286). The houses are five in number, and given that both sets of heroes enter the first of them soon after breaking off an eastern ball game and placing an object corresponding to Venus in the attic of Xmucane's house, it seems likely that they correspond to the five different 50-day intervals (at the heart of larger 90-day intervals) when Venus has completed its last 27 days in the east and has yet to reach its first 13 days in the west. In effect, Venus (or its eastern aspect) remains safe in the sky while the gods responsible for it risk their lives in the underworld.

After a stay in one of the underworld houses, the heroes always face an athletic contest with their hosts in which their lives are at stake. The first four contests are ball games (D. Tedlock 1985:112-113, 137-140, 142, 146-147) and the fifth requires leaps across the mouth of a fire pit (D. Tedlock 1985:148-149). I take it that these five games belong to the end of the 90-day stage, when Venus has begun appearing in the west but has not yet reached the stage (in the second column of the table) when it is securely assigned to the role of evening star. The court used for the ball games belongs to the Lords of the Underworld, and its logical location would be on the western edge of the earth, opposite the eastern ball court belonging to One and Seven Hunahpu and their sons. In either location Venus would be close to the horizon and elusive, like a ball seen rising above the side walls of a court by an outside observer.

Severed heads come into play on five different occasions in underworld games, three of them real and two artificial. One Hunahpu's head is cut off by One and Seven Death and placed in a tree near their ball court, and Hunahpu's head rolls twice, once on the ball court and once when Little Hidden Sun cuts it off as part of a magic show (D. Tedlock 1985:113, 143-144, 153). The artificial heads enter the action when One and Seven Death trick Hunahpu and Little Hidden Sun into playing with a booby-trapped ball that has a coating of crushed bone and thus resembles a skull, and when Little Hidden Sun tricks One and Seven Death into playing a game with what they believe to be Hunahpu's head when in fact it is merely a carved squash (D. Tedlock 1985:112, 138-139, 145-147).

On five different occasions Hunahpu and Little Hidden Sun hunt birds with a blowgun. In a group of three episodes, they shoot *Wuqub' Kaqix,* or

"Seven Macaw," out of his tree, then encounter his son Zipacna while they are out hunting birds, and finally shoot birds in order to feed his other son, *Kab'raqan,* or "Earthquake" (D. Tedlock 1985:91-92, 98, 100-101). In a separate group of two episodes, they shoot birds to feed their elder brothers, One Monkey and One Artisan, and shoot a falcon that comes to their ball court with a message (D. Tedlock 1985:120-121, 132). They defeat Zipacna, Earthquake, and their brothers by trickery rather than by shooting them, but in each of these episodes their bird-hunting serves as a cover—and, for the reader, a metaphor—for their malevolent intentions. The five hunting episodes together call to mind the middle and lower rows of five illustrations each that run across the pages of the Dresden Venus table. The gods of Venus wield dart-throwers in the middle row, while the lower row shows darts piercing five different victims. Some of these darts may be metaphorical rather than literal, since darts serve as a general metaphor for conquest or subordination in Mixtec codices. But judging from the alphabetic Popol Vuh, its hieroglyphic predecessor would not have depicted weapons of this kind, whether literal or not. Instead, it would have shown the Venus gods armed with blowguns, the same weapons that are wielded by the classic Maya counterparts of Hunahpu and Little Hidden Sun (Coe 1978:13).

Seven Macaw is merely wounded when Hunahpu and Little Hidden Sun shoot him, necessitating a later episode in which they come before his house with a plan to finish him off (D. Tedlock 1985:92-93). Astronomically, he corresponds to the seven stars of the Big Dipper (D. Tedlock 1985:360), and in order to get near him the twins must join an elderly couple named *Saqi Nim Aq* and *Saqi Nim Tzis,* "Great White Peccary" and "Great White Coati," who could be the Quiche equivalent of the pair of peccaries that occupy one of the zodiacal houses of the Bonampak murals. On completely independent grounds, the Brickers (in press) have located this particular house in the eastern portion of Leo, which happens to be nearer to the bowl of the Big Dipper (used by Western stargazers to locate Leo) than any other part of the zodiac. In the alphabetic Popol Vuh, the narrative moment that brings the twins near Seven Macaw would correspond to an astronomical moment in the hieroglyphic version that brought Venus into the house of the Great White Peccary and Coati.

If the episode of the peccary and coati belonged to a set of parallel episodes marked by the return of Venus to the same moment in its synodic period, then the next episode would take place farther along on the zodiac, given that the Venus period exceeds one full year by 219 days. Each of the 13 zodiacal houses on pages 23-24 of the Paris Codex is assigned 24 days, and a distance of nine houses (totaling 216 days) comes close to filling the bill exactly. At that distance beyond the house marked by a peccary is the one containing the Pleiades (Bricker and Bricker in press), and it so happens that the very next house to be mentioned in the Popol Vuh belongs to the Omuch' K'ajolab', the "Fistful of Boys," who are destined to take the role of the Pleiades (D. Tedlock 1985:96-99, 336). Zipacna buries these boys beneath the ruins of their own house, an event that probably corresponds to one of the two heliacal settings of the Pleiades, but after Hunahpu and Little Jaguar Sun avenge them they make their first appearance as the actual Pleiades, which would correspond to a heliacal rise. Other Popol Vuh episodes probably have zodiacal aspects, but this case, combined with that of the peccary and coati, is the clearest.

More could be said on the subject of Venus, but the evidence already presented makes a strong case that the hieroglyphic Popol Vuh contained a Venus table with a general resemblance, in both its calendrical dimensions and its narrative structure, to the one in the Dresden Codex. Clues to the subject of a hypothetical table other than the ones dealing with Mars and Venus are given by the part of the alphabetic version that deals with Moon Blood, the mother of Hunahpu and Little Hidden Sun. Among all the characters in the story of the sun, moon, and stars she is the only one whose story involves an explicitly lunar time interval. After the skull of One Hunahpu spits in her hand and makes her pregnant, her father discovers her condition when six moons have passed (D. Tedlock 1985:115). Six synodic moons is the length of the more common of the two types of groups into which lunar periods are arranged in the Dresden eclipse table (pp. 51-58; see Lounsbury 1978:789-795). Not only that, but when Blood Moon is sent to gather maize by Xmucane, she begins her prayer before the single cornstalk with the following invocation (folio 17r):

X Toj, x Q'anil,
x Kakaw, ix pu Tziya

Precious Toj, precious Q'anil,
precious Cacao, and precious Cornmeal

She thus names two successive days on the 260-day calendar, *Q'anil* and *Toj,* but she reverses their order.[12] This is not merely the result of a momentary lapse on the part of some scribe, since the order of cacao and cornmeal in the second line fits the order of day names in the first line. *Toj* is a day of payment on the Quiche calendar, and cacao pods once served as currency; *Q'anil* is a day for the harvest of maize, and from that harvest comes cornmeal (B. Tedlock 1982:114-115). The explanation for the reversal would seem to lie in Blood Moon's lunar character, since by Lounsbury's reckoning (1978:796) the Dresden eclipse table begins on the day *13 Muluk (Toj* in Quiche) and then, at the end of an interval of 11,959 days, arrives at *12 Lamat (Q'anil* in Quiche). In effect, then, Blood Moon might be invoking, by means of metonymy, the calendrical patrons of all possible moons or groups of moons, from the beginning to the end of an eclipse table.[13] Among the intervening dates specified in the Dresden table are *Muluk* and *Lamat* days with numbers other than 13 and 12, which helps explain why she invokes Toj and *Q'anil* in general rather than by specific numbers.

The sun, or at least the sun of the present age, does not appear until the end of the story, but its coming is presaged in two different incidents. The first of these is the appearance of an opossum who is referred to as *mama,* "grandfather" or "old man" (D. Tedlock 1985:145, 288). This is the term used by the contemporary Quiche for the bearers of new solar years, who are shown as opossums in the new year's almanac of the Dresden Codex (pp. 25-28). The opossum of the Popol Vuh makes four streaks in the dawn sky, signifying that there will be four types of year beginning on four different days. The Quiche names for these days are *Kej, E, No'j,* and *Iq',* and they are equivalent to the days that begin the years of the Dresden almanac, which are *Manik', Eb, Kaban,* and *Ik'.* In a later episode Hunahpu and Little Hidden Sun disguise themselves as itinerant actors (D. Tedlock 1985:149-153), which is a role taken by the year-bearing gods of the classic Maya (Thompson 1970:277). Both this episode and that of the opossum happen late in the story, and the only dates in the Dresden Venus table with a year-bearing potential are also late. The first such date comes in the last column of the third page, and the other three are clustered on the last page.

One last bit of calendrical evidence bearing on the hieroglyphic Popol Vuh occurs at the very end of the story of the sun, moon, and stars. Hunahpu and Little Hidden Sun, having avenged the death of One and Seven Hunahpu at the hands of One and Seven Death, go to the place where they lie buried (D. Tedlock 1985:159). The remains of Seven Hunahpu (unlike those of One Hunahpu) include his head, and the twins are able to speak with him. They promise that his day will be the first one ever to be kept holy by human beings. From this we may guess that in the historical section of the Popol Vuh, when the Quiche ancestors burn incense on the occasion of the first rising of Venus as the morning star (D. Tedlock 1985:181), they do so on a day named Junajpu. At a more general level, the twins are instituting a custom still followed among the Quiche, who use Junajpu days in general to honor the dead. They choose days of this name to visit cemeteries, where they pray that the souls of the departed may become sparks of light and one day rise out of the underworld and into the sky (B. Tedlock 1982:124).

The twins may succeed in honoring Seven Hunahpu, but they are unable to bring him completely back to life (folio 32r):

Xawi xere uwach xraj uxik, xtzonox k'ut chire
ub'i' ronojel, uchi, utzam, ub'aq uwach xuriq
nab'e ub'i',
xa k'u skakin chik xch'ataj wi.

He had wanted his face to become just as it was, but when he was asked to name everything, and once he had found the names of his mouth, his nose, the eyes of his face, there was very little else he could say.

At one level these words refer to Seven Hunahpu's state of decay, but at another they can be read as a straightforward description of the face that forms [insert artwork] the glyph for the Yucatec day *Ahaw* (at left), equivalent to Quiche *Junajpu*. In the present context, the bar-and-dot version of the number seven, though it lacks a nose, becomes a simple face as well. Whatever the case with the number, the writers of the alphabetic Popol Vuh may be giving us an origin story for the glyph we have come to know by the name *Ahaw*. If so, then their words can also

Figure 19.1. Glyph for Ahaw *(left).*

be read as a comment on the relationship between the spoken word and hieroglyphic characters. In effect, they are saying that even the dead can speak, at least to the extent that words can find form in hieroglyphic characters. But visible though the words of the dead may remain after they themselves have decayed, it is not in the nature of such words to reconstitute full images of living faces.[14] Hieroglyphic characters are, so to speak, skeletal.

Having paid their respects to their uncle, the twins abandon their responsibility for Venus and move on to greater things. Hunahpu takes a solar role during the day, but Little Hidden Sun takes over at night, when the sun passes through the underworld (D. Tedlock in press). The pattern for this division of roles was set during their previous adventures: whenever one of them took the lead, it was Hunahpu who did so on the surface of the earth, whereas it was Little Hidden Sun who always knew what to do in the underworld (D. Tedlock 1985:91, 143-145, 153). The full moon, which contemporary Quiches compare with the sun in both its appearance and its movement, probably belongs to Little Hidden Sun,[15] with the other phases belonging to Blood Moon. That could explain why the authors of the Popol Vuh, when they describe the specific occasion of the first dawn, assign the sun to Hunahpu and the moon to Little Hidden Sun (D. Tedlock 1985:160). When the twins rehearsed for this performance by letting themselves be burned, they faced each other (D. Tedlock 1985:149), which is to say that they were in the same relationship as the sun to the full moon.

All in all, it seems quite likely that the hicroglyphic Popol Vuh, like the Dresden Codex, contained a Venus table, an eclipse table, and a new year's almanac. It may also have contained sections corresponding to the Dresden Mars table and the zodiacal almanac on pages 23-24 of the Paris Codex. If it had pages devoted entirely to the 260-day calendar, like the 1722 "Count of Days" and pages 2-22 of the Dresden Codex, they might well have come at the beginning, just as Xpiyacoc and Xmucane come into the alphabetic narrative ahead of the gods who take astronomical roles. If the illustrations of this hypothetical codex differed from those of the known codices, they may have had a greater resemblance to classic Maya painting, at least in the case of the Venus table. Indeed, if language is any indication, the Quiche were less modified by Mexican influences than the Yucatec. The alphabetic books written in the latter language contain considerably more words of Nahua derivation than does the Popol Vuh.[16] In any case, it is clear that the Quiche Maya and Yucatec Maya shared a common written tradition. The names of the Quiche gods who serve as the patrons of writing give eloquent testimony to this: they are none other than Jun B'atz' and Jun Chuen.

ACKNOWLEDGMENTS

The research that made this paper possible was supported, in part, by a fellowship and translation grant from the National Endowment for the Humanities. Anthony Aveni, Victoria and Harvey Bricker, Floyd Lounsbury, and Barbara Tedlock have lent patient ears.

NOTES

1. Citations of the Popol Vuh text refer to the manuscript, which is accurately paleographed in Schultze Jena (1944) and reproduced in facsimile in Ximénez (1973). Translations, with some changes, are from D. Tedlock (1985). For all Quichean texts given in the present paper, I have followed the new alphabet decided upon by native speakers of Quichean languages (see Academia de las Lenguas Mayas de Guatemala 1988). Sounds are approximately as in Spanish, except that q is like the Hebrew qoph, tz is like the English ts, x is like the English sh, and ' indicates the glottal stop (when it follows a vowel) or glottalization (when it follows a consonant).

2. The sources for this gloss are tzucuba and tzuqueh in Varea (1929) and Ximenez (1985).

3. Yucatec words are in the orthography of the Diccionario maya cordemex (Barrera 1980).

4. Excerpts from the text of the Rab'inal Achi have been converted to the orthography described above (note 1), and they have been emended by means of a comparison with a 1913 manuscript version of the play, a copy of which is currently in use in Rabinal (the original is in the Latin American Library at Tulane University). I have made further emendations, together with my translation, with the help of Jose Leon Coloch of Rabinal, the current master of the drama, who permitted me to tape-record his own recitations of selected passages.

5. For a facsimile of the Dresden Codex see Thompson (1972); parenthetical Dresden Codex references are to the page numbers of the manuscript itself.

6. The Cakchiquel text given here has been converted to the orthography described above (note 1) and incorporates emendations.

7. Lounsbury's argument (1985:52-53) that the -que in Xbalanque (the spelling used in the Popol Vuh manuscript) might be q'e, or "sun," is confirmed by Haeserijn (1979), who has contemporary speakers of Kekchi calling the sun b'alamq'e when it is hidden at night, whereas they call the daytime sun saq'e, "light (or white) sun."

8. The same pun works in Yucatec: one of the Yucatec terms for "net" is k'an, and the Yucatec name for the day in question is K'an (Barrera 1980). The great antiquity of this Popol Vuh scene is indicated by the presence, at the foot of the cornstalk on the tablet of the Temple of the Foliated Cross at Palenque, of the glyph known as the K'an cross. The inscriptions in the three temples of the Cross group tell (in outline) the story of the classic Maya equivalents of the pregnant woman and her twin sons; for a further discussion of the relationship between these inscriptions and the Popol Vuh, see D. Tedlock (in press).

9. In reckoning these two directions as above and below rather than north and south I follow the work of Bricker (1983, 1988), but I avoid the terms zenith and nadir, which involve the same ethnocentric error

by which the Mayan terms for east and west, which apply to the sides of the horizon marked out by the sun's solstitial rising and setting points, are confused with cardinal points (B. Tedlock 1989). I suspect that in astronomical contexts the "above" term refers to the celestial meridian (or the higher part of it) rather than to a point directly above the observer, and that the "below" term refers to the unseen continuation of the line of the meridian beneath the observer.

10. I thank Anthony Aveni for informing me of the visibility of Venus during solar eclipses, and Victoria Bricker for calling my attention to the representation of this event in the Dresden Codex.

11. In formulating my statements concerning the timing of the observable movements of Venus I have consulted Closs (1978:154) and Aveni (1980:83-86).

12. While working on my translation of the Popol Vuh, I discarded the possibility of a calendrical inter-pretation of Blood Moon's prayer because of this reversal (see D. Tedlock 1985:118 for the result).

13. If this is correct, then the Dresden version of the eclipse table would not be transitional or corrective, as Lounsbury (1978:796) has suggested, but quite possibly canonical.

14. For more on the relationship between sound images in Maya thought, see D. Tedlock (1988).

15. The idea of a male lunar deity is not a late import from Mexico, as some have thought, but is present in Classic Maya iconography (Schele and Miller 1986:306).

16. On this point compare Campbell's list of Nahua-derived words in the Popol Vuh (1983:83-85) with the "Nahuatl" entry in the index to Edmonson's translation (1982:215) of the Chilam Balam of Tizimin.

BIBLIOGRAPHY

Academia de las Lenguas Mayas
1988   *Lenguas mayas de Guatemala: documento de referencia para la pronunciación de los nuevos alfabetos oficiales.* Guatemala: Instituto Indigenista Nacional.

Aveni, A. F.
1980   *Skywatchers of Ancient Mexico.* Austin: University of Texas Press.

Barrera Vásquez, A.
1980   *Diccionario maya cordemex, maya-español, español-maya.* Mérida: Ediciones Cordemex.

Brasseur de Bourbourg, C. E.
1862   *Rabinal-Achi ou le drame-ballet du tun.* Collection de Documents dans les Langues Indigènes de l'Amérique Central 2, Part 2. Paris: Arthus Bertrand.

Bricker, H. M., and V. R. Bricker
in press   Zodiacal References in the Maya Codices. Paper delivered at the conference "Astronomy in the Maya Codices," Colgate University. To appear in *The Sky in Mayan Literature*, ed. A. F. Aveni. New York: Oxford University Press.

Bricker, V. R.
1983   Directional Glyphs in Maya Inscriptions and Codices. *American Antiquity* 48:347-53.
1988   Phonetic Glyph for Venus: Reply to Closs. *American Antiquity* 53:394-400.

Bricker, V. R., and H. M. Bricker
1986   The Mars Table in the Dresden Codex. *Middle American Research Institute Publications* 57:51-80.

Brinton, D. G.
1885   *Annals of the Cakchiquels.* Philadelphia: Library of Aboriginal American Literature.

Campbell, L.
1983   Préstamos lingüísticos en el Popol Vuh. In *Nuevas perspectivas sobre el Popol Vuh*, eds. R. M. Carmack and F. Morales Santos, pp. 81-86. Guatemala: Piedra Santa.

Carmack, R. M.
1973   *Quichean Civilization: The Ethnohistoric, Ethnographic, and Archaeological Sources.* Berkeley: University of California Press.

Closs, M. D.
1978   Venus in the Mayan World: Gods, Glyphs, and Associated Astronomical Phenomena. In *Tercera Mesa Redonda de Palenque,*

eds. M. Greene Robertson and D. C. Jeffers, pp. 147-165. Monterey: Pre-Columbian Art Research Center.

Coe, M. D.
1978   *Lords of the Underworld: Masterpieces of Classic Maya Ceramics*. Princeton: The Art Museum, Princeton University.

Edmonson, M. S.
1982   *The Ancient Future of the Itza: The Book of Chilam Balam of Tizimin*. Austin: University of Texas Press.

Haeserijn V., E.
1979   *Diccionario k'ekchi' español*. Guatemala: Piedra Santa.

La Farge, O.
1947   *Santa Eulalia: The Religion of a Cuchumatán Indian Town*. Chicago: University of Chicago Press.

Lounsbury, F. G.
1978   Maya Numeration, Computation, and Calendrical Astronomy. *Dictionary of Scientific Biography* 25(1):759-818.
1985   The Identities of the Mythological Figures in the Cross Group Inscriptions of Palenque. In *Fourth Palenque Round Table*, eds. M. Greene Robertson and E. P. Benson, pp. 45-58. San Francisco: Pre-Columbian Art Research Institute.

Nash, M.
1967   *Machine Age Maya: The Industrialization of a Guatemalan Community*. Chicago: University of Chicago Press.

Roys, R. L.
1967   *The Book of Chilam Balam of Chumayel*. Norman: University of Oklahoma Press.

Schele, L., and M. E. Miller
1986   *The Blood of Kings: Dynasty and Ritual in Maya Art*. Fort Worth: Kimbell Art Museum.

Schultze Jena, L. S.
1944   *Popol Vuh: Das heilige Buch der Quiché-Indianer von Guatemala*. Stuttgart: W. Kohlhammer.

Stuart, D.
1987   Ten Phonetic Syllables. *Research Reports on Ancient Maya Writing 14*. Washington, DC: Center for Maya Research.

Tedlock, B.
1982   *Time and the Highland Maya*. Albuquerque: University of New Mexico Press.

in press   The Road of Light: Theory and Practice of Mayan Skywatching. Paper delivered at the conference "Astronomy in the Maya Codices," Colgate University. To appear in *The Sky in Mayan Literature*, ed. A. F. Aveni. New York: Oxford University Press.

Tedlock, B., and D. Tedlock
1985   Text and Textile: Language and Technology in the Arts of the Quiché Maya. *Journal of Anthropological Research* 41:121-146.

Tedlock, D.
1985   *Popol Vuh: The Mayan Book of the Dawn of Life*. New York: Simon and Schuster.
1988   Mayan Linguistic Ideology. In *On the Ethnography of Communication*, ed. P. V. Kroskrity, pp. 55-108. Los Angeles: University of California at Los Angeles Department of Anthropology.
1989   Writing and Reflection among the Maya. 1992 Lecture Series Working Papers 4. College Park: University of Maryland Department of Spanish and Portuguese.
in press   Myths, Maths, and the Problem of Correlation in Mayan Books. Paper prepared for *The Sky in Mayan Literature*, ed. A. F. Aveni. New York: Oxford University Press.

Thompson, J. E. S.
1970   *Maya History and Religion*. Norman: University of Oklahoma Press.
1972   *A Commentary on the Dresden Codex*. Philadelphia: American Philosophical Society.

Tozzer, A. M.
1907   *A Comparative Study of the Mayas and the Lacandones*. New York: Macmillan.

Varea, F. de
1929   *Calepino en lengua cakchiquel*. Typescript paleography by William Gates, in the Gates collection of the library at Brigham Young University, Provo, Utah, of a 1699 manuscript copy by Francisco Ceron, in the library of the American Philosophical Society, Philadelphia.

Ximénez, F.
1967   *Escolios a las historias del origen de los indios*. Sociedad de Geografía e Historia de Guatemala Publicación Especial 13. Guatemala.
1973   *Popol Vuh*. Facsimile edition with paleography and notes by A. Estrada Monroy. Guatemala: José de Pineda Ibarra.

1985   *Primera parte del tesoro de las lenguas cakchiquel, quiché y zutuhil, en que las dichas lenguas se traducen a la nuestra, española.* Ed. C. Sáenz de Santa María. Academia de Geografía e Historia de Guatemala, Special Publication 30. Guatemala: Tipografía Nacional.

XX

The Future of Tikal

Christopher Jones

The University Museum of Archaeology and Anthropology, University of Pennsylvania

Will Tikal last for a thousand years? The future of Tikal, like that of the rest of the planet Earth, is at present hostage to the political tension of the world as a whole. To guess what the site will signify to our descendants a thousand years from now is to guess at trends in social evolution. One would like to believe that the present apparent trend toward reintegration and brotherhood will continue in spite of setbacks, but it is also possible to imagine a future in which this somehow never happens. Tikal might be allowed to fall apart and melt away into a footnote in world history.

In February of 1986, thirty-one members of The University Museum and I visited Tikal and other Maya sites in Guatemala. After the tour, I stayed to meet with the newly appointed Technical Commission of the National Tikal Project to discuss the formulation of plans for the future of Tikal and other archaeological sites in northern Guatemala.

Three large archaeological projects have come and gone at Tikal: The University Museum of the University of Pennsylvania from 1956 to 1969, the Tikal National Park Service from 1972 to 1979, and the National Tikal Project from 1979 to 1985. All three have effected profound changes by clearing and excavating large areas of the site center. They have brought Tikal into view of the world, but they have each left problems of maintenance and repair. The commission feels that what is needed now is a period of rest. This would allow for the development of a permanent system of maintenance and protection, an integration of the data from the three projects, and time to assess the growing significance of Tikal in world history.

The most important structure at Tikal at present is Temple I, also called Structure 5D-1 or the Temple of the Giant Jaguar (Fig. 20.1). It has become the principle image of Guatemala and as such is watched closely by the government and the Guatemalan

press. It is generally recognized that some of the strength and success of the image is due to the restoration of its front during the 1960s by The University Museum, which brought out from obscurity the strong convergent lines of the terraces. The terraces were rebuilt on the left side of the stairway using freshly quarried stone cut like the original masonry. The right-hand terraces were left more in their eroded condition, and thus the two sides of the temple provide a sense of time depth for the viewer.

From time to time, a dramatic article appears in the press, telling of the imminent collapse of Temple I. Indeed, some blocks of outer masonry high on the rear of the temple have become severely undercut by erosion through the years. In 1986, scaffolding was erected to begin a major new consolidation of the terraces. This type of preventive maintenance will have to be a major part of the Tikal budget for as long as the government wishes the temple to last. It has become clear, incidentally, that the restored terraces built with fresh stone last longer and present fewer maintenance problems than the consolidated ones.

The side walls of the Temple I front stairway have become riddled with large holes dug by wasps into the dry, powdery chalk stone. Pounds of powder get swept up from the plaza floor at the base of the walls every year. For several years, the powdering was almost stopped by spraying the walls with water during the height of the dry season and thus maintaining the moisture content. This was discontinued, however, and the walls are now severely undercut.

Another problem with the stairway is that the stair treads themselves have worn away to nothing on the narrow exposure of stairs, where hundreds of tourists climb, holding on to the chain. One solution to this problem would be to close the stairway permanently. Another, and better one, I think, would be to completely reconstruct the stairway from top to

Figure 20.1. Temple I, Tikal, in 1988. It was built ca. A.D. 733 to cover the burial chamber of Ah Cacao, ruler of Tikal (A.D. 682-733). Note the thatch roofs over the stelae in the Great Plaza.

Figure 20.2. North Acropolis summit behind Structure 5D-33 in 1980. Note cracks and slumping in Acropolis wall to the left.

bottom. This would allow climbers to use many paths and not wear down one. The wide stairway of Temple II across the plaza has not been worn by traffic, probably because it has no chain and no set path for climbing. Complete reconstruction would also replace and repair the threatened side walls of the stairway. Lastly, the lines of the temple would be immeasurably improved and brought closer to the original.

During the consolidation work on the rear terraces of Temple I, there are plans to investigate the rear exit of the long plaza-level tunnel which The University Museum excavated through the temple in the early 1960s. The ancient Maya fill through which the tunnel was dug is an extremely solid and compacted mass of limestone blocks and wet-laid mix-

ture of mud and white earth. The tunnel is narrow and low. While excavation was going on, there was never any indication of tunnel failure or entry of water through the fill, and there has been no structural failure since then.

In the North Acropolis, on the other hand, the tunnels have caused cracks and slumping to appear in the floors at the top of the Acropolis (Fig. 20.2). When these were discovered in 1980, the Museum sent down its tunnel plans and sections, which revealed that the problem lay, not in the carefully repacked fill of the deep, wide Acropolis trench itself, but in the tunnels dug into the sides of the trench. These had been dug into less solid Maya fill than that of Temple I and so began to collapse. In the same year government crews reopened the tunnels and repacked them with stones and solid fill. Five years later, however, new cracking was spotted in the front part of the Acropolis top. This time, I traveled down to Tikal and, with the aid of the drawings, the supervisor and I were able to determine that a front tunnel had been missed in 1980. A shaft has been dug to reach it, and it is being refilled in the same manner as the previous ones. No new cracks have occurred in the meantime in the part of the Acropolis that had been repaired earlier, so it appears that the tunnel problem has been resolved. Although this is an example of how excavation for scientific purposes can create severe problems for preservation, it is also an example of how communication can solve those problems.

Other archaeologically caused problems resulted

Figure 20.3. Lost World Pyramid, west side, in 1988. Note the dry white powdery and decaying limestone under the thatched roofing.

Figure 20.4. Temple V in 1969, before the brush was cleared from the roof comb.

from the investigations undertaken by the other projects. In the late 1970s, the east side of the 30-m-high "Lost World Pyramid" collapsed after the National Tikal Project had cleared the forest cover from the structure (Fig. 20.3). Although the west and north sides were relatively well preserved and have been impressively restored, the east side was full of wide cracks and crevasses that allowed the tropical rain torrents to pour down into the pyramid. The early Maya builders of the pyramid had not yet developed the engineering skills of Temple I, so the pyramid fill is loose piles of rough rocks without a binding matrix. Attempts have been made to tie the crevasses together with new mortar and overlapping stones, but it is not yet certain whether the pyramid is stabilized.

The Technical Commisssion has reported on another danger that seems to be the fault of early explorers. Sometime long before The University Museum came to dig, someone had tunneled upward from the room of Temple V to the top of the huge roofcomb mass, thus allowing water to enter the otherwise sealed roofcomb chambers (Fig. 20.4). Cracks have developed between the massive rear wall and side walls of the roofcomb, indicating that the rear wall is in danger of peeling away from the front and crashing down to the plaza level 30 m below. When Oscar Quintana, the coordinator of the commission, visited the Museum in December 1986, we were able to give him detailed architectural drawings of the temple by the Guatemalan archaeologist Miguel Orrego, completed for the Museum in

the 1970s. These drawings will be a great help to the engineers who must devise a plan to save the building.

Natural forces are also threatening the ancient Maya architecture. Forestry experts on the Technical Commission are faced with deciding which of the great forest trees at Tikal pose threats to the structures. Especially troublesome are the top-heavy old trees that have been left exposed to winds by the cutting of their neighbors (Fig. 20.5). Many of their tall silhouettes ring the restored areas of the site, ready to rip out sections of masonry when they fall. A large program of selective topping and cutting has been proposed.

The erosion of carved stone monuments and exposed stucco sculpture is also a major problem for Tikal, as it is all over the world (Fig. 20.6). In the tropics, the stone is exposed to torrential rains, then to dessication during the dry season. The alternation between wet and dry has an effect similar to that of heat and cold in the north. A few years ago, the government decided to take the temporary step of erecting palm thatching over each carved monument at Tikal. The same was done at Quirigua and (by Honduras) at Copan. These pole-and-thatch structures severely transform the aspect of the site and cast shadows that ruin photography. However, it is certain that some protection must be provided to halt the documented erosion that has occurred in the hundred years since the forest canopy was removed.

A permanent solution to the problem of monument erosion is going to be expensive and radical.

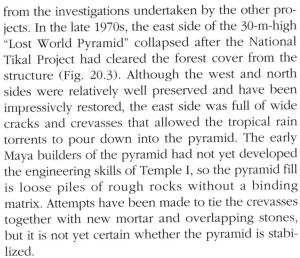

Figure 20.5. Temple I and Central Acropolis in 1969. Tall trees at the edges of cleared areas are particularly vulnerable to winds.

One approach is to remove the original stones to roofed museums and replace them with cast copies. The technology of casting is certainly able to create perfect replicas, and the originals can be displayed in better light and explained more creatively as treasures of human history than they are now. Furthermore, in a museum building at Tikal they can be better protected, not only from weather but also from vandalism and theft. Another solution is to leave the stones in place and erect permanent roofs over them, perhaps of translucent fiberglass, with single supports placed less obtrusively behind each stone. These, however, would intrude the modern world into the ancient scene. A third solution is to harden the stones against erosion, using a silicon solution. Although this has been tested for several years on uncarved monuments with no sign of adverse effects, it is not yet considered advisable to commit the carvings to this hardening process.

For the present, I think the thatch roofs should stay. They are cheap as well as easily maintained and replaced. Furthermore, they symbolize a reverence for the ancient monuments, protecting them from harm with the same materials the Maya would probably have used for such a purpose.

During the summer of 1987, the Technical Commission built a new road around the northern peripherry of the site to a new parking lot behind Temple IV. For a few months, all vehicular traffic within the site was stopped. The plan is to have people either walk from the entrance up through the site or take a bus directly up to Temple IV at thc far western limit of the site and walk back to the hotel through the various restored areas of the ruin. The walk is not extensive, measuring about 2 km back to the hotel. At Teotihuacan, one must walk 1.7 km from one end of the site to the other, and at Chichen Itza, 1.1 km.

Figure 20.6. Stela 13, a monument to Kan Boar, ruler of Tikal (A.D. 457-488). These small, early stelae are made of particularly hard limestone.

Because of complaints by the hotel guides and tourist agencies, however, the plan was temporarily rescinded. Much can be said for working again on the concept of excluding vehicles from Tikal. The crowds of parked buses in the main gathering place behind Temple II detract from the majesty and quiet of the Great Plaza. Many of the roads go along the site's ancient causeways, which should be selectively restored, cleared, and displayed as causeways. This cannot be done effectively with the raised vehicular roadway winding among them. In several areas, the roads are steep and very dangerous when wet, especially where cars gun their motors to climb the incline behind the North Acropolis. With proper rest facilities within the site, well-maintained and guarded paths, and a finished system of peripheral roadways, the plan would greatly improve the ambiance, elicit more respect and awe from its visitors, and do much to protect the buildings and monuments from damage.

In addition to its focus on Tikal, the Technical Commission is responsible for the protection of the ruins in the whole northern part of the Peten Province of Guatemala. Large and small archaeological parks are being created around the major ruins, some covering hundreds of square kilometers of virgin forest. These include the sites of Naranjo, Nakum, Topoxte, Yaxha, El Zotz, Río Azul, Xultun, Uaxactun, and Piedras Negras. Most of these have buildings about to collapse from erosion. They are ravaged from looting and from the work of early archaeologists. All desperately need protection from the rapidly increasing pioneering and commercial development of the region.

Guatemala has long known that it is in its national interest to protect the remains of Maya civilization and to promote its greatness in the eyes of the world. This realization was crucial to its committment to financial cooperation with The University Museum in the excavation and restoration of Tikal from the 1950s on. The interest is clearly both economic and political. The economic lesson was relearned in the last decade, when tourist revenues dried up almost completely during the fighting and violence. Not so obvious is the political cohesiveness that pride in a great Maya past can give to a nation that is racially divided.

To save Tikal, therefore, is not just of enormous value archaeologically, but can be justified as a step toward expanding human consciousness. The task that the Technical Commission has before it is to reach out to all our descendants, a thousand years from now and beyond.